THE CRISIS OF
SCHOOL VIOLENCE

THE CRISIS OF SCHOOL VIOLENCE

A NEW PERSPECTIVE

MARIANNA KING

Michigan State University Press | East Lansing

Copyright © 2021 by Marianna King

 The paper used in this publication meets the minimum requirements of ANSI/NISO Z39.48-1992 (R 1997) (Permanence of Paper).

Michigan State University Press
East Lansing, Michigan 48823-5245

LIBRARY OF CONGRESS CATALOGING-IN-PUBLICATION DATA
Names: King, Marianna, author.
Title: The crisis of school violence : a new perspective / Marianna King.
Description: East Lansing : Michigan State University Press, [2021]
Includes bibliographical references and index.
Identifiers: LCCN 2019057392 | ISBN 978-1-61186-379-6 (paperback)
| ISBN 978-1-60917-654-9 (PDF) | ISBN 978-1-62895-414-2 (ePub)
| ISBN 978-1-62896-415-8 (Kindle)
Subjects: LCSH: School violence—Psychological aspects.
Bullying—Prevention. | Violence in mass media—Psychological aspects.
Classification: LCC LB3013.3 .K494 2021 | DDC 371.7/82—dc23
LC record available at https://lccn.loc.gov/2019057392

Book design by Charlie Sharp, Sharp Des!gns, East Lansing, MI
Cover design by Shaun Allshouse, www.shaunallshouse.com
Cover art: One glowing balloon like moon shining in the dark night isolated above other dim balloons over white background with window reflections 3D rendering by masterzphotofo. Used with permission from stock.adobe.com.

Michigan State University Press is a member of the Green Press Initiative and is committed to developing and encouraging ecologically responsible publishing practices. For more information about the Green Press Initiative and the use of recycled paper in book publishing, please visit www.greenpressinitiative.org.

Visit Michigan State University Press at *www.msupress.org*

*This book is dedicated to my mother,
Edith Irene Sabadosh Banks,
who taught me right from wrong.*

CONTENTS

ACKNOWLEDGMENTS · ix

INTRODUCTION: The Crisis · xi

CHAPTER 1. The Causes of Violence: Standard Explanations · · · · · · · · · · · · · · · · 1

CHAPTER 2. Standard Practices: Necessary but Not Sufficient · · · · · · · · · · · · · · 17

CHAPTER 3. Paolo Freire and the Question of Human Nature · · · · · · · · · · · · · · 41

CHAPTER 4. The Culture of Violence · 55

CHAPTER 5. The Culture of School Violence: The School Environment · · · · · · · · · · 83

CHAPTER 6. School Rampage Shooters: More Lethal Than Ever · · · · · · · · · · · · 107

CHAPTER 7. Media Reality · 131

CHAPTER 8. Fun and Games: A Virtual Reality · 161

CHAPTER 9. The Brain's Response to Electronic Entertainment Media · · · · · · · · · 191

CHAPTER 10. The Future of Violence · 215

CHAPTER 11. What We Can Do: The Opportunity · 221

APPENDIX. School Violence Prevention Resources · 227

NOTES · 231

BIBLIOGRAPHY · 295

INDEX · 333

ACKNOWLEDGMENTS

Special thanks to J. Spencer Herz, long-time friend and intellectual companion, who provided editorial advice as good as the advice he gives about life. Ursula Rose, a rose by any other name, and Jeffrey S. R. Patterson, attorney extraordinaire, also gave critical and helpful feedback. Anna Bryson consistently helped with her support and intelligent comments, and Myra Horton continued to amaze with her insights. Gratitude also is due to John Camponeschi, Erwin Young, Pamela Potvin, Tom Harris, Pam Harris, Sheila Velez, Aileen McLoughlin, Kathy Hope, Francis Ferranti, Keean Davis, Cherry Lindsay, Erin Bourdo, and Kathleen Bernath for their helpful comments. My brother Frank Banks, Martha Ann Lategan, Janet Black, and Arvilla Wheldon gave ongoing heartfelt support. Also, thanks to Whitney Glenn, Brandon J. Gallegos, Virginia Silcox, and Mary Carmel Hoffman for providing exceptional technical assistance and moral support. Finally, thanks to Julie Loehr, editor at Michigan State University Press, for her understanding.

INTRODUCTION

THE CRISIS

> It is my conviction that nothing enduring can be built on violence.
> —Mahatma Gandhi

Schools in the United States are in crisis. They must deal with severe budget cuts, poor student performance, burned-out teachers, and aggressive students. Bullying continues at unacceptably high rates, and rampage school shootings continue to shock the country.

In the early 1980s, only 3 percent of adults in a national survey identified violence and crime as the most important problem facing this country. By the 1990s, violence was viewed by half of the respondents as the most serious problem—more serious than the high cost of living, unemployment, poverty, homelessness, and health care. By 1994, violence, along with a lack of discipline among students, was identified as "the biggest problem" experienced in public schools.[1]

Why is it important to understand school violence? School violence harms children physically, emotionally, mentally, and spiritually. School violence creates a cauldron of mean-spiritedness and also promotes poor academic performance. It is important to understand school violence because schools are the crucibles of the future.

School violence includes vandalism, physical assaults, aggravated thefts, suicide, bullying, and rampage shootings. This book concentrates on the most harmful forms of school violence—bullying and rampage school shootings. The National Center for Education

Statistics reports that at least 20 percent of school children report being bullied and 9 percent report one or more physical attacks.[2] As will become clear in later chapters, there is good reason to believe that these statistics underreport the problem.

The damaging results of bullying can last a lifetime and also can be lethal. Young people who are chronically bullied may resort to suicide. In addition, most rampage school shooters were bullied.

At the same time, few school violence prevention programs work. Tremendous resources are directed to preventing and reducing school violence; however, researchers and practitioners are at a loss to explain this violence. The National Resource Center for Safe Schools concludes: "We have learned that we cannot identify with certainty those students who, for reasons clear only to themselves, will assault their teachers and peers."[3] The National Academies of Science point out that many school shooters present an anomaly because they come from peaceful communities and stable, loving families. They have concluded that it is "impossible" to adequately explain why school shootings occur.[4] Media accounts and academic investigations refer to these and other mass murders as "senseless." The literature that deals with school shootings is punctuated with the unanswered question: Why?

The Crisis of School Violence answers this question. This interdisciplinary book investigates school violence from a broad array of disciplines dedicated to understanding human behavior, including anthropology, archaeology, history, psychology, sociology, media studies, and the cognitive neurosciences. This broad approach answers this question and also identifies the primary causal factor in the escalation of bullying and the emergence of rampage school shootings, which is a new form of violence.

School violence prevention programs usually address symptoms rather than the more deeply rooted causes such as the human need for respect, equality, and justice. School violence is a crucible for future aggressive and violent behavior in other settings such as the home, the workplace, and public places. The progeny of rampage school shootings are rampage shootings in other public places.

Other books have not raised key questions and so have not been able to provide key answers. For example, what is the relationship between human nature and aggressive behavior? Why is the problem most pronounced in the United States? Why is bullying escalating? How does the brain respond to violence in electronic entertainment? Why don't school violence prevention programs work? Without effective prevention what is the future of violence? What can we do?[5]

It is necessary to identify the root causes of violence in order to prevent it. For this reason, *The Crisis of School Violence* explores the question of human nature. Are human beings violent by nature? Prevailing theories about causes of violence are discussed, and the standard practices based on these theories are analyzed. Most theories are based on psychology. However, a larger perspective is required that takes social and economic forces into account. For this reason, the culture of violence and the violence industries, especially the violent electronic entertainment industries, are investigated. The book also describes the future of violence, a probable scenario if prevention efforts continue to be inadequate.

This book is a call to action. The Chinese character for crisis is the same as that for opportunity. The crisis in our schools offers the opportunity to examine the problem critically and to transform schools into crucibles of humanization and peace. The extent to which the reader takes action determines the extent to which school violence is prevented.

It is that simple.

CHAPTER 1

THE CAUSES OF VIOLENCE: STANDARD EXPLANATIONS

> Violence begets violence.
> —Martin Luther King Jr.

Many times when we read or hear about brutal acts of violence, they are described as "senseless." This chapter helps to make sense of violence.

What is violence? The word "violence" is derived from the Latin *violare*, which means "to violate." Researchers agree that violence is associated with an activity or behavior that involves force or the threat of force.[1] Violence is defined as "the threat, attempt, or use of physical force by one or more persons that results in physical or nonphysical harm to one or more persons."[2] Violence is the "intentional use of physical force or power, threatened or actual, against oneself, another person or against a group or community that results in injury, death or physical harm."[3] The National Television Violence Study defines violence as "any overt depiction of a credible threat of physical force or the actual use of such force to physically harm an animate being or groups of beings."[4]

Inherent in the threat of force or the use of force is the goal of gaining power over another. Violence is defined as "the use of force to gain dominance over another or others."[5] Power is intrinsic to violence. It is its essential element.

Violence differs from aggressive behavior, which is "often less extreme and more normative and is not necessarily limited to physical harm."[6] Studies have rarely differentiated aggressive behavior from violent behavior.[7] This book is concerned with aggression as well as violence. Although less lethal than violence, aggression springs from the same roots and can be harmful.

Most violence occurs between family and friends in this country.[8] The rate and seriousness of violence are greater for adolescents and young adults than for all other age groups.[9] In the 1960s research showed that boys and men committed violence ten times more often than girls and women. Two-thirds of all crime is committed by young men between the ages of twelve and twenty-eight.[10]

There is concern about a "new female offender," one who is more ruthless and violent than in the past. By the year 2000, this ratio had changed to four to one.[11] Much of this increase has to do with violence perpetrated by girl gang members.[12]

The prevalence of violence among young people in general has been increasing over time. In addition, children are committing violent crimes at younger ages.[13] is some evidence that the fastest growing group of murderers is five-year-olds.[14]

Why is violence among young people escalating? Why are younger children more socially aggressive and more violent?

Common Sense Understanding

What causes violence and its escalation? Our understanding of the causes of violence is strongly influenced by our families, communities, and media accounts. The following discusses causes listed by students, parents, and teachers. These explanations tend to be laundry lists. However, some major themes emerge.

A survey of teachers in over two thousand school districts in the United States conducted by the National School Board Association revealed that 77 percent of the respondents hold changes in families as responsible for increased violence in our society. The factors cited include an increasingly inhumane society in which children do not receive loving care; children and families live in poverty; and children are raised in homes where there is violence, abuse, and addiction. Related factors include lack of parental discipline and supervision, lack of parental concern about student behavior, lack of conflict resolution skills, and a lack of a clear and consistent disciplinary response at home, at school, and in the courts.[15]

These cited reasons are actually symptoms of underlying causes. What causes dysfunctional families, poverty and an increasing inhumane society? A recurring theme among explanations for violence is that young people may act violently because of unexpressed anger.[16] The critical question is, what causes such anger? To what extent is young people's anger a reflection of witnessing and experiencing massive amounts of media and video-game death and destruction? To what extent is their anger caused by anticipating an environmentally depleted future? To what extent is anger caused by living in poverty and experiencing other forms of injustice?

Biological Explanations

Some people claim that violent behavior is caused by biological or genetic factors. One of the earliest attempts to link genetics and violent behavior occurred in the 1960s when researchers believed they had discovered a propensity for violence in men born with an extra Y chromosome. These studies attracted a lot of attention at the time. However, further examination of XYY males showed that they did not display any substantial violent tendencies. In addition, XYY males are very rare and so only account for a very small portion of increases in violence.[17]

In his book, *On Aggression*, Konrad Lorenz (1966) documented aggressive activity in the animal kingdom. He also documented the mechanisms that keep aggression in check. He argued that humans do not have appropriately evolved mechanisms to inhibit their aggressive impulses. He believed that, until the invention of weapons, these inhibitory mechanisms did not develop because human beings were not capable of doing each other harm. Later research suggests that humans, conditioned by their social environments, have more inhibitory control over their use of aggression than Lorenz suggested.[18]

Some research involving twins suggests that there is a genetic component to individual differences in rates of aggression. For example, a study of identical and fraternal twins in adoptive homes in England and Wales found that variation in antisocial behavior could be explained by genetic factors. This study supports the conclusion that some individuals have "a greater genetic predisposition toward aggression than do others."[19] However, most studies about the genetic contribution to aggressive behavior have yielded few positive results. Miles and Carey (1997), for example, did a meta-analysis of the available research and found that there is no measurable genetic effect.

There is no particular center in the brain that produces aggression. Rather, the brain has neural systems that facilitate aggression, and it has the frontal lobe system that inhibits aggression and controls impulses. Damage to the prefrontal cortex impedes decision-making and increases impulsive behavior. Studies of violent criminals have revealed diminished activity in the frontal lobes if this system is damaged, disconnected, inactive or not fully mature. There is a tendency for people convicted of murder to have reduced activity in the prefrontal cortex.[20] Brain pathways must function effectively so that people can control the expression of negative emotion. If people experience reduced activation in the amygdala, which plays a role in the regulation of emotion, they may not be able to inhibit the negative emotions that lead to aggressive behavior.[21] For example, the autopsy of sniper Charles Whitman, who shot and killed people from a University of Texas campus tower, revealed a tumor pressing into his amygdala.[22]

Males of all ages, ethnicities and cultures are more physically aggressive than females. In animals, testosterone is linked to social aggression in the animal kingdom. Reducing testosterone in the alpha male by castration eliminates his dominant social status, and injecting testosterone causes him to regain his social status. However, administering testosterone to males with less social status does not usually result in their taking over the alpha male position. This indicates that there is not a direct relationship between testosterone and position in the dominance hierarchy.[23] Testosterone levels, which are inherited, frequently have been studied as a factor in human male aggression. Studies have found that testosterone heightens dominating and aggressive behavior.[24] In humans there is some evidence that high testosterone males are more likely to be socially aggressive and thrive on competition, making them more likely to have a sports career or lead a successful company.[25] Teenage boys and adult men with high testosterone levels have a tendency to be delinquent, use hard drugs, and be aggressive or bullying in response to frustration.[26] High testosterone levels often correlate with irritability, low tolerance for frustration, assertiveness, and impulsiveness. These are qualities that can tend to lead to more aggressive responses to provocation.[27]

A person's testosterone level will not necessarily be a good predictor of aggressive behavior. In addition, high levels of testosterone may promote socially aggressive behavior, but there is little evidence that it promotes violent behavior.[28] An exception is that some studies have found a prevalence of high testosterone levels in violent male sex offenders.[29] While testosterone heightens dominating and aggressive behavior, aggressive behavior also boosts testosterone levels.[30] For example, a study of male college basketball fans before and after a big game showed that testosterone swelled among the victorious fans and was diminished among the losing fans.[31]

So men who live in cultures that promote competition and aggression experience increases in testosterone levels. The extent to which testosterone increases is mitigated by the social environment. Compare, for example, Margaret Mead's description of the peaceful South Sea Islander men with militant terrorists from patriarchal cultures. What needs to be considered is the extent to which the social environment of the virtual world of violent video games, which embody dominance and winning, raise testosterone levels.

Steroids are at times cited as causing violent behavior. Many studies have verified that the negative side effects of anabolic steroids used by athletes, termed "steroid rage," include mood swings and aggressiveness. In some cases the resulting violent outbursts have resulted in murder by young men who had no history of violence.[32]

Research suggests that thrill-seeking may be a motive in enacting violence. People who are involved in antisocial behavior tend to be physiologically under-aroused, as indicated by lower resting heart rate levels. Such people may seek excitement to compensate for under-arousal in order to bring some physiological balance to their system. It has been demonstrated that violent offenders have lower resting heart rates than nonviolent offenders.[33] This suggests that for these people thrill-seeking may be a more important motive for violence than for other criminal behavior.[34] This factor may be at work in "thrill killings," a new form of violence.

Other biological risk factors include the use of licit and illicit substances. Crack cocaine is especially notorious in shutting down the abuser's ability to feel empathy or compassion.[35] Alcohol can unleash anger and aggressive responses.[36] People who have been drinking commit four out of ten violent crimes and three in four acts of spousal abuse.[37] Alcohol is connected to the majority of homicides. Some studies show that as many as 90 percent of young murderers used alcohol or drugs before the killings.[38] Alcohol can be a catalyst, triggering violent behavior, but it does not cause violence.

We need to ask about the cause of wanting to overindulge in alcohol. And what is the cause of the anger that is often released by alcohol? What is present and what is lacking in people's lives that leads to alcohol abuse and to murderous rage? Similarly, with drug abuse, what is it about social conditions that has led to an epidemic of substance abuse? Answering this question requires looking at quality of life issues and their relationship to such market forces as the entertainment industry and the advertising industry.

We also need to look at the role of food and of substances that pass themselves off as food. Some people believe that sugar is a gateway drug to alcohol abuse. In 1986, the best-selling book *Sugar Blues* explained how refined sugar is alien to the human body, and its use, and especially its overuse (abuse), relates to a host of problems. These include hyperactivity, problems concentrating, addiction to sugar, and aggressive behavior. It is significant that Michael Carneal, the fourteen-year-old who killed three people in a Paducah, Kentucky, school, said that it helped him to get "sugared up" before the shooting. In 1978, typical teenage males in the United States drank about seven ounces of soft drinks daily. Nowadays teenagers drink from three to five times that amount. This is equivalent to thirty to fifty teaspoons of sugar each day. In addition, about 20 percent of one and two-year-olds now consume soft drinks.[39] Many of these soft drinks contain caffeine, which contributes to hyperactive and aggressive behavior, especially when combined with sugar. Sanctioned by the Food and Drug Administration, food manufacturers have been using sugar as cheap filler in processed foods for decades. These processed foods do not list sugar as an ingredient. Coupled with a very high rate of soft drink consumption and other sugared products, this has resulted in an epidemic of childhood-onset diabetes as well as increased aggressive behavior. Morgan Spurlock, in his documentary video, *Supersize Me*, documented the results of his eating only food from fast food restaurants for three months. He reported fatigue, depression, mood swings, irritability, an inability to focus, and a general sense of not feeling well. Essentially, processed food filled with chemicals and sugar is not natural to the human body and is not good for the body. And what is not good for the body is not good for the brain.[40]

Environmental neurotoxins, such as nicotine and lead, also may play a role in aggressive behavior. There is research support, for example, that nicotine affects the fetus. Smoking by pregnant women infuses nicotine into the fetal bloodstream, damaging the central nervous system and thus lowering the amount of serotonin available to the brain. This places children at especially high risk of delinquency.[41] Lead is another widespread neurotoxin. Studies have linked exposure to lead with criminal behavior.[42] A lead increase of just one microgram per deciliter of prenatal blood has been found to be associated with a 7.8 percent increase in arrests. Lead poisoning damages the brain by inhibiting synapse formation, which reduces the travel of neurotransmitters and lowers arousal of the cerebral cortex.[43] A weakened prefrontal cortex tends to impair decision-making and increase aggressive behavior. People convicted of murder tend to have reduced activity in the prefrontal cortex.[44]

The fifty or so neurotransmitters, the chemical messengers in the brain that allow nerve cells to communicate with one another, have been studied in relation to violent crime.[45] The most thoroughly studied are dopamine, norepinephrine, GABA and serotonin. Serotonin, the most well-known neurotransmitter, plays a key role in mediating aggressive and violent behavior. Serotonin is one of the chemicals that serve as a messenger from the body's nerve cells. It is produced in the brain from one of the essential amino acids derived from food.[46] Axions are the carriers of such messages, and dendrites receive the messages. Serotonin must jump the synapse, the space between axions and dendrites, for the brain's communication. Depleted serotonin increases aggressive behavior, and increased serotonin reduces aggression and increases peaceful interactions. People with low serotonin levels are prone to suicide and to impulsive violent acts.[47] Research into the effects of serotonin levels is new. It is unclear if there is a genetic basis for low serotonin levels or if this deficiency is caused by a lack of adequate nutrition. Also, it is not known at this time how much influence the social environment has on serotonin production.

In some cases biological explanations may be necessary. However, they are not sufficient to the extent that they are not linked to the social and economic reality. For example, distressed social conditions, such as poverty, may trigger violent behavior in people who are genetically at risk.[48] In addition, people who are most exposed to neurotoxins tend to be poor and subject to insufficient nutrition and other stressors, including environmental hazards. Neurotransmitter deficiency can be linked to insufficient prenatal care and to malnutrition, both of which are most often linked to low socioeconomic status. These deficiencies, coupled with the emotional, physical, and environmental stress associated with poverty, at times, sparks violent behavior. Nowadays, however, the debate about biological factors is framed not so much as nature versus nurture but rather nature and nurture. People make choices about displays of aggression conditioned by their social environments. Culture plays "a critical role in determining the extent to which people are 'able' to inhibit aggression."[49]

Biological theories no longer see crime as biological destiny. The larger understanding sees biological risk factors combined with such influences as malnutrition, substance abuse, lack of health care, poverty, and the overarching risk factor of a social environment that condones, promotes, or rewards violent behavior. The more risk factors from the social environment, the more likely a person will behave violently. Paul Billings, a clinical geneticist at Stanford University, points out that it is not the genes that cause violence in society, but it is the social system.[50] Stressful, modern-day living in itself contributes to the biology of violence. Stress-induced aggressive behavior has been documented in countless studies of animal and human behavior. This risk factor for violent behavior is worsened when coupled with poor nutrition, food additives, sugar, caffeine, and other substances that create internal stress and confound the working of the body and the brain. This internal stress, compounded by external stress, can lead to violence.

Psychological Explanations

Current research and prevention approaches rely heavily on the discipline of psychology and tend not to take a broader interdisciplinary perspective into account. Peter Gross, in *The Psychological Society* (1978), describes the broad societal emphasis on a psychological interpretation of events, evident in psychology being one of the most popular college majors.

What does psychology have to say about the causes of violence? A popular psychology textbook defines aggression as "any physical or verbal behavior intended to hurt or destroy, whether done reactively out of hostility or proactively as a calculated means to an end."[51] This definition sidesteps the question of what causes the hostility. It also ignores the question of power.

The general aggression model is a psychological model of behavior that is a cousin of sociology's social learning theory. The general aggression model posits that social knowledge structures develop learning processes over time. Aggression, based on this model, is largely based on the activation of aggression-related knowledge structures in memory, such as scripts and schemas. A number of studies have demonstrated that aggressive people have a "hostile attribution bias," tending to interpret ambiguous social events in a relatively hostile way. This bias carries the expectation that other people will react to potential conflicts with aggression.[52] The question is—Why do some people develop this view of the world?

Psychological factors that trigger aggression include the frustration-aggression hypothesis. According to this hypothesis, frustration occurs in situations in which people are prevented from attaining their goals. An increase in frustration leads to a greater probability of aggression. Frustration creates anger, which may generate aggression, especially if an aggressive cue, such as a gun, is present. Other negative or aversive stimuli, including physical pain, foul odors, hot temperatures, and cigarette smoke, can evoke an aggressive response.[53]

The role of hot temperatures in instigating aggression especially has been studied. It has been shown that people are more prone to aggressive or violent behavior as the temperature rises.[54] Because of this, climate change and rising temperatures need to be taken into account when assessing what the future of aggression and violence will be.

Psychology has made a significant contribution to the understanding of violence. However, its scope is neither broad enough nor deep enough to develop a truly valid understanding. A psychological interpretation is inherently limited because it is only one of the social sciences that seek to understand and to explain human behavior. Psychological theories and practices may be necessary. However, they are not sufficient.

Other Expert Opinions

What do experts and practitioners in the field have to say about causes? Examples of their standard explanations include the following laundry lists.

"Violence often results from a complex interaction of environmental, social, and psychological factors such as the learned behavior or responding to conflict with violence, the effects of drugs or alcohol, the presence of weapons, the absence of positive family relationships and adult supervision."[55]

Another researcher concludes: "The complex interaction between poverty, racism, alcohol and other drugs, the loss of jobs with decent wages in our inner cities, gangs, inadequate handgun regulation, lack of personal opportunity and responsibility, disinvestment in schools and after-school activities, and family violence plays a critical role in our culture of violence."[56]

Poor parenting practices, particularly harsh physical punishment, have been associated with the development of aggressive and violent behavior.[57] Dr. Ron Slaby, a psychologist at Harvard University, explains that poor child-rearing practice creates antisocial behavior in children before age six. This causes tantrums and chaos at home initially, and the behavior continues in school as bullying, delinquency, and dropping out of school.[58]

A survey about the causes of school violence identified the number one cause cited as a lack of parental discipline and control. The second leading cause identified was the breakdown in family structure and dysfunctional lifestyles.[59] School principals most frequently identify the cause of school violence as a lack of parental supervision and a lack of parental involvement with the schools.[60]

Poor child-rearing practices are risk factors because they are an abridgement of the child's power and sense of personal survival. A related explanation is that violence is intergenerational. That is, child abuse and neglect by parents causes their children to abuse and neglect their children.[61] However, family dysfunction, lack of parental involvement, and child maltreatment are not the causes of violence. Rather, they are the symptoms. We need to discover the causes of family dysfunction, child abuse, and lack of parental involvement.

The California Attorney General's Policy Council on Violence Prevention determined that violent behavior is rooted in the multiple contexts of individual, family, and community and social conditions that can converge to increase the risk for violence.[62] Further, the council concluded that poverty, a sense of hopelessness, isolation, and educational decline are social conditions that sow the seeds of violence.[63]

The Office of Juvenile Justice and Delinquency Prevention of the US Department of Justice concludes: "It is widely accepted that the increase in delinquency and violence over the past decade are rooted in a number of interrelated social problems—child abuse and neglect, alcohol, drug abuse, youth conflict and aggression, and early sexual involvement—that mainly originate within the family structure."[64] Because of such beliefs, the US Department of Justice has created the Strengthening Families Program, which emphasizes parent training.

It is clear that single-parent families, especially impoverished ones, experience more dysfunction and disruption than families headed by two parents. High rates of violence occur among families that experience minimal father care.[65] The US Bureau of Justice Statistics has reported that about 60 percent of imprisoned juveniles did not grow up with two parents.[66] Lack of attachment to parents, especially to fathers, is correlated to antisocial behavior for adolescent girls and boys.[67] There is a correlation between the absence of a father and violence that holds for all ethnic groups, income levels, and locations.[68] Single parent households have become more and more prevalent. Since 1970, the proportion of households with both parents has declined substantially. In 1970, 64 percent of African American children lived with two parents, compared with 35 percent in 1997. Comparable figures for white children are 90 percent and 74 percent.[69] This helps to explain increased violence among young people.

The US Department of Justice relates: "The dramatic increase in the number of teenagers murdered during the last two decades has been attributed to various factors, including the rise in child poverty, expansion of gang activity, spread of crack cocaine and drug market competition, and increased availability of guns."[70] This conclusion gets closer to the truth because it taps the surface of the influence of poverty and its relationship to the market economy. The unanswered question here is—What causes child poverty, gang activity, drug use, and increased availability of guns?

What causes school violence? In asking this question, the Center for the Study and Prevention of Violence concludes that "personality characteristics and typical reaction patterns, in combination with physical strength or weakness in the case of boys, are quite important for the development of these problems in individual students (making them more likely to become victims or bullies). At the same time, environmental factors such as the teachers' attitudes, routines, and behaviors play a major role in determining the extent to which the problems will manifest themselves in a larger unit such as the classroom or the school.[71]

Researchers have discovered three key findings about what triggers violent behavior in schools. The largest portion of violent incidents started with an opening move. This consisted of an unprovoked contact or interference with another's possession that was seen as a minor affront. However, the conflict escalated from there. Most incidents began in the school or home, with the greatest number occurring between youngsters who knew one another. The third finding was that the most common goal of violent acts was revenge. The justifications offered by the young people indicated that their behavior stemmed from a value system in which violence is acceptable.[72]

Some of these answers may be valid, but they do not get to the heart of the problem. Why do bullies want to feel more powerful than their victims? Why do they feel a need to have power? Why is there a pecking order in schools? How does this hierarchy impact the school system and society in general?

What causes school shootings? To quote a popular introductory sociology text, "Schools do not create the violence; in most cases, violence spills into schools from the surrounding community."[73] A critical question that this quote prompts is, "What causes violence in the surrounding community?" Researchers have pointed out that most explanations for youth violence fail to acknowledge the role of the community, or such structural variables as family income.[74] Investigations into school shootings tend to focus on early childhood factors, dysfunctional families, availability of weapons, and bullying experiences in school. There also is mention of violent media and video games. Several authors have created profiles of school shooters that concentrate on psychopathology and its kindred, including raging hatred and deep anger.[75] The focus on psychopathology is echoed by media accounts that label the shooters as "disturbed" or "crazy." These explanations in some cases may be necessary. However, they are not sufficient because they do not take into account the larger social and economic forces at work. Some researchers who have investigated school violence conclude: "We have learned that we cannot identify with certainty those students, who, for reasons clear only to themselves, will assault their teachers and peers."[76]

The most thorough investigation of school shootings has been conducted by the National Research Council. They conclude that it is "impossible" to adequately identify the causes of school shootings.[77]

A Broader Prism

A broader prism of understanding is necessary to identify the causes of violence and its proliferation. To understand school violence, we need to look at the causes of violence in the larger society. School violence is a symptom of deeply rooted societal injustice. In order to eradicate school violence, the deeper problems need to be addressed from a broad social scientific perspective.

It is important to frame a social problem within a theoretical framework in order to arrive at effective ways to prevent or intervene with the problem. Much of the ineffectiveness of prevention programs can be traced to the problem not being understood deeply or broadly enough by program designers. This lack of a critical approach is evident in the fact that school violence prevention programs do not work well, especially in terms of long-term effectiveness.

Sociological Explanations

To better understand the causes of violence, we need to take sociological theories into account. Sociological studies have established that poverty, unemployment, and racial discrimination are correlated with violent crime. The following sociological theories help to clarify the causes of violence. At times theories have overlapping areas of agreement, and sociologists tend to rely on more than one theory to help explain social phenomena.

The two major sociological theories that address social change and conflict are functionalist theory and conflict theory. The structural-functional approach sees society as a complex system whose parts work together to promote solidarity and stability. It sees social structure as any relatively stable pattern of social behavior. This approach is interested in any structure's social functions, that is, the consequences of any social pattern for the operations of society as a whole. Most sociologists favored the structural-functional approach until the mid-1950s. In recent decades, its influence has declined, in part because it was unable to explain the social upheaval of the 1960s. Critics point out that by focusing attention on social stability and unity, structural functionalism ignores inequalities of social class, race, ethnicity, and gender. As such, they argue, functional theory is conservative by nature. According to Robert Merton, functional theory "is merely the orientation of the conservative social scientist who would defend the present order of things."[78]

Many people explain violence in terms of "the survival of the fittest." Herbert Spencer, the originator of functional theory, did a disservice by converting Charles Darwin's "survival of the fit" into "survival of the fittest."[79] The implication of Spencer's distortion is that, by nature, human beings compete, must be aggressive, and even overpower others, in order to survive. Changing the word to "fittest" has had an enormous influence on people's thinking about human nature and violence, and is used extensively to explain or justify violence.

Karl Marx originated conflict theory, also known as critical theory. This perspective sees society as marked by conflict between unequal groups over limited resources, including the resource of power. The conflict perspective has become more widespread since the 1960s, when social scientists were challenged to explain such social movements as the student movement, the Black Power movement, and the feminist movement. Whereas Marx concentrated on conflict between social classes, conflict theory now is applied to social conflict between people, groups, societies, and nations. Conflict theory is the theoretical framework which best explains violence domestically and internationally because it analyzes who has power over whom and why. Conflict theory is concerned with the social order being forcibly imposed by the powerful on the less powerful. Capitalism reinforces hierarchy, with competition for resources, including the resource of power, resulting in conflict. This theory can be applied at a microlevel, such as bullying in schools, and at the macrolevel, such as war. Marx concluded that all aspects of social life and ideology emanate from a society's type of economic system. He wrote: "The mode of production of material life determines the general character of the social, political and spiritual processes of life. It is not the consciousness of men that determines their being but, on the contrary, their social being determines their consciousness."[80] The economic system of a society is the foundation that generates other social phenomena, such as ideology, world views, fashion, and language.

Contemporary conflict theorists give emphasis to the great inequalities of power and resources in US society and how this inequality along class, ethnicity, and gender lines shapes a broad array of social problems. Conflict theory focuses on why and how hierarchies of dominant and subordinate groups are established, maintained, and replaced.[81] They argue that the great wealth of corporations and the poverty of many workers create an exploitative and conflict-ridden system. This social order appears to be stable on the surface but harbors conflicts generated by inequality.[82] Karl Marx's ideas appear to be most applicable to the problem of school violence, which is intricately connected to media hegemony. He recognized the power of the printed word and mass communication. A Marxian analysis especially applies to the power of the electronic media to shape consciousness and influence behavior.

In the 1950s C. Wright Mills pointed out that a small group of people, the "power elite," in business, government and military institutions make our society's most important decisions.[83] For decades, sociological research has verified the reality of a "power elite" or "ruling elite."[84] A core idea of Marx is encapsulated in his writing, "The ruling ideas of any age are the ideas of the ruling class."[85] This quote is especially salient when considering the media's influence on ideology and consciousness. The media has tremendous ability to create and to shape consciousness, to forge ideologies and to create world views.

To what extent do the media shape our beliefs and our world view? And who owns the media? These questions are connected to questions at the heart of conflict theory—Says who? And, who benefits? Who benefits from a particular pattern or social arrangement, and at whose expense? Conflict theorists strive to answer such questions by identifying practices the dominant groups have established, consciously or unconsciously, intentionally or unintentionally, to promote and protect their interests.

Conflict theory is integrated with other theories. An example is the biological theory that addresses the role of lead and other neurotoxins in violent behavior. Conflict theory's broader perspective would pay close attention to ecological and structural issues stemming from race and class hierarchy and forms of economic production that characterize American cities.[86] In other words, the poorer one is, the more one is likely to be exposed to toxins. Conflict theory also would conclude that violent behavior resulting from eating bad food made in the name of profit is more concentrated among the poor and among children and adults who are heavily exposed to food and junk food commercials on television.

Symbolic interaction theory also is useful in understanding the causes of violent behavior. This approach focuses on the way that people define reality, how they make sense of the world, how they experience and define what they and others are doing, and how they influence and are influenced by one another. Meaning evolves through interactions with others. An example of conflict theory's integration with symbolic interaction theory in analyzing interpersonal displays of power, such as bullying.

Social learning theory is derived from symbolic interactionism. Social learning theory explains the development of the self through the learning and acquisition of roles and labeling and the dynamics of interpersonal interaction. Social learning theory contends that the likelihood of people committing acts of violence increases when they associate with others who commit violent behavior. Social learning includes media imitation, definitions of violence being justified, and less punishment for violent behavior.[87]

Social learning theory is entwined with phenomenology, the European-based method of social inquiry. Phenomenology is interested in the social construction of reality and how the worldviews of individuals and groups are formed. Phenomenology's approach is helpful in understanding how the media are able to construct an electronic virtual reality.

Some of the other major sociological theories that address violence have been developed in recent decades. Theories of especial interest include general strain theory, control balance theory, social disorganization theory, routine activities theory, social geometry theory, and feminist theory.

The core idea of general strain theory is that if you treat people badly, they may become upset and respond with criminal behavior, including violence.[88] General strain theory describes types of negative treatment (strain) most likely to result in crime, why negative treatment increases the likelihood of crime, and why some people are more likely than others to respond to negative treatment with crime. Strains include the failure to achieve core goals that are easily achieved through crime as well as parental rejection, child abuse and neglect, negative school experiences, low-paying jobs, homelessness, abusive peer relations, criminal victimization, and experiences with discrimination. Negative treatment contributes to negative emotions, including anger, frustration, and depression. These emotions create pressure for corrective action, with crime being a possible response. In other words, crime may be a way to reduce strain or to escape from it.[89] Anger, especially situational anger, plays a central role in general strain theory. Studies of violent incidents find that such incidents typically begin with one person treating another in a way that is perceived as negative, such as insulting one's honor, resulting in a dispute.[90] Studies of high school and middle school students have found that most of the violent incidents at school began with one student provoking another, such as pushing, hitting, or insulting them.[91]

The questions here are: What motivates bad treatment? Why do students provoke each other? What causes a negative reaction? What causes the anger that triggers the violence?

Control balance theory has a lot in common with general strain theory. This theory looks at issues of control imbalance that ultimately result in violence. Perpetrators of violence experience a "control deficit." That is, they are the objects of control more often and to a greater extent than they control other people or things. Examples include being insulted or demeaned. They adapt, but when events bring their weaknesses to the fore, they think about performing deviant acts as a way to change things, to gain control. Control balancing involves the potential perpetrator weighing the perceived gain in control to be achieved from deviant behavior. Violence is usually committed by those with small control deficits or small control surpluses, or by those with larger control imbalances who possess relatively weak self-control.[92]

Control is, essentially, power. Why are control and power important to human beings? Control balance theory is akin to the "locus of control," in which people perform well when they experience a sense of self-empowerment.

Social disorganization theory sees social disorganization in terms of weakened social networks that usually tie community residents to each other and the relative inability of these ties to regulate the nature of the activities that occur in a neighborhood and the neighbors' unwillingness or inability to make use of these networks. The degree of social disorganization in a neighborhood is determined by the degree of economic disadvantage and residential stability.[93] Social disorganization theory mostly is concerned with violent offenses classified as Part I of the FBI Uniform Crime Reporting program. This includes murder, rape, robbery, and aggravated assault.[94]

Routine activities theory concludes that three things generate violence—wanting something from someone, wanting to punish someone, or wanting to preserve one's identity.[95] The rational choice approach posits that only personal attacks and other behavior the person finds offensive trigger aggression. This involves an attribution of blame, loss of face, or deterrence. Attribution of blame is essential to whether a negative experience leads to aggressive behavior. Aggression is seen as instrumental rather than expressive.[96] Social geometry theory is often used to explain gang formation and activity. This theory is applied to blood feuds, which involve a reciprocal exchange of killing. This theory addresses what can happen if one's sense justice has been violated. The lethality of violence is a direct function of social distance. If the social distance between gangs is increased, more violence is predicted. If there is increased social contact, less violence is predicted.[97] Feminist theory recognizes that the inability to attain equality through legitimate channels may result in violence. Also, violence against women may occur when masculine status is threatened. The 2002 Violence Theory Workshop sponsored by the National Institute of Justice illustrates how the issue of sexism tends to be ignored as a factor. The workshop's publication noted: "Although most of the papers dismissed gender, it is the most consistent variable across all forms of violence."[98]

It has been found that the most common goal of violent acts in schools is revenge. The teasing in the shower, the insults, the pressure to act a particular way are the problems students must live with every day and the situations that may provoke aggression or violence. Other research finds that over 40 percent of the young people surveyed reported that they could not control anger and would fight when provoked. The justifications offered by the youth indicated that their actions stemmed from a value system in which violence is acceptable.[99]

Standard explanations have some basis in fact. Factors such as family dysfunction, maltreatment, and problems engendered by poverty may contribute to violent behavior. However, these so-called causes of violence actually are symptoms. These symptoms are linked to deeper dynamics that constitute the cause of violence. Social and economic forces that cause, condone, or promote violence need to be considered. We need to investigate the culture of violence that spawns such industries as the weapons industry and the violent video game industry. We need to understand how our culture socializes boys according to what Barbara Ehrenreich calls "the warrior ideal" and what happens when these men and boy warriors are disempowered socially, politically, and economically.[100]

The Root Cause

These theories and research consistently reveal interpersonal violence may be prompted when a person is treated badly, abused, disrespected, or disempowered by people and social processes and institutions. In order words, violence may result if a person is treated unjustly. The root cause of violence is social injustice. This injustice manifests itself in personal relationships, the family, the school, the workplace, the criminal justice system, the economic system, and other societal institutions. Social injustice shows itself as oppression and as systems that allow power over others. Power over others is the central fact of violence. To direct violence toward another is a violation, an injustice. Violence embodies power and always has a violator and a victim.

The 1967 President's Commission on the Causes and Prevention of Violence identified social injustice as the root cause of violence. The commission judged that the criminal justice system had to be constructed, reformed, and developed in ways that would enable it to deliver justice reliably and well. They also concluded that, in order to meet the challenge of violence, the social order must make violence both unnecessary and unrewarding. To make violence unnecessary, our institutions must provide justice, giving everyone a satisfactory stake in the community and the nation.[101] This root cause extends itself to injustice experienced interpersonally as well as socially and economically.

Our desire for justice is part of our human nature. This conclusion is borne out by the facts. Crime rates are higher (and happiness rates are lower) in countries with a great disparity between rich and poor.[102] Also, it has been repeatedly demonstrated that reducing poverty and discrimination reduces street crime for many poor ethnic groups.[103] Recognizing the key role of social injustice in violence, Martin Luther King stated that peace is not only the absence of conflict but also the presence of justice. From the playground to the Middle East there can be no peace without justice.

CHAPTER 2

STANDARD PRACTICES: NECESSARY BUT NOT SUFFICIENT

> Everything from lollipops to lobotomies has been called prevention.
> —Anonymous

During the past thirty years an impressive amount of energy and money have been invested in preventing school violence. These programs, based on standard explanations, have yielded only modest results. Many schools offer prevention programs that are inadequate and ineffective. Many have violence prevention training in name only. As a ten-year-old bully expressed it: "The school does have a bullying prevention program but I do not know anything about it. There are posters in the lunchroom, but I don't pay attention to them."[1]

Standard practices tend to mirror standard explanations about the causes of violence. As such, these practices tend to focus on counseling and life-skills training, such as communication and problem-solving. Interpersonal relationships are the focus, addressed through such programs as anger management, conflict resolution, and mediation. For example, about half of the character-building and mentoring programs were found to be effective. However, this applied to only one "externalizing behavior" on the part of the students studied.[2]

The heart of the problem is that standard practices address symptoms rather than causes. Some standard practices may be necessary. However, they are not sufficient. This is demonstrated by the almost universal flaw of community and school violence prevention programs—they do not work.³ An example is the 2010 US Department of Education research that instituted standard practices in forty middle schools, which found no statistically significant impacts between high-risk youth in treated schools and control schools.⁴ The US Department of Justice also reports that progress has not been made in reducing serious violent crime in schools.⁵ The Injury Prevention Center at Johns Hopkins University reviewed evaluations of three widely used curricula—Positive Adolescent Choices training, the Violence Prevention Curriculum by Deborah Prothrow-Stith, and the Washington, DC, Community Violence Prevention Program—and found no evidence that the programs resulted in long-term changes in violent behavior. A survey of fifty-one programs found that fewer than half even claimed to have reduced levels of violence.⁶

Risk Factors and Protective Factors

The concept of risk and protective factors was created in order to better understand and address youth violence. Risk factors are characteristics or situations that increase the probability of a young person becoming a victim or a perpetrator of violence.⁷ Protective factors, such as nurturing parents and early childhood education, encourage the development of healthy and productive human beings. Programs try to reduce risk factors while providing protective factors that are missing from a young person's environment. Researchers conclude that the chance of a successful adolescence is not high until the number of protective factors far exceeds the number of risk factors.⁸ The reasoning is that these cumulative risk factors, especially if they are not mitigated by protective factors, make delinquent or violent behavior more likely.

A study of thousands of middle school children found that children with more than five risk factors probably have, at most, one protective factor. As such, the more effective programs address multiple risk factors while creating protective factors. The study recommended programs that promote interactive, personal, positive relationship building to increase protective factors for at-risk young people.⁹ It was found that having just one long-term relationship with a parent, family member, or community member such as a friend, neighbor, minister, teacher or mentor, to whom the child could talk about difficulties, is such a strong protective factor that it could override other risk factors.¹⁰

The problem with this paradigm is that risk factors are symptoms of the problem, not the causes. Because of this, programs tend to address symptoms. They may ameliorate some violence, but they do not prevent it. The prevailing ideology focuses on the family as the origin of violent behavior. This focus is reflected in the emphasis on family-centered prevention programs. For example, the family strengthening program is intended to reduce or buffer "the known, overlapping precursors of conduct and substance use problems in adolescents that originate in the family."[11] The problems, however, do not originate in the family. Families do not cause violence. Dysfunctional families are symptoms of a broader social and economic framework that is defective.

The Cambridge Study in Delinquent Development found that the percentage of young people convicted for violent crimes increases only 3 percent for those with no risk factors versus 31 percent for those with four risk factors. These risk factors included low family income, large family size, low nonverbal IQ, and poor parental child-rearing behavior.[12] All these risk factors tend to be especially evident in impoverished families. Poverty, accompanied by the lack of health, housing, education, employment, and recreation, is one of the most powerful risk factors.[13] Almost all of the other listed risk factors, such as pregnancy complications, parental criminality, academic failure, delinquent peers, and community disorganization can be traced to family poverty. The degree to which poverty is a risk factor is evidenced by the fact that violent crimes are most prevalent in low-income communities.

The US Department of Justice's Office of Juvenile Justice and Delinquency Prevention conducted a meta-analysis of sixty-six studies to identify the most significant risk factors in five domains: individual, family, school, peer-related, and community and neighborhood factors. They discovered that individual risk factors include pregnancy and delivery complications, low resting heart rate, poor health, history of treatment for mental or emotional problems, hyperactivity, aggressiveness, and attitudes that are favorable to antisocial behavior.[14] School factors include academic failure, low bonding to school, truancy, and frequent school transitions. Peer-related factors include delinquent siblings, having friends with weak social ties, delinquent peers, and gang membership.[15] Family risk factors include a family history of problem or antisocial behavior, family conflict, abuse, and low parental involvement. Community risk factors include community disorganization, economic deprivation, and the availability of drugs and firearms.[16]

The elements in each level of this analysis, from individual to community, point to risk factors associated with poverty. The question is—What causes poverty?

It is noteworthy that exposure to violent entertainment and video games is seldom identified as a risk factor and when it is identified as a risk factor its influence is not adequately explained. This book's chapters about media and video game violence make a case for these influences being risk factors and provide in-depth analyses.

Protective factors are characteristics of situations that mitigate the risk of becoming a victim or perpetrator of delinquency or violence.[17] Protective factors identified at the individual level include positive social orientation, self-identified religiosity, and emotional well-being. A peer protective factor is having friends who participate in prosocial activities, and school protective factors include being engaged in school and clear rules for behavior. Family protective factors include family connectedness, sharing in regular activities with parents, and parental monitoring.[18] The most powerful protective factors are positive parenting, early childhood education, and mentoring. In many ways, prevention strategies try to provide what effective parents and communities provide in the course of a child's life.[19] Protective factors help to develop resilience in children. Resiliency includes the attributes of social competence, problem-solving skills, autonomy, and sense of purpose.[20] Social competence includes the qualities of responsiveness, flexibility, empathy, communication skills, a sense of humor, and other prosocial behavior. As a result, resilient children tend to develop more positive relationships with others, including friendships.[21]

One of the most powerful protective factors is quality early childhood education. Early child education programs constitute primary prevention and act as strong protective factors. Evidence has been accumulating that providing early child development opportunities for children, especially low-income children, help to prevent later delinquent behavior. This is because these programs focus on brain development, literacy, prosocial skills, life-skills training, parent training, and coordination of community services.[22]

The Perry Preschool Program in Ypsilanti, Michigan, is a model project that provides early childhood education to disadvantaged children from age two to four. This program addresses the relationship between childhood poverty and school failure by promoting the child's intellectual, social, and physical development. Such high-quality programs include weekly home visits, and monthly group meetings for teachers and parents.[23] The curriculum views children as active and self-initiated learners; the classroom does not exceed twenty children and has at least two staff people. In addition, the staff is highly trained, made social service referrals, and had frequent contact with parents. Evaluation of the program has revealed reduced delinquency, less involvement in serious fights and police contact, fewer school dropouts, and higher rates of graduation and higher income. The long-term results showed that at age twenty-seven the program's participants showed a 50 percent lower number of criminal arrests.[24]

Family

The family can be a risk factor or a protective factor. Social scientists conclude that maltreatment of children today essentially is the result of poorly trained adults who treat children within the context of the violence they themselves experienced as children. Family factors that have been identified include parental criminality, child maltreatment, poverty, poor family management practices, poor family bonding, and parent-child separation.[25] What causes poorly trained parents?

Parenting and the family have been identified as highly influential protective factors. Because of a belief in an intergenerational cycle of violence, a variety of programs considered to be primary prevention programs address intervention with parents and families. Researchers have found that many of the most promising violence prevention strategies are family interventions that teach parenting skills and improved family relationships.[26] An especially important protective factor is early positive parental involvement with children. Schedler and Block, at the University of California, Berkeley, studied and followed a group of children ages three to eighteen.[27] They found that a very significant protective factor is warm and supportive mother's involvement with the child. Positive parental involvement with the child predicted long-term positive outcomes.[28] Protective factors within the family include caring and support, high expectations, encouraging children's participation in family life, and encouraging responsibility.[29]

In response to such research findings, the US Department of Justice's Office of Juvenile Justice and Delinquency Prevention Programs created the Strengthening Families Program for Parents and Youth. The program's family sessions provide problem-solving, reinforcement, and skills practice, such as using consequences when their children break rules. During family sessions, parents and children practice communicating with respect, identify family strengths and values, learn to solve problems and be responsible, and plan enjoyable family activities.[30]

It may be necessary to act on these listed factors. However, it is not sufficient. A question is—What causes family risk factors?

School

School can be a risk factor or a protective factor. Effective schools embody some protective factors that parallel family protective factors, such as nurturing and clearly stated rules that are backed up with consequences. A few studies have explored the role of teachers as protective factors in the lives of children who overcome great adversity.[31] Inspiring teachers often teach activities that promote cooperation and reduce prejudicial behavior. These include nonviolence, compassion and empathy, fairness, trust, justice, tolerance, self-respect and respect for others, and appreciation of controversy.[32] Research with older adolescents has found that "meaningful, instrumental activity" promoted by schools is as powerful a protective factor as social support.[33] Part of this meaningful activity is the development of critical thinking. The ability to think critically relates to recognizing social justice issues as they occur and create links between these issues and classroom instruction. Decades of research, including recent neurobiological research, suggests that complex thinking can be most effectively fostered in classrooms in which social norms of interdependent exploration, flexibility, and complexity are facilitated.[34] Young people want to belong and to contribute. When schools ignore the basic human needs of belonging, bonding, and participating, they become "ineffective, alienating places."[35] A school with no effective violence prevention program is a risk factor.

Community

Community risk factors include community disorganization, availability of drugs and firearms, and exposure to violence and ethnic prejudice.[36] Low-income communities constitute risk factors. Community protective factors include bonding with adults and having resources available. This coalesces with the idea that "the whole village raises the child," with adults volunteering as well as advocating for comprehensive school and community services.

Strengthening Families

Since the early 1990s, a lot of attention has been given to parenting strategies termed "strengthening families" initiatives.[37] Many researchers and practitioners believe that improving parenting practices is the most effective way to reduce delinquency and violent behavior. Researchers believe that the three family intervention strategies effective in reducing risk factors and increasing protective factors are parent training, family skills training, and family therapy.[38] Some examples of these program approaches follow.

The rationale of family strengthening programs is that one must improve the family environment and the parents' ability to nurture and to provide appropriate learning opportunities for their children in order to reduce risk factors. This has involved changing how families interact with one another, such as using communication training and teaching them problem-solving and listening skills. The most successful family strengthening programs combine parent skills, child skills, and family skills. The program has shown some success in increasing children's positive behavior and prosocial skills, improving parenting skills, enhancing the family environment by clarifying family rules, and decreasing family conflict.[39] Three years of follow-up study, through the ninth grade, found significantly less substance abuse among young people at some test sites.[40] However, the long-term success of the program is unknown.

Nurturing Parenting Programs focus on teaching parents that praising a child is a nurturing parenting practice while berating a child is an abusive parenting practice. The strategy that is often identified as most likely to prevent injuries to children is parenting education for adults and adolescents before they become parents.[41] The development of empathy is considered the single most desirable quality in nurturing parenting.[42]

The initial Nurturing Parenting program was evaluated by collecting data one year after parents completed the program. The results indicated that parents were more empathic to the needs of their children and they had changed their attitudes about the use of physical punishment.[43] The study noted the personality characteristics of participating parents, such as aggression, intelligence, and anxiety. However, it did not note how many of the participating parents were single mothers and how many were poor. In addition, it is not known how effective this intervention was after the first year.

Training in parenting skills can reduce negative behavioral problems by improving parental monitoring and supervision, but it has been found to only indirectly improve family relationships.[44] As some researchers have observed: "Overall, there is sufficient evidence that these programs work for children from infancy to five years. However, there is no evidence that these programs work with older children."[45] There is growing evidence that the effectiveness of many of the most popular parenting programs has not been demonstrated. In fact, the most marketed family and parenting programs may even be counterproductive.[46] Although some family and parenting programs have shown some positive effect, it is very difficult to sustain the benefits over time because of the overarching negative influence of living in impoverished families and communities.

Life Skills

The Dropouts and Social Skills program in Seattle, Washington, schools worked with at-risk children in the areas of proactive classroom management, family management, academic support, conflict resolution, and peer resistance skills. The program demonstrated 39 percent less involvement with antisocial peers and 19 percent less tobacco use.[47] The extent these reductions in negative activities reduced violent behavior and the long-term effects are unknown.

The Violence Prevention Project of Boston's Department of Health and Hospitals started the first community-based violence prevention program in the country in 1986. Its strategies include training youth agencies how to teach adolescents about the risk of violence and preventative measures they can take and using community networking to create a new community ethos in support of violence prevention. Such programs raise public awareness of the problem, coalescing local resources into a cohesive force for change. They also expand the types of programs in which at-risk young people can be taught about nonviolent conflict resolution. A formal evaluation of the original program showed a positive impact on students. When interviewed, they reported having fewer fights during the past week.[48]

Accountability Programs

The Office of Juvenile Justice and Delinquency Prevention created programs and approaches that hold juvenile offenders accountable for their behavior. The juveniles are referred by law enforcement agencies or those who cooperate with law enforcement officials to protect students and school personnel from drug, gang, and youth violence. During the past decade, more attention has been rightly given to the role of teaching accountability to young people. Accountability-based programs work with juvenile offenders referred by law enforcement agencies. It has been found that such programs work more effectively when they are part of a comprehensive and collaborative community approach, including students, parents, faculty and staff, community residents, law enforcement and juvenile justice authorities, elected officials, and business representatives.[49] Programs emphasize the meaningful involvement of students, parents, and other school/community partners to avoid operating in isolation. School/community-based teams can design goals and objectives to address the identified priorities, allowing schools to select and implement programs that have been evaluated.[50] Key elements of effective accountability-based programs include an emphasis on student involvement and meaningful responses that are specific to the offender and the offense, and graduated sanctions appropriate to the seriousness of the misconduct and the history of the offender. Unfortunately, few programs are able to fulfill all of the accountability-based program goals and even fewer have been evaluated sufficiently to determine their effectiveness.[51]

In recent decades, researchers and policy makers have realized the need for a more comprehensive and strategically designed approach to prevent violence. In 1993, the Office of Juvenile Justice and Delinquency Prevention launched a national training initiative to implement the creation of a continuum of juvenile delinquency prevention, early intervention, and graduated sanctions strategies. This approach helped to move the emphasis away from "troubled youth," which blamed the young person, to the realm of the local community and to providing more networked, direct services. The continuum starts with prenatal prevention and includes community-based prevention services centered on risk and resource assessment, immediate interventions, and a range of graduated sanctions that include institutional care and aftercare services.

Best Practices for Violence Prevention Programs

During the past two decades a number of "best practices" programs intended to prevent youth crime have emerged. These "research-based" or "evidence-based" programs have tended to be evaluated more than other programs. Researchers analyzed forty-six programs that were evaluated effectively and identified nine program principles leading to positive outcomes for young people. They include quality of implementation; caring, knowledgeable adults; high standards and expectations; parent/guardian participation; community involvement; holistic approaches; youth as resources and service-learning; work-based learning; and long-term services, support, and follow-up.[52] Best practices include early childhood education, parenting skills, mentoring programs, mediation, and some conflict resolution programs.[53] Similarly, the Centers for Disease Control identifies best practices as parent and family strengthening, home visits, social and cognitive strategies, conflict resolution skills, and mentoring. These practices include social and cognitive strategies, programs that clarify and communicate norms about behaviors to children and teach social competency skills, such as communication skills and problem-solving. Even though these programs are the most successful, they are only moderately effective. For example, mentoring programs show about a 50 percent success rate in reducing youth violence.[54]

Parenting

A considerable amount of research indicates that strengthening parenting competence and increasing parental involvement in children's school-related activities helps to prevent children's behavioral problems and promote social competence. Evaluation of such parenting programs showed that the participants' gains lasted for at least one year after they completed the programs.[55] However, the long-term effectiveness of these programs is unknown.

Cognitive Skills

Social and cognitive skills development or the "problem-solving" approach centers on social and emotional learning in children and in the skills parents can use to contribute to their development. The social-cognitive approach to preventing violence, based on more than twenty years of research on specific interpersonal cognitive problem-solving skills, is considered to be primary prevention for children aged four to eight and for their parents. This approach focuses on thinking processes rather than the behaviors themselves. This approach to childrearing deals with social cognition and adjustment. Its theme is that interpersonal cognitive skills play a critical role in the social adjustment of both parent and child. The purpose of this problem-solving program is to strengthen the capacity of children to solve problems that may lead to violence or other negative behavior.[56] Preschool and kindergarten teachers are trained to teach skills through games, role play, and dialogs applied to real life. An evaluation study showed that children exposed to the interventions in preschool improved their problem-solving skills more than children who were not so trained. The children were more likely to show a decrease in impulsive and withdrawal behaviors, gains still apparent when measured four years later.[57] Problem-solving skills are key in children developing self-confidence, self-esteem, and an overall improved sense of competency. Children with problem-solving skills are able to think abstractly, reflectively, and flexibly and are able to try alternate solutions to problems. Autonomy refers to an "internal locus of control," "sense of power," "self-efficacy," and "self-esteem."[58] These qualities lend themselves to resilient children developing a "sense of a compelling future."[59] They have a sense of purpose and future that is accompanied by healthy expectations, a success orientation, and educational aspirations.[60]

Mentoring

Mentoring is the pairing of a young person with a volunteer who acts as a supportive, nonjudgmental role model. The background and experience of mentors vary. They are community residents, local business owners, high school seniors, college students, senior citizens and teachers. Mentoring activities include tutoring, cultural enrichment, social skills development, job-shadowing, life experience sharing, and sports coaching. Mentoring has a range of positive effects. Most students relate that mentors help them to learn to succeed, improve their grades, avoid drugs, increase their respect for others, improve their relationships with parents and teachers, and choose a career path.[61]

Big Brothers Big Sisters is the oldest and best-known mentoring program in the United States, maintaining 75,000 active matches between adults and children. The program predominantly services ten to fourteen-year-old disadvantaged young people from single-parent households. The purpose of the program is to give these children the opportunity to develop a friendship with an adult volunteer mentor. The mentor and the child meet for three or four hours a week to engage in a variety of activities that they enjoy, such as sports, cultural activities, and outings. These clubs are engaged in comprehensive strategies to help children build self-esteem, acquire positive values, and pursue productive goals. The relative success of mentoring programs demonstrates a need for one or more close supportive relationships.

An eighteen-month follow-up study of the Big Brothers Big Sisters programs showed that participating young people were 46 percent less likely to start using drugs, 33 percent less likely to hit someone, and demonstrated improved school attendance and performance and better peer and family relationships.[62] These recommendations are embodied in the Blueprints developed by the Center for the Study and Prevention of Violence.

Blueprints Best Practices

In 1996 the Center for the Study and Prevention of Violence at the University of Colorado Boulder identified and replicated youth violence prevention programs that they found to be effective. The Blueprints programs include, among others, prenatal and infancy home visitation by nurses, the Incredible Years Series, intensive family therapy, Promoting Alternative Thinking Strategies (PATHS), and Big Brothers Big Sisters of America.

Their Blueprints for Violence Prevention identifies violence prevention and intervention programs that meet a strict scientific standard of program effectiveness. These model programs have been effective in reducing adolescent violent crime, aggression, delinquency, and substance abuse.[63] In order to be a Blueprint program, the program must demonstrate a sustained effect at least one year beyond participating in the program.[64] However, their long-term effectiveness tends to be unknown. Note that, as with parenting and family programs, the success of Blueprints programs is significantly compromised when participants live in an impoverished environment.

Visiting Nurses

The Nurse-Family Partnership program sends nurses to the homes of low-income, first-time mothers to improve their health, parenting skills, and the health of their babies for two years. The program helps women improve their prenatal health and the outcomes of pregnancy, improve the care provided to infants and toddlers, and improve women's own personal development, giving especial attention to the planning of future pregnancies, women's educational achievement, and participation in the workforce. A fifteen-year follow-up study reveals that there were 7 percent fewer reports of child abuse, 31 percent fewer subsequent births, 44 percent fewer maternal alcohol and drug abuse problems, and 56 percent fewer arrests on the part of fifteen-year-old children.[65]

Incredible Years

The Incredible Years series is a comprehensive set of developmentally based curricula for parent, teacher, and child training. The curricula are designed to promote social competence and prevent conduct problems in children aged two to eight, at risk for or presenting conduct problems, defined as high rates of aggression, defiance, and oppositional and impulsive behavior. Trained facilitators use interactive presentations, videotape modeling, and role-playing techniques to encourage group discussion, problem-solving, and sharing of ideas.[66]

The Incredible Years training for parents emphasizes parenting skills known to promote children's social competence and reduce behavior problems such as how to play with children, helping children learn, effective use of incentives, effective limit-setting, and strategies to handle misbehavior. The advanced program includes effective communications skills, anger management, and problem-solving between adults. The teacher training emphasizes effective classroom management skills such as the effective use of teacher attention, praise, proactive teaching strategies, and how to teach empathy, social skills, and problem-solving in the classroom. The children's curriculum emphasizes skills such as emotional literacy, empathy, friendship skills, anger management, problem-solving, and how to be successful at school.

Program evaluation of eight hundred children and their parents show significant increases in parent-child interaction and parental attitudes, a reduction in violent forms of discipline, and reduced child conduct problems. Teachers increased positive management skills, a positive classroom atmosphere, and bonding with parents. Children increased conflict management skills and social competence, as well as improved academic engagement and school readiness. Effects have been maintained for three years following program participation.[67]

Intensive Family Therapy

Various forms of intensive family therapy programs have had some success. The Dysfunctional Families and Therapy program was developed by the University of Utah to reduce referrals to foster care. The program provided twenty-six to thirty hours of direct service, which included an intervention plan, positive reinforcement of the individual child, information and guidelines that focused on interpersonal skills and needs, such as communication and parenting skills, and identification of social support. After five years, the group demonstrated a 34.6 percent reduction in foster care referrals.[68] Although the results are promising the program has a number of inherent limitations. The thirty hours of intensive individualized service probably created a "halo effect" which, in itself, promoted positive results. The reduction in recidivism into foster care is an indicator of program effectiveness. However, it does not directly measure a reduction in delinquent or violent behavior. Another problem is the treatment cost of $22,000 per family.[69]

Promoting Alternative Thinking Strategies

Promoting Alternative Thinking Strategies (PATHS) is an innovative intervention designed to promote social and emotional competence and reduce aggression and behavior problems in the classroom. A key objective is to reduce emotional and behavioral problems. The program is based on two decades of prior research that indicated an increased need for universal, school-based curriculum to promote emotional competence. Social and emotional competence had not been considered a necessary component of education in the past, but its creators felt that it had become as critical for the basic knowledge repertoire of children as reading, writing, and arithmetic because of the increasing complexity of the world.

Knowledge of the neurobiological development of the brain was heavily influential in the development of PATHS. The program's design includes attention to developmental models of brain organization.[70] Information is initially transmitted to the frontal lobes for processing and interpretation, then the frontal lobes transmit messages back to the limbic system to modify emotion signals and to the sensory-motor cortex to influence potential actions. The frontal lobes are heavily involved in decision-making, integrating data involving emotions with knowledge-based information. In early childhood, there are few interconnections between the limbic system and the frontal lobes. What results is the "terrible twos" in which children frequently hit, bite, or kick when they feel angry. As children mature, increasing neuronal interconnections evolve between the frontal lobes and the limbic system. This is important regarding self-control because the frontal cortex becomes increasingly able to regulate impulses from the limbic areas and modify actions. Between the ages of five and seven, a shift occurs in which the frontal areas achieve significant dominance in exerting emotional self-regulation and self-control. These developments do not automatically occur but are heavily influenced by environmental input throughout early childhood. If these networks do not develop in an optimal manner, children do not have the neuronal structure necessary to control their actions in response to strong emotional signals. So, PATHS teaches children to practice strategies for self-control, identifying and labeling feelings, expressing feelings, delaying gratification, reducing stress, controlling impulses, reading and interpreting social cues, communication skills and empathy.[71]

Social and emotional competence includes the expression, understanding, and regulation of emotions.[72] PATHS is designed to enhance the social and emotional competence of children and to facilitate self-control, emotional awareness, and interpersonal problem-solving skills.[73] An evaluation of the program shows it is effective in increasing management and understanding of emotional experiences.[74] More specifically, it has been shown to improve self-control, improve understanding and recognition of emotions, increase the ability to tolerate frustration, decrease anxiety and depression, decrease conduct problems and aggression, and instilling the use of effective conflict resolution methods.[75]

Boys and Girls Clubs

According to a Columbia University study, Boys and Girls Clubs have been effective in increasing rates of school attendance and improving academic performance. The clubs in public housing projects have reduced the juvenile crime rate by 13 percent.[76] Another study involving thirty-three Boys and Girls Clubs found that involvement and regular attendance of high-risk youth in club activities were effective in improving behavior and performance at school.[77] The litmus test of the clubs is a measure of the long-term reduction in juvenile crime and violence. The results are very mixed, tending to show that these programs may work in the short-term but not over time.

Security Measures

Many people, including school administrators, think that violence prevention means establishing safety features in the school environment, such as security officers, surveillance cameras, barbed-wire fences, and a front entrance security gate. The January 2018 school shooting in Marshall County High School, Kentucky, for example, was followed by instituting metal detectors and talk of stationing the National Guard in schools. This notion of school security also includes emphasizing safe school planning and crisis management. While these components may be necessary for school violence prevention in some settings, they are not sufficient to prevent violence. They merely intervene.

School prevention programs typically emphasize school safety issues, control, and crisis management. Often preventive measures consist of surveillance cameras and school resource officers, who are law enforcement officers. These practices tend to focus on promoting school safety, addressing children's grief, and the development of community crisis response teams.[78]

School resource officers are prepared to deal with weapons and violent behavior. They are trained to counsel students about law-related problems and support services, teach classes on the law, and serve as role models. These officers have been most successful in settings where their role is clearly defined and well understood by students, teachers, and staff, and where they have received extensive training. In their most expansive role, they act as referral agents to other groups, such as law enforcement, social services, and tutoring services.[79] These officers tend to be placed in tough schools and also in schools that are relatively affluent and can afford them. The critical problem with school resource officers is that they tend to be an indication that the horse is already out of the barn and that school violence is a well-established fact on campus.

Counseling

Counseling and therapy are often applied to reducing and preventing violence in schools and in society at large.[80] The usual form of individual and family counseling at times has beneficial results. However, its effectiveness in the long-term, especially for young people living in troubled environments, is unclear. While it is important to provide young people with access to school psychologists and counselors, research shows that programs that focus exclusively on counseling, especially group counseling, have little impact on their delinquent and criminal behavior.[81]

Group counseling for children who bully involves group therapeutic treatment, including anger management and conflict resolution. Research confirms that these groups are often ineffective at best. Such efforts often are counterproductive, with group members' behavior deteriorating as they serve as role models and reinforcers for each other's antisocial behavior.[82] These groups do not work because bullying is not about anger or conflict but power.

Conflict Resolution

Conflict resolution is especially popular in school programs. Many conflict resolution programs are based on the premises of *Getting to Yes*, by Roger Fisher and William Ury. The book began by asking what is the best way for people to deal with their differences.[83] Conflict resolution centers on the conclusion that responsible behavior is the hallmark of an emotionally intelligent person and that it depends, above all else, on the absence of coercion.[84] Conflict resolution programs recognize that conflict is natural and that people can learn new skills to deal with conflict in appropriate, nonviolent ways. The bedrock of conflict resolution is reciprocity and fair play.[85]

The principles of conflict resolution emphasize separating the people from the problem, developing perspective by understanding that different points of view exist, and sharing feelings and emotions. This process includes focusing on interests rather than positions, inventing options for mutual gain, and using objective criteria to negotiate a fair standard rather than the arbitrary will of either side.[86]

Researchers recommend that, within this context, teachers need to give up the inclination to exercise forceful authority over students, without abandoning the responsibility to maintain order. Because teachers are responsible for promoting acceptable and successful behaviors in young people, they need to transfer responsibility to students for choosing behaviors that fit within acceptable standards.[87]

Conflict resolution programs in schools usually fall into one of three models: mediation, curriculum integration, or peaceable schools.[88] The mediation program trains adults and/or students to act as neutral parties who help disputing young people to reach resolutions. The peaceable classroom is a whole-classroom approach that incorporates conflict resolution into the core subjects of the curriculum and into classroom management methods. Peaceable classrooms are the building blocks of the peaceable school.[89] Some researchers conclude that the peaceable school approach, which incorporates the other three approaches, has the greatest potential to help bring about long-term change.[90]

Criticisms of conflict resolution include its being too late in the development of young people whose "social skills deficits" begin in childhood. Also, these "deficits" may not be the root of interpersonal violence.[91] Bullying, for example, is not about conflict but power. Some programs in conflict resolution may defuse an initial situation before it worsens. However, conflict resolution programs attempting to curtail bullying do not work.[92] Conflict resolution does not answer the questions that need to be addressed in order to prevent these initial situations from happening. A truer form of violence prevention would ask the question of why students are so prone to bullying and physical aggression. What are the characteristics of the culture of violence that promote aggressive and violent behavior in young people?

Peer Mediation

Peer mediation programs frequently are used in school violence prevention programs. They train young people to act as mediators in school by listening, communicating, identifying, and arriving at nonviolent solutions to conflicts.[93] Most evaluations of these programs have not been properly designed and few have shown positive results or long-term success.[94] Some researchers have flatly concluded that peer mediation programs do not work.[95] Peer mediation may be appropriate in cases of conflict between students. However, it is not recommended in bullying situations.[96] The messages that mediation sends, such as, "You're both partly right and partly wrong," are inappropriate. The appropriate message to the child who bullies is "Your behavior is inappropriate and won't be tolerated." Also, facing one's tormentor in a mediation session may be very distressful for the victim and may inhibit the victims from even participating in the program.[97]

Best Practices for Schools

The Safe Communities—Safe Schools program of the Center for the Study and Prevention of Violence at the University of Colorado, for example, recommends five components of safe schools. These include developing a social support team, which is a small team that is a repository of information and can take action, and implementing only proven effective programs. The other three components are forming a planning team, doing a safety assessment, and developing a crisis management plan.[98]

A meta-analysis of 149 school-based programs found that successful programs shared a number of common features. The report notes that it may be important to provide students with access to school psychologists and counseling. However, programs that focused exclusively on counseling, especially group counseling, had little impact on students' criminal and delinquent behavior. Programs that built skills were much more likely to have positive results, such as reducing school disorder. This study found that the successful programs recognized the importance of building school capacity to support innovation, communicated clear messages about acceptable and unacceptable behavior, and enforced rules consistently. The programs emphasized responsible decision-making and problem-solving and taught critical thinking skills to help high-risk students consider alternatives to delinquent behavior.[99]

Other widely accepted principles for peaceful schools include making violence prevention a long-term priority for the school. Students, teachers, and parents should plan and assess violence prevention activities, and programs should include school and community coordination.[100]

Olweus Bullying Prevention

The most effective school-based prevention programs often are modeled after the Olweus Bullying Prevention program. The program has received attention since the late 1980s in Japan, England, the Netherlands, and Canada. There are now hundreds of programs modeled on the Olweus approach both internationally and in the United States.

In Norway in the early 1980s, public attention was captured by the suicides of three young boys who took their lives after being persistently bullied. This horrific event resulted in a national campaign against bullying in the Norwegian schools and the development of the Olweus Bullying Prevention Program, which involved 25 percent of the children in Norway.[101]

The program includes students in elementary and middle schools. All students within a school participate in most aspects of the program. The program involves school staff, students, and parents in school-wide, classroom, and individual interventions. Faculty and staff survey students anonymously to determine the nature and prevalence of the school's bullying problem. They increase supervision of students during breaks and conduct school-wide assemblies to discuss the issue. Teachers receive in-service training on how to implement the program.

The program raises awareness about bullying, improves peer relations, intervenes to stop intimidation, develops clear rules against bullying behavior, and supports potential victims. School-wide rules and sanctions that emphasize a climate intolerant of bullying behaviors are reinforced by regular classroom discussions. The program clarifies norms and teaches social competency skills. Individual students receive consistent supervision. This often is accompanied by parent involvement and mental health interventions.

An important premise of this prevention program is that bullying behavior can be redirected into a positive direction through a systematic restructuring of the social environment. This restructuring results in fewer opportunities for bullying and fewer or smaller rewards, in the form of prestige or peer support, for displaying such behavior. In addition, positive, friendly, and other prosocial behavior is encouraged and rewarded.

The program is built around some key principles derived from research on the development and modification of problem behavior, especially aggressive behavior. The program strives to develop a school (and ideally, a home) environment characterized by warmth, positive interest, and involvement by adults; firm limits to unacceptable behavior; to apply nonhostile and nonphysical negative consequences; and to help adults to act as authorities and positive role models. Adults are encouraged "to emulate an authoritative (not authoritarian) adult-child interaction model in which they take responsibility for the students' total situation, including both academic learning and social relationships in school."[102]

The first and most comprehensive evaluation of the program was conducted with 2,500 elementary and middle school students in Bergen, Norway, between 1983 and 1985. Results revealed that the frequency with which students reported being bullied and bullying others decreased by 50 percent. Other antisocial behavior, such as vandalism, fighting, theft, and truancy decreased by about 15 percent during this time. A well-implemented program results in significant improvements in the social climate of the class, reflected in students' report of improved order and discipline, more positive social relationships, and a more positive attitude toward schoolwork and school.[103] In addition, program effects appeared to be cumulative. For some of the outcome variables, the program effects were more marked after twenty months of intervention. Evaluations of programs in the United States, England, and Germany have produced somewhat more modest findings.[104] A key factor to consider regarding Norway's better ability to reduce bullying compared to the United States is that Norway is more peaceful than the United States and does not promote a culture of violence.

The Achilles' heel in the Olweus program is that the adults "take responsibility for the students' total situation, including academic performance and social relationships in school." In the classroom, teachers and other school personnel introduce and enforce classroom rules against bullying and hold regular classroom meetings with students to discuss bullying. Students can be involved in both formulating and enforcing the rules that govern them and in deciding what the consequences are. However, giving all authority to an adult in such matters obstructs the child's natural growth toward more independence, responsibility, and competency. This shortcoming is partly why the Olweus program, after almost forty years in operation in a relatively peaceful culture, has only a 50 percent success rate.

A widely recognized example of a bullying prevention program heavily influenced by the Olweus model is the Bully-Proofing Your School approach. Emphasis is on creating a caring school community. School staff is trained in conflict resolution and methods of intervening in bullying situations. Teachers learn how to work with victims and bullies. Students learn social problem-solving techniques in a nine-session curriculum, followed-up by sessions in middle school. Children who engage in bullying are taught leaderships skills, and victims are taught more effective social skills. In addition, parent support groups are available.[105]

Bully Busters

Another widely used program is the Bully Busters training program. It describes itself as a research-driven bullying prevention curriculum that enables staff to begin reducing bullying and to positively affect school climate. The training focuses on characteristics of students who bully and their targets; how to use appropriate interventions in bullying situations; how to develop prevention policies that work; and how to help students involved in bullying (bullies, victims, bystanders). A 2010 study shows that the Bully Busters effectively increases teachers' knowledge and use of intervention skills and their efficacy, and reduces classroom bullying.[106]

Stop Bullying Now!

The Stop Bullying Now! program recommends best practices based on a review of bullying prevention programs and feedback from educators. The focus is on the social environment of the school and requires the efforts of everyone in the school. The program includes assessing the extent of bullying by administering an anonymous questionnaire to students about bullying. The program obtains staff and parent buy-in to support bullying prevention and forms a representative coordinating group that develops simple, clear rules about bullying that help students become aware of adult expectations. The program suggests weaving bullying prevention into the fabric of the school environment.[107]

Second Step

Second Step is a widely used program that is based on social-emotional learning. The program discusses empathy and role-learning. However, like many prepackaged school violence prevention programs, the program's effectiveness is compromised significantly because it does not consider how effectively the entertainment media teach attitudes, values, and behaviors. Programs of this nature may be necessary. However, they are not sufficient because they do not address the omnipresent social learning projected by the electronic entertainment media. Chapter 7, "Media Reality" and chapter 8, "Fun and Games," explain how the effects of the electronic entertainment media supersede the efforts of such programs.

Democratic Classrooms

Democratically facilitated classrooms help to improve learning and behavior. Student decision-making in the classroom and student-driven learning are highly effective. Teachers' modifying their classroom management and teaching styles, such as incorporating the use of cooperative learning methods and promoting interactive learning, improves academic performance and may prevent delinquent behavior.[108]

A pivotal study of school violence, conducted by the National Institute of Justice, resulted in a 50 percent reduction in the time that teachers spent dealing with disruptive students. The key reason for this success was that the project was student-driven and focused on student-level problem-solving. Students identified and prioritized problems through open class discussions, analyzed the problems using a variety of information-gathering methods, and then formulated responses and brainstormed solutions using the information previously collected. Finally, the students were empowered by having the opportunity to define the problem and devise ways to address it.[109] This study demonstrates how a classroom environment that nurtures student empowerment and self-empowerment is a key factor in reducing aggressive behavior. Student-driven learning is democracy in action.

Intrinsic to democratic classrooms are critical thinking and discussion of real-world problems, such as social justice. Teachers need to recognize social justice issues as they occur and create links between those issues and classroom instruction. Decades of research, including recent neurobiological research, suggests that complex thinking can be best fostered in classrooms in which social norms of interdependent exploration, emotional safety, flexibility and complexity are established.[110] These programs are effective because young people need to be empowered by knowledge of their world and by having a voice in their own governance. This need for democracy is demonstrated in the classroom and on the world stage.

Teaching students responsibility is effective in school settings. One program that showed some success was for middle school students who demonstrated low achievement, disregard for rules, and low bonding to school and family. For two years, the program focused on reducing the students' cynicism and increasing their sense of competence by increasing the link between their actions and the consequences of those actions. This effort focused on such risk factors as inconsistent rewards and low monitoring. Only 10 percent of the student participants were later involved in criminal acts and arrests, compared to 30 percent of students who did not participate. This suggests that holding children accountable can reduce antisocial behavior.[111]

Democratic classrooms show that young people respond positively to shared decision-making, personal acknowledgement, respect, skills development, and responsibility.

The Arts

Researchers have investigated music theater workshops, native dance programs, mural projects, playwriting, and service projects through the arts. They have found that art in its various forms is a protective factor and helps young people to develop resiliency. Art is a deterrent to delinquency, and it enhances youth development. The arts are empowering because they help children better understand their world and cultural heritage and develop artistic skills, they facilitate decision-making and problem-solving skills.[112] The arts also give children opportunities to express themselves and make a contribution to the world.

Families and Schools Together

A program that links families and schools in raising children successfully is the Families and Schools Together (FAST) program. Many parents feel alone, too busy to connect with their children, lacking support from other adults. The FAST program reaches out to entire families and organizes multifamily groups to increase parent involvement with at-risk young people. A four-year follow-up study found that about 23 percent of the children improved in just eight to ten weeks. The areas of improvement were conduct disorder, reduced from 85 to 53 percent; anxiety/withdrawal, from 81 to 55 percent, and attention span problems, from 83 to 51 percent.[113]

Developing School Capacity

Building school capacity is considered to be a best practice and is a key element in preventing school violence.[114] Research has shown that "effective school-based programs should focus not just on students but on the school itself as well."[115] The most effective strategies are very comprehensive in nature. These involve the entire school as a community working to change the climate of the school and the norms for behavior.[116] Developing school capacity includes developing the capacity to implement, develop, and evaluate school violence prevention programs. Building school capacity is a key part of the process and the part least implemented.

Community Involvement

There is a recent increased recognition of the important role of the community. In the mid-1990s, the US Department of Justice shifted its emphasis from "troubled youth" to a risk and protection assessment of the community, as well as the family. There is an emphasis on "proximal social settings," which concentrates on improving the attitudes, skills, and practices of people working with young people and modifying the organizational climate of the school and community.[117] Because of this, there have been efforts to create comprehensive programs that involve collaborative relationships among schools, service providers, law enforcement, and faith communities. This makes sense, considering the large degree in which the school and community are entwined.

The themes among these recommendations are to develop effective programs. The programs should be comprehensive, encompassing the school, home, and the community. The programs appear to be most effective when they have a broad scope, involving such components as moral reasoning, anger control, social skills development, and collaborative problem-solving methods.[118]

The major failing of these programs is that they address the symptoms rather than the causes of school violence. The recommendations and the programs built around them may be necessary, but they are not sufficient. A major obstacle to reducing school violence is that effective violence prevention programs require time, resources, and money. Although dedicated teachers, administrators, and parents give of their time and resources, more money needs to be allocated to schools.

Program Evaluation

The effectiveness of most school-based violence prevention programs is uncertain at best.[119] The vast majority of violence prevention programs have not been evaluated, and their long-term results have been called into question. Most of the programs that have been evaluated have been found to be ineffective.[120] Studies show that the usual components of school violence prevention efforts, such as conflict peer mediation and individual counseling do not work very well.[121] In addition, researchers' claims about the success of standard practices vary and are due, in part, to faulty research methods.[122] The relatively few programs that have been evaluated well have tended to show short-term positive results, but few have results that last over time.[123]

In fact, some programs may do more harm than good. Some researchers point out: "Not only have programs that have been earnestly launched been ineffective, but some of our seemingly best ideas have led to worsening the behavior of those subjected to the intervention."[124] It has been found that children wrongly placed in targeted programs may actually worsen. For example, conflict resolution for children exposed to high levels of violence may increase their anxiety, depression, and aggression.[125]

More evaluation of school-based interventions is essential to establishing and maintaining effective prevention programs.[126] It is necessary to implement research-based programs with demonstrable success. However, this is not sufficient to prevent school violence. The litmus test of the insufficiency of research-based violence prevention programs is that, despite incredible efforts and resources, school violence has not diminished.

What Works—Sort Of

What is necessary as well as sufficient for school violence prevention programs to be effective? Programs that work acknowledge the human need for acceptance, respect, competency, creativity, and making a contribution to the world. Carl Rogers's idea of "unconditional positive regard" is that acceptance is a fundamental human need without which learning is diminished. Unconditional positive regard, or respect, helps to create classrooms that are more inclusive and intellectually rigorous. As one educational theorist explains, in schooling, "unconditional respect is every student's entitlement. It provides the foundation for meaningful teaching and learning."[127]

Respect needs to be taught in terms of ethnic diversity and physical ability, and also in terms of sex and gender. Learning how to achieve egalitarian relationships is "as critical to students as reading, writing, math, and the use of computers."[128] Violence against girls and women needs to be incorporated in violence prevention curricula, including ways to give boys and young men the emotional and intellectual support for non-violence.[129] The appendix of this book includes resources for gender education, such as "Dreamworlds," a video that shows how music videos promote a rape culture.

Democratic classrooms are accepting, inclusive and respectful. Young people welcome democratic practices in the classroom. They want to be empowered and make contributions to the world. The elements of democracy, such as respect and shared decision-making, are intrinsic to justice. Our human nature requires justice—justice in our relationships and in the social order. These program elements are effective because they are aligned with the needs of human nature. Why this is so becomes clearer in the following chapter.

CHAPTER 3

PAOLO FREIRE AND THE QUESTION OF HUMAN NATURE

> Nothing is to be preferred before justice.
> —Socrates

To understand and to prevent violence it is necessary to clarify and understand the elements of human nature. Many people argue that violent behavior has always been a part of human nature because it is part of our biological makeup and has been necessary for survival. As the following research reveals, violence is not part of our nature. The research also shows which qualities of human nature have been necessary for our survival. In order to arrive at a valid understanding and explanation of human aggressive and violent behavior, both need to be placed in the context of a broad social scientific inquiry, including the disciplines of history, economics, psychology, sociology, media studies, cognitive neurosciences, and the study of culture.

Our perception of the qualities of human nature is overshadowed by the dominant misconception that Darwin wrote about "the survival of the fittest." Herbert Spencer, a predominant early sociologist, interpreted Darwin's theory as "the fittest," but Darwin actually was writing about "the survival of the fit." This distinction is significant because "fittest" implies competition. The notion of the survival of the fittest has wielded tremendous influence on modern ideology, resulting in a widespreat belief that it is natural for human beings to be competitive, self-interested, and ready for battle. As the following research shows, this is not the case. It is essential to understand what our nature is because violent behavior is a response to our basic nature being violated. Let us begin an exploration of what it is to be human by visiting the work of Paolo Freire.

Paolo Freire

Paolo Freire was an internationally renowned educator and educationist theorist. His theory of education is detailed in such books as *The Pedagogy of the Oppressed* and *Education for Critical Consciousness*. Freire's writings work toward "the creation of a world in which it will be easier to love."[1] His work in educational theory and practice necessarily involves an exploration of the nature of violence and what it is to be human. He concludes that it is our vocation to become more fully human. As such, it is inherently violent to obstruct the fulfillment of this vocation. Central to Freire's theory of education is his concern with violence as an expression of oppression. He investigated the process through which nonliterate native people in Northern Brazil developed a critical consciousness. This exploration led him to discover the conditions under which people come to practice critical consciousness and to experience themselves as creators and transformers of the world.

Freire is concerned with the violence inherent in educational institutions that inhibit the expression and development of the students' humanity. These institutions inhibit our vocation to become "more fully human." In order to accomplish this, he proposes that education is the practice of freedom rather than domination. This advocacy for education that liberates is shared globally with other renowned educators, including Ivan Illich, Frantz Fanon, Loris Malaguzzi, and Miles Horton. Central to the work of these liberatory educators is their advocacy and facilitation of critical thinking, which is necessary for democracy.

Freire discusses "banking" education versus "problem-posing" education, which is a constant unveiling of reality. The liberatory educator poses reality as a question and a process rather than a given, and facilitates self-directed learning and creativity. He identifies and describes the inherent violence in the relationship between the "bank teller" teacher and the student in which the teacher presents him/herself as "the necessary opposite" of the student, rather than as a partner in unveiling the world. Freire's advocacy for "co-intentional education" is predicated on the nature of the oppressive character of all non-reciprocal relationships. In this way he is an advocate for democratic classrooms and learning experiences.[2]

The banker educator's task is to "fill" the students with the contents of his or her narration, the contents of which are detached from reality. They are "disconnected from the totality that engendered and could give them significance."[3] Banking education turns students "into 'containers,' into 'receptacles' to be 'filled' by the teacher. The more completely he fills the receptacles, the better a teacher he is. The more meekly the receptacles permit themselves to be filled, the better students they are."[4] Intrinsic to this process is objectification of the student. This non-reciprocal process reduces the child to an object and so is inherently violent. Freire's intent was "to call the attention of true humanists to the fact that they cannot use banking educational methods in the pursuit of liberation, for they would only negate that very pursuit."[5]

According to Freire, true education occurs when the teacher and students together are involved in "the quest for mutual humanization." Education "must begin with the solution of the teacher-student contradiction by reconciling the poles of the contradiction so that both are simultaneously teachers and students."[6] "Through dialogue, the teacher-of-the-students and the students-of-the-teacher cease to exist and a new term emerges: teacher-students with student-teachers... They become jointly responsible for a process in which all grow."[7] Such highly reciprocal relationships are deeply democratic. Freire writes that, apart from inquiry, human beings cannot be truly human. In order to be more authentically human we must express our human nature. One way that we do this is to question the world. This is especially prevalent in children, who are full of questions.

Freire notes that a characteristic of the ideology of oppression is to project an absolute ignorance onto others. This, in turn, legitimizes obstructing their will and taking away their power to make decisions. He notes that to alienate people "from their own decision-making is to change them into objects."[8] The process of objectification can be facilitated by language, such as assigning labels and names that connote a nonhuman status. These labels include "gooks," "bitches," and, as some law enforcement officers call criminals, "maggots." Once people are objectified, it is easier to exploit and harm them. This is amply evidenced by the My Lai Massacre, domestic violence, and police brutality.

Imposing hierarchy and objectifying people are part of the dynamic of demonstrating power. In a reciprocal relationship, one does not have power over another. In a truly reciprocal relationship, there is no violence. Freire further points out that the more students work at storing the deposits the teachers deposit in them, the less they develop their critical consciousness. Critical consciousness "would result from their invention in the world as transformers of the world."[9]

Loris Malaguzzi, founder of the Reggio Emilia schools, has observed children acting on this desire to transform the world. He observed that "children realize that the world is multiple and that other children can be discovered through a negotiation of ideas. Instead of interacting only through feelings and a sense of friendship, they discover how satisfying it is to exchange ideas and thereby transform their environment."[10] The desire to engage in reciprocal relationships, to ask questions of the world, and to create and transform the world is essential to being human.

Another important contribution Freire has made to the study of violence is the concept of "horizontal violence." The negative stereotypes and actions of the dominant society against oppressed people are so powerful that the oppressed cannot help but internalize these and develop self-hatred. During times of duress (and the poor always live under duress), people tend to project this self-hatred horizontally against others in their group, others who are like them. This phenomenon is abundantly evident in domestic violence, Hispanic gang killings, and witchcraft in Indian communities. Statistics bear this out. Ninety-four percent of homicides involve victims and offenders of the same ethnicity.[11]

The question of who benefits from oppressive forms of education and systems needs to be asked. Freire writes that banking education serves the "interests of the oppressors, who care neither to have the world revealed nor to see it transformed."[12]

Freire's model of liberatory education derives from and promotes the consciousness, efficacy, empowerment, and humanization of students. To what extent is the human desire to explore and transform the world nurtured by schools? To what extent do schools empower students to become more fully human? How can students be empowered in the classroom so that they do not feel the need to overpower others? Liberatory classrooms are based on problem-posing education, facilitating self-directed learning and creativity. These classrooms promote democracy and reciprocity, from which naturally spring forth harmony and respect.

It is not easy to facilitate such education in a contemporary classroom, which tends to be overcrowded and attended by students who have been raised on bank-teller educational methods and systems. As a friend of the author commented, "Take a classroom of thirty hyperactive teenagers right after a sugar-filled lunch and see if you can imagine some program that would accomplish Freire's ideas." This comment points to the need to institute this method during the earliest years of school and to work to establish this approach throughout the child's school years. To a great degree, this has been accomplished by such schools as the Emilia Reggio, Waldorf, and Montessori schools. This can be accomplished for public schools by increasing funding and making more resources available to schools.

Human nature needs to be taken into account in order to facilitate education and also to understand violent behavior and to prevent it. When our efforts to live according to our nature are thwarted, violent behavior may result. Therefore, we must ask, What is human nature? What are the essential elements of being human?

The experience of Freire and other liberatory educators has led them to conclude that it is human to learn, to thrive, and to contribute to a social environment that is democratic and cooperative and nurtures creativity, humanization, and transformation. To what extent is such a conclusion borne out by social scientific research?

What is Human Nature?

There are common misconceptions about the nature of human beings. Some of these misconceptions are due to lack of adequate evidence, misinterpretations or distortions of early research, and simply habit of thought. Textbook responses to the question of human aggression are typified by the following statement. "Evolutionary analysis suggests that a drive for survival may have endowed many or most species with an innate predisposition toward some forms of violence."[13]

As noted, Darwin wrote about "the survival of the fit."[14] The widespread belief that he wrote about "the survival of the fittest" introduced an entirely different perspective on the question of human nature that focused on hierarchy and competition. This ideological perspective, perpetrated by Herbert Spencer, supported his functionalist perspective of sociological theory which supported the status quo of capitalism and its engine, competition.

The work of Konrad Lorenz often is cited to support the argument that human beings are aggressive by nature. However, Lorenz argued that human beings, unlike other members of the animal kingdom, do not have appropriately evolved mechanisms to inhibit aggressive impulses. He believed that these inhibitory mechanisms failed to evolve because, until the invention of artificial weapons, humans could not do each other much harm.[15] What Lorenz did not address is the logical corollary of his premise. That is, human beings did not evolve mechanisms to inhibit aggressive impulses simply because humans tend not to have aggressive impulses. Also, it is significant and revealing that it took eons for human beings to invent artificial weapons.

More recent research suggests that humans have more inhibitory control over their use of aggression than Lorenz suggested. The research concludes that humans make choices about aggressive behavior that are conditioned by their culture and social environments. In other words, cultures themselves play a crucial role in determining the extent to which people are able to inhibit aggression. This needs to be taken into account when we analyze the influence of the violent electronic culture and the "culture of violence."

Some people think that the work of Stanley Milgram demonstrates that people have an innate capacity toward aggression to the point of cruelty. In this experiment, people were told by authority figures that memory and learning could be improved by administering supposed electric shocks to people. The major rule they followed was to increase the level of shock each time the learner made an error until the learning was errorless. Most participants complained and protested, and repeatedly insisted they could not continue. Although the experimental situation produced considerable conflict in the participants, the majority of participants obeyed the authority fully.[16] The applicability of this research, however, is limited because its purpose was to discover conditions under which people obey authority figures. The research failed to acknowledge that the participants were raised in hierarchical institutions. Within this matrix of hierarchy, obedience to authority is ingrained. In addition, the interpretation of this research was isolated from the social and political reality and influence of "the culture of violence." This culture emphasizes hierarchy, competition, personal power, rewards for aggression, and is reinforced by media violence. The subjects' ability to inflict pain needs to be understood within the context of this culture, especially because of the desensitizing effects of media, notably the global riots in 2020 against police brutality and injustice. The subjects were socialized within a potent matrix of hierarchy and aggression, and they responded accordingly.

The frequent argument that people are violent because of a hunter/gatherer past is false because for hundreds of thousands of years humans did not hunt and kill. This conclusion is backed up by the field of military psychology, which posits that resistance to killing one's own species is a key factor in human combat. The research of General S. L. A. Marshall showed that only 15 to 20 percent of World War II riflemen fired their weapons at an exposed enemy soldier. Many of them packed their rifles so that they would not shoot or shot over the heads of the enemy.[17] Although Marshall's findings have been somewhat controversial, every study since that time has validated his basic premise. As Lt. Colonel Dave Grossman observes: "Paddy Griffith's data on the extraordinarily low killing rate among Napoleonic and American Civil War regiments, Richard Holmes assessment of Argentine firing rates in the Falklands war, the FBI's studies of non-firing rates among law enforcement officers in the 1950s and 1960s, and many other individual and anecdotal observations all confirm that humans, by nature, are not close-range, interpersonal killers."[18] This historical and contemporary research back up the conclusion that killing another human being is contrary to human nature. Our innate sensibility is not to kill.[19] The aversion to killing another human being is such a deep part of us because it is necessary for the survival of the human race. People may kill in self-defense or when experiencing alcohol-induced rage. Otherwise, only sociopaths, damaged human beings, kill. Some people are driven insane by being forced to kill or otherwise suffer from emotional trauma,[20] as evidenced in the fact that as many as 50 percent of returning veterans from Iraq and Afghanistan suffer from posttraumatic stress disorder and other mental problems.[21]

So, what is human nature? The essential elements of human nature are demonstrated by people in ancient societies, preliterate people, and the behavior of young children.

When did we become human? Anthropologists believe that we became human about four million years ago. This is the time that *Australopithecus* departed from the rest of the animal world.[22] Our earliest human forebears were not hunters. *Australopithecus* species were entirely scavengers.[23] What do early societies reveal about human nature? The earliest human groupings originated as many as 200,000 years ago. They were highly integrated bands of extended families of thirty to forty people.[24] This form of community constitutes about 99 percent of human social history.[25] Also, 99 percent of human history consists of vegetarian societies. Neither *Homo erectus* nor Neanderthal people had spearpoints, which indicates that they did little hunting.[26] Contrary to the widespread belief that early humans were hunter/gatherers, the earliest humans were foragers and scavengers.[27]

The primary concern of these earliest societies was survival. The qualities and behavior that ensured their survival included cooperation, harmony, respect, equality, empathy, and justice. All these qualities inhere in the spirit of democracy, hence its popularity. The ancient desire for justice, which stems from the spirit of equality, is evident in the fact that humankind's first written document was Hammurabi's Code of Law, a code of law and justice. In addition, history is permeated with mass riots and rebellions against injustice, notably the global riots in 2020 against police brutality and injustice. This desire for justice also is evident in that the most common goal of violent acts in schools is retribution.[28] Revenge, or "getting even," is a mutated form of justice. It is not part of human nature. Many species imitate retaliatory aggressive responses. However, no parallel has been demonstrated in humans.[29]

Around 35,000 years ago, during the Upper Paleolithic period, the foundation for the most ancient of religions, the religion of the Goddess, was established.[30] The worship of female deities appeared in every area of the world.[31] Goddess worship has continued throughout history in various forms.[32] In 2008 a goddess figure, "The Venus of Hohle Fels," was unearthed in a cave in southwestern Germany. This figure is similar to, but even older than, previously discovered Paleolithic sculptures of women. Ancient reverence for the Mother Goddess continued through later Neolithic religion, about 10,000 years ago.[33] For example, the Indigenous peoples of the Andes worshipped Pachamama, the fertility goddess who presided over planting and harvesting and caused earthquakes.[34] The Sumerians wrote many poems about their mother goddess Ninhursag.[35] Homeric Hymns praise Gaia, "the Mother of All," and Native Americans revere Mother Earth. These goddess cultures were not matriarchal. Following earlier social forms, they were egalitarian. In these early cultures, power was shared between women and men. In fact, there is no evidence that matriarchy as a female version of patriarchy ever existed.[36]

The next stage of human group development was the tribe, during which people were scavengers and involved more in gathering than in hunting.[37] Tribal life was based on economic cooperation and gender equality. Tribal members tended to live peacefully with themselves and other tribes. Competition was ritualized in contests of singing and athletics but was discouraged in daily life.[38]

In the 1970s, informed by the discovery of new evidence about Goddess worship, anthropologists challenged the earlier generalizations that male dominance and status was universal in early societies. They discovered that male dominance was far from universal. They found societies in which sexual asymmetry did not carry characteristics of dominance or subordination. People were considered equal and treated each other equally. There tended to be a division of labor based on gender. However, one task was not considered more important than another. There was mutual respect for work done. The roles of men and women were considered complementary. They were different but equal. There were no status differences and an absence of hierarchy.[39]

Archaeological evidence also has laid the myth of male dominance to rest.[40] These cooperative classless, harmonious societies survived until about 8,000 to 10,000 years ago, the time when agriculture was established and towns began to be created. Early towns had houses that showed little variation in size and furnishing. Also, the absence of streets or a palace leads to the speculation that there was neither hierarchy nor central political authority and that authority was shared among inhabitants. Catal Huyuk in Turkey was an early town that existed at that time in which there is no evidence of blood sacrifices nor evidence of a military caste. In all of Catal Huyuk there is no evidence of warfare over a period of one thousand years. The excavation of Catal Huyuk revealed an egalitarian society. In the earliest periods, men and women had the same social status. There was a balance of power. The absence of streets, a large plaza or a palace, and the uniform six of dwellings at Catal Huyak demonstrate that there was no hierarch or central political authority.[41]

Intergroup aggression was virtually nonexistent for many millennia. Between 12,000 and 50,000 years ago when population density grew, competition for resources intensified, resulting in increased intergroup conflict.[42] Catal Huyuk is believed to represent a transitional stage between goddess-centered and patriarchal societies because these communities lived harmoniously while neighboring regions were warfaring.[43]

As recently as 10,000 years ago, chiefdoms were established and war was introduced. We do not see social classes until this time with chiefs controlling and distributing resources.[44] This form of society introduced hierarchy and social classes, including a warrior class. There is evidence that such early forms of status differences and hierarchy began to instill more aggression and violence in these societies.[45] It appears that the more status differences in a society, the more violence occurs.[46] This illustrates how hierarchy is contrary to human nature and so promotes violence. These patriarchal societies are newcomers to human history. The creation of patriarchy, "the rule the fathers," occurred between about 3100 BC and 600 BC. Lerner concludes that it is likely that the development of warfare "during periods of economic scarcity fostered the rise to power of men of military achievement."[47] Patriarchy was epitomized in ancient Rome, in which the head of the household was allowed to kill anyone in his household with impunity.

Human Qualities

Humanity's long history of living in groups created a human need to belong and to be accepted.[48] As one anthropologist explains: "Our ancestors began to understand how to preserve peace and order.... They came to judge behavior that systematically undermined the social fabric as wrong, and behavior that made a community worthwhile to live in as right."[49] Peace and order were necessary for survival, and people who engaged in wrong behavior were expelled. The need to belong and fear of rejection are part of our social heritage. The extreme and most dreaded form of rejection in ancient societies was ostracism, sending the person alone into the wilderness to almost certain death. It is no wonder that shunning and rejection elicit strong emotional responses.[50] Nowadays rejection can result in murder and school shootings. Most killers, including school shooters, have a history of social rejection, ranging from shunning to childhood neglect. For hundreds of millennia human beings lived in social groups that relied on cooperation, harmony, equality, mutual respect, democracy, and harmony. This is our nature. It is our nature because it has been essential to our survival. These qualities still are necessary for our survival. Because they are necessary for survival and so ancient, they may even be genetically embedded in us.

The behavior of later preliterate, geographically isolated people illustrates the human need for harmony. In the 1920s, Margaret Mead found that violence was alien to the South Sea cultures she studied.[51] Current evidence of this can be seen among contemporary tribespeople who live in relative isolation, such as Inuit peoples and the Lepchas of the Himalayas. An example of a contemporary form of such a society can be gleaned from a television program called *Meet the Natives*.[52] Four men from a gatherer-hunter tribe in Tanna, an island in the South Pacific, visited families in Montana, New York, and California. Compared to their hosts, their faces were softer, their jokes and laughter more frequent, and their kindness and compassion was consistently evident. Their hosts loved them.

Our nature evolved from an ancient, deeply embedded way of living that existed for eons. This way of living was egalitarian, compassionate, cooperative, just, and peaceful. Survival also required members to be responsible. Fisher and Ury, in *Getting to Yes*, conclude that responsible behavior is the hallmark of an emotionally intelligent person.[53] They also point that that responsible behavior depends, above all else, on the absence of coercion.[54] Coercion and its more extreme form force represent the opposite of the democratic principles that were practiced by human beings for millennia. The popularity of democracy and its sister, freedom, is clear considering their persistence throughout the ages and people's willingness to die for them.

When our human nature is violated, we feel anger, the primary emotion that triggers aggression and violence. When people's nature is violated and not allowed to be fulfilled, over time, this can culminate in fury and violence. Humanistic personality theorists, such as Abraham Maslow, Carl Rogers, and Karen Horney, concluded that the motivation for behavior comes from a person's unique innate qualities and learned tendencies to develop and to change in positive directions toward the goal of self-actualization. In his hierarchy of needs, Maslow describes human needs. At the base of this pyramid are our physiological needs, such as those for food and water. If these needs are met, we are prompted to move up the pyramid to other needs, such as receiving love and enjoying self-esteem. He concluded that compassion and empathy are integral to human nature.

Beyond this, said Maslow, lies the highest of human needs—to actualize one's full potential.[55] Self-actualization is closely aligned with Freire's conclusion that our human vocation is to become more fully human. In the same light, Carl Rogers stressed the importance of unconditional positive regard in raising children. He writes that unconditional positive regard is also essential in adulthood because concern about seeking approval interferes with self-actualization.[56]

A corollary is the person's need to feel unconditional positive self-regard and self-acceptance. Karen Horney believed that people have a "real self" that requires favorable social conditions to be actualized. These include an atmosphere of warmth, the goodwill of others, and parental love of the child as a "particular individual." If these favorable conditions are not present the child develops a basic anxiety that inhibits expression of feelings and prevents effective relations with others. Coping with this anxiety involves resorting to interpersonal defenses, which produce movement toward others, such as excessive compliance or self-effacing behavior. Coping also includes action away from others, such as detachment or isolation, and action against others by arrogant, narcissistic, or aggressive behaviors.[57]

The peaceful and cooperative behavior of children also gives us insight into human nature. The tendency for cooperation and harmony is still present and especially evident among young children when the learning environment allows it. Toddlers as young as eighteen months share with each other without being prompted by adults. As observed by a teacher in a Reggio Emilia school, "When we see young children cooperating, we notice a sort of ethic: they do everything they can to keep the situation stable and ongoing. . . . Of course, conflicts also exist. Clashes of principles and ideas can be very rich, but do not necessarily need to be expressed through a direct confrontation. Sometimes children feel the disparity of their views but they hold back to maintain the harmony of the group functioning. . . . Sociable emotions have a strong role to play in this complex development."[58]

The human response to nonhierarchical, democratic social processes also was illustrated by Kurt Lewin's ground-breaking research in the 1930s. He investigated the responses of ten-year-old boys to autocratic, laissez-faire, and democratic leadership styles. The boys in the groups run by an autocratic leader exhibited the most destructive individual reactions, displaying a very high level of aggression. They showed up to thirty times more hostility than they did under laissez-faire or democratic forms of social groups. The boys were more likely to destroy their own property and showed more scapegoating behavior, focusing on weaker individuals as displaced targets for their frustration and anger. In the democratically run groups, members worked most efficiently and showed the highest levels of interest, motivation, and originality. When discontent arose, it tended to be openly expressed. Democracy promoted more group loyalty and friendliness. There was mutual praise, more friendly remarks, more playfulness, and more sharing.[59]

Democratic processes and balance are entwined with one's sense of personal power. This sense of a locus of control—that is, the belief that the outcomes of one's actions are dependent on what one does rather than on external, social factors—is also inherently human.[60] The concept is closely related to a sense of self-efficacy and self-empowerment.

Bandura's research in the 1970s revealed that self-efficacy is the belief that one can perform adequately in a particular situation. Judgments about one's self-efficacy influence how much effort the person expends and how long he or she persists when faced with difficulties in life situations. These concepts are entwined with one's sense of self-worth, self-respect, and self-empowerment.[61] This is especially important during adolescence, which is a time that young people develop mastery, social identity, and autonomy.[62]

Self-efficacy is closely connected to the human desire to make a contribution to one's community and the world. Human survival is dependent on democratic principles and behavior. Democracy requires responsible attitudes and actions. Because of this, early human survival was grounded in the individual's responsibility to the group, the idea that each bears responsibility for all. This helped to ensure the survival of the species and is evident today in such popular youth programs as service learning.

The human need to create is evident throughout history, from cave paintings to current artistic and technological innovations. It is innately human to want to create and to contribute to the world. Matthew Fox writes: "Pessimism comes from the repression of creativity. To not be able to contribute one's gift is to feel despair, whose violent results can be seen everywhere: in self-hatred, increased crime, the drug trade, fear and alcoholism."[63]

The human capacity and need for love are backed up by social scientific research.[64] Some researchers suggest that human beings are programmed biologically to care for one another in order to ensure psychological and biological evolution. The need for love and the capacity for love have implications for classroom teaching as well as for violence. Not surprisingly, students who feel unconditionally accepted by their teachers are more likely to be interested in learning and to enjoy challenging academic tasks.[65]

The opposite of love is disrespect, hatred, and abuse. Early childhood abuse is characteristic of more than half of the convicted murderers in the United States. Many of the school shooters also experience early abuse, which is compounded in their lives by continued abuse in the form of bullying.

The need for justice and fairness is intrinsically human. When we perceive unjust or unfair treatment, we tend to respond with feelings of anger. This response is exhibited by not yet fully socialized children declaring, "That's not fair!" Anger is the response to injustice. According to many psychologists, anger results from disrespectful treatment.

Human beings are imbued with an inherent sense of self-worth and self-respect, which is generated by and entwined with the need for love and justice. When our innate human nature is violated, we respond with anger, the emotion that sparks interpersonal violence.

Self-respect is an essential human characteristic. Research shows that aggression may result from the desire to maintain self-esteem and buttress one's positive self-concept after an ego-threatening event.[66] The importance of respect is demonstrated by young people in the ghetto murdering a person who has "dissed" them and by Mafia men's preoccupation with "honor." The motto of the notorious MS-13 gang is: "Loved by some, hated by others, respected by all." Some of the school shooters were seeking respect as well as responding to rejection. Michael Carneal, after killing three people and injuring five in West Paducah, Kentucky, said, "People respect me now."[67]

Revenge is a mutated form of justice. It is derived from the need for respect and for justice. Revenge is "vengeance again" or "getting even." The phrase "getting even" illustrates a desire to make things equal and, therefore, just. In our society, revenge is sanctioned and even rewarded by social norms and values. This socialization, which is reinforcement by media messages, mutates the human need for justice into revenge. A central motivation for many school shootings is revenge. In fact, researchers found that more than half of school shooters had revenge as a motive.[68]

It is the nature of human beings to be cooperative, to share and live in harmony, express mutual love and respect, be creative, contribute to the community, and live with democracy and justice. These human qualities were engendered hundreds of thousands of years ago. Their purpose is to ensure the survival of the human group. Now their purpose is to ensure the survival of the human race.

Peaceful Schools

The school violence prevention programs that are aligned with human nature, that promote competence, social bonding, responsibility, shared decision-making, and unconditional regard, are the most successful. To the extent that schools institutionalize oppression, that is, the suppression of human nature, they violate human nature and promote violence. A telling story concerns a teenage boy in Buffalo, New York who was apprehended in his attempt to blow up his high school. Earlier in the school year, the boy had written an English class essay suggesting that the Columbine killers were rebelling against an oppressive environment.[69]

The spiritual dimension of human nature is beyond the scope of the present writing. Suffice it to say that Jesus is called "the Prince of Peace," Mary is "the Queen of Peace," and all major world religions have the Golden Rule at their center.

Liberatory education derives from and promotes the consciousness, efficacy, empowerment, and self-actualization of students. In other words, liberatory education helps children to fulfill their vocation to be human. To what extent do schools meet our need, in Freire's words, "to become more fully human"? To what extent is the human desire to explore and transform the world nurtured by teachers and schools? To what extent do schools and school violence prevention programs address these needs?

Children need to develop in accord with their true democracy-loving, self-empowered, empathic, and cooperative natures. To the extent that schools do not address these human needs, they institutionalize violence and foster its expression. While aspects of school violence prevention programs may be necessary they are not sufficient if they do not take into account how human nature is compromised by the culture of violence and the industries it generates.

CHAPTER 4

THE CULTURE OF VIOLENCE

The love of money is the root of all evil.
—1 Timothy 6:10

Since World War II, industrialized countries have experienced significant increases in crime rates.[1] The character and magnitude of violence in the United States has increased so dramatically that it has been characterized as "the culture of violence."[2] After the mass murders at Columbine High School in Littleton, Colorado, President Clinton stated that "every one of us must take responsibility to counter the culture of violence. The government must take responsibility to counter the culture of violence."[3] In a pastoral statement, "Confronting a Culture of Violence," Archbishop Michael Shuen notes that the culture of violence reveals a spiritual crisis, and he quotes Pope Paul VI, "If you want peace, work for justice."[4] Rather than honoring life this culture destroys life. The culture of violence, by definition, is a violation against our human nature.

The United States is the most homicidal country among developed nations. It has "a particularly notorious history with respect to lethal violence,"[5] with a very high murder rate relative to the modernized world as far back as data is available.[6] By 1996 the United States' homicide rate of 5.7 persons in 100,000 was three times higher than any other developed country.[7] By 2016, the rate was 6.3 per 100,000.[8] Firearms are used in almost 70 percent of US murders compared to 7 percent of murders committed in England. The rate of rape in the United States is three times greater than England.[9] Murder is the second leading cause of death in the United States and the primary cause of death for young black people.[10] Homicide is between five and ten times higher for young black men and black women.[11] More than 50,000 people die each year from violence in the United States.[12] For every homicide, there are an estimated one hundred assaults, many resulting in serious injury.[13] More than twenty-five million more suffer nonfatal injuries from violence.[14] In other words, about one in fifteen people in this country is injured by violence each year.

There is a new character to violence now. Violence is no longer concentrated just in cities but has spread to suburbs and rural areas. Violence is not as confined to poor communities as it used to be. It used to be that dangerous public places were known. Nowadays dangerous episodes occur in the post office, on commuter trains, and in fast food restaurants. Violence has become more extreme. There are more guns, and altercations result in death more frequently. Mass murders, such as school rampage killings, are more lethal, claiming more lives. The emergence of the "serial killer" is a barometer of the culture of violence. "Thrill killings" also have become part of the lexicon. An example is the case of two Phoenix gunmen who blasted at lone pedestrians from the window of their car. One of the perpetrators called it "random recreational violence."

In recent decades we have seen significant increases in police violence, especially in black communities, which signifies horizontal violence. Law enforcement increasingly is using combat maneuver tactics and "weapons of war."[15] Police brutality and killings in black communities have been getting a lot of media coverage in recent decades, as have the riots that that resulted from law enforcement perpetrators consistently receiving acquittals and dismissed charges.

A litmus test of whether a culture is violent is the death penalty. The United States is the only industrialized Western country, apart from South Africa, that has the death penalty. Almost all death row prisoners are penniless. Over 40 percent of them are black compared to the 12 percent of people in the United States who are black.[16] In 1993, there were 2,825 death row prisoners.[17] By 1997, there were 3,335 death row prisoners.[18] Currently, there are more than 3,600 death row prisoners in the thirty-seven death row states.[19] The execution of one death row prisoner costs $3 million to $10 million, whereas the cost of a life sentence is $500,000.[20] The death penalty has not proven to be a deterrent. "No one who kills, by permanent or temporary insanity, through jealousy, drug addiction, robbery, alcoholism, retardation, brain damage, chemical imbalance, rape, revenge, a feeling of no way out or rage, thinks of the death penalty at the time of the murder."[21] In fact, the murder rates go up in death penalty states immediately after an execution.[22] Despite these facts, the death penalty is widely accepted, illustrating that revenge is a predominant dynamic in the culture of violence.

Hierarchy in major institutions, such as the family, school, and workplace, as well as public life, typifies the culture of violence. In addition to school violence, workplace violence is a problem in the United States. This is the only country in which postal workers have gone "ballistic" in workplace mass murders. Hierarchy embodies a structure that displays dominance and power over others. Hierarchy constitutes threat and obstacle to egalitarian and democratic relationships and institutions. It is a way in which the culture of violence inhibits the expression and manifestation of human nature.

The culture of violence is unjust. Despite being the world's wealthiest economy, the United States has one of the poorest economic and social rights record among high-income countries. Child poverty and infant mortality are higher than any other comparable country. Black women are four times more likely to die during childbirth than white women. Health and education disparities, particularly among minority people, continue to be wide.[23] The federal budget of the United States contains the largest military budget in the world.[24] Military spending displaces tax money otherwise spent on basic human needs, such as food, medical services, jobs, and education. For these reasons, the United States ranks as one of the lowest countries on the Global Peace and Sustainability Index, which factors in indicators such as human rights records, military expenditures, and relations with other nations. A concentration on terrorism and war shapes the consciousness of people by creating fear and anger. War is based on the premise that violence is an acceptable way to deal with conflict. The influence of a war consciousness and militarized economy fan out into all aspects of life, including play, fashion, talk, and behavior.

A Brief History of Youth Violence

Most violent crime in the United States is committed by young people. Youth violence in the United States is particularly lethal compared with other industrialized countries.[25] Between 1957, the year the FBI started tracking data, and 1992, the per capita murder rate doubled in the United States.[26] From 1960 to 1970, violent crime increased by 126 percent.[27] By 1970, the violent crime rate was 5.1 per 100,000 people.[28] From 1960 to 2000, U.S. crime rates experienced a steady and, at times, dramatic increase. The overall adolescent violent crime arrest rate doubled between 1966 and 1975.[29] This startling increase happened during the Vietnam War and its aftermath, a time of political unrest and turmoil. The violent crime rate in the mid to late 1970s was static; it reached 10.2 per 100,000 people by 1980.[30]

By 1984, an epidemic of youth violence was evident.[31] From 1984 to 1994, the youth violent crime rate again doubled.[32] The beginning of the growth of youth violence in the 1980s began with at-risk children. By the 1990s, it had spread to more groups with different profiles. Youth violence also became more lethal, with more altercations ending in death. Youth violence peaked in 1994. In 1995, it decreased by 3 percent, 6 percent in 1996, and then 4 percent in 1997. Despite considerable efforts, youth violence still remained 49 percent greater than in 1988. In comparison, the adult violent crime rate had increased 19 percent.[33]

A Brief History of Violence

The crime wave that began in the early 1980s did not fall until 1998.[34] This dip in violence can be attributed to a relatively robust economy, a large youth cohort graduating into maturity, 100,000 additional police officers on the beat through the Community Policing Program, a "get tough" three-strikes policy on sentencing, and the Million Man March, which had a very positive impact in black communities.[35] Youth violence also had been curtailed by the US Department of Justice's creation of the Office of Juvenile Justice and Delinquency Prevention and channeling of a lot of money into youth programs. In addition, during that time, advances in gun legislation, although weak and partial, may have accounted for some of the reductions in homicide.[36]

Although violent crime decreased by 1998, it still was 133 percent greater than the 1965 rate, and 166 percent greater than the 1995 rate.[37] By 2005, violent crime was on the increase. Murders were up between 5 percent and 13 percent in mid-size cities. On a Memorial Day weekend in Milwaukee, twenty-eight people were shot. As a police department spokeswoman commented: "People used to settle disputes with their fists. Now they settle them with guns."[38] By 2005, the homicide rate among young people climbed to nine deaths per 100,000 people, and the following year the violent crime arrest rate among young men was 521 arrests per 100,000 people.[39] By 2014, the homicide rate was 5 per 100,000 people, with 3.5 attributed to firearms.[40] The 2016 murder rate rose 8.4 percent from 2015, and aggravated assault rose by 4.7 percent.[41]

Suicide

In addition to an alarming rate of homicide, the culture of violence experiences a suicide rate that is among the world's highest. In the United States, for every two people who die from homicides, three people die of suicide. It is the eleventh leading cause of death in the nation. For adolescents, it is the third leading cause of death.[42] About one-quarter of the general population has seriously considered suicide at some time in their lives. About 4 percent of people in this country actually have attempted suicide.[43] Suicide makes up the largest portion of annual gun deaths.[44] About 63 percent of all adolescent suicides are committed with a firearm.[45] Research has repeatedly demonstrated that depression is a key precursor to suicide and has also explored the strong relationship between the presence of guns in the home and suicide. One of the more startling facts is that the first year after the purchase of a handgun, suicide is the leading cause of death among gun purchasers.[46]

Between 1979 and 1991, the rate of teenage suicide increased 31 percent. In 1991, teenagers committed suicide at the rate of 11 per 100,000 youth.[47] By 2014 the rate was 13.4, a 24 percent increase since 1999.[48] Suicides among young people are a barometer of the degree of severity of the culture of violence. In the year 2000 in the United States, suicide was the third leading cause of death for fifteen- to twenty-four-year-olds.[49] By 2018 it was the second leading cause of death for adolescents, ages 15 to 19.[50] To what can we attribute this shocking increase? This question will be explored further in later chapters that discuss the effects of media violence and violent video games.

Youth Violence

Historically, when young people in the United States were called juvenile delinquents, their crimes were perpetrated mostly on property, not people. The most frequently committed crimes were car theft, larceny and arson. However, in recent decades, violence has become a more significant component of juvenile crime.[51] The Council on Crime in America has concluded: "Each generation (of juveniles) is roughly three times as violent as the one it succeeds."[52] Youth culture has become a culture of disrespect as well as aggression and violence. Youth culture exemplifies "a culture in which disrespectful behavior becomes a legitimate way for people to treat each other."[53] This culture of disrespect tends to be characterized by hostility, sullenness, a lack of empathy, and irresponsibility.

The attitudes of young people reflect the culture of violence. A survey of high school students reveals their readiness to use violence as a means of resolving interpersonal conflict. Fourteen percent of the students said they had hit a parent or guardian and 13 percent had hit or pushed a teacher or other adult at school. Over 9 percent said that they had been physically attacked or hurt in the past month, with about 5 percent being hurt badly enough to have seen a doctor.[54] In response to fictitious stories about conflicts, many students chose violence as the option of first resort. In one story, "A guy Neil hardly knows tells the principal that Neil has been selling drugs at school." Almost 7 percent of the boys said that Neil should threaten him for telling lies, and almost 15 percent of the boys said that Neil should "beat the guy up."[55] Other attitudes revealed by the survey includes 91 percent of the students agreeing that if a girl sees someone flirting with her boyfriend she should fight with her, and about 49 percent agreeing that it sometimes is necessary to fight with people who are rude or annoying.[56] Early exposure to sexual behavior, alcohol and substance abuse, and violent entertainment media and games, coupled with the consciousness of contemporary world problems, has resulted in many young people being aggressive, discourteous, sarcastic, and sullen. Much of contemporary youth culture is characterized by cynicism and irresponsibility, as well as sex, drugs, and rock 'n' roll. Alienated and estranged young people mirror and perpetuate the culture of violence.

The United States is first among developed countries in homicides of juveniles.[57] An American seventeen-year-old is ten times more likely to commit murder than his or her Canadian counterpart.[58] For people between the ages of fifteen and twenty-four, the homicide rate of 15.2 per 100,000 people is higher than the combined total homicide rate of eleven industrialized nations.[59] The US rate of youth violence is five times higher than the other twenty-five developed countries combined, and nearly double the rate of the next highest rated country.[60] In the early 1990s, when violent crime peaked, the homicide rate for young men in the United States was seventy-three times greater than the rate in similar industrialized nations.[61] Since the 1980s, violence among young people has become more extreme and has claimed more fatalities. The Denver Youth Survey looked at high-risk youth and delinquent behavior and, over a fifteen-year span, saw that "the level of injury from violent offenses increased substantially. The prevalence of victims of violence in need of hospitalization or being left unconscious almost doubled (from 33 to 58 percent). This increase corresponded to an increase in the use of weapons."[62]

What does account for the increase in violence and in the use of weapons? Since the early 1990s school shootings have been more heinous, claiming many more victims. The question is—Why?

The perpetrators of violent crimes are becoming younger. By 1994, juveniles aged twelve or younger who committed violent crimes grew 32 percent. Those aged thirteen and fourteen increased by 49 percent. The largest increases were for the most serious charges.[63] In 1996, it was reported that five-year-olds had become more involved in violent crime.[64] Currently, offenders under the age of fifteen "represent the leading edge of the juvenile crime probe, and their numbers have been growing."[65] Violent crime arrests, for example, increased by 94 percent between 1980 and 1995 for those under age fifteen, compared to 47 percent of older young people.[66]

Violent behavior has tended to be predominant during adolescence. Early studies generally found the prevalence of male violent behavior starts to show itself at age twelve and peaks at ages fifteen to seventeen. However, researchers have yet to see a decline in males' self-reported involvement in serious violence in late adolescence.[67] This indicates that the period of time in which young men tend to display violent behavior is longer. What are the possible implications of an extended duration of peak prevalence rates? If the duration of peak prevalence rates is extended, there is likely to be higher levels of violent crime at a later point in time.[68]

Gangs

The rate of youth violence is more fully understood when considering the prevalence of gangs, which have proliferated rapidly since 1980. At that time, there were about 2,000 gangs with 100,000 members in 296 cities. By 1996, there were between 23,000 and 31,000 gangs with 700,000 to 846,000 members in 4,800 cities and towns in all fifty states.[69] In a survey of seven hundred communities nationwide, 40 percent of the suburban communities and non-metropolitan towns and cities said gangs were a factor in the violence in their schools.[70] Homicide reports from major cities document a resurgence in both gang and non-gang homicides. Also, there was a slow but steady increase in robbery and assaults that resulted in injuries.

It is commonly accepted among researchers that young people "who perceive particular deficiencies in their lives often seek to compensate by joining gangs."[71] Many people believe that young people join gangs because they come from impoverished minority communities and from families characterized by absent parents. This explanation is not sufficient, however, because "most youths from such areas, such groups, and such families do not join gangs."[72]

Although many theorists and, at times, gang members themselves, talk about how gangs act as families for the young people, the attraction is both deeper and more practical. Gangs are embedded in the culture of violence and a capitalist economy. Poor young people can earn minimum wage by working at McDonald's or be unemployed. An alternative is to make hundreds of dollars a day selling crack cocaine. In a number of ways, gangs are microcosms of capitalistic enterprises. The values of corporate America are accepted on the streets, and gangs are mimicking capitalist techniques. A business card at a drug bust in a California crack house said, "If you offer good, high quality, uncut cocaine at a reasonable price, Southern California will beat a path to your door. This is our guiding principle—why not give us a try."[73] Aside from money, another attraction to gang membership is acquiring and displaying power, often through firepower. Many sociologists concur that gangs tend to form in communities with limited legitimate opportunities for success.[74] Membership in a gang may be lucrative, but it also confers a kind of identity that suggests "power, fearlessness, and domination."[75] Poor and working-class men especially tend to adhere to "the warrior ideal." Joining gangs is a path to manliness, a path to power. Gangs are a way to compensate for not having access to the power and resources that more privileged people have in the culture of violence.

Serial Killers

Serial killers were fairly common from 1900 to 1940, and then the rate dipped until the mid-1960s. Serial killings increased dramatically in the later 1960s, as did the homicide rate in general.[76] Notorious serial killers, such as Son of Sam and the Golden State Killer, sparked a new wave of fear among the general public. Violent crime increases during times of war, so it is reasonable to speculate that the Vietnam War is connected to the resurgence of this kind of violence.

Rampage Shootings

Non-sanctioned rampage shootings, that is, rampage shootings not sanctioned by government action, originated in the United States. The 1966 University of Texas tower shooting was followed by two school rampage shootings in the 1970s. The first public rampage shooting occurred in 1982. There were two public rampage shootings in 1986, five in 1991, eleven in 1992, nine in 1993, fifteen in 1994, nineteen in 1999, and thirteen by 2006.[77] Since the latter part of the twentieth century, the number and the deadliness of school and public shootings have increased at an alarming rate, with the United States being the global leader of rampage shootings. Data for 171 countries from 1966 to 2012 show 31 percent of public mass shootings occurred in the United States. The global average was 1.7 attacks per year.[78] In the United States between 2003 and 2013, there were 161 active shooter incidents, an average of thirteen incidents a year.[79] Since 2013, rampage shootings have increased exponentially in the United States. A 2015 special report by the Public Broadcasting Service's *News Hour* reports that now there is an average of one rampage shooting each day. Lankford suggests that it is possible that cross-national differences in the availability of weapons helps to explain the differences in rates of mass shootings in different countries.[80] Citizens and elected representatives are focusing on more gun control as a remedy for rampage shootings.

Children

Homicide is the only major cause of childhood death that has increased during the past forty years. Although deaths of children resulting from accidents, congenital defects, and infectious diseases have been falling, homicides of children are increasing and now rank second or third (depending on the age group) and account for one in twenty-three deaths of children.[81] More than 60 percent of the young people in the United States have been exposed to violence each year, either indirectly by witnessing a violent act; learning of a violent act against a family member or neighbor; or experiencing a threat against their home or school. The types of violence include being threatened with a weapon or experiencing injury, sexual victimization, maltreatment, and dating violence.[82] Children in the United States are more likely to be exposed to violence and crime than are adults. Almost half of the children and adolescents in this country were assaulted at least once in the past year, and more than one in ten were injured in an assault. One in four were victims of robbery, vandalism, or theft.[83] One in ten children suffer from maltreatment and one in sixteen are victimized sexually.[84] Over 2,000 children in the United States die of child abuse and neglect each year, and most are younger than five years old.[85]

The perpetrators of violent crimes are becoming younger. By 1994, the number of juveniles aged twelve or younger who committed violent crimes grew by 32 percent. The number of those aged thirteen and fourteen who committed violent crimes increased by 49 percent. The largest increases were for the most serious charges.[86] Currently, offenders under the age of fifteen "represent the leading edge of the juvenile crime probe, and their numbers have been growing."[87] Additionally, violence committed by children at even younger ages is on the rise.[88] A small but substantial proportion of children are involved in serious violence before reaching adolescence. In study samples, children as young as ten years have committed serious violent crime.[89] A Rochester, New York, study discovered that by age twelve, 19 percent of the boys and 15 percent of the girls reported involvement in violent behavior.[90] By 1996, it was reported that five-year-old children had become more involved in violent crime.[91] Bullying has increased among toddlers, and in recent years, many preschool and early school-age children meet the diagnostic criteria for conduct disorders. Conduct disorders have been found to be a stable trait over time for many preschool children and appear to be the most important behavioral risk factor for antisocial behavior in adolescence. This behavior is a predictor of the development of drug abuse in adolescence, as well as juvenile delinquency, depression, school dropout, and violence.[92]

Women and Girls

Although young men have the highest rates of mortality, violence against girls and women is severe. Homicide is the leading cause of death for young black women and the second leading cause of death of young white women.[93] The culture of violence is especially dangerous for women. On any given day, about 41,000 victims of domestic violence stay in emergency shelters or temporary residential living centers. About 40,000 women and children need other kinds of services, including counseling. An additional 21,683 make hotline calls about crises or emergencies each day.[94] Females are at least three times more likely than males to be victims of family violence.[95] Each year nearly four million women are beaten to death, and the estimates of women who were physically assaulted by male partners or cohabitants approaches five million.[96]

By 1990, the rape rate in the United States was higher than any previous year. It was eight times higher than in France, fifteen times higher than in England, twenty-three times higher than in Italy, and forty-six times higher than in Greece.[97] In 2016, rape or assault with the intent to commit rape totaled 95,730 women, 4.9 percent higher than 2015 and 12.4 percent higher than 2012.[98] Over 20 percent of surveyed high school girls reported past physical or sexual abuse, the majority of which occurred at home. Abused girls are more than twice as likely to develop depression than girls who report no abuse, and they are at double the risk of eating disorders.[99]

Violence against women contradicts those elements of human nature that embody the principles of protecting life, cooperating and sharing, and compassion and empathy. Violence against women continues to be epidemic, with new forms of violence occurring, such as break-up violence and revenge porn, despite considerable resources devoted to stopping it.

Since the late 1980s, there has been growing concern about the emergence of a "new female offender," who is more ruthless and violent than in the past. Arrest statistics show that females account for a growing number of violent offenders. In 1966, the ratios of male to female offenders was in excess of ten to one.[100] In 1983, the ratio was five to one, and by 1999, it was three to one.[101] At this time, the ratio is about four males who commit violent crime to one female.[102] The increase in violent crime committed by girls and women indicates that females are not immune from the powerful influence of the culture of violence. In many settings, from gangs to the workplace, girls and women have become more aggressive and more male-defined in their attitudes and behavior. That is, they have adopted attitudes that are traditionally associated with males. As one researcher notes, young women and girls "appear to have a distorted sense of equality, that to be equal they must emulate males."[103] In "Girls Gone Skank," Patrice Opplinger points out that girls are increasingly taught to go to outrageous lengths in seeking male attention. She writes that instead of advancing women's empowerment, popular culture seems to be backsliding into the blatant sexual exploitation of women and girls at younger and younger ages.[104]

Poverty

The culture's most critical problem is disparity of income. A prime example of economic injustice is the polarity of wealth and poverty in Washington, DC, the capital of the Western world. The affluent and extremely influential live in the northwestern section of Washington, DC. However, over half of DC residents are black, and many of them poor. These people exhibit the highest rate of infant mortality, the shortest lifespan, and the highest incidence of AIDS in the United States.[105]

The culture of violence creates crime. However, there is no doubt that poverty is a prime factor in criminal and violent behavior. Homicide rates in the United States fell in the 1960s until 1973 when the country was at full employment. Greater equality of income is a deterrent to crime.[106] By the late 1980s, one in every four schoolchildren came from a family on welfare.[107] Since the turn of the century, Americans have become even poorer, and national rates of severe poverty have climbed sharply.[108] More children are living in relative poverty in the United States than in any other economically advanced nation. The rise in severe poverty strikes children the hardest. Children under age five are twice as likely to be living in severe poverty. By 2004, one of three Americans with incomes less than 50 percent of the poverty threshold was a child.[109] This compares to one in five children living in poverty in 1980.

The New Poverty

The culture of violence promotes the love of money yet increasingly obstructs access to it. For decades, the income of the entire US population fell, except for a very small class of highly affluent Americans. Researchers describe a "sinkhole effect" in which "families and individuals in the middle and upper classes appear to be migrating to lower income tiers that bring them closer to the poverty threshold.[110] According to the Pew Research Center, by 2013 the wealth gap between upper-income people and middle-income families was 660 percent. By 2016, 43 percent of American households could not afford such basics as housing, food, childcare, or health care.[111] Black and Latino families who achieved middle-class markers, such as a college degree and well-paying job, still lag behind their white counterparts in terms of wealth.[112]

Hunger in the United States is a consistent problem. In 2009, forty-nine million households lacked consistent access to adequate food, the highest since the US Department of Agriculture began tracing "food insecurity" in 1996. The increase of thirteen million Americans was much larger than even the most pessimistic observers anticipated. About 506,000 households with children faced "very low food security," up from 323,000 households in 2008.[113]

By 2015, 43.1 million people lived in poverty, which is 13.5 percent of the U.S. population.[114] By 2019 the poverty rate was 16.7 percent. This compares to the 20 percent poverty rate in South Africa.[115] The poverty rate for black people in the United States is 21.7 percent.[116]

Many of impoverished people are chronically unemployed. Unemployment results in untold hardships. A clear indication of this suffering is that for every one percent increase in unemployment, there is a 0.8 percent increase in the suicide rate. Research of the University of Oxford and the London School of Hygiene and Tropical Medicine also shows that with a 3 percent increase in unemployment there is a 28 percent increase in deaths from alcohol abuse.[117]

Everyday Life in the Culture of Violence

The culture of violence diminishes the quality of life, which is reflected in everyday life.

What is everyday life like in the culture of violence?

The culture is characterized by "rankism." In *Somebodies and Nobodies*, Robert Fuller analyzes how millions of people are irreparably damaged because of shabby treatment by someone in power. This treatment includes a boss humiliating an employee, a teacher disrespecting a student, a parent yelling at a child, or a policy officer violating a person's rights. Fuller sees increased rankism as a trend toward plutocracy.[118]

There is a taken-for-granted quality in the culture of violence which renders expressions and signs of aggression and violence invisible. The environment itself communicates danger and threat. This ranges from such displays of power as "muscle cars" to brand names of clothing, such as "Rampage" and "Cruel Girl." Rubbermaid advertises a storage container as "Brute," which also is the name of a male cologne. The culture of violence has popularized symbols of death. Skulls are very popular images, especially among the young. A widely available cigarette lighter with a skull on it reads: "Love kills." Military metaphors, reflecting the economic basis of the culture of violence, abound. During a recent Fourth of July, a radio ad on KBOM, "The Bomb," referred to fireworks as "Master Blasters." The announcer commented, "Hope you're having an explosive good time." An internet weather reporting service describes itself as giving "rapid fire updates." Often evident are a high police and security officer presence, security cameras, and signs. These include "Neighborhood Watch," "Beware of dog," "Trespassers will be prosecuted to the full extent of the law," and "If you can read this (*sic*) you're in range." Other collective representations are bumper stickers such as "God, guts, and guns make this country great." Another bumper sticker, which appears to be related to road rage, is "Keep honking. I'm reloading."

Humor and Language

Aggressive social behavior in the culture of violence shows itself as, among other things, humor and language. Much of the humor in the culture of violence communicates hierarchy. Things considered funny by many people are "put-down" humor, snarking, and trolling. Put-down humor, from school hallways to the Comedy Central stage, characterizes the culture of violence. This humor often includes vicious comments about people, sex jokes that denigrate women, and a lot of profanity. Put-down humor is based on hierarchy. "Snark" is "a tone of teasing, snide, undermining abuse, nasty and knowing," "a method that attempts to steal someone's mojo, erase her cool, annihilate her effectiveness. . . . Snarkers like to think they are deploying wit, but mostly they are exposing the seethe and snarl of an unhappy country, releasing bad feeling but little laughter."[119] Another example of vicious humor is trolling on the internet. Young hackers pull such pranks as teasing the parents of a child who has committed suicide or sending flashing lights into a Website for epileptics, sometimes resulting in visitors having seizures.[120]

Violence is normalized in the culture of violence, so much so that references to violence and war have become invisible. "He threw me under the bus" is a common expression, as are "I almost died laughing," "I was so mad I could have killed him," "I'll take a stab at it," and "Well, just shoot me!" The word "fight" is used often, such as in a literacy campaign called "Fight for the Write" and the "fight breast cancer" campaign. Toothpaste "fights" cavities and Ora-Vet advises the pet owner to "fight" their dog's bad breath. It is natural in the culture of violence to find military metaphors and expressions, such as "I was blown away," "right on target," and "battle of the bands." Advertisements mimic this. For example, the "guts and glory all new Ram rebel truck" is designed to "break formation." Similarly, Viktor Rolf advertises its "perfect gift" as the "Flowerbomb." Lysol toilet bowl cleaner claims that it "blows other brushes out of the water."

Language reflects internalized violence. Interpersonal interaction and social relations in the culture of violence often are aggressive and may consist of "power plays." The culture of violence places a premium on displays of power in its various forms, from driving muscle cars to bullying. The everyday language of the culture of violence is very revealing in its use of variations of the word "kill." Examples include "killer cookies," which are very good cookies, an organic bread is called "Dave's Killer Bread," and the "Killer Shake" is produced by Killer Products. In the culture of violence, "killer" means exceptionally good. Common expressions include "You slay me," "You're killing me here," "to die for," and "drop-dead gorgeous." A new variation is to use the word "kill" in terms of accomplishment, such as "I killed that interview." In another example, an article from a women's magazine points out how the author was doing so well that she was "killin' it." Killer in the culture of violence means very effective or very good. It is no surprise that advertisements use violent words and expressions. For example, an ad for an immune system enhancer reads: "Unleash the Natural Killer in You."[121] This reflects the common belief that killing is natural to human beings. Another example is a newspaper headline that read: "Jazzy New Little Suzuki SX4 SportBack Packs a Nice Punch."[122] The Ford F-150 pickup is advertised as "Built Ford Tough," and Movie Gallery advertises that it is "Kick butt guaranteed." Olay anti-wrinkle cream is offered at a "knockout price," and a migraine medicine exclaims that "Not many things knock you out like a migraine but you can knock out a migraine with Relpax."

The word "power" is utilized by advertisers. Advertisements frequently proclaim that power inheres in their products. The label of an energy drink, "Powerade," describes it as a "Mountain Blast Thirst Quencher." A cereal ad tells the consumer to "Power up with a unique blend of protein and fiber," and an ad for eggs advises the consumer to "Power your day the right way." Another example is a magazine advertisement for "ImmPower," an immune system enhancer. A magazine, *Delicious Living*, featured a headline: "Raw Power, 6 Fresh Asian Recipes."[123] Hierarchy also is commonly expressed in everyday phrases such as "king of the hill" and "top dog." The culture of violence, although thought of as a democracy, is embedded with language signaling the contrary. Consider "Dairy Queen," "Burger King," and "Budweiser, king of beers."

Objectification is the process of reducing a person to an object or an animal, to a nonhuman status. A tendency in popular culture is to use objectified language that reduces human beings to things. Objectification is evident in language, such as "gook," a term used by American military people for North Vietnamese villagers, and in school, "geek." Talk overheard in high school corridors includes, "You're dead meat." Law enforcement officers are known to use such phrases as "maggots" referring to criminals. In an episode of the television show, *Alaska State Troopers*, a trooper wanted the public to disperse from a crime scene and said to another officer: "Let's get the meat out of here." If people are objectified, that is, dehumanized, it is easier to exploit and oppress them. Language is our primary symbolic system and so plays a key role in the creation of worldviews. Such language and talk reflect and reinforce a culture that promotes the status of products while lowering the status of human beings. In other words, things are more important than people.

The lack of regard for women is evident in talk, such as calling girls and women "candy ass," "dogs," "pigs," "chicks," "bitches," and so on. Women especially are objectified in the culture of violence. "Bitch" has become such a part of the language that women at times refer to each other as "bitch" in a matter-of-fact and not necessarily angry way. Referring to women as animals exemplifies how women are denigrated in the culture of violence. It is disheartening that many girls and women are male-defined to the extent that they call each other such names. Although not to the extent as females, males are objectified in the culture also. This includes referring to a man as a "hunk" or a "stud."

The American culture's fascination with technology also shows up in objectified language. Part and parcel of this process of objectification is human-machine metaphors, which have especially proliferated since the use of computers. These include, among many others, "That's how my head is wired" and "That doesn't compute." Other examples include: "Jack me up," "I felt like punching the guy's lights out," and "No one keeps you revin' like 7-11." At the same time, the advertising industry increasingly personalizes products. Examples include a magazine ad for Canon cameras that states: "What was Canon thinking when they developed a digital SLR with the personality of a film camera?" Temperpedic describes its removable cover as "New skin. Same soul." Dodge claims its cars are "born Dodge" and they have "future muscle." It is revealing that the culture of violence reduces humans to animals and objects while products have personality and soul. This reflects Marx's idea of "commodity fetishism" in which capitalism values products more than living beings. The problem with using objectification is that over time these labels and images take on a life of their own and become part of everyday talk. They become internalized, which is part of a desensitization process. This relates to Paolo Freire's concern with reducing human beings to objects and its consequences. One consequence is that it is easier to diminish, exploit, bully, rape, and murder people who are objectified and thus are considered to be somehow less than human.

The use of military metaphors and similes in the culture of violence reflects Marx's conclusion that the economic basis of a society generates phenomena such as language. Examples include phrases such as "pick your battles," "blown away," "the front line of prevention," and candy named "Warheads," which has a label showing the head of Wally Warhead, a cartoon character, being blown apart. Balloons labeled "Water Bombs" include a water bomb launcher. The Daily Coin had a recent story entitled "The Fed out of Bullets?" which discussed problems in mortgage lending.[124] Such language reflects the culture of violence and reinforces it. A lot of idioms center on guns and shooting, such as "Give it a shot," "Let's shoot for ten o'clock," "He shot himself in the foot," "on target," "Let's aim for," and "straight shooter." This focus also manifests as product names and product labels, such as Robinson's "Fruit Shoot" drink.

Language among young people in particular is diminished. They frequently use hyperbole, such as the words "perfect," "awesome," and "great," which, by definition, are rare states. This exaggeration is related to the tendency of media entertainment to engage in hyperbole, exaggeration, and sensationalism. In an appendix to his novel *1984*, George Orwell predicted that the use of language would become increasingly limited to the point of words deteriorating into "duckspeak," which consists of a series of quacking sounds. The book's characters use such phrases as "supergood" and "superplusgood" instead of such words as "excellent" and "superlative." The deterioration of language clearly is evident in the loss of words. Rather than using words such as "said," "exclaimed," "queried," and the like, young people use the word "went," such as "Then, he went 'I like that movie a lot.'" Many young people, especially young men who have spent a lot of time watching cartoons and playing violent video games, use sounds, especially explosion sounds, to express themselves. People living in the culture of violence witness and experience violence in virtual worlds and also in everyday real life. People witness bad behavior, from rudeness to road rage. They observe surveillance cameras and warning signs. They see aggressive driving, muscle cars, and cars that look like military vehicles, such as the Hummer. They also see men who have hyper-masculine bodies and adults and children who wear camouflage military clothing. Experiencing and witnessing everyday life in the culture of violence creates varying degrees of fear, dread, anger, and alienation. This affects the consciousness of people living in the culture of violence, whose peace of mind already is disturbed by awareness of world problems and nuclear and environmental threats and disasters. Fear is reinforced by news accounts of violent crime and, for many, by violence they experience in their lives. A poll revealed that that 35 percent of children ages six to twelve fear their lives will be cut short by gun violence.[125]

Alcohol and Other Drugs

Over half of all perpetrators or victims of murder have consumed alcohol before the homicide.[126] This is not to say that alcohol causes violence, but it has the ability to trigger explosive emotions, especially anger.

Alcohol is the most pervasive drug in the United States. About twenty million adults abuse alcohol and more than half started drinking heavily when they were teenagers. Alcohol abuse can start before age twelve and it, along with the use of marijuana, is common among high school students. In addition to damage done to the body, alcohol is involved in 10,000 teenage traffic fatalities each year with an additional 40,000 people injured.[127] When young people use alcohol and also have a gun available, the risk for violence increases greatly. In a youth suicide study, victims who killed themselves with firearms were about five times more likely to have been drinking than those who used other means.[128] Drinking is one of the most important problems facing today's college students. This problem is linked to campus crime and sexual assault, especially date rape. Many students are binge drinkers, with consequences for health as well as for behavior.[129]

Use of alcohol and drugs has been documented since early human history. However, these substances were most often used in ritual ceremonies and celebrations or, at times, to communally "let off steam." The phenomenon of youthful and widespread abuse of these substances is peculiar to modern societies, particularly the culture of violence. The evolution of drug use and abuse since the 1960s mirrors changes in society. People in the

'60s were more interested in mind-altering or mind-expanding drugs, such as marijuana and LSD. Life has sped up since then, reflected now in the use of stimulant drugs, such as cocaine and methamphetamine. The continuing deeply rooted human desire for expanded experience and higher experience is evident in the current widespread use of MDMA or "Ecstasy." The name says it all. A desire to experience different domains of consciousness and feeling is part of our spiritual nature. The current epidemic of substance abuse appears to be a mutation of a spiritual impulse that is denigrated by a violent culture in which everyday life is difficult.

In the 1990s juveniles were involved in about 14 percent of all drug arrests. Between 1991 and 1995, juvenile arrests for drug abuse violations increased 138 percent.[130] The most heavily used illegal drugs among young people are marijuana, stimulants (cocaine, crack, speed), LSD, PCP, opiates, heroin, and such designer drugs as Ecstasy.[131] In 2000 the Food and Drug Administration had an annual budget of only $1.4 billion to regulate pharmaceutical drugs, which resulted in 50,000 to 100,000 deaths each year from overdoses and improper use. At the same time, government agencies were spending up to $40 billion a year to fight the illegal drug trade, which caused between 8,000 and 10,000 deaths from drug overdoses.[132]

Other violence results from the drug trade, however. Gang violence over drug market turf may trigger violence. However, violent behavior is usually not committed while under the influence of an illicit drug. The drug that is most frequently associated with violence is alcohol, the legal drug.

What is it about the culture of violence that results in young people abusing alcohol and drugs in epidemic proportions? How happy are people who live in the culture of violence? A 2016 survey found that the United States ranked fiftieth among the world's nations. The happiest countries are Norway, Sweden, and Iceland, countries with mixed economies.[133]

Food

The underlying basis for feeling good physically and for good health is food. Food affects mood and can be linked to depression and to aggressive behavior.[134] *Super Size Me* (2004), a documentary by Morgan Spurlock, described his physical and emotional decline during a period of time eating at fast food restaurants. He reported fatigue, mood swings, irritability, an inability to focus, and a general sense of not feeling well. Also, he gained over twenty pounds.

In addition to contributing to aggressive behavior, sugar is the underlying reason for so many people in the United States being overweight. There is an epidemic of obesity in this country.[135] The United States has the highest obesity rate of any industrialized nation.

More than half of all adults and about one-quarter of children in the United States are now classified as obese or overweight.[136] The average boat passenger now weighs 185 pounds, up from 160 pounds in 1960.[137] In the past twenty years, the number of overweight children has tripled. Twice as many US children are obese nowadays compared to the 1970s.[138]

The average teenage boy drinks fifteen teaspoons of sugar, and the average girl drinks ten teaspoons of sugar in soft drinks on a daily basis.[139] In 2002, forty-nine million gallons of soda were consumed. Twelve to nine-year-olds drink an average of two cans of soda a day.[140] Every day 2,235,616 pounds of sugar is consumed by people in the United States in their breakfast cereals. Every person in the United States eats an average of sixty-four pounds of sugar yearly.[141]

A study of incarcerated delinquents showed that by removing fast food and sugar from their diets, antisocial behavior, including assaults and rule violations, decreased 47 percent.[142] Interestingly, Michael Carneal, a rampage school shooter, admitted to "getting sugared up" before the shooting. Another school shooter, Kipland Kinkel, concluded that violent media and video games as well as "sugary cereal" contributed to his rampage.

A high consumption of sugar displaces a natural hunger for wholesome foods. It has been estimated that youngsters in the United States, at best, eat half of the recommended amount of fruit and vegetables. Consumption of sugar, including processed food that has sugar as a filler, is the overall factor in the Type II diabetes among children as well as obesity. An added health risk is that high blood sugar is a more accurate heart disease predictor than cholesterol. According to the *British Medical Journal*, the higher your blood sugar level, the higher your risk of heart disease and other serious health problems, such as diabetes.[143]

The hyper-consumption of sugar-based food products is fueled by the average child in the United States seeing 10,000 food advertisements per year, 95 percent of them for fast food, soft drinks, candy, and sugary cereals. These are high-profit and nutrition-poor products.[144]

Another likely contributor to poor health in the United States is how food is processed and changed. Since the 1990s, the European Union has refused to allow sales of US beef in Europe.[145] Whereas European Union countries are considering legislation that requires labeling Genetically Modified Food (GMO), the United States does not require such a label that identifies food as having been modified genetically.[146] Arguments against GMO foods include the possibility that people may grow ill or die from unexpected allergies to such food, the food stream may be contaminated, and unknown long-term effects of eating genetically modified.[147] It is reasonable to wonder if GMO foods contribute to dysphoria and aggressive behavior.

A country's infant mortality rate is about the best indicator of overall physical health. In the United States, the infant mortality rate has doubled in the past decade. The report,

"U.S. on List of UNICEF's Worst Countries For Kids," points out that the United States fares worst of all twenty-one developed countries in terms of health and safety, measured by rates of infant mortality and accidents and injuries. On overall criteria, the United States scored second worst, next to England.[148] Bad food and lack of food are the primary reasons why people in the United States experience poor health and a shorter lifespan than other industrialized countries. At 77.5 years the US life expectancy is lower than Cuba. It also is lower than England, France, and Canada.[149] Another key factor is that US health care is the most expensive and the worst performing among industrialized nations.[150] The lack of infrastructure and preparedness became clearly evident during the Coronavirus pandemic in 2020.

The Violence Industries

The culture of violence generates violence industries. The culture of violence and the violence industries are mutually reinforcing and perpetuating. The violence industries are industries that directly and indirectly contribute to and promote violence. In order to more fully understand the culture of violence, we need to look at the effects of the violence industries. The licit violence industries include the electronic entertainment industry, the toy industry, the alcohol industry, the weapons industry, and the war industry. The products of these industries work together synergistically. They not only sustain the culture of violence but also guarantee it. Of course, illicit violence industries, such as the illegal drug industry and the quasi-legal pornography industry also are integral to the culture of violence, but it is beyond the scope of this book to discuss them. Needless to say, their intent is the same as the licit violence industries—to make profit. The electronic entertainment industry and video games have been researched extensively and criticized for contributing to violence. Their impact will be discussed in ensuing chapters.

Corporate Crime

Corporate crime can be seen as a violence industry because of the harm it causes its victims as well as the economy. The public has little knowledge of the enormous financial and human losses that occur because of corporate crime. Deviance and criminality have become normal in big business due to the pressure to produce massive profits at the expense of all other considerations.[151] Stuart Hill, in his book *Corporate Violence*, explains how the mandate of corporations is "profit at any cost." He points out that doing business as usual can be an evil that takes on "a certain banality."[152]

"Crime in the suites" is more deadly than "crime in the streets."[153] Although corporate crime is more lethal than crime in the streets, corporate crime is met with no punishment or with minimal punishment such as relatively small fines. Street crime, however, is addressed in increasingly punitive and unjust ways. A good example is banks laundering billions of dollars in heroin money during the civil war in Afghanistan in the 1980s, providing financial services for the Saudis and other US allies who funded the Taliban. These banks remain in business. Yet, California's "three-strikes" law that sentences people convicted of three felonies to life in prison results in such injustices as that of the man who tried to run out of a store with a few golf clubs who faces life behind bars for his misdeed.[154]

The magnitude of violence generated by corporate crime overshadows aggressive behavior and the lawbreaking transactions associated with street crime. Whereas burglary and robbery cost about $4 billion a year, white-collar fraud costs the country about $200 billion a year.[155] The FBI places street homicide at 24,000 victims a year, while more than 56,000 Americans die every year on jobs in corporate settings or from such malfeasance as occupationally induced cancers.[156] These massive expenditures devour much of the nation's wealth, impose an extraordinary strain on taxpayers, and take money from such necessary expenditures as education and economic development.

Corporate violence as well as corporate crime and its results have been well documented during the past few decades. Indirect violence such as the suffering caused by the Enron scam to direct violence caused by the Ford Pinto debacle have fallen within the public radar.[157] Researchers have concluded: "The violent or 'physical' costs—the toll in lives lost, injuries inflicted, and illnesses suffered—are perhaps the gravest and certainly the most neglected of the damages that corporate lawlessness imposed on the American people."[158]

The link between corporate crime and street crime is a long-ignored connection that is particularly important. In the last forty years, money laundering, tax fraud, environmental crimes, occupational hazards, and a host of other corporate crimes have played a central role in the growth of street crime and the drug trade. Corporations are complicit in directly facilitating those crimes and by indirectly creating social problems that give rise to crime.[159]

Over time, lack of employment opportunities in high-crime communities has been worsened by corporate policies—some illegal, some legal—that discriminate against minority people, cheat government agencies out of tax dollars, pollute the environment, and discourage investment in low-income communities. By 1991, with crime rates reaching record levels, job discrimination against minority people cost the economy about $165 billion a year in lost employment opportunities.[160]

The Toy Industry

From the perspective of conflict theory, it is not surprising that the war economy of the United States has generated war games, war toys, and war-themed video games. Such an economy, as pointed out by Barbara Ehrenreich, creates a "warrior ideal" as a model of behavior for boys and men. War play is an activity almost exclusive to boys.[161] As a result, boys identify with warriors, and girls identify with Barbie-type dolls. Integral to this process of gender socialization are war games, including toy guns and action figures. Playing with violent toys and war toys helps to set the stage for future alignment with weapons and aggressive behavior. In the culture of violence, G.I. Joe–type toys are the most popular doll for boys, and the toy gun industry alone nets well over $100 million a year.[162]

Why are war toys so appealing? One explanation is that war play allows children to feel powerful. "At an age when children can feel helpless and out of control … this sense of having control and power can be very important.[163] It is in the nature of human beings to want to feel and be capable and effective. During childhood, this quality of efficacy is developed. At the same time, children learn how to cooperate. The importance of the child's emerging sense of personal power is amplified by the culture of violence and its imposition of hierarchy and competition. These cultural forces too often result in personal power becoming mutated into a desire for power over others.

Another key reason for the proliferation of war games is encased in and promoted by the culture of violence and its industries. One of the first toys advertised on television became a national best-seller after it appeared during *The Mickey Mouse Club* in 1955. The Burp Gun manufactured by Mattel was a realistic reproduction of the automatic machine gun used in World War II. With the help of television advertising, the leading toy producers no longer created products that emulated adult life and taught basic skills like engineering sets, model trains, and baby dolls. The new marketing strategies brought in a flood of toys that simulated activities familiar in movies and television. An example is the G.I. Joe action figures which were marketed through the *G.I. Joe: Great American Hero* cartoon.[164] As a result, G.I. Joe was the favorite doll of boys for over three decades and G.I. Joe–type dolls have maintained a remarkably high level of popularity. With the Federal Communications Commission deregulation of children's television programming in 1983, toy manufacturers could develop thirty-minute cartoon commercials for their products. The sponsors, companies in the toy industry, introduced action figures based on popular cartoon characters. The World Wrestling Federation, in their words, sold action figures "with bone-crunching action" to children ages five and older.[165] By 1987, the sale of violent toys had soared by more than 600 percent.[166]

The effects of early play, compounded by the effects of violent media, have a profound effect on children. Many best-selling toys increasingly are linked to children's electronic media. In addition to violence, many of these toys promote sexy behavior and consumption. The most popular toy for girls is Barbie and Barbie-type dolls. The ratio of the Barbie dolls sold in the United States since 1959 to the number of Americans born since then is 5:1.[167] Barbie is the standard of beauty, which presents several problems. If she were a real woman, she would be seven feet tall and have a triple E bra cup size. This tendency toward exaggerated body types is also evident in video game heroines, such as Lara Croft's impossible physique. Girls literally cannot measure up. No doubt the Barbie syndrome is a key factor in bulimia and anorexia. Bratz dolls and Disney princess dolls also narrowly focus girls into play scripts about shopping, appearance, and being sexy, including being thin and wearing make-up and adult clothing. Advertising slogans like "Beauty is our duty" encourage girls to act older at younger ages and to imagine that how they look determines their value. This promotes rigid gender stereotypes, negative self-image, and eating disorders in girls. These dolls, coupled with the relentless and artificial media projections of feminine beauty, have contributed to more and more women being unhappy about their appearance.[168] Barbie and other dolls, as well as the projected media standard of beauty, have significantly contributed to bulimic and anorexic problems among girls and women. Indirectly, this manufactured standard of beauty relates to violence against women who do not physically measure up to such impossible standards.

The Alcohol Industry

The alcohol industry is another violence industry. Alcohol is involved in most cases of violence,[169] and most of the country's prisoners used alcohol or drugs while committing their offense.[170] In a youth suicide study, victims who used firearms were about five times more likely to have been drinking than those who used other means.[171] These stark figures afford a glimpse into the world of violence that alcohol helps generate. Undoubtedly, many acts of domestic violence and child abuse also are committed under the influence of alcohol. We could say that alcohol does not kill people, people kill people, but this does not explain away the key role that alcohol plays in violent crimes.

The Prison Industry

Prisons, especially privately owned prisons, constitute a violence industry. Fyodor Dostoevsky once wrote: "The degree of civilization in a society can be judged by entering its prisons."[172] The United States is now the world's top jailer, surpassing the Soviet Union and South Africa.[173] Prisons in the United States hold record numbers of poor, jobless, uneducated, and unskilled people. Their numbers triple the projected growth of the general US population.[174]

This huge increase in prisoners does not reflect a nationwide crime wave. The vast majority of people entering state prisons have been convicted of a nonviolent crime, often a drug charge.[175] Over half the offenses committed by the people in US prisons are for petty crimes involving no injury or threat of injury. Another 30 percent are jailed for crimes, that is, crimes, that are criminal offenses but not serious crimes. The remainder has been convicted for serious crimes, including stealing over $10,000 to murder. Of these 20 percent, about five percent committed very serious crimes such as rape, manslaughter, or kidnapping.[176] In 1984, just 30 percent of federal prisoners were drug offenders. By the turn of the century, it was 57 percent.[177]

Prisons are violent institutions that breed violent individuals. As psychiatrist Seymour Halleck says, "If one systematically and diabolically tried to create mental illness, one could probably have constructed no better system than the American prison system."[178] Prisons generate violence within prison walls and in the larger society. The National Council on Crime and Delinquency concludes that incarceration makes an individual "more alienated, more prone to violence, and less capable of re-entering productive society."[179]

Studies consistently reveal the ways in which the prison industry perpetuates crime.[180] A student of the author who was a prisoner in a state prison summed up the problem well. He said, "In the United States, it is a crime to be poor. And the poorer we are, the more criminal we are. Most prisoners are young, poor, and black. About 80 percent of the people who go to prison are not able to afford an attorney and are forced to rely on underpaid and overworked public defenders.[181]

The burgeoning of the prison population has resulted in private companies contracting with the government to construct and manage prisons. The private prison industry, blatantly based on profit, has wreaked even more havoc, suffering, and death than government-run facilities. The Corrections Corporation of America (CCA), the country's largest private prison company, has a record of continuing abuses and deaths. Examples are rampant. Prisons guards at CCA's Cibola County Correctional Center in New Mexico tear-gassed nearly seven hundred prisoners who had staged a daylong nonviolent protest of conditions at the facility.[182] Jurors in Columbia, South Carolina, found that guards at a CCA juvenile prison had abused a young person confined there and that their use of force was so malicious that it was "repugnant to the conscience of mankind."[183]

Prisons harbor and generate violence. They create more anger and feelings of disenfranchisement among inmates who then are more likely to engage in violent behavior in prison and when they are released. Prisons also create violence because of the stratified nature of the justice system and the ensuing connection between prisons and the perpetuation of poverty.

The Weapons Industry

The United States has a national gun culture, and given that the United States has the world's largest supply of privately owned weapons, it is no surprise that much of the toy industry is devoted to war toys and war games. There are approximately forty-four million gun owners in the United States. Twenty-five percent of all adults and 40 percent of households own at least one firearm. These owners possess 192 million firearms, of which sixty-five million are handguns.[184] The United States continues to have the highest rate of firearm-related deaths among industrialized countries.[185] It is estimated that annually handguns killed forty-eight people in Japan, eight in England, thirty-four in Switzerland, fifty-two in Canada, fifty-eight in Israel, twenty-one in Sweden, forty-three in Germany, and 10,728 in the United States.[186] Austria has two gun deaths per 100,000 people, France has three, Canada has five, and the United States has 40.[187] About 80 percent of violent deaths can be attributed to firearms.[188]

During the 1990s, the cycle of gun use accelerated as young people acquired guns to protect themselves from other armed youth, real and imagined. Death by firearms ranks as the fifth leading cause of death for five to nine-year-old children, and the second leading cause of death for children ages ten to fourteen.[189] About 60 percent of these deaths are attributed to interpersonal violence.[190]

The ready availability of firearms provides the means for school shooters to carry out their plans. Without access to guns, none of the school tragedies could have taken place. A researcher comments: "Guns are a critical risk factor. When juvenile homicide tripled in this country in just ten years, all of the increase was in gun-related killing. There was no increase in juveniles stabbing or beating one another to death. Guns are not the cause of the violence, but they provide the means."[191] Research confirms that many school-age children in the United States can easily obtain a firearm, even though laws forbid the sale of firearms to minors.[192] About 14 percent of male juveniles report carrying a gun outside the home. In the inner city, the problem is more severe. One study revealed that 22 percent of inner-city youth carry weapons. About 88 percent of convicted juvenile offenders report carrying guns.[193] The US Department of Justice reports: "A teenager in the United States today is more likely to die of a gunshot wound than from all the 'natural' causes of death combined."[194] Fights that used to involve fists have become deadly exchanges.

Assault rifles have become notorious because they are used in rampage shootings. The International Association of Chiefs of Police, the International Brotherhood of Police Officers, and the Fraternal Order of Police all supported renewal of the assault weapon ban. However, in 2004, the Senate voted ninety to eight against the reauthorization bill after the National Rifle Association urged its defeat.[195] The 1994 Assault Weapon Ban had outlawed nineteen types of military-style assault weapons, which include AK-47s, Uzis, and TEC-9s.[196] Banning these weapons was shown to reduce lethal violence.[197] Between 1993 and 1996, for example, gun-related homicides declined by 33 percent, including a 35 percent drop in handgun homicides.[198]

The weapons industry is one of the most dangerous industries in the United States.[199] And, it is doubly dangerous because of its clear motive for profit at any cost. Gun deaths have not abated because of the lift of the assault weapons ban and also because of the work of gun lobbyists. Critics of the industry have demonstrated that in order to rejuvenate gun sales, the industry started making more powerful pistols.[200] In addition, beginning in the mid-1990s, gun manufacturers were producing smaller guns for small hands.[201]

Currently the gun industry is exempt from the federal health and safety regulations applied to virtually every other consumer product on the market. This means that a federal agency cannot set minimum safety standards, issue recalls on defective merchandise, or mandate safety warnings. In addition, gun manufacturers are not required to label their products to ensure that guns that are defective can be identified and traced. The only protection gun consumers have against manufacturers of defective guns is to file a lawsuit after the victim has been injured or killed.[202] In 1997, during the first national symposium on gun industry reform, Sarah Brady, chair of the Center to Prevent Handgun Violence, stated: "We are here today to tell you about an industry whose secrecy, opportunism, cynicism and disdain for consumer protection make it the next logical target for reform in America. That industry, although it contains some respectable and responsible companies, also has a chief executive who boasts about marketing tools of mass murder."[203] Dennis Henigan, director of the Legal Action Project of the Center to Prevent Handgun Violence, has noted that the American legal system has long imposed penalties on those whose irresponsible conduct leads to violence. He has said: "Without withdrawing an iota of responsibility from the criminals who commit the crimes, we must also hold accountable the industry that provides them with the 'tools of the trade' with no thought of anything but its own profit motive."[204]

The increased availability of guns to young people has had devastating consequences for families, schools, and communities. In addition to the tremendous human suffering caused by these fatalities and injuries, gunshot wounds account for approximately $40 billion in medical, public service, and work-loss costs each year.[205]

The War Industry

In 1942, at the height of World War II, the United States experienced an 89 percent increase in "acts against common decency." A documentary film entitled *The Youth Problem* attributed this to the stress of living during a war and an "unraveling view of the world."[206]

This consciousness still holds today and is compounded by the awareness of the threat of nuclear annihilation.

The economic basis of the United States is a military-industrial complex that has a militarized budget and a militarized foreign policy. The nature of a society's economy, as Marx pointed out, shapes worldviews. An economy dominated by military spending fosters a militarized ideology that tends to accept violence as a normal and acceptable way to resolve conflict.

After World War II, President Eisenhower coined the term "military-industrial complex," noting that in the United States industries and the military were becoming entwined. He warned that "we must guard against the acquisition of unwarranted influence, whether sought or unsought by the military-industrial complex." He noted: "Every gun that is made, every warship launched, every rocket fired signifies in the final sense a theft from those who hunger and are not fed, those who are cold and not clothed. . . . This is not a way of life in the true sense. Under the clouds of war, it is humanity hanging on a cross of iron."[207]

The United States has the largest war budget in the world.[208] The cost of the war against Iraq and Pakistan/Afghanistan has cost over $1 trillion dollars. This is larger than that of all other national defense budgets in the world combined.[209] Desert Storm cost about $90 billion a year. Including a nuclear arsenal, troops in Japan and Europe, and about one million men and women under arms, the total US annual war budget in the early 1990s was about $150 billion.[210] By 2003, it was $776 billion and comprised 46 percent of the Federal budget.[211] What do our federal tax dollars pay for? In 2010, they paid $1,440 billion for military expenditures comprising 54 percent of the federal budget, the largest military budget since World War II. This includes $380 billion for interest on our national debt. About 80 percent of this $380 billion is estimated to be created by military spending.[212] The federal budget approved by Congress in 2010 contained the largest military budget since World War II, $1,372 billion.[213] The fiscal year 2021 Federal budget allocated 47 percent for military expenditures, which total over $15 billion.[214]

Since the year 2001 Twin Towers attack, there have been remarkably few terrorist attacks in the United States. Even though a study by the highly respected Rand Corporation concludes that "there is no battlefield solution to terrorism,"[215] since that time national defense spending has doubled.[216] Even the conservative Brookings Institution proposes a 33 percent cut.[217] Former Defense Secretary Robert Gates has criticized bloated Pentagon expenditures and spoke against weapons systems with huge cost overruns as well as swollen and unnecessary bureaucracy. He asked, "Does the number of warships we have and are building really put America at risk when the US battle fleet is larger than the next thirteen navies combined, eleven of which belong to allies and partners?"[218]

By 2019 the United States had a national debt of $21.9 trillion, and most of the debt has been created by military spending.[219] According to independent analysts, the United

States' war economy has placed the social fabric as well as the economy of the country at risk. According to Moody's Investors Service, in early 2011, the United States lost its top-notch credit rating. The ratio of interest payments to general revenue was at levels that "invariably require fiscal adjustments of a magnitude that, in some cases, will test social cohesion."[220] A usual argument in support of war is that it creates jobs. Actually, a war economy tends to create low-paying, short-term jobs. Cutting the military budget would create more jobs.[221] Because joblessness has a direct relationship to crime, creating more jobs would reduce crime.

What is the human cost of the war industry? In addition to lives being compromised and shortened in the United States, there have been thousands of US military deaths in Iraq and Afghanistan. In addition, the total number of Iraqi people killed is over 655,000.[222] It is unclear how many Afghan people have been killed.

A highly militarized economy creates violence indirectly as well as directly. The war industry consumes resources that would otherwise be used to enhance the quality of life and preserve it. War generates poverty and endorses the idea that violence is normal. It generates a mean-spiritedness which is characteristic of the culture of violence. This culture generates industries that facilitate aggression and promote violent behavior. The culture produces world views, attitudes, beliefs, and behavior that are contrary to human nature. This is of particular concern because human nature evolved to protect the human race and ensure its survival.

CHAPTER 5

THE CULTURE OF SCHOOL VIOLENCE: THE SCHOOL ENVIRONMENT

> The environment teaches.
> —John Dewey

Schools are embedded in the culture of violence and perpetuate it. School violence ranges from malicious teasing to physical aggression to school shootings. The most prevalent form is bullying and the most notorious is rampage school shootings.

Bullying among children is not new. It has been documented in literary works, such as those of Charles Dickens, for hundreds of years. Such films as *The Little Rascals* and *Mean Girls* give adults a glimpse into the world of bullying. However, the current reality is harsher. Many schools are no longer a haven of safety and security. The problem of bullying has been increasing steadily for the past forty years and has taken on a more sinister character.

The first rampage high school shooting happened in 1974, but rampage school shootings were infrequent until the 1990s. Since that time rampage school shootings have become more lethal and also have graduated into public places at an alarming rate.

What has happened to create such a culture of school violence in this period of time?

Schools are a microcosm of the larger culture. Like families, schools can be the cradle of democracy or infamy. Violent schools are crucibles of future violence. School campuses have become dramatically more violent in the last three decades. School-associated violent deaths reached their peak during the 1992–1994 school years with 105 victims.[1] The

1999–2000 school year saw thirty-two school-associated violent deaths.[2] Between 1999 and 2006, the average annual number of violent deaths on school campuses decreased to 20,[3] probably due to security and programmatic responses to the 1999 Columbine massacre. This catastrophic event created an alertness among both school personnel and students that resulted in intervening and obstructing more violence from occurring. However, by the 2007–2008 school year, violent death has again increased to forty-three violent deaths on school campuses.[4] The rate of annual reported violent crimes is highest for middle schools at forty-one incidents per 1,000 students. In elementary schools it is twenty-six incidents and for high schools twenty-two incidents.[5] About one-quarter of schools reported no violent crimes, and about one-quarter reported twenty or more violent crimes. The range in the number of crimes reported by schools vary by school characteristics. For example, a larger percentage of city schools report twenty or more violent incidents. In the 2007–2008 school year, 36 percent of city schools report this high rate compared to 24 percent of suburban schools, 21 percent of town schools, and 14 percent of rural schools.[6]

A History of School Violence

The problem of school violence came to light with the 1978 release of the *Safe School Study Report to Congress*, which revealed shocking statistics. The report indicated that about 282,000 students were physically assaulted in secondary schools every month. This translates into 1.3 percent.[7] By 2007, the rate of being attacked increased to 12 percent.[8] The report also noted that about 5,200 teachers were physically assaulted in secondary schools every month.[9] This compares to an estimated 16,000 teachers thirty years later in 2008.[10] The Safe School Study did not include school shootings because campus homicides were a new and rare event.

Since the early 1990s, nearly half of all teens believed that their schools had become more violent.[11] By 1993, 25 percent of schools reported that, as a result of violence, students had suffered injuries that required hospitalization or had died.[12] More than half of the surveyed students were in a physical fight during the previous six months and 10 percent in the past month. About six percent were hurt badly enough to be seen by a doctor.[13] The 1992–1993 school year peaked in school-associated violent deaths. About nine percent of the students said that within the past month they had been physically attacked and hurt while at school.[14]

Nineteen percent of high school students in 1994 identified violence as the biggest problem where they go to school.[15] By 1998, 25 percent of middle school and high school students reported that their schools had very serious problems of social tension and violence.[16] During that time the number of adolescent homicide offenders who claimed multiple victims increased dramatically.[17] About 39 percent of school children reported feeling very safe at school, and 42 percent felt somewhat safe, while 12 percent reported not feeling very safe at all. Students reported being less concerned about extreme violence than the everyday violence manifested in bullying.[18] About 80 percent of adult respondents said that violence was a serious problem in school, and 40 percent of the parents of high school seniors stated they were "very or somewhat worried" about their child's safety while in school or going to and from school.[19]

One-third of all teachers and two-thirds of teachers from poor-quality schools believe that teachers are less likely to challenge or discipline students as a direct result of the threat of violence.[20] About 14 percent of students surveyed admitted they had hit a parent as well as a teacher.[21] A poll conducted by the American Psychological Association revealed that 40 percent of the young people surveyed expressed concern about a potentially violent classmate.[22] These students also indicated that the threat of violence made them less inclined to pay attention in class.[23]

By 1996, one in ten teens reported a fear of being shot or otherwise hurt by classmates who carry weapons to school.[24] This fear is not unfounded, considering that by 1990 nearly 20 percent of high school students reported they had carried a weapon at least once during the preceding month.[25] Many students carry a weapon for protection. About 36 percent of male students and 21 percent of female students interviewed that they would feel safer in a fight if they had a knife.[26] By the end of the 1990s, high school seniors worried most about violence—more than drug abuse, economic problems, poverty, race relations, or even nuclear war.[27]

In the 2007–2008 school year, there were forty-three school-associated violent deaths. During that year 32 percent of middle school and high school students reported being bullied.[28] That school year was the first time that crimes on school campuses exceeded crime away from school. At school there were twenty-six violent crimes per 1,000 students compared to twenty violent crimes off campus.[29]

By 2013 there were forty-eight school-associated deaths.[30] This is remarkably close to the forty-seven school-associated deaths in 1999,[31] despite concerted efforts to reduce and prevent school violence during those fourteen years. For 2018, the US Department of Education reported that there were thirty-eight school-associated violent deaths, and 20 percent of the students reported being bullied.[32]

The School Environment

What does the school environment teach? In addition to the three Rs, it teaches hierarchy, non-negotiable power, obedience, competition, and aggression. Hierarchy's offspring, disempowerment, characterizes the culture of school violence. "To oppress" means to push down. So, by its very nature, hierarchy is oppressive. Olson, in her book *Wounded By School*, writes that most schools embody Old School Culture, which is "a set of old-fashioned ideas and attitudes in school that construct teaching as hierarchical and learning as passive."[33] This criticism of Old School Culture is aligned with Paolo Freire's concern about "the pedagogy of the oppressed."[34] How dissonant is Old School Culture with human nature and with liberatory education? The expression and use of power are intrinsic to hierarchy. Hierarchy extends from the culture of violence to the school board to the administrators to the faculty and to the students.

The students themselves replicate hierarchy through social status and displays of power in the form of bullying. This hierarchy is maintained with status boundaries and cliques. An unprecedented emphasis on competitive sports in schools has played a key role in defining school hierarchy, with "jocks" often at the top of the social ladder. Anthony Solomon, a school shooter in Rockdale County, Georgia, said he could understand the Columbine killers "wanting to shoot the jocks and preps."[35] According to the National Research Council, the social hierarchy among students in schools has become more exclusive and rigid over time.[36] This, in part, accounts for increased rates of school violence because, as anthropological evidence shows, the more status differences in a society, the more violence.[37]

Often these displays of power by bullying demonstrate a mean-spiritedness that has a chilling effect on the classroom and school environment. This climate is worsened by the fact that more than 8 percent of high school students attempt suicide each year and 17 percent report that they have seriously considered attempting suicide.[38]

The looks of the school reinforce the presence of power and authority. Many are large concrete blocks, often surrounded by a barbed-wire fence. They look like factories or prisons. Many school environments are influenced by "the Columbine effect," that is, instituting security measures and infrastructure. Physical security measures, surveillance cameras, metal detectors, and gun-free school zone signs are often evident. This physical environment proclaims danger and threat as well as control. Between 1999 and 2016, the use of security cameras increased from 19 to 81 percent. Locked entrances increased from 75 to 94 percent.[39] Such measures are widespread, even though multiple studies show that increased security measures do not significantly increase school safety, often making students feel less safe at school.[40] Many school security measures are implemented without consulting the empirical evidence and without considering the fiscal consequences. Another negative outcome is socializing students toward a society of control and authority.[41]

The culture of school violence increasingly is characterized by the presence of uniformed security guards and, in some cases, police officers. As of 1998, forty states had launched plans to put law enforcement personnel on campuses and to add police or school safety officers to their administrative teams.[42] By 2005, 68 percent of high schools had school resource officers.[43] In addition, as of 2018, at least eight states allow teachers to carry weapons on campus.[44] Between 2001 and 2005, there was an increase in the use of security cameras from 39 percent to 58 percent. Correspondingly, during this time, the percent of locked school entrance doors increased from 38 to 53 percent.[45] The presence of security infrastructure and law enforcement officers communicates that the school environment is not safe. It communicates fear as well as control.

The hallways of school buildings often are cavernous, amplifying the already sugared, caffeinated, and food-additive fueled loud and rapid talk of the students. There are a lot of expletives and such exchanges as "You're dead meat." Loud bells, signifying authority, periodically punctuate this cacophony. Many school hallways have posters with slogans such as "Murder the Spartans!" and "Slaughter the Vikings!" These are visible reminders that schools are becoming more centered on sports, many of which are aggressive. Also, school sports are an arena in which girls are learning to be more male-defined, reflected in unisex clothing, demeanor, and language.

There is little variation in students' clothing style. The t-shirt and jeans fashion worn by both boys and girls resembles a uniform, although girls tend to show more flesh. Boys and, at times, girls wear army fatigues and khaki clothes. The majority of students and many of the teachers wear the dark colors of black and blue. Gray and beige also are preponderant. Black, blue, gray, and beige are depressive colors and also the colors of bruises, apparently communicating that they feel depressed and possibly bruised and battered.

The sense of oppression and the aggressive feelings engendered in the culture of school violence are shockingly clear when considering the stories of middle school teachers related to the author. They related that students in their classes cheered when they heard of the Columbine massacre.

Hallways feature vending machines, which contain merchandise with additives, sugar, and caffeine, all of which are increasingly associated with ADHD and aggressive behavior.[46] Cafeterias are tending to provide more and more junk food, heavy in sugar and fat, which contribute to hyperactive behavior, inability to concentrate, obesity, and diabetes, which is reaching epidemic proportions among children.

Class disruptions are problems in many classrooms. Such disruptions interfere with learning and erode the educational development of many students. Student misbehavior, at one point or another, has interrupted teaching in most eighth grade classrooms and in more than half of all twelfth grade classrooms. About one in four students report that these disruptions interfere with their learning.[47] These disruptions also cause continuous stress for teachers who already experience constraints and burnout because of budget cuts, large classes, and fewer resources.[48]

This mix of problematic behavior is compounded by exposure to radiation, which is especially harmful to children. Radiation exposure is experienced in schools located near cell towers and that use Wi-Fi. The dangerous effects of such exposure have been documented for decades by hundreds, perhaps thousands, of studies in the United States and internationally. Exposure results in behavioral problems, such as increased aggression and learning difficulties, such as difficulty in focusing. Other effects include depression and health problems, including cancer. Physicians for Safe Technology acknowledge these deleterious effects and recommend safeguards, such as prohibiting construction of towers near schools. They report, for example, that educators in California have initiated legislative action and that a Colorado middle school that banned Wi-Fi relates that students are happier, experience less stress, and perform better academically.[49]

School Staff

Teachers also face risks on school campuses. By the late 1990s, national surveys revealed that about 11 percent of teachers reported being victims of violence in and around schools.[50] Eleven percent of grade school teachers and nine percent of high school teachers were threatened with injury in 2015, and nine percent of grade school teachers and two percent of high school teachers were physically attacked.[51] It is noteworthy that younger students are acting more aggressively toward their teachers.

In 1977 about 5,200 teachers were attacked each month.[52] By 2008, 16,000 teachers were attacked each month.[53] Threats to teachers and classroom disruptions have resulted in a new low in teacher job satisfaction, with almost one-third thinking about leaving the profession.[54] There has been a trend of teachers and administrators in many large cities seeking early retirement because they do not want to deal with the increase in school crime and violence.[55] At times this is coupled with school administrators not reporting violent incidents for fear their schools will be labeled "persistently dangerous" by the No Child Left Behind Act and thus face possible loss of funding.[56] How many schools underreport violence because of this?

Many, if not most children, are reluctant to report bullying because of fear and also because help is not available. School risk factors for bullying include schools in which bullying is tolerated because of a lack of adequate adult supervision and where teachers, other staff, and students have indifferent or accepting attitudes toward bullying.[57] Many children question the commitment of teachers and administrators to stop bullying. In a study of ninth grade students, only about 35 percent believed that their teachers were interested in trying to stop bullying, and 21 percent felt that their teachers were not interested. The remaining 44 percent of the students reported that they did not know.[58] As a student on a CNN special about bullying stated it: "Teachers need to step in."[59] Reluctance to report bullying also is due to many children's lack of confidence in school personnel's handling of incidents and reports. In a survey of high school students, 66 percent of those who had been bullied believed that staff responded poorly, and only 6 percent felt that these problems were handled very well.[60] Leary and his colleagues conclude that bullying is typically ignored by school administrations.[61] The problem is thus compounded because if students observe bullying behavior going unchecked, they will learn to regard bullying behavior as acceptable.

Mean-Spiritedness

An unidentified risk factor for school violence is school board members, administrators, and teachers who themselves are bullies. This bullying is less readily obvious and more sophisticated, such as political bullying. However the goal is the same—power over others. Demonstration of power over others sustains hierarchy and non-democratic processes in the boardroom, office, classroom, and playground. A school climate characterized by bullying has negative effects for everyone, not just the bully and the victim. Entire schools and communities also are affected.

This mean-spiritedness is reflected in the following survey results. A survey of high school students' attitudes about the use of violence and nonviolence demonstrates this climate. About 38 percent indicated that they disagreed with the statement, "If someone called me a bad name, I would ignore them or walk away. About 21 percent disagreed with the statement, "I don't need to fight because there are other ways to deal with anger," and 15 percent disagreed with "When you are so mad that you want to hurt someone, it's always best to find another way to handle your anger." About 45 percent more boys than girls disagreed with these statements.[62] Additionally, more than 81 percent of the students agreed with the statement, "If a girl sees someone flirting with her boyfriend, she should fight with her." Seventy-four percent agreed with "It's okay to hit someone who hits you first." Almost 49 percent agreed with "Sometimes it is necessary to fight with people who are rude or annoying." About 43 percent agreed with "If I'm challenged, I'm going to fight." And 26 percent agreed with the statement, "If someone steals from me, the best way to handle it is to beat the person up."[63] Young people increasingly are defining social problems in hostile ways, adopting aggressive or violent methods of interaction, and seeking few facts or alternatives before acting. They tend to give a high priority to aggressive solutions and believe that violence is legitimate, effective, and socially approved.[64]

The emotional life of students contributes palpably to the culture of school violence. Fear is a pervasive experience among the victims of bullies.[65] It also affects the children who witness the bullying. This fear has basis in fact, considering the rate of bullying and the presence of guns and other weapons. Since the 1999 Columbine massacre, many students report being afraid of such an incident in their schools.[66] An eleven-year-old boy, living in Colorado twelve years after Columbine, commented that students are not made fun of so much now "because people know nowadays that people aren't scared to walk into a school and start shooting." When asked if he ever feared shootings at his school, he responded, "Yes, because on 4/20 a lot of people try and reenact Columbine."[67] Like 9/11, 4/20 is a shorthand code that has become part of everyday language for children in Colorado.

Weapons

The presence of guns in schools is part of the culture of school violence. By the mid-1990s an estimated 270,000 guns were brought to school each day in the United States.[68] A recent study in rural South Carolina found that students' gun ownership was linked with rates of bullying.[69] By 1995, 61 percent of school districts, especially urban districts, cited weapons as a problem. At that time 9 percent of eighth grade students, 10 percent of ninth grade students, and 6 percent of twelfth grade students report carrying a weapon, such as a gun, knife, or club to school at least once during the previous month.[70] By 2006 about 65 percent of school homicides resulted from gunshot wounds.[71] In the mid-1990s, about 7 percent of students reported being threatened or injured with a weapon. About 19 percent of eighth graders reported being threatened with a weapon and 9 percent reported being injured. At every grade level, black students and Hispanic students are more likely than white students to report being threatened or injured with a weapon at school.[72] Some surveys indicate that being threatened by weapons decreased from 12 percent to 6 percent between 1992 and 2004.[73] In 2016 about 6 percent of high school students reported they had been threatened or injured by a weapon on school property during the previous twelve months.[74] Part of this decrease is due to the increased presence of resource officers and metal detectors. Despite these security measures, by 2017 about 11 percent of students reported carrying a weapon and 6 percent reported being threatened by a weapon.[75]

Drugs

The culture of school violence also features drug use and abuse among students. About one-third of high school students report that someone has offered, sold, or given them an illegal drug at school.[76] About 6 percent of students claim to smoke marijuana on campus, and 22 percent admit to smoking marijuana elsewhere. Five percent admit to drinking alcohol on campus, and 43 percent state that they drink at school or elsewhere.[77] In a national poll, almost half of public high school students reported that drugs were a serious problem in their schools.[78]

Violence Against Girls

Bullying is predictive of sexual harassment and homophobic teasing.[79] Sexual harassment and dating violence, which emerge during adolescence, color the school environment. Almost 6 percent of high school girls and 9 percent of older adolescent girls experienced dating violence in 2008.[80] By 2011 about 48 percent of middle school and high school students had experienced some form of sexual harassment in person or via texting or social media. It is so prevalent that it is considered "the new normal."[81]

Suicide

Students attending violent schools often experience depression and fear. The extreme manifestation of depression, suicide, creates a shadow over the school environment. By 2005, 17 percent of high school students in the United States reported that they had seriously considered attempting suicide during the year preceding the survey. More than 8 percent of students reported that they had actually attempted suicide one or more times during the same period.[82] The connection between bullying, depression, and fear has created a new term—bullycide.

Bullying

Bullying has been receiving national attention since the mid-1990s. It is recognized as a serious problem in schools throughout the United States and in other industrialized countries. Bullying often is viewed as a more urban phenomenon. While some research supports this conclusion, other research shows little variation in rates of bullying among urban, suburban, and rural schools. However, this conclusion may be confounded by reporting methods.[83]

Bullying is not a part of normative development for children and teenagers. It should be regarded as a precursor to more serious aggressive or violent behavior.[84] Bullying is a manifestation of hierarchy, a demonstration of power and control. Bullying is defined as the "use of one's strength or status to intimidate, injure, or humiliate another person of lesser strength or status."[85] Bullying often is committed by a school's elite in defense of their social position or by individuals reacting to a perceived threat.[86] The American Medical Association defines bullying as "a pattern of repeated aggression with deliberate intent to harm or disturb a victim despite apparent victim distress and a real or perceived imbalance of power."[87] Dan Olweus states that bullying entails an imbalance in power and strength. Bullying is aggressive behavior or intentional "harm doing" that is carried out repeatedly over time.[88]

An eleven-year-old boy was asked to define violence, and replied, "When you lose control over something, you need to get power back so you use violence."[89] As a ten-year-old boy put it, "Bullying is where one kid picks on another kid. Or when a group picks on one kid. This can be from calling them names all the way to beating them up and taking things from them. Also bullying can be not letting others play a game with you, not letting them be part of your group. Just being mean to them."[90] A fifteen-year-old reformed bully commented: "Bullying was satisfying. It gave me more confidence. And I kind of felt powerful."[91] The themes of power and domination characterize the literature that describes bullying. Felson, for example, writes: "For the bully, dominating the victim is an accomplishment, a way of demonstrating power to himself and others."[92]

Bullying consists of negative actions that intentionally inflict injury or discomfort upon another person. These actions can be carried out physically, verbally, or, increasingly, through the internet. Bullying includes using a weapon, threatening with a weapon, striking, kicking, spitting, throwing objects, excluding someone, removing and hiding belongings, and making threatening gestures, such as staring fixedly at someone who is unwelcome.

Bullying can include racial bullying, directed at someone because of racial identity, and sexual bullying, which has negative sexual or gender implications.[93] A 2005 Harris poll found that 90 percent of gay and lesbian teenagers say that they have been bullied in the past year. Nearly two-thirds of these students feel unsafe in school.[94] About 14 percent of middle school children are the victims of hate-related words, and about 37 percent report being victims of hate-related graffiti.[95] There is a thin line between bullying and hate crimes, exemplified in the case of Lawrence King, a small fifteen-year-old boy who lived in Oxnard, California. He started showing up for class at the E. O. Green Junior High School dressed in women's accessories and make-up. He wore stilettos and at times chased the boys around the school in them. He was then ridiculed even more, and the boys in gym class would shove him around the locker room. "Random people would come up to him and start laughing," a friend related. One day in class another student shot and killed Larry.[96]

Girls report being bullied by both boys and girls, whereas boys typically are bullied only by other boys.[97] Girls are more involved in relational bullying or teasing (emotional bullying).[98] Emotional bullying follows a similar pattern to physical bullying, reaching a peak among six to nine-year-old children. About a third of children in this age group report being teased in the past year, with the number decreasing steadily thereafter.[99]

Children typically report different kinds of bullying in different age groups. Older students tend to bully younger students, thus enacting hierarchy. Bullying is most likely to occur in elementary schools and middle schools, occurring most frequently from the sixth to the eighth grade.[100] Younger children, fifth through eighth grade, are more likely to be hit, shoved, kicked, or tripped than older children. Older children are more likely to tease and gossip about one another.[101] The highest rates of victimization tend to be among eighth grade students. Children report being bullied less often as they get older. Most studies have found that rates of bullying decrease fairly steadily through elementary grades, middle school, and into high school, although bullying occurs frequently but temporarily during the first year of high school.[102] Most bullying occurs in the playground, the classroom, hallways and corridors, the gymnasium, the locker room, and the bathrooms. The great majority of bullying occurs when adults are not present, so there is a tendency to underestimate its prevalence.[103] Children are present about 85 percent of the time. The involvement of other children ranges from joining in the bullying, to passively observing, to actively intervening to stop the bullying. About half of the students admit that they do not try to intervene, apparently out of fear of reprisal or feeling that their efforts would be futile.[104] Student reports of bullying tend to be inaccurate because victims often remain silent because of fear of retaliation.[105]

Part of the problem with the persistence of bullying is that it has a self-generating nature. The attackers and, at times, the attacked, often engage in physical fighting. About 56 percent of high school students state: "Anyone who avoids fighting is going to get picked on even more."[106] In keeping with the warrior ideal of male socialization, about 28 percent of the high school boys state: "If I walked away from a fight, I'd be a coward."[107] Almost half of the male students stated that they were concerned that their friends would think that they were afraid if they refused to fight.[108]

Cyberbullying

Cyberbullying is the most rapidly expanding abusive behavior among school children. Fully 95 percent of teens are online, and 80 percent use social media.[109] Cyberbullying has a peak risk period for children ages 14 to 17. About eight percent of this age group report experiencing internet harassment.[110] A Canadian study shows that one in four middle school children have been cyberbullied,[111] and in the United States, that number approaches 37 percent.[112] Other estimates are that 50 percent of teens and young adults report some form of digital abusive behavior.[113] A European Union study found that about 54 percent of young people in their countries who use Facebook report being cyberbullied.[114]

Cyberbullying is intrusive, damaging, and widespread. It occurs when "a child, preteen or teen is tormented, threatened, harassed, humiliated, embarrassed or otherwise targeted by another child, preteen or teen using the internet, interactive and digital technologies or mobiles phones."[115] The youngsters often change roles, with bully becoming victim.[116] Social networking websites, chat rooms, instant messaging, and blogs are likely areas where cyberbullying occurs. It includes the cyberbully offering up the victim for sex to online adult sexual predators.[117] Cyberbullying consists of direct attacks and also cyberbullying by proxy, using others to help cyberbully the victim, either with or without the accomplice's knowledge.[118] Cyberbullying could be "trash talk" or humiliating someone, such as superimposing the victim's head on a naked body.[119]

A good deal of cyberbullying is conducted outside school, but it often involves children who attend the same school. Children repeatedly targeted with offensive and threatening messages can become very distressed, and can lead to major depression, self-harm and suicide.[120] Children have killed each other and committed suicide after being involved in cyberbullying.[121] Adolescent girls are four times more likely to be victims of cyberbullying than boys.[122] About 8 percent of cyberbullying victims report feeling suicidal. Bullycide is highest among middle school children.[123] Cyberbullying may rise to the level of a misdemeanor cyber-harassment charge or, if the child is young enough, may result in the charge of juvenile delinquency.[124] Most of the time cyberbullying does not go that far. However, parents at times try to pursue criminal charges.[125]

How Much Bullying Is Going On?

How much face-to-face bullying takes place in schools? Bullying tends to be underreported for a variety of reasons. Adults in school environments tend to be uninformed about conflict among students. Students see and fear violence more than teachers do.[126]

Another factor that impedes accurate reporting is that the No Child Left Behind Act stipulates that if a school is designated as dangerous for two concurrent years, it is "persistently dangerous" and faces possible loss of funding so school violence is probably more prevalent than reported statistics indicate.

The most comprehensive study of bullying was conducted in the 1980s by Dan Olweus in Norway and Sweden among six to fourteen-year-old students. Fifteen percent of the students reported being involved in bully/victim problems.[127] These findings need to be assessed, however, in the light of Norway not having a culture of violence and having a relatively low youth crime rate.

A variety of studies during the past twenty years reveal different rates of bullying. Although some of these differences can be explained by variations in research and reporting methods, the statistics generally reveal high rates of bullying and consistent increases. A 1992 study by the Centers for Disease Control found that, nationally, half of boys and one-quarter of girls reported being physically attacked by someone at school. Over 16 percent of students had been involved in a fight at school.[128] One-third of all students in eighth and tenth grades reported they had been threatened with physical harm, and 14 percent had been robbed. About one-quarter of students in grades 3 through 12 nationwide reported being kicked, bitten, or hit by another student at school the previous year.[129] By the mid-1990s, 36 percent of high school students reported that they spent a lot of some of the time worrying about being the victim of a crime.[130]

There are be regional differences, although minor, in the rate of bullying. By 1997, 27 percent of students surveyed in small Midwestern towns indicated that they had been bullied the previous year, and 88 percent of the students had observed bullying.[131] During that same time, about 25 percent of school children in the rural South indicated they had been bullied or bullied regularly.[132] This is consonant with another study of a rural North Carolina high school that showed that 20 percent of high school students reported being victims of violence.[133]

A few years later, a 2001 national study found that 30 percent of students are involved in bullying, either as a bully (13 percent), a victim (11 percent), or both (6 percent).[134] In 2003 the National Center for Education Statistics reported increases in the percentage of students victimized by bullying from 1999 to 2001. During this two-year span the percentage of being bullied increased from 5 to 9 percent for white students, 4 to 8 percent for Hispanic students, from 3 to 7 percent for non-Hispanic students, and remained at 6 percent for black students.[135]

Nearly half of the middle school students surveyed in Virginia reported being bullied in the previous month. About 15 percent of the students reported being bullied at least once a week, and 7 percent reported being bullied several times a week.[136] In a similar vein, in 2001, a national study of sixth to tenth graders revealed that 23 percent were bullied.[137] By 2005, 28 percent of middle school students and high school students reported being bullied, with 24 percent of them sustaining injuries.[138]

By 2015 about 21 percent of students ages twelve to eighteen reported being bullied at school. The US Department of Education reports that between 2005 and 2015 bullying decreased from 28 to 21 percent.[139] This translates to a decrease of 0.7 percent a year. By 2016 about 28 percent of twelve to eighteen-year-old youngsters reported being bullied.[140] Forty-seven percent of third-grade students reported being bullied in 2017, with 51 percent reporting relational aggression, such as being ignored or excluded from play.[141] As many as 77 percent of students report being bullied verbally.[142]

Academic Performance

There is a correlation between high rates of bullying and poor academic performance. In schools with high levels of bullying problems, students tend to feel less safe and are less satisfied with school life. This means that, for many students, and particularly for the victims, the classroom is no longer a place of concentrated work and learning. Nor is it necessarily felt to be a safe haven. *A Nation At Risk*, a 1983 study of the quality of schools in the United States, revealed the following: Forty percent of seventeen-year-olds cannot draw inferences from written material. Only 20 percent can write a persuasive essay. Only 30 percent can solve mathematical problems requiring several steps, and one-third (half in urban schools) fail to master even the basics in reading, math, and science on the National Assessment of Education Progress examination.[143] Another study revealed that 63 percent of the students reported that they would learn more at school if they felt safer.[144] This undoubtedly contributes to high drop-out rates. Although poor performance indicates other influences, such as heavy entertainment media consumption, it also is a barometer of violence in schools. A national study discovered that 22 percent of students in grades 3–12 were less eager to attend school because of threats or acts of violence. Sixteen percent of students reported they were less willing to talk in class, and one-quarter of the students believed that the violence they experienced or witnessed had a detrimental effect on the quality of their education.[145]

Bullies

Bullies tend to share some common characteristics. These children tend to have impulsive, hotheaded personalities and are easily frustrated. They have difficulty conforming to rules and view violence in a positive light, as a way to solve problems. They also tend to be physically stronger than their peers.[146] Bullies also are more apt to perform poorly in school and to drink and smoke.[147] The most salient feature of many bullies is their lack of empathy.[148] Bullying is about power and control, not conflict and anger. As such, the widespread use of conflict resolution and anger management classes does not work in preventing bullying.[149] The more essential issues of children seeking power over others and the causes for their lack of empathy need to be addressed in order to prevent bullying.

Students' reasons for gun ownership appear to be linked to rates of bullying. High-risk gun owners, those who own guns to gain respect or frighten others, reported higher rates of bullying than low-risk gun owners, those who owned guns to feel safe or to use in hunting.[150]

Bullies often engage in other delinquent behavior, such as vandalizing property, shoplifting, skipping school, and using drugs. Bullying is related to other antisocial behaviors, such as fighting, drinking alcohol, smoking, poor school performance, truancy, and dropping out.[151]

A perpetrator's bullying behavior does not exist in isolation but may indicate the beginning of an antisocial and rule-breaking behavior pattern that can continue into adulthood. Bullying is predictive of future destructive and violent behavior, including workplace bullying. This early aggression, if unchecked, also is linked to adult criminal behavior.[152] About 60 percent of males who were bullies from grades 6 through 9 were convicted of at least one crime as adults. This compares with 23 percent of males who did not bully. As many as 40 percent of these former bullies had three or more convictions by the age of twenty-four, compared to 10 percent of the others.[153] By age thirty, one in four boys who bully have a criminal record.[154] In other words, schools that tolerate bullying are schools that are crucibles for future violence.

A 2005 study discovered that four-year-old children were involved in relationship aggression, harming others through purposeful manipulation and damage to relationships. Relational aggression tactics used by preschoolers include not allowing a child to play with the group, threatening to not play with a child unless certain demands are met, and refusing to listen to someone with whom they are angry.[155] A 2008 study of 2,000 children revealed that the "trajectory of victimization" begins as early as age two.[156] Teachers say that toddlers repeatedly use stand-over tactics and resort to punching and biting others to get their way. Some hit, push, punch, and shove children, usually those who were smaller.[157] Because of this early introduction to bullying, as a bully, victim, or bystander, the entire span of a child's school experience is negatively affected.

Girls are less likely to bully than boys.[158] However, the gender gap has closed somewhat in recent years. Bullying among girls is being reported at earlier ages. Girls as young as four use social aggression to maintain dominance, compared to boys who tend to use physical aggression. These girls are perceived by their peers as more social, as well as more aggressive than the average child. "These preschool 'Queen Bees' are the controversial children who receive a substantial number of both 'like' and 'dislike' nominations from their peers. As such, they are the children with a strong social impact, perceived by other children as more sociable and also as more aggressive than the average child."[159] Older girls also tend to not use physical means of bullying. They use more subtle and indirect ways of harassment such as slandering and manipulating friendship relations. These forms of bullying may be more difficult for adults to detect.[160] Whereas boys are more likely to be physically bullied, girls are more likely to report indirect bullying, such as being the targets of rumor-spreading, sexual comments, and social exclusion. This bullying may be more damaging than physical abuse.[161]

Gang activity, a factor in the rate of bullying, is prevalent in many schools. By the late 1990s about 15 percent of middle school children report that street gangs were present at school.[162] By 2005, 21 percent of students between the ages of twelve and eighteen reported gangs in their schools.[163] Thirty-seven percent of school resource officers reported an increase in gang activity in their schools.[164] Gangs contribute to a climate of fear in the community and in schools. Gangs can be seen as the organized manifestation of bullying in groups.[165] The lure of gangs is that membership confers an identity that suggests "power, fearlessness and domination."[166] Students express such concerns as fearing gang disruptions at school, encountering gang members on the way to and from school, receiving threats, being harassed by gang members, and perceiving the presence of more weapons related to gang activity.[167] Seventy percent of surveyed gang members admitted that their members assaulted students and half of them admitted that members of their gangs had assaulted teachers.[168]

Case Studies

Tony is eight years old, has a Mohawk haircut, and frequently is seen riding his bike around his neighborhood. Tony's family is a working-class family with two children. They live in a small rural town, with a population of less than 5,000 people, in a farming community. Two six-year-old twins, Dylan and Bella, are afraid of Tony because he threatened to shoot their mother when they would not let him borrow a toy. Dylan and Bela's parents talked to Tony, who appeared to be intimidated and serious about the adult encounter. Tony's parents said they were not aware of his bullying behavior. Tony then told his parents that the two neighbor boys who live next door beat him up while the parents were working. They were nine, ten, and eleven. War toys were strewn across their porch and front lawn.

Sammy is twelve years old. He is the youngest of three children in a middle-class family. Sammy is big for his age. At the age of eight, Sammy began to play video games, many of them violent games that belonged to his older brother. Unknown to his parents, within a year he was playing violent games for two or more hours a day. He began bullying when he was ten. He started to push younger, smaller children around and call them names. When he was eleven he got into a few fights after school and also started bullying other boys his age. By age twelve his bullying came to the attention of the school principal who arranged for a parent conference. His parents were bewildered because, for the most part, Sammy was a good boy. He did his chores and was responsible for taking care of the dog. He also got good grades at school and seemed to be generally well liked. The principal recommended that Sammy see the school counselor for two months. After the counseling sessions were completed, his bullying abated somewhat. Within several months, however, Sammy's bullying accelerated. The school had no bullying prevention program so the principal referred Sammy to a therapist in the community.

Daniel began teasing other children in the sixth grade after he and a neighborhood friend had a growth spurt while their neighbor, Courtney, did not. "We were taller and just naturally started making fun of her," says Daniel, now fifteen. "When she didn't do anything about it, we drove in more and more.... It felt cool to not be made fun of and to be the one making the fun." At no point did Daniel think of himself as a "mean bully." He says, "I thought of myself as a playful bully: I bullied with a smile on my face." At one point his teasing went too far and the next morning he was summoned by his middle school dean to talk with and apologize to Courtney and her mother. Daniel's mother wondered, "Where did I go wrong?" She grounded him from playing "his beloved video games" for two weeks. Since that time Daniel has become a leader in his school's chapter of Peace-Jam, a nationwide student organization that studies the deeds of Nobel Peace Prize laureates. He has become a champion of those in need. "I always end up befriending the people being bullied," he says. "It's satisfying to help people out."[169]

Victims

Younger and weaker students are more often exposed to bullying. But bullying is generally directed to children who are somehow different. This includes "nerds," and girls who are especially pretty. A good deal of bullying is carried out by older students toward younger ones.[170] Victims often tend to be cautious, sensitive, and insecure children who have problems asserting themselves among their peers. Children who have been victims of maltreatment (neglect, physical, or sexual abuse) are more likely to be victimized by their peers.[171] Victims of bullying receive a clear message that they are not valued or accepted. Bullying typically occurs in the presence of others, thus including an element of public humiliation. This communicates a profound disrespect and has consequences. Bullying may seriously affect children's psychosocial functioning, academic work, and health. Consequences include feelings of shame, humiliation, anxiety, low self-esteem and depression,[172] and some symptoms may last a long time.[173] Victims may complain of headaches and stomachaches and have trouble sleeping or frequent nightmares. They tend to be quiet, sensitive, and passive and may appear to be sad, depressed, moody, or anxious. They frequently are socially isolated and lonely.[174]

Boys who are bullied often are physically weaker than their peers.[175] Bullies tend to target especially vulnerable children who have been victims of child neglect and abuse.[176] Although many people believe that children with certain physical characteristics, such as wearing thick glasses or having freckles and red hair, may be prone to victimization, recent research suggests that children with such disabilities as stammering, cerebral palsy, and muscular dystrophy may be more likely targets of bullying.[177] This bias is reflected in such expressions as "That's so lame," or "That's so bipolar."

Nationwide, many students missed at least one day of school during the preceding month because they felt unsafe at school or traveling to or from school. The Center for the Study and Prevention of Violence reports that about 500,000 high school students nationwide stay home at least once a month because of fear of bullying.[178] This feeling is especially predominant among Hispanic and Black students.[179]

Some consequences of bullying may persist into adult years. Olweus found that those who had been bullied were more depressed and had lower self-esteem than their peers who were not bullied. These results continued even though they were no longer victims of bullying and no longer showed other signs of victimization.[180]

Rather than face teasing at school, some youngsters take their lives. About 12 percent of victims express suicidal thoughts or engage in suicidal behavior.[181] A study of Australian children who were bullied at least once a week were twice as likely as their peers to "wish they were dead" or admit to having a recurring idea of killing themselves.[182] In September 2010 alone, three middle school students committed suicide due to being bullied about being gay.[183]

Warning signs of bully victimization include returning from school with torn and damaged clothing; unexplained cuts, bruises, or scratches; having few friends; being afraid of going to school; losing interest in school; and not doing well academically. A once happy child can suddenly become withdrawn and feign illness to avoid school.

Case Studies

Jason was a happy and precocious child. At age five he entered kindergarten. He wore glasses and was very short for his age, and the boys in his class teased him about this. The bullying accelerated by the third grade. Boys would tease him and at times push and punch him. He was afraid to tell his teachers because he thought he would be even more rejected by his classmates. He also feared retaliation. Jason's parents were very supportive and loving and the bullying did not reach extreme proportions, so Jason managed to do well academically and to make friends. This social environment, coupled with Jason's high intelligence, resulted in his deciding to become the class clown. He discovered that he was talented in juggling and magic tricks. He did magic tricks, told jokes, and made fun of himself. During high school he was the mascot for the football team, did well academically, and was well liked.

Christine was fourteen years old and a first-year high school student in a small rural town. She was born in the town and was popular and well regarded by young people and adults, because she was a good student, excelled in sports, and was a youth leader in her church. She also was the leader of a small group of affluent, popular girls who liked to target girls who were less attractive and less popular. Christine took an especial dislike to a new girl in school, Pat, who was overweight and very shy. Christine texted little poems, such as "Pat is fat. Pat looks like a rat," to her circle of friends who laughingly shared the message with others. Some of the girls showed some of the message to Pat, who felt terribly humiliated and even afraid. The texted messages and laughter continued throughout the fall school term. Pat's shyness became even more painfully evident, and she was suffering so much that at times she was distraught. She was close with her parents and told them about the problem. The parents contacted the principal of the school who concluded that Pat was the problem. Her parents transferred her to another school the following week.

Billy was twelve years old and had been bullied since he entered middle school. Billy was slight of build and more soft-spoken than his peers. He was an intelligent boy and made good grades in school. He spent a lot of time with his grandmother, Susan, who had a BA degree in geology and, because of the economy, made ends meet by cleaning houses. Susan also was an animal advocate and provided foster care for abandoned animals until they were adopted. Billy had a special affinity with animals, and he was able to work with those animals who had been mistreated or abused even though they might not respond positively to other people. Like many children, at times Billy preferred to stay home instead of going to school because he did not want to deal with bullying confrontations. He said that he did not like to talk about it.

Page is now a senior in high school. She was a victim of bullying from middle school until her sophomore year in high school. She said, "I was a hairy kid; very hairy arms and big eyebrows." She said that kids in middle school started calling her Chewbacca and making fun of her. She said at this point she refused to show any hair. She said she "would wear hoodies everyday so no one could see my arms and I would not make direct eye contact with anyone." She had to transfer schools, and the bullying actually got worse. Students called her a werewolf, even her "so-called new friends." They would make snide comments to her like: "Show me the full moon" or "look out, here comes the werewolf." This is when she started to bully in return, feeling it was her only way to deal with it. She had gone to her parents, and they told her it was "no big deal." She also told the school staff, and she felt "they could care less." She made fun of anyone's imperfections, such as being overweight or having acne. Now she shaves and waxes, and most of the students do not even remember bullying her. She said, "I'm pretty sure it crippled me emotionally." She is still self-conscious and less outgoing now. Because this was such a big part of her life, she is also now thinking of getting a werewolf tattoo to remind her to be strong.[184]

Leila, now fourteen, said that eighth grade was very difficult for her. She was a friend of Brie, which made her a target. Other girls started rumors about her and her friends, saying they were "sluts." They made fun of her because of her acne. She didn't bully back because she did not feel there was a need for more drama and her mother had told her to try to ignore them. It wasn't until the group of girls "called and texted her over 50 times in one day threatening to beat her up" that her mother called the school demanding they step in. The bullies were called into the principal's office including girls who were threatening her. From that point forward the girls left her alone. Leila said that there was no bullying prevention program at her school.

Tyler was a shy teen. He spent a lot of time on his own, a quiet young man. "He was always by himself with his iPod in his ears," said a former high school classmate. "He was quietly hilarious," a pal said of Tyler. He also was a gifted musician, playing the violin. When he picked up his violin, he came alive. "There was deep emotion when he put that bow to his violin. That's how he expressed himself," said a friend. At the age of eighteen Tyler attended New Jersey's Rutgers University. One day his roommate webcammed him in an encounter with a man in their dorm room and streamed it live. The cyberbully wrote, "I went into Molly's room and turned on my webcam. I saw Tyler making out with a dude. Yay." Two days later he tweeted he was going to secretly webcam Tyler again and share it with his internet chat group. The next day Tyler committed bullycide by jumping to his death from the Washington Bridge into the Hudson River.[185]

Bully-Victims

Bully victims, who comprise about six percent of students, frequently display the social-emotional problems of victimized children, and they also may display the behavioral problems of bullies. Bully-victims report more loneliness and problems with classmates, as well as poorer academic achievement and more frequent alcohol use and smoking than other students,[186] Bully-victims share many characteristics with passive victims, but they also tend to be hyperactive and may have problems concentrating.[187] These children tend to be quick-tempered and try to fight back if they feel insulted or attacked. They also may tend to bully younger or weaker children.[188]

Mike, a ten-year-old victim-bully commented: "I have been bullied. I was hurt and sad and didn't think that anyone wanted to be friends with me. I picked on other kids because it made me feel a lot better about myself when I put others down. I felt that I had some kind of power and control over others."[189]

The connection between bullying and being bullied is most dramatically exemplified by the many school shooters who were bullied.[190] Rather than take their own lives, bully-victims are among those who become school shooters, seeking redress and revenge. A study in the year 2000 found that 67 percent of school shooters felt bullied by their peers.[191] By 2006, 71 percent of the school shooters reported being bullied.[192] Case studies of bully-victims are included in "School Shooters," the next chapter.

Creating Peaceful Schools

Schools are not only microcosms of the culture of violence, they are perpetrators of the culture. Many schools embody hierarchy and generate violence. Schools also can foster democracy and peace. School culture can support and promote violence, or it can evolve into a culture that sustains healthy and harmonious relationships.

There are a variety of recommendations necessary to create peaceful schools. The American Medical Association advocates more resources to increase the ability of schools to provide safe and effective education programs. This includes programs to teach respect and tolerance, sensitivity to diversity, and interpersonal problem-solving; violence reduction curricula, including materials about the effects of violence and aggression; policies to eliminate bullying and other aggressive behavior; and parental involvement.[193] Similarly, the Center for the Study and Prevention of Violence recommends high academic expectations and performance, high levels of parental and community involvement, effective leadership by administrators and teachers, few—but clearly understood and uniformly enforced—rules, after-school, extended-day programs, and promotion of character education and good citizenship.[194]

The 1987 Schoolyard Bully Practicum at Harvard University identified the following ways to mediate bullying:

1. for students in anger management, assertiveness training, and behavior modification training, behavior contracts signed by students and parents;
2. emphasis on discipline that stresses right behavior;
3. friendship groups that support children who are bullied;
4. close monitoring of cafeterias, playgrounds, and bullying "hotspots";
5. classroom and school activities that build self-esteem.[195]

The National Resource Center for Safe Schools has identified essentials for creating safe schools. The following are their recommended components of safe school planning:

1. creating school-wide prevention and intervention response planning;
2. developing school policies and understanding legal considerations;

3. establishing rules against bullying that are publicized and posted school-wide, accompanied by sanctions;
4. providing student and adult mentors who assist victims and bullies to foster mutual understand and appreciation for differences in others;
5. creating a buddy system that pairs students with a friend or older buddy on whom they can depend for help;
6. establish an on-campus parents' center that recruits, coordinates, and encourages parents to be involved in the school;
7. providing classes for adults in parenting skills;
8. creating a positive school climate and culture;
9. implementing ongoing staff development;
10. ensuring quality facilities and technology;
11. fostering school/law enforcement partnerships;
12. instituting links with mental health/social services;
13. fostering family and community development;
14. acquiring and utilizing resources.[196]

International studies have shown that the most successful approaches to safe schools are built around four major principles—a community-based approach, a focus on the school atmosphere, a problem-solving partnership model, and the holistic use of multiple strategies.[197] Such recommendations and programs built around them may be necessary. However, they are not sufficient. Research covering a twenty-year time period shows that few school violence prevention programs work. This failure is demonstrated by the lack of progress in reducing serious violent crime in schools.[198] To a great extent this lack of progress results from addressing symptoms rather than fundamental causes.

In order to understand causes, we need to understand the human need for respect, equality, and justice. A democratic society is a just society, and a just society is a peaceful society. As Martin Luther King reminded us: "There can be no peace without justice." This maxim applies to schools as well. How can schools embody justice and teach democracy? What would a school culture be like that promotes peaceful and healthy relationships? What more is necessary?

To the extent that a school culture prohibits the humanization of students, that is, to the extent that it violates human nature, it is a violent school. In order to be safe and productive, schools need to acknowledge and honor the requirements of human nature, which include democracy and peace. Our nature includes the need for respect, empowerment, harmony, the freedom to create, and to be responsible for each other. Programs that address these needs include character education and training in empathy, respect for diversity, gender sensitivity, self-empowerment, democracy, responsibility; they also provide opportunities to make a meaningful contribution to the life of the community.

A pivotal study of democratic classrooms showed a 50 percent reduction of violence and a 50 percent reduction in the time that teachers spent dealing with disruptive students. The key reason for this success was the project was student driven and focused on student-level problem-solving. Students identified and prioritized problems though open class discussions, analyzed the problems using a variety of information-gathering methods, and then formulated responses and brainstormed solutions.[199] In other words, the students were empowered by having the opportunity to define the problem and the solution. In Freirian terms, they were allowed to "name their world" and to change it.[200] In order to be healthy and productive, a school needs to embody democracy. Democracy is an umbrella that covers self-respect, respect for others, egalitarianism, shared decision-making, empowerment, and responsibility. Another necessary element is to have the resources to become peaceful and productive. School violence will continue to grow if schools continue to be underfunded.

These recommendations are necessary to make schools healthy, safe, and peaceful. However, they are not sufficient. To be sufficient, these efforts also need to take into account the powerful influence of the violence industries, especially violent electronic entertainment media. The following chapter investigates the most extreme form of school violence—rampage school shootings.

CHAPTER 6

SCHOOL RAMPAGE SHOOTERS: MORE LETHAL THAN EVER

> Is there any relationship between unleashed violence at Columbine and the terror rained down on Serbia—including the use of cluster bombs and depleted uranium?
> —Richard Deats

Rampage school shootings are mass murder tragedies that point to deeper, sociological undercurrents and problems. In light of Freire's paradigm, school shootings raise intriguing questions: What is the symbolic and real significance of school campuses being the scene of such violence? Why did rampage school shootings escalate in the 1990s? Why have they become more lethal? What larger social and economic forces have been in effect in the last five decades?

To answer these questions, let us look at the problem from an international and historical perspective. The United States has been the scene of the great majority of mass murders in schools, with five times the total of the Philippines, the second highest country. This corresponds with the United States leading the world in firearm ownership, which appears to be connected.[1]

Internationally, there are only a handful of school mass murders. However, they are occurring more frequently in other countries, such as Germany, Bosnia, and Argentina.[2] The first international incident occurred in 1975. A student in Ontario, Canada, killed two students, injured thirteen, and shot himself.[3] In 1996, a twenty-eight-year-old Australian man killed thirty-five and wounded nineteen in a public school.[4] In 1999, a seventeen-year-old student injured five in the Netherlands. In 2000 in Germany, a sixteen-year-old student killed a student and injured himself. The following month, a five-year-old student in Ontario, Canada, stabbed six students. In 2001 a teenage boy in Kenya killed sixty-seven and injured nineteen students by arson.[5] In 2002 Robert Steinhazuser killed sixteen people and himself at the Gutenberg High School in Erfurt, Germany. The attack motivated the German government to raise the age for owning recreational firearms from eighteen to twenty-one.[6] The next international incident occurred in Finland in 2007, closely following the Virginia Tech tragedy. The Finland rampage shooting was initiated via email by fourteen-year-old Dillon Cossey in the United States, a victim of bullying. Dressed in body armor and armed with several guns, Dillon was arrested after it was discovered he planned to attack Whitemarsh High School in suburban Philadelphia. Still, he was able to incite Pekka-Erik Auvinen of Finland to commit a rampage shooting. This Finnish student killed six students, two staff, and shot himself.[7]

The Anomaly

The recurring question among researchers, school personnel, students, parents, and media is "Why?" How are these acts of ultimate violence to be explained?

The US Congress asked the National Academies' National Research Council to research lethal school violence. The National Research Council concluded: The "violent incidents that galvanized congressional concern seemed to many to be new and unique as well as urgent and specific."[8] We must ask what caused this "new and unique" violence.

Dr. Dewey Cornell, profiling antisocial youth and violent juvenile offenders, describes rampage school shooters as "the most puzzling because they often appear to be normal youngsters whose acts of violence surprise us."[9] Regarding Adam Lanza, one of the most lethal school shooters, a researcher concluded: "It's still unclear what motivated the Newtown shooter."[10] Another investigator refers to "the mystery" of what causes rampage school shootings.[11]

Violent behavior is often attributed to youngsters from impoverished communities. What is so striking about most of the school shootings is that they do not happen in poor communities but in ones that are relatively affluent and peaceful. The National Research Council report writes: "What is startling . . . is that some portion of the lethal violence observed happens not in economically marginalized communities, but in ones that are relatively well off economically, socially and politically. . . . It would be hard to attribute the shootings in these areas to economic or social disadvantage."[12] Only a few rampage school shooters experienced early school failure that often precedes delinquent behavior. Most were not considered by the adults around them to be at high risk for this kind of behavior. Unlike other violent juvenile offenders who show an early onset of delinquent behavior, school shooters tend to display delinquent behavior shortly before the shooting.[13]

The National Research Council concluded it is "impossible" to determine the causes of school shootings.[14] A study conducted collaboratively by the US Secret Service National Threat Assessment Center, the US Department of Education, and the US Department of Justice concluded that there is no accurate or useful profile of "the school shooter,"[15] a finding echoed by other researchers.[16]

To begin unlocking the secret to why some young people become rampage shooters, let us look at the history of school shootings in the United States and the shooters' salient characteristics.

A Brief History of School Shootings

In 1966 Charles Whitman, a twenty-five-year-old student at the University of Texas was the first rampage school shooter. He first killed his mother and his wife and then, from a sniper position in a tower on campus, he gunned down forty-five people, killing fourteen. His father was very strict, was obsessed with guns, and encouraged his son to shoot. Charles became the youngest Eagle Scout in US history and at eighteen joined the Marines. Whitman had psychological problems and reportedly stopped taking his medication. An autopsy revealed a small tumor on his brain.[17] Before this rampage, people felt they were comfortably removed from such deadly mayhem. "He was our initiation into a terrible time," an Austin merchant said.[18]

The earliest known case of a middle school or high school shooting occurred in 1974 in Olean, New York. Anthony Barbaro, a student, brought guns and homemade bombs to his school, set off the fire alarm, and shot at the janitors and firemen who responded to the alarm. He killed three children and injured eleven more children.[19]

In 1979, seventeen-year-old Brenda Spencer killed two adults and wounded eight children and a police officer by firing a gun from her home, which was across the street from an elementary school in San Diego, California. Her parents were separated. She apparently had an unloving mother and an emotionally distant father, who allegedly sexually molested her. There also is some indication that she had experienced brain damage due to a head injury, and she displayed symptoms of a conduct disorder.[20] Her father, when hearing of the shooting, was incredulous. She had experienced bullying at the school and did the shooting after drinking some alcohol.[21] When the six-hour standoff finally ended, she was quoted as saying, with a shrug, "I don't like Mondays."[22]

School shootings were rare in the 1980s. There were only six rampage shootings during that ten-year period.[23] Between 1986 and 1990, seventy-five people were killed on school campuses. About two hundred people were severely injured, and 242 were held hostage.[24] In 1987, Nathan Ferris, age twelve, was an honor student in Missouri. Nathan was incessantly teased to the point of torment. One day he took a pistol to school, and when a classmate made fun of him, he killed the boy and then turned the gun on himself.[25] An especially lethal incident involves twelve-year-old Patrick Purdy. In 1989 he opened fire on an elementary school playground in Stockton, California, killing five children and wounding thirty others.[26]

In the 1990s, school shootings became part of a mean-spirited cultural landscape of the United States. During the 1992 and 1993 school year, school-associated violent deaths erupted at an unprecedented rate. Fifty people were killed in school-related violence during that nine-month period of time.[27] School-associated violent deaths peaked between 1992 and 1994 with 105 victims.[28] The year 1994 witnessed the beginning of a dramatic increase in rampage shootings.[29] There were two rampage shootings in 1992, four in 1995, and eight in 1998.[30] During this time forty people were killed in multiple-victim school shootings.[31] This increase in multiple-victim homicides in schools also occurred in youth violence happening outside of the school setting. Outside the school setting, the number of adolescent homicide offenders who claimed multiple victims also increased dramatically between 1992 and 1994.[32] Researchers concluded that "there is little doubt that the number of student rampages increased over time."[33] By 1995 school shootings had come to national attention and raised many questions about causes and interventions.[34] Between 1994 and 2000, rampage school shootings had increased by over 600 percent.[35]

Rampage shootings peaked in 1997.[36] However, the years 1997 through 1999 experienced a cluster of school rampage shootings. The copycat effect clearly was evident in the rampage school killings in 1997 in February, October, and on December 1 and December 15. In 1998, rampage killings occurred in April, and two happened on May 19 and May 21.[37] Killings in the Southeast were especially notorious during that time. This cluster of shootings was especially lethal in Kentucky, Arkansas, Mississippi, Georgia, and also in Colorado. In 1997 in Pearl, Mississippi, Luke Woodham killed three people and injured seven. Two months later in Paducah, Kentucky, Michael Carneal killed three people and injured five. Two weeks later, in Arkansas, Jason Todd injured two students.[38] In 1998, there were thirty-eight murders on school campuses and an additional quarter of a million children were "seriously injured" by school violence.[39] Part of this cluster may be attributed to the copycat effect and part to the national gun culture. However, as we shall see, more factors are at work.

The year 1999 witnessed the Columbine killings, and three additional shootings that resulted in injuries but no fatalities.[40] Columbine has triggered copycat rampages and rampage attempts since the time it occurred. About one month after Columbine T. J. Solomon, fifteen, was depressed about breaking up with his girlfriend and claimed that he had "no reason to live anymore." He injured six people, aiming low with an intention not to kill people. In December of 1999 in Oklahoma, Seth Trickey, thirteen, walked up to a group of students at his school that he did not know and began shooting. Later, he said he did not know why he did it. He was an honor student who others regarded as funny and nice. He was well liked and not a loner. Trickey has not been able to provide a plausible reason for his actions.[41]

There were at least twelve thwarted attempts in 1999 alone, not including thwarted attempts that were not reported. Examples include a May 13 plan of four middle school children to slaughter everyone at a school assembly and a May 20 shooting rampage that resulted in four injuries.[42] Attempted or thwarted school shootings are more numerous than the actual events. They tend to be prevented because students and staff now are more alert to the potential danger when a student discusses plans or desires with classmates. Also, some state and local gun-free school zone legislation may mandate the use of weapon detectors. Prevention also has been helped to some extent by the use of see-through book bags and the presence of school resource officers.

In 2000, there were thirty-two school-associated violent deaths at school, including twenty-four homicides, sixteen of which involved school-age children.[43] In February 2000, a six-year-old boy pointed a gun at a classmate, and said, "I don't like you," and killed her. The children had argued the day before, and the victim had slapped the perpetrator. Reportedly, he wanted to get revenge by scaring her with the gun. The boy had been left in the care of an uncle so that his mother could work two jobs.[44]

On March 5, 2001, Andy Williams, fifteen, in Santee, California, killed two students and wounded thirteen other students. He had been bullied to the point of torment. His parents were divorced and he lived with his father, with whom he did not have a close relationship.[45] Two days later, in the second school shooting committed by a girl, Catherine Bush, fourteen, shot the head cheerleader in the shoulder. Catherine has been teased maliciously at a previous school, so her parents transferred her to a smaller, private school, where she was similarly tormented. Catherine had been betrayed by the victim who revealed the content of emails. She suffered from periods of depression.[46] Later in March of 2001, Charles Andrew Williams opened fire in a high school bathroom in Santee, California, killing two students and wounding thirteen. At the time this was the country's deadliest school attack since Columbine.[47]

Some of the most lethal acts of gun violence have occurred since 2004, the year the ban on assault weapons was lifted. From the year 2000 to 2006, there was an average of 6.4 school shootings annually. From 2007 to 2013, the average rose to 16.4 per year.[48] The year 2007 was also notably lethal. That year included Seung-Hui Cho at Virginia Tech, the University of Illinois rampage, and the attack on the Amish school.

The most heinous rampage school shooting occurred in February 2018 at the Marjory

Stoneman School, in which seventeen people were killed. This occurred three months after the most lethal public rampage shooting in Las Vegas, Nevada, in which fifty-seven people were killed by an adult in a concert setting. Since that time the incidence of rampage school shootings has grown exponentially. Now hundreds of rampage school shootings and rampage public shootings occur every year. In 2018 there were ninety-seven mass school shootings. In 2019 there were a total of 434 school and public mass shootings, in which 1,643 people were injured and 517 were killed. One hundred sixteen of these mass shootings were rampage school shootings.[49]

The Psychology of School Shooters

National headlines have sensationalized the murders committed on school campuses. Many of our popular conceptions come from media accounts of the incidents and "expert" opinion about the causes. Most researchers hypothesize that the shootings are due to problems with the shooters' parents and aversive early childhood experiences. However, with few exceptions, "little evidence was unearthed to indicate that the perpetrators' families had an unusual number of problems, and the perpetrators themselves often absolved their parents of any responsibility for their actions."[50] Many people concur with popular media accounts that school shooters are "crazy." Some psychologist researchers contend that most of school shooters have mental problems, ranging from depression to psychosis. Ferguson, for example, concludes that mental illness is at the root of school shootings.[51] Langman, for example, contends that the traits of a "psychopathic shooter" are narcissism, a lack of morality, anger problems, sadism, and a lack of remorse.[52] He writes: "A teenage boy from a good home who idolizes Hitler and fantasizes about killing off humanity does not make sense.... Something was wrong within the minds of the school shooters."[53] This raises the question—what has caused these traits? To find the answer we must discover what caused something to be "wrong" with the shooters' minds.

There is evidence of mental disturbance in some school shooters.[54] A study found that about 50 percent were psychotic and 30 percent were sociopaths. They displayed narcissistic and sadistic behavior and had no empathy.[55] Other researchers estimate that the number of perpetrators who have psychological problems range from 5 percent to 67 percent.[56] Other researchers contend that most rampage shootings are committed by people who are not ill.[57] The study of shooters conducted by the US Secret Service National Threat Assessment Center, the US Department of Education, and the US Department of Justice concluded that few of the attackers had been diagnosed with a mental disorder, and less than one-third of them had histories of drug or alcohol abuse.[58] Other researchers concur, concluding that psychosis is rarely a factor.[59] Care must be taken in giving diagnoses such as personality disorder to adolescents because a number of symptoms of such disorders are within normal range during adolescence.[60] Rampage shooters often are described as psychopathic because of their apparent lack of empathy for the victims and a lack of remorse for their actions.[61] As will become clear in the following chapters, a lack of empathy is displayed by young people heavily exposed to violent electronic entertainment media, especially violent video games. Depression appears to be the most common psychological problem experienced by school shooters. One study shows that approximately 30 percent of the shooters were known to be depressed.[62] Why they were so depressed, and why are so many young people are depressed to the point of committing suicide?

Considering the tenets of human nature, killing itself can be considered a crazy act. Killing another human being is contrary to human nature, so someone who is enraged enough to commit mass murder perhaps may be considered crazy at that time. From this perspective, rampage killing, by definition, is an insane act. As such, rampage shooters may be temporarily insane at the time of the shooting. Many of the school shooters appeared to experience dissociation during and immediately after the shooting. A number of shooters later reported that it seemed to be a dream. Kip Kinkel said: "It didn't seem real."[63] Immediately after his rampage, fourteen-year-old Andrew Wurst said: "None of this is real."[64] Dissociative amnesia is a state preceded by a period of trauma and victimization. The appears to be a mechanism by which the shooter does not take responsibility for the killing.[65] This response is in keeping with human nature. Some attorneys have used insanity as a line of defense, but the courts seldom uphold these arguments. In the middle of a rampage which left three people dead, Andrew Wurst yelled, "I'm crazy, man! I'm crazy, man!" but the judge found him to be mentally competent.[66] Kip Kinkel, who killed his parents and then killed two more people and wounded twenty-two, later said, "I don't know what's wrong with me. Something's wrong in my head."[67]

Among those shooters who were psychologically vulnerable, what pushed them over the edge? Kip Kinkel suggested the cause was "role-playing games, heavy metal music, violent cartoons, TV [and] sugared cereal."[68] To an extent, he was right. However, it's not that simple. We need to ask what confluence of events and factors lead to such behavior. What experiences lead to the massacres? What pushed them to the edge? And, the ultimate question is—What is the primary causal factor?

As with youth violence in general, researchers and others tend to compile laundry lists of causes. The most frequently cited reasons for shootings include mental illness, a gun culture, a problematic family setting, bullying, and exposure to media violence.[69] School shootings also have been variously attributed to social moral decline, lax gun laws, the "Goth" movement, and interpersonal rejection.[70] Other research reveals that these risk factors include a preoccupation with weapons and fantasy, depression, uncontrolled anger, and suicidal ideation.[71]

Anger has been listed as a risk factor. Langman contends that the shooters were experiencing "existential rage directed against the conditions of their existence."[72] The underlying question is—What causes rage of such magnitude?

It is common to blame the parents in these cases and to lay much of the responsibility at their feet. In 1998, for example, the Senate Committee on the Judiciary concluded that parents are the most effective means to prevent youth violence. However, many shooters come from stable, loving families. Typically, the parents of school shooters are bewildered by their children's behavior.

Risk factors seldom occur in isolation. Leary and his associates note the relevance of cumulative risk factors. They conclude: "Although rejection in one form or another was implicated in most of these episodes, the shooters also tended to be characterized by one or more of the three other risk factors that we investigated—psychological problems, an interest in guns and explosives, and a fascination with death."[73] The unanswered questions these conclusions have raised have to do with the causes and configuration of accumulated risk factors. The so-called causes are actually symptoms. We need to ask what causes social moral decline, social rejection, interest in guns, a fascination with death, and so forth. This leads to the question of how these symptoms are related to and nurtured by the culture of violence and its industries.

Assessing cumulative risk factors, protective factors, and resilience is an approach that focuses on children with life situations and experiences that may put them at risk for future maladaptive behavior. Some children display remarkable resilience and are less vulnerable to risk factors than other children. The risk assessment perspective helps to explain why some children experiencing cumulative risk factors act out through school shootings. As risk factors accumulate, the likelihood of problem behavior increases because of the reinforcing nature of multiple risk factors. As such, risk factors become more influential as they accumulate.[74] The Columbine shooters illustrate the cumulative risk model. They were bullied at school, had easy access to guns, and had disinterested or abusive parents. These risk factors, coupled with exposure to the violence industries, place people at risk of enacting aggression or violence. For children, there is a comorbidity among risk factors. Because risk factors seldom occur in isolation, children who experience one risk factor often experience a variety of other risk factors.[75] From this perspective, the key is to identify and to also rank which risk factors are most influential in order to find the primary causal risk factor.

We need to recognize the role of broader cultural factors affecting children outside the home.[76] The culture of violence presents risk factors that penetrate the home environment as well as the school environment.

Standard Practices

The National Research Council recommends that research should focus on serious bullying in school, firearms, signs of developing mental health problems, the effects of student attacks on teachers, and the effects of rapid change in increasingly affluent rural and suburban communities.[77] This theoretical and research emphasis on firearms and mental health have influenced legislation as well as school violence prevention programs. Legislation has been put in place that comes down on perpetrators. For example, Mississippi has made murder on school property a capital crime, and some states require a seventy-two-hour holding period for students who bring guns to school.[78] President Clinton's response to increased juvenile crime was recommending more prosecutors.[79]

School rampages kindled a new awareness of the importance of preventing bullying. An entire industry has arisen that provides software and instruction about preventing bullying. However, few of these programs work in the short-term or, especially, the long-term. Some of the prescribed interventions may be necessary. However, they are not sufficient. Prevention programs that do not address the influence of the culture of violence, the violence industries, the culture of school violence, and the needs of human nature are not effective.

Shared Characteristics of Shooters

In order to understand and prevent school shootings, we need to investigate why some children become school shooters. What makes these young people different? We can get closer to an answer to these questions by assessing the characteristics they tend to share. All the school shooters were socialized within a culture of violence as well as a culture of school violence. Researchers have compiled lists of characteristics the shooters appear to share. However, this research does not take into account background awareness of the overarching threats facing our world every day that are seldom discussed. These include environmental destruction and the threat of nuclear annihilation. Very young children talk about their fears. However, as children get older, these fears are sublimated and not as easily acknowledged. Nonetheless, this sublimated awareness exists and contributes to creating a worldview that is dark, ominous, and dangerous.

Juveniles delinquency and juvenile crime rose during and after World War II. This indicates that war and consciousness of war contribute to more antisocial feelings and behavior. It is no coincidence that school shootings escalated shortly after Operation Desert Storm in the early 1990s. Awareness of war and the attendant fear tended to heighten the influence of the warrior ideal as a model of male socialization. In *Bowling for Columbine*

(2002), Michael Moore points out that, on the day before Columbine, more bombs were dropped on Kosovo than ever before, that 20 percent were manufactured in Littleton, the home of Columbine High School. Living with the consciousness of "the forever war" is a risk factor.

During that time, school culture was becoming more hierarchical. There was an increased presence of exclusive student groups in the form of cliques and, in some cases, gangs. A number of school shooters left videos and writings that expressed their hatred of the "jocks and preps," and they claimed some among their victims.

Before 1987 school shooters typically were young black males in inner city schools.[80] Of the 134 mass shooters between 1966 and 2006, three were female, and 98 percent of the shooters were male.[81] And, with very few exceptions, the perpetrators have been white.[82] Kalish and Knoll point out that the shootings occur in a "culture of hegemonic masculinity" in the United States, which creates a sense of aggrieved entitlement that is conductive to violence.[83] Eric Madfis writes about "triple entitlement" and homicidal anger, in which white heterosexual masculinity makes life losses more unexpected and therefore more shameful.[84] Since 1987 the great majority of school shooters have lived in small, rural towns with a gun culture. Katherine S. Newman's analysis of school shootings uses a social ecological approach, asking the question of what these relatively affluent rural towns have in common. She discovered an emphasis on conformity, masculinity, and guns.

The US Secret Service National Threat Assessment Center, the US Department of Education, and the US Department of Justice have concluded that there is no accurate or useful profile of "the school shooter." However, they have found the following characteristics tend to be shared.

1. Attacker ages ranged from eleven to twenty-one, with most being between the ages of fourteen and eighteen.
2. They came from a variety of racial and ethnic backgrounds, with about one-quarter of them not being white.
3. They came from a range of family situations, from intact families with numerous ties to the community to foster homes with histories of neglect.
4. Their academic performance ranged from excellent to failing.
5. They had a range of friendship patterns, from socially isolated to popular.
6. Their behavioral histories varied, from having no observed behavioral problems to multiple behaviors warranting reprimand or discipline.
7. Few attackers showed any marked change in academic performance, friendship status, interest in school, or disciplinary problems at school prior to their attack.

8. Few of the attackers had been diagnosed with a mental disorder, and less than one-third of them had histories of drug or alcohol abuse.[85]

The case studies developed by the National Research Council's Committee on School Violence revealed similarities among the eight shooters they studied: All the shooters were boys. Five had recently begun hanging out with delinquent friends. Five experienced a recent drop in school grades. Five had engaged in previous serious delinquent acts, and the other three in minor delinquent behavior. They concluded that six of the eight boys studied exhibited serious mental health problems, ranging from clinical depression to personality disorders. All the boys had easy access to guns and played violent video games. Only one was a loner, and only two were gang members.[86]

The US Secret Service's assessment of twelve shooters identified risk factors of poor parenting, access to guns, and a rejection event. They concluded, however, that there was no clear profile of the shooters.[87]

Cornell concurs by pointing out that there is no single profile of the school shooter. His work has focused on three major categories of violent youth. The first group is the five percent of the youth who kill someone because they are mentally ill, suffering from psychosis and delusions that guide their behavior. The second group are the antisocial youth. About two-thirds of the juveniles who commit murder have a long history of delinquent behavior, with problems evidence in early childhood. They are aggressive, from disadvantaged homes, and dysfunctional families. The third group comprises the group who are most involved in school shootings. These young people "often appear to be normal youngsters whose acts of violence surprise us." They may be intelligent and capable, but not satisfied with their achievements and often feel unfairly treated by others. They feel lonely and isolated although they may have some friends. These young people are "emotionally troubled and conflicted-alienated, angry and depressed."[88]

Leary and his associates offer a tentative profile of the student who may be prone to violence against his peers. "The typical shooter is a male student who has been ostracized by the majority group at his school for some time, and has been chronically taunted, teased, harassed, and often publicly humiliated. Moreover, he probably demonstrates one or more of the three risk factors . . . an unusual interest in guns and explosives; a fascination with death, Satan, and other "dark" themes; or psychological problems that are characterized by depression and/or a personality disorder that involves antisocial behavior, poor impulse control, or sadistic tendencies."[89]

What causes this fascination with guns, dark themes, depression, and antisocial behavior? What is the connection between this dark worldview and depression? What is the connection to violent behavior? A fascination with guns, death, and depression are symptoms and not the cause of the shootings. How are these symptoms related to a culture of violence and its industries?

Commonalities shared by many of the school shooters include a history of maltreatment, especially in early childhood. Studies have found that being abused or neglected as a child substantially increases the likelihood of future crime and delinquency.

Children who are the victims of bullying receive a clear message that they are not valued or accepted. Because bullying typically occurs in the presence of others, there is an element of public humiliation. This communication of a profound disrespect has consequences. According to the research of Luckenbill and Doyle, aggressiveness is most pronounced when it involves an attack in a public setting.[90] Rampage shootings, in part, result from displaced aggression after experiencing public humiliation.[91] In other words, the human nature of rampage shooters has been violated by disrespectful behavior and, because the schools did not stop the violence, the shooters developed a deep sense of injustice. Over time the shooters' outrage was fueled by the violence industries and culminated in mass murders. Research clearly identifies the role of bullying in school shootings. Between 68 percent and 93 percent of school shooters described feeling persecuted, bullied, or threatened by their peers prior to the attack.[92] Most of the school shooters had experienced "an unusually high amount of bullying or ostracism that was particularly relentless, humiliating, and cruel."[93] About half of those who reported being bullied were simultaneously involved in romantic rejections.[94]

At the same time, the shooters had an "intense concern" about their social standing in their schools. In other words, they were concerned about being respected. It was "almost always about shielding themselves from physical victimization, including bullying or other personal humiliation."[95] They were "intensely interested in defending or elevating their social standing. They believed that they were being ignored, or were under attack, or had been unjustly treated.[96]

A group of children who are set apart from other children are those who experience "rejection sensitivity." Children who expect to be rejected tend to perceive more hostility and rejection in ambiguous comments than those who are not so sensitive. These children may behave aggressively and experience increased interpersonal difficulties. This causes them to be rejected by peers more often, which deepens the psychological damage. They may become very distressed and then act out.[97]

In testimony presented to the House Judiciary Committee after the Columbine shootings, Dr. Cornell described the shooters as "deeply resentful, ruminating over perceived injustices."[98] To shield themselves, in order to protect their esteem and self-respect, most of the attackers had revenge as a motive. One study showed that more than half of the attackers had revenge as a motive and another study revealed that almost three-quarters of the shooters were motivated by revenge.[99] One high school shooter was quoted as saying,

"I wanted to get as much revenge as I could."[100] More than three-quarters were known to hold a grievance at the time of the attack, and many communicated with others about these grievances prior to the attack.[101] One shooter said: "I killed because people like me are mistreated every day. I did this to show society: Push us and we will push back.[102] Revenge is "getting even," a mutated form of justice. Revenge is an especially prevalent value in a culture that promotes hierarchy and "the warrior ideal" as the model for male behavior. Violent masculinity often is aligned with gaining esteem and respect and saving face. These values are encased in attitudes that portray violence as an acceptable, if not preferable, way to express anger and to seek justice.

Some of the shooters have threatened suicide, others have asked to be killed, some have committed "suicide by cop," and some have actually killed themselves. About 75 percent of the shooters threatened to kill themselves, made suicidal gestures, or tried to kill themselves.[103] About 17 percent of school shooters actually commit suicide.[104] Kip Kinkel of Springfield, Oregon, who killed four people and wounded twenty-five others, was tackled by students when he tried to kill himself. He then begged people, "Kill me! Kill me!" Michael Carneal of Paducah, Kentucky, notoriously also asked bystanders to kill him during his rampage.

Lack of empathy is common among school shooters during the incident and afterward. For example, when Jamie Rouse took aim at his football coach and fired, he was smiling.[105] One witness said that fifteen-year-old Charles Andrew Williams had a smile on his face as he opened fire, killing two students and wounding thirteen.[106] Commenting about Golden and Johnson, who had just engaged in mass murder, a witness said, "There's very little emotion on their faces."[107] When apprehended, Andrew Wurst, who had just shot four people, "acted as if the whole thing was a big joke."[108] When Michael Carneal and Andrew Golden were in court facing their crimes, their "eyes looked dead, they betrayed nothing physically or emotionally that would suggest they had just gunned children in cold blood." Similarly, Kip Kinkel, who killed his parents as well as students, betrayed no emotion in court.[109] This is common among young people who appear in court on murder charges.[110]

Many school shooters present themselves as warriors, dressed in commando garb, and almost all utilize a pseudo-commando style.[111] The pseudo-commando is a type of mass murderer who kills in public during the daytime, plans his offensive, is prepared with a powerful arsenal of weapons, and expects to be killed during the shooting.[112] He feels deep anger and resentment and feels grossly and unjustly mistreated. Revenge fantasies become the last refuge of the pseudo-commando's wounded self-esteem and ultimately enable him to commit mass murder and suicide.[113]

Many rampage school shooters are, in part, motivated by recognition and fame. In the aftermath of a mass shooting, the perpetrator generally receives a great deal of media attention. Some shooters have sent messages or released manifestos to media outlets, which have given them a kind of celebrity status.[114] The news media should do everything possible not to glamorize and sensationalize these shootings because of this quest for fame and because of the copycat effect. However, because of competition and the profit motive, this is not going to happen.

Steinberg points out that many young people are "Nintendo kids." She points out that each school shooter between 1996 and 1999—the time she was writing about—was highly fascinated by violence and that addiction to violently graphic movies and video games was a major component in their lives.[115] Similarly, McGee and DeBernardo noted that many school shooters grew up with G.I. Joe games and combat video games.[116] This entertainment seldom is recognized as a shared characteristic and will be discussed in detail in the following chapters.

Researchers consistently have been puzzled by the anomaly presented by many school shooters from stable families and affluent communities. Most were not considered by the adults around them to be at high risk for this kind of behavior. Although other violent juvenile offenders tend to show an early onset of delinquent behavior, school shooters tend to display delinquent behavior shortly before the shootings. Considering that many of the shooters appeared, in most respects, to be normal, relatively affluent young people, the question remains: what is the primary causal factor in their becoming mass murderers?

Case Studies

In 2003 the National Research Council conducted six case studies of school shooters. The following case studies draw from their research and also include other sources of information. These school shooters were chosen here because they are representative of the shared characteristics described above.

Michael Carneal
December 1, 1997 / Heath High School, Paducah, Kentucky / Age 14

Michael Carneal opened fire on a prayer group in the lobby of Heath High School, killing three students and wounding five others. He had experienced unrequited love, and the girl who rejected him was the first person he shot.

Paducah is a mixed-class community in which professionals, such as lawyer John Carneal, were in the top stratum. The Carneals were described as actively involved in all aspects of community life. They opened their home to their children's friends, who were frequent guests at the Carneal family dinner table. Michael Carneal appeared to be a fairly normal boy but in other contexts, especially the harsh social world of high school, he was uncomfortable and constantly looking for approval and respect from both students and adults.[117] He talked about "doing something big."[118]

Michael was a victim of bullying. He was of slight build and wore oversized glasses with big frames. A journal he kept for his English class reflected sadness, loneliness, and rage against classmates.[119] He had friends but was a fringe member of several groups, which is not unusual for fourteen-year-old boys. Also, he had a girlfriend.[120] Michael displayed some problem behavior before the shooting. He had accumulated five discipline infractions during the school semester. However, he was not identified as a problem student, and the school faculty who knew him were shocked when they heard that he was the shooter.[121]

When asked in a police interview whether he had read or seen anything like his shooting spree, Carneal said he had seen the movie, *The Basketball Diaries*. The lead figure in the movie takes revenge on a Catholic school priest who had abused him by shooting the priest and classmates to the cheers of his friends.[122] Carneal asked victims, "Do you deserve to die?," a quote from the movie *Natural Born Killers*.[123] Also, Carneal spent much time in the middle of the night using the internet. His taste for violence included sites of how-to instructions for making weapons and rehearsals of violent attacks. His writings began to reflect a fixation on violence. He killed a dog and commented: "This is my first kill."[124] Carneal reputedly was a violent video game addict. He had been playing video games since he was a child and spent many hours playing violent video games. These games included *Mortal Kombat*, *MechWarrior*, and *Doom*. He especially liked *Doom*, which pioneered immersive 3D graphics. It featured a lot of interactive violence and satanic imagery. The parents of three of the girls he killed sued Sony Computer Entertainment, which produces equipment for these types of video games.[125]

Although he had never fired a real pistol in his life, Carneal had practiced killing thousands of people by playing video games in virtual reality.[126] During the shooting, he slowly fired three shots and then five shots in rapid succession. Every bullet struck a fellow student. According to the FBI, the average experienced law enforcement officer, at a range of seven yards, hits with less than one bullet in five. An FBI agent commented, "Nowhere in the annals of law enforcement or military or criminal history can we find an equivalent achievement."[127]

He told the police that he shot his classmates because he was tired of being picked on. Speaking with psychologists and psychiatrists later, he said that patterns of harassment went back to elementary school. His grades fell in the eighth grade because he was called "gay" and "faggot" numerous times after a school publication's gossip column stated that he likes another boy. Such a stigma would be very difficult to contend with in a Southern community with conservative social mores.[128] He said that it was an attention-getting act that he thought would bring him the power and the respect that he deserved.[129] He did not believe that his peers respected him, and he felt that taking guns to school would increase their respect. He was quoted as saying, "People respect me now."[130]

Although Carneal had not been diagnosed with a mental illness before the shooting, he was depressed. Forensic psychiatrists and psychologists found him to be able to understand the consequences of his actions but concluded that he was mentally ill at the time of the shooting. Apparently, he was disassociating at the time because he told a psychiatrist that he felt like he was in a dream.[131] However, the prosecution's team determined that he was not mentally ill.[132] He was reported to exhibit odd behaviors and a sense of paranoia. He reported unreasonable fears. He told one psychiatrist that he thought he heard people in the prayer group talking about him. As he walked on a quiet college campus the Friday before the shooting, he remarked, "Boy, you could really get mugged out here." Knives were discovered under his mattress after the shooting.[133] His behaviors could be a natural result of years of being bullied and heavy exposure to dark and dangerous movies and virtual video game reality. During the shooting, he yelled for someone to kill him but made no attempt to kill himself. He was judged "guilty but mentally ill."[134] He is in prison, where he has attempted suicide at least twice.[135]

Andrew Golden and Mitchell Johnson
March 24, 1998 / Jonesboro, Arkansas / Ages 11 and 13

On Tuesday, March 24, 1998, just a few minutes after fifth period had started, Andrew pulled a fire alarm at Westside Middle School, home of "The Warriors." As students exited the building they were met with a hail of gunfire. Four students and a teacher died in the shooting, and nine people were wounded.[136] Mitchell and Andrew fired fewer than thirty rounds and struck fifteen people. They were dressed in camouflage.[137] Mitchell Johnson was the leader of the two.[138]

Mitchell Johnson was new to the school in Jonesboro, having moved from Minnesota. His mother had been married three times. As a child, he was sexually molested by an older neighborhood boy and in Minnesota had been caught molesting a two-year-old girl. A psychologist concluded that it was an isolated incident.[139]

He was repeatedly teased for being fat. In addition to being bullied, he was known to bully others. Mitchell claimed to be a gang member and projected a tough image to protect himself against bullying. He was described as tough and mean-spirited.[140] He had told a friend that he "had a lot of killing to do."[141]

He also liked to play violent video games that involved guns.[142] He played gruesome games like *Mortal Kombat*.[143] He owned only two rap CDs, Tupac Shakur's *All Eyez on Me* and Bone Thugs-n-Harmony's lyrics about mass murder. Mitchell took this music to school and sang lyrics over and over, playing a cassette in the bathroom about "coming to school and killing all the kids."[144]

Mitchell's father had an explosive temper, but Mitchell got along well with his stepfather. His teachers described him as a normal child, and many of the adults at school commented how polite and respectful he was. He was also a good student. His mother said: "He truly was a good kid." The parents of both boys said that they were raised in a loving manner.

About a month before the shooting, Mitchell started to call sex-talk lines on his father's credit card. His father was furious, called the police and threatened that Mitchell might have to move back to Minnesota with him. Mitchell felt "hopeless" and since that time experienced a downward spiral. Two weeks before the shooting, Mitchell tried out for the basketball team but was not accepted because of self-mutilation, having carved his initials on his shoulder. Then, his girlfriend broke up with him.[145]

Andrew Golden was eleven years old at the time of the shooting. Andrew was the center of his parents' world and also was close to his grandfather. The Golden family were avid hunters, and Andrew was given a shotgun for Christmas the year he turned six. As a toddler, Andrew posed for photographs dressed in camouflage with a rifle.[146] In addition, he was a heavy video game player.

Around the neighborhood, Andrew had a reputation for being "mean-spirited" and was fond of killing cats in his backyard. Like Mitchell, Andrew was known as a good boy but also had a darker, more hostile side.[147] He was found to lack empathy and to be highly impulsive.[148]

Andrew, slight in stature, was thought to have been bullied. After the shooting rampage, he said he felt that he was picked on.[149] Reportedly he also was tired of his teachers' "crap" because they exercised authority over him.[150] The boys were in different grades and were not close friends. However, they rode the same bus on the long ride home. Many believe that their plans were conceived there.[151] They were convicted as juveniles and served their time until they reached twenty-one.

Andrew Jerome Wurst
April 24, 1998 / Edinboro, Pennsylvania / Age 14

Andrew Jerome Wurst killed a teacher and wounded another teacher and two students by gunfire. Before going to a school dinner-dance, he left a suicide note at home and picked up a pistol.

Andrew Jerome Wurst was described as "a typical middle school student."[152] He lived in a relatively affluent community and was a member of a stable, two-parent family. Andrew, like other boys, watched television and played computer games. He also liked heavy metal, with Marilyn Manson and Nine Inch Nails being among his favorite bands. Andrew said that he was having ideas about suicide since he was ten but could not say why.[153] The violent video games that Andrew played included *Cheap BMW 3 Series, Rain Seen, Resident Evil 2, and Black Wolf Breeds*, among others.[154]

In his statement to the police, Andrew said, "I died four years ago. I've already been dead, and I've come back. It doesn't matter anymore. None of this is real."[155] A psychiatrist later said that Andrew thinks he is real but that everyone else is unreal. Andrew stated he had returned from the future and had "a mission to prevent something terrible that has happened or that will happen in the future." He was not sure what the mission was, but he knew that he had an "arch enemy" who would try to prevent him from accomplishing it.[156] It is noteworthy that this perspective parallels many violent video game scenarios in which gamers are on warrior-hero missions.

A psychiatrist concluded that Andrew did not suffer from a delusional disorder or show symptoms of any major psychiatric illness. He said that Andrew had a history of emotional upset, which was characterized by "depressed moods associated with aggressive and suicidal ideation."[157] Andrew remains in prison.[158]

Kip Kinkel
May 21, 1998 / Springfield, Oregon / Age 15

Kip was regarded as a "little class clown." He was short in stature, physically clumsy, and suffered from learning disorders. He was bullied consistently and struggled to keep pace with his older sister who was socially and academically successful.

Kip was placed on a behavioral management plan because of aggressive acts on the playground and also because of his cruel teasing of classmates. He was placed in a gifted learner program in fourth grade because of his aptitude in math and science, but he struggled with other subjects, only being able to learn a few words in Spanish,[159] a frustrating cognitive disparity.

In middle school he was bullied so much that he took karate lessons to protect himself. He visited pornography sites on the internet and sites that described bomb-making, which was becoming more and more fascinating to him. He also was drawn to guns. His father had bought his son two BB guns, three knives, and a 336 Marlin. In the next few years, he assembled a stockpile of guns, which was confiscated by his father.[160]

He was overheard remarking "Hey, that's pretty cool," when he learned about the school shootings in Mississippi, Kentucky, and Arkansas. Kip was rejected by a girl he had a crush on and told friends he fantasized about putting a bomb under the bleachers and "hitting" the cafeteria with his .22 and talked about joining the army so he could know how it felt to kill people. On May 20, Kip had taken a gun to school, got caught, and was expelled. Later that day, he shot and killed both of his parents.[161] He later said, "I had no other choice. I didn't want to. I loved my dad but I had to. I didn't know what else to do. I couldn't do anything else."[162]

The next morning, wearing a cap with the logo of his favorite band, Nine Inch Nails, he secured two guns to his chest, and then returned to school and opened fire on students in the cafeteria. He killed two students and wounded twenty-five more. Kip and attorneys agreed to plead guilty and reserve testimony about his mental state for the sentencing hearing. In his written plea, he wrote: "My mind is clear and I am not sick." He is serving a sentence of 111 years in prison with no chance of parole.[163]

Dylan Klebold and Eric Harris
April 20, 1999 / Littleton, Colorado / Ages 18 and 17

On April 20, 1999, at 11:30 A.M., Dylan and Eric hid semiautomatic weapons, shotguns, rifles, and bombs beneath their trench coats and then ran through the school, yelling and shooting. When they reached the library, they killed their largest number of victims—twelve students and a teacher, and wounded twenty-three students—for a total of thirty-four victims.[164] They carried out a complex attack they had planned for over a year, which involved a sequence of bombs and shooting. Most of the bombs did not detonate so they had to improvise.

The culture of school violence had a role. One observer commented that "bullying was so rampant at Columbine High School that the school had a toxic culture."[165] Both boys had been ostracized, taunted, and bullied, particularly by athletes. Evidence collected after the shooting indicated that the incident was, in part, retribution for how they had been treated by other students.[166] However, they also were bullies. They bragged in their diaries how they picked on freshmen and "fags."[167]

Harris had been rejected by the Marines a week before the attack and was turned down by a girl whom he had asked to the prom. He was on medication for depression.[168] Both boys were heavily addicted to living in the virtual worlds of such ultra-violent video games such as *Doom* and *Quake*. Their rampage, copied by dozens of later shooters, mimicked the rampages of the splatter games they had played so often. Both boys were so immersed in a world of media violence that they were said to have memorized nearly the entire dialogue from the movie *Natural Born Killers*.[169]

Eric Harris identified with Hitler and hurled insults at minority people. He "could not tolerate a world he viewed with contempt but had power over him."[170] The day before the rampage, they sent an email to the local police declaring that their revenge against those who ridiculed them had been accomplished. They blamed parents and teachers for turning their children into "intolerant sheep" and then announced their own suicide. In videotapes, the boys recounted episodes of ostracism and teasing. "I'm going to kill you all," Klebold said. "You've been giving us shit for years."[171] A final report concluded that they were angry, bitter young people who had access to guns and were spurred by images of violence to act out their anger against classmates who fit in better than they did.[172]

Klebold and Harris were influenced by Michael Carneal, and they, in turn, influenced many copycat attempts and actual shootings. After the Columbine tragedy, other students called in bomb threats, wore trench coats to school, or used the internet to praise what Klebold and Harris had done. Only ten days later, on April 30, people feared a major shooting rampage event that would mark Hitler's suicide in 1945. Schools in Arizona, New Jersey, Michigan, North Carolina, and Washington, DC, closed to investigate potential threats. In Hoyt, Kansas, on February 5, 2001, three students who admired the Columbine killers were arrested for planning an attack on their high school. In their homes were bomb-making materials, floor plans of the school, ammunition, and a modified assault rifle. Each also possessed a black trench coat.[173]

In *Bowling for Columbine*, Michael Moore points out the proximity of nuclear weapons production facilities to the Columbine School and its possible role in affecting the attitudes and behavior of the killers. In a similar vein, the US Secret Service concludes that Seung-Hui Cho of Virginia Tech notoriety had knowledge of his country developing as a nuclear military threat.[174]

Anthony Solomon

May 20, 1999 / Rockdale County, Georgia / Age 15

oExactly one month after the Columbine High School massacre, Anthony B. Solomon Jr., known as T. J., opened fire with a .22-caliber rifle on the commons area of his high school. He discharged twelve shots, emptying the rifle, and, running from the building, he pulled out a .357 magnum handgun and fired three more shots. He did not kill anyone but wounded six students. T. J.'s actions came as a complete surprise because he had not exhibited any problem behavior, came from an upper-middle-class, churchgoing family, and because Heritage High School was rated as one of the best high schools in Georgia.[175] He was reportedly depressed because of a break-up with his girlfriend and claimed that he had "no reason to live anymore." He had been bullied by a football player and feared becoming the school "wuss."[176]

Contributing factors included a high rate of gun ownership in the South, T. J.'s pride in being able to use a firearm, and the influence of his favorite rock group, Korn. One music rating service classified Korn as "post-grunge, alternative metal, heavy metal," and it was described as "ominous, gloomy, nihilistic, aggressive, detached, visceral, bleak, angry, hostile."[177]

Also, T. J. was obsessed with Columbine, which is thought to play a role in instigating the murders.[178] T. J. had written, "There aren't many words that I can say, to describe how I feel. One big question everybody probably [is] wondering about now is WHY?! Well, for the sake of my brothers and sisters related to the trench coat mafia, that will have to remain a mystery to the public eye. I have been planning this for years, but finally got pissed off enough to really do it."[179] In an interview, the assistant prosecuting attorney said, "Columbine . . . showed a way that T. J. could gain power; he could be in control.[180]

Psychological testing after the event revealed depression that was thought to partly emanate from his parents' divorce and his mother being emotionally "cold."[181] However, because symptoms were not evident before the shooting, it was not clear if depression was a preexisting condition or one prompted by the murders. Also, it was not clear how much the dark worldview projected by violent media and video games contributed to T. J.'s depression.

Seung-Hui Cho

April 16, 2007 / Virginia Polytechnic Institute and State University (Virginia Tech) / Blacksburg, Virginia / Age 23

Four days before the anniversary of Columbine, Seung-Hui Cho enacted the most horrific school shooting rampage yet experienced.

The parents of victims dismissed Cho as "crazy." For example, a father who lost his daughter at Virginia Tech said: "I don't think you can stop every crazy person. But some of the [documents] show what these crazy kids did."[182]

Cho was diagnosed with emotional problems, and his behavior was odd, even bizarre at times. The shootings occurred when he was off his medication. It was discovered that he was "lost between the cracks" and that the system failed him, not responding to his increasingly strange behavior and his failure to keep counseling appointments. He had a lifelong history of severe social impairment. He was born in South Korea. He was sick and very quiet as a young child. He had few friends. His social difficulties became worse when his family moved to the United States. He was teased in school because he could not speak English.[183] He very rarely spoke, and when he did speak, his comments left his peers bewildered. He told his roommates that he had an imaginary girlfriend named Jelly, a supermodel who lived in outer space. He also claimed that he and Vladimir Putin had grown up together in Moscow.[184] This is not to say that his rampage was solely caused by emotional problems. Like other school shooters, he had legitimate grievances. Social isolation and teasing worsened his already troubled nature. Like other rampage shooters, he had developed a deep sense of rage.

Just as the proximity of nuclear weapons production facilities affected the Columbine shooters, Cho was affected by a wider, political dynamic. He had developed a sense of his country being bullied and treated unjustly on the world stage.[185] In a "multimedia manifesto" he mailed to NBC News, he expressed his distress and rage.[186] Cho's emotional instability and sensitivity, coupled with his own experience of being bullied, was catalytic in releasing his deadly rage.

Nikolas Cruz
February 14, 2018 / Marjory Stoneman Douglas High School / Parkland, Florida / Age 19

On February 14, 2018, Nikolas Cruz perpetrated one of the most lethal school shooting up to that time, killing seventeen people and wounding seventeen others.

He was one of two boys adopted by Roger and Lynda Cruz who had moved into the affluent community of Parkland, Florida. When the father died, the boys began a reign of terror in the neighborhood that lasted for years. Nikolas, the older brother, was very moody and prone to explosive anger. He took delight in torturing animals and provoking everyone on the block. He killed squirrels with a pellet gun and picked fights with other neighborhood children constantly. His classmates referred to him as "weird," and adults referred to him as "troubled." In high school, his behavior became increasingly bizarre, withdrawn, and hostile. He tore up a classroom, threatened classmates, and sent disturbing Instagrams displaying his arsenal of weapons and showing a gun's holographic laser sight pointed at a neighborhood street. He trained his two dogs to be weapons used to threaten neighbors.[187]

His mother, among the only people with whom he was close, died in November 2017, causing him to be deeply depressed.[188] Although close to his mother, he had hit her with a vacuum hose when she confiscated his Xbox. Dressed in a military uniform, he approached his mother with an air gun and said, "Drop to your knees, b_ _ _ _ , I'm going to blow your f_ _ _ _ _ brains out."[189]

Cruz experienced very significant rejection events. He was adopted, and then when he was a teenager, both his parents died unexpectedly, a rejection event of some magnitude. Several months before the shooting, he was rejected by a girl with whom he was infatuated, and then he was expelled from school for fighting and because he was carrying bullets in his backpack.

On Valentine's Day, wearing a hat with the words "U.S. Army," Cruz walked into Marjory

Stoneman Douglas School and became the most notorious rampage school shooter in American history.[190] The Marjory Stoneman Douglas High School shooting has renewed calls for national gun reforms. It also sparked walkouts and rallies of tens of thousands of people, most of whom were young people.[191]

Discussion

Researchers and others express confusion about the primary cause of rampage school shootings and have been unable derive an accurate and consistent profile of the shooters. The media tend to report the mass murders as "senseless," and many people conclude that the shooters are crazy. Researchers have created lists of risk factors, and some researchers recognize that the shootings result from the cumulative effect of a combination of risk factors.

The research investigating school shootings tends to rely on psychological explanations and, in so doing, does not take the "big picture" into account. Psychological explanations may be necessary, but they are not sufficient. A key deficiency is not taking into account how the consciousness of many people, especially since the early 1990s, has been impacted by war and the fear of terrorism. This is compounded by worry about environmental deterioration and the many other problems presented by a troubled world.

The culture of violence and its offspring, the culture of school violence, are contrary to human nature and human needs. Human nature calls for acceptance and respect. As a matter of sheer survival, human nature calls for empathy and compassion for others. It also calls for self-preservation, felt as a need for personal power, a sense of efficacy, and the ability to contribute to the community. And, perhaps above all, it calls for justice.

At heart many young people recognize that school is oppressive and violates their nature. School is violent to the extent that it violates or prohibits the humanization of students and staff. The shooters' rage at the schools is evidenced by school staff members being shot in many of the rampages. Students who are especially sensitive to rejection are probably emotionally sensitive in general. As such, they are less resilient and more vulnerable to the effects of the culture of violence and the culture of school violence.

These factors and the confluence of other shared characteristics bring us closer to an explanation for school shootings. However, none of the research or speculation has been able to identify the primary causal factor in school shootings. Therefore, the question remains—Why do some children become school shooters?

Researchers have concluded that there is no single profile of the school shooter. Other juvenile murderers tend to exhibit a number of high-risk factors, including poverty and living in a violent community. School shooters present a striking anomaly. Most had no previous delinquent activity, and the majority had stable families and lived in relatively affluent and peaceful communities.

Understanding rampage school shootings is critical for a number of reasons. The deaths are terrifying to victims and witnesses, and family and friends experience relentless grief. It also is important to understand these rampages because they signify a deep crisis in our schools and society that demands to be resolved.

We can search for the primary factor by looking at the sudden escalation of rampage school shootings during the 1990s. What was happening in the world, and what new factors emerged during that time?

A poll conducted in 1999 revealed that the public saw the Littleton school shooting as a sign of deeper problems in the United States. Forty-seven percent viewed the shootings as a serious problem. Over half the respondents felt that neither the government nor society could do anything to prevent similar acts of violence.[192] As the following chapters show, this is not the case. The following chapters shed light on the causes of rampage shootings, this "new and unique" violence. This will be accomplished by looking at "new and unique" electronic entertainment media and technology prevalence and related research. After reviewing relevant research, the primary causal factor will be identified and the question "Why?" will be answered.

CHAPTER 7

MEDIA REALITY

> We are products of our products.
> —Jean-Paul Sartre

The culture of violence is a media-saturated culture. In order to understand the culture of violence, we need to recognize the primacy of the media as a source of influence. Many people cite media violence as part of the problem. However, few realize the full magnitude of the media's impact.[1] Since the middle of the twentieth century, electronic entertainment has become part of taken-for-granted everyday life. At the same time, children and adults routinely assume that everyone else is more strongly influenced by the media than they are.[2] In fact, people expect others to be more influenced than themselves.[3] In certain ways the entertainment media can be effective in teaching positive cognitive and social skills. They can provide examples of compassion, understanding, human diversity, nonviolent problem-solving, and harmonious relations with others. But this seldom happens. Instead, entertainment media tend to trivialize and glamorize violence.[4] The media consist of movies, videos, music, music videos, television, and other screen technologies. Because television is the most pervasive medium, this chapter will focus (a word that has become more prevalent since television) on it.

Music and Music Videos

In the meanwhile, another pervasive mass medium that warrants attention is music. Music and singing have always played an important role in learning and the communication of culture. Socrates says in Plato's *Republic*, that "musical training is a more potent instrument than any other, because rhythm and harmony find their way into the inward places of the soul, on which they mightily fasten."[5]

Music videos combine music with images, many of them violent, sexist, negative, destructive, and morbid. Prominent themes of music and music videos advocate and glamorize alcohol and other drugs, graphic violence, sex that focuses on control, and violence against women.[6] The average teenager from age seventeen to eighteen listens to over 10,500 hours of rock music, much of it violent.[7]

"Dream Worlds," a series of educational videos, shows how music videos and music television portray women as scantily clad, sex objects and nymphomaniacs, constantly seeking men's attention, as well as depicting women who are chained and bound. Such music videos have helped to create a "rape culture."[8]

Sexual content has become more explicit, denigrating, and violent since the 1960s. The rock band Nine Inch Nails released a song titled "Big Man with a Gun" that describes a sexual assault at gunpoint. Another example is Marilyn Manson, whose lyrics include: "Let's just kill everyone and let your god sort them out," and "Who says date rape isn't kind?" A recent "Hot 100" song called "Rockstar" by Post Malone includes the following lyrics: "I've been f_ _ _ _ _ _ hoes and poppin' pillies. / Man, I feel just like a rockstar." In general, pop treatment of sex is "shockingly regressive."[9] Such hatred, dark visions, and violence against women "are widespread and unmistakable in mainstream hip-hop and alternative music."[10] This hatred and violence is even honored; for example, *Rolling Stone* awarded Best New Artist to Manson in 1997. Another MTV favorite is Eminem, who wrote a song in which he described killing his child's mother and dumping her body in the ocean. Hip-hop and "gangsta" music embodies violence, breaking the law, and a profound misogyny. Song titles reflect hip-hop's disturbing trend. These include "Women and Bitches," "Bitch Niggaz," and "Shut Up and Give Me Your Bone Marrow." The favorite CD of Kip Kinkel, who killed his parents and then went on a school-shooting rampage, was Nirvana's *Nevermind*. The lyrics are lush with nihilism: "Death / With violence / Excitement / Right here / Died / Go to hell . . . Take a chance / Dead."

Although little research has been conducted about the effects of violent music, the existing research shows a link between this music and violence. For example, a 2003 study of five hundred college students showed that violent music lyrics increase aggressive thoughts and hostile feelings. The researchers concluded: "There are now good theoretical and empirical reasons to expect effects of music lyrics on aggressive behavior to be similar to the well-studied effects of exposure to TV and movie violence and the more recent research efforts on violent video games,"[11] a conclusion backed by other research.[12] A laboratory study in Germany found that male participants who listened to misogynistic song lyrics gave more hot chilis to a female than a male confederate. A follow-up study found that these male participants recalled more negative attributes of women and reported more feelings of vengeance compared to participants who heard neutral lyrics. Man-hating songs had similar effects on female participants.[13] Considering that many more lyrics are misogynistic than man-hating, the effect of listening to such lyrics "is likely to become even more pronounced and could probably lead to even more severe aggression against women, such as rape or other forms of aggressive assaults."[14]

A Virtual World

For over four decades, media researchers have recognized the powerful ability of the media to create a "media reality."[15] George Gerbner, the founder of American media studies, conducted the longest running study of the effect of television violence on light, medium, and heavy television viewers. This research shows that heavy television viewers, who watch four or more hours a day, tend to perceive the world in ways that are consistent with television images and messages.[16] Heavy viewers especially are prone to believe that they lived in "a mean and threatening world." Their immersion in mainstream entertainment media results in a frightening worldview, which is reinforced by the sensationalist emphasis of media news and its focus on violence and crisis. The various media interact and wield influence synergistically. The more that people are immersed in media reality, the more they experience a virtual world. Their real world is entwined with an electronic reality that is increasingly seamless. This constitutes an electronic construction of reality.

The creation of media reality is facilitated by the media's format and perspective. In 1958, two psychiatrists, interested in television's ability to simulate social interaction, coined the term "parasocial interaction."[17] Parasocial interaction is a key component in television's ability to be an instrument of social learning and a creator of worldviews. Phenomenology is a useful tool to understand the media's power to create and to develop worldviews. Phenomenology's purpose is to understand the relationship between individual consciousness and social life.[18] Phenomenology is interested in how social reality is not a given, but rather is socially constructed. Rather, this method of investigating social reality asks how the interaction between people and the world is "mutually formed and forming."[19] An example is children raised on violent media who, when they become adults, become media creators and producers who create violent media. Thus, the beat goes on.

The extent to which one is influenced by the media depends on the age when exposure began, what was watched, for how long, if viewing was solitary, what the content was, and how realistic and engaging the images were. The worldview of consumers is shaped, in part, by the "sub-universes of meaning" to which they are exposed through the media. Such sub-universes are entwined with real world experiences to create a person's worldview. An example is avid watchers of soap operas who acquire the attitudes and opinions of the characters.

Phenomenologists are interested in how features of the taken-for-granted everyday world become, in effect, invisible. The proliferation of media forms, genres, and products has resulted in mutually reinforcing relationships that make the boundaries between the real world and the mediated world more seamless. For many people, the electronic surroundings have resulted in a virtual reality.

A related dynamic is resonance. Resonance is a term used by physicists and mechanical engineers. Resonance occurs when an external force periodically is applied that is equal or nearly equal to one of the natural frequencies of the system on which it acts. This results in the system oscillating with larger amplitude than when the force is applied at other frequencies.[20] The term was borrowed by George Gerbner to further explain the media's ability to construct and to amplify social reality. Resonance may occur when an event in the real world resembles a similar situation experienced in a virtual world. Like a mechanical system's resonance, the results may amplify the real-world event and may result in violent behavior.

Hegemony

Many people think that the purpose of the media is to entertain and to inform. Actually, the basic purpose of the media is to make profit.[21] By 2016 the global electronic entertainment and media revenue reached $1.8 trillion, projected to reach $2.2 trillion by 2021.[22] The media industry is comprised of fewer than fifty corporations, most of them colossal.[23] The hegemony of the media operates through "gatekeepers" and "agenda setters" who determine, to a great degree, what we see and hear. This process has become even more concentrated and constricted since the major corporate mergers that began in the 1980s.

Herbert Schiller, a pioneering critical media analyst, pointed out how the media industry is engaged in cultural imperialism. American media corporations earn at least half of their profits from global sales. New and expanding markets have emerged in countries that have abandoned state control of media and distribution. Global media markets continue to expand.[24] This results in the culture of violence proliferating globally.

The format of television news affects how people think about the world. This format gives viewers the impression that the world is unmanageable and that events just seem to happen. Television news gives the public only the most superficial facts about events in the world.

The news industry also is primarily motivated by profit. Neil Postman, author of *Amusing Ourselves to Death*, points out how the news is a "cash cow" that follows the sensationalism and inaccuracies of non-news programs. He writes: "News shows are on the air from early morning until late at night, and there is no lack of realism depicting the violence in the human condition. Rapes, muggings, terrorism, and drug-related murders and kidnappings are the currency of the evening news. And with the proliferation of pseudo-news tabloid shows, young eyes can feast on wall-to-wall horror, and the horror can feast on young minds."[25] Mainstream media news also blurs real-world reality because the news industry has its own profit-motive agenda. Media researchers have found that newscasts "are distorting what they claim to represent, and in the process are adding to our social problems."[26]

Children's Programming

The media are teachers. What do they teach? Media violence is one of the post potent influences in teaching that force, especially the use of deadly force, is the primary, if not the only way to solve conflict and problems.[27] For a variety of reasons, children find television to be much more attractive than the three Rs. School is skill centered, requires course content, is graded by age, has prerequisites for knowledge, is reflection centered, requires a response, and takes place in a group setting. Television is attention centered; programs are elective and not graded. No prior knowledge is required; no response is required. The content is emotion centered, and learning often takes place in a solitary setting.

For most children, the entertainment media occupy more of their time than the classroom. By 1990, the average American child aged two to five was watching over twenty-seven hours of television each week.[28] It's estimated that children in the United States now spend between five and seven hours a day in front of a screen.[29] This constitutes up to 44 percent of their waking hours. Infants are exposed to television virtually at birth. About 68 percent of children under the age of two actively use screen media, mostly television and video games.[30] Babies as young as fourteen months of age are seen to observe and incorporate behavior seen on television.[31] Some evidence indicates that infants can imitate behavior from television that is presented in a simple and instructional manner. This early ability to imitate continues and can manifest as the "copycat effect," which is evidenced by school shootings.[32] Until age four many children are unable to distinguish fact from fantasy in television programs and continue to be unable to do so after age four despite adult coaching. For young children, television is a source of information about how the world works. Their earliest and deepest impressions are of a television world in which violence is commonplace and usually portrayed as "powerful, exciting, charismatic and efficacious."[33] Among young children, violent media elicit a fear response that may be long-lasting, linked to PTSD, and negative responses can occur after only one exposure.[34] The ability of the media to create reality is especially a problem for young children. Many children confuse fantasy and reality, and some children appear to be obsessed with specific action figures and series, such as Star Wars and Power Rangers, and are unable to focus on other activities. At the same time, the quality of play becomes less creative and imaginative and is more often imitative.

In children's programming, and increasingly in adult entertainment, violence presented as fun. Cartoon violence introduces children to television violence at a young age, and then sets the tone for what they expect from it in later years. Children who watch television identify more with the characters that are their own gender. Stereotyped perceptions of what it means to be male—to control, to be powerful—have become part of our national mythology. The "warrior ideal" is glorified in the media, evidenced by behavior and by many boys and men wearing combat fatigues as everyday clothing.

Girls, on the other hand, are bombarded with messages to be slender, sexy, beautiful, and attractive to males. An example is Miley Cyrus, at age seventeen, giving a provocative strip pole performance on national television. The influence of such sexualization is evidenced by girls at younger ages dressing and acting in sexually provocative ways.[35]

What is it like for children to grow up in a media reality? By 1980, violence, defined as "physical aggression," occurred more than twenty-one times per hour on Saturday morning children's programs.[36] The *UCLA Television Violence Monitoring Report* concluded that Saturday morning children's programs contain "sinister combat violence."[37] Estimates are that children who watch three to four hours of noneducational television per day will witness over 8,000 murders on television by the time they finish grade school.[38] By age eighteen, a child in the United States will see 200,000 acts of violence and 16,000 murders in the media.[39] In this virtual world, television characters are murdered at a rate 1,000 times higher than real world victims.[40] Between 1982 and 1991, the number of violent acts per television hour remained at about five per hour. In 1992, the number of violent acts doubled to ten per hour. The year 1994 saw an average increase to fourteen violent acts an hour.[41] Television violence since that time increasing became more graphic,[42] and children's programming, particularly cartoons, displayed up to twenty-five violent acts hourly."[43] Between 1982 and 1999, television violence in all programming increased 780 percent. At the same time teachers have reported nearly a nearly 800 percent increase of aggressive acts on the playground.[44]

Meanness, aggression, and violence in media affect children more deeply than adults.

As Diane Levin explains: "Young children experience violence whenever they feel endangered and unsafe—by things that undermine the sense of safety of their thoughts, feelings, bodies, or who they are. Demeaning language (such as 'put-downs'), gender and racial stereotypes, abuse of power (for instance, when one group exploits another), and deviousness (for example, when advertisers mislead children) can undermine a child's sense that the world is a safe and just place."[45]

Children's cartoons and fantasy programs lay the foundation for adult viewing. Media reality is "entertainmentized," from children's cartoons to the evening news.[46] This is a world of hyperbole, exaggeration, the unlikely, the impossible, and one in which violence is fun. From sitcoms, to soap operas, to commercials, to the so-called news, exaggeration is the norm.

This world also is one of sex, drugs, and rock 'n' roll. The average teenager nowadays witnesses about 16,000 televised sexual per season, most often having no consequences. This worldview is reinforced by young people being exposed to about three alcohol ads each day, a number that triples for black and Hispanic children.[47]

A media reality that glorifies violence glorifies the expression of power. It is natural for young people to seek power, especially if they live in such institutions as the family and school that often do not allow enough expression of personal power. Indeed, the expression of power may be punished within an institutional framework.

Adult Programming

The "mean and threatening world" of television dominates the airwaves for both children and adults. From adult cartoons to prime-time programming to the evening news, programing is saturated with violence. In the seven-year period between 1994 and 2001, the rate of television violence increased by 286 percent.[48] There were fourteen acts of television violence an hour in 1994, and by 2001, there were forty.[49] Media violence is increasingly realistic, horrific and prevalent. Content includes more realistic murders, rape scenes, and torture scenes. Other disturbing trends include the hero being the most violent character. In addition, there is more violence directed against children.[50]

Sexual themes are more explicit and plentiful. More rapists, fetishists, and sexual predators are appearing with increasing frequency.[51] Violence against women in music videos, commercials, and entertainment media is rampant. The media commits violence against women by projecting and spotlighting a standard of beauty that, in large part, is the media's own creation and rarely possible to attain. The video, *Beauty Mark: Body Imaging and the Race for Perfection*, illustrates how damaging this campaign is on the self-esteem, health, and well-being of girls and women.[52] Women, much more frequently than men, use the word "perfect." This is aided and reinforced by advertisers using the word "perfect" in food and cosmetics ads during the past forty years or so. Vanity Fair Napkins advertises "the perfect napkin, whether you're serving fish sticks or lobster tails." A recent one-page magazine article in a women's magazine contained the word "perfect" eleven times. This is reflected in the relentless standard of beauty and physical perfection women are subjected to. It also reflects many women feeling that they need to be perfect in motherhood and work as well as in appearance. The media has had tremendous impact in creating this quest for perfection, which, by definition, is almost impossible.

The entertainment media also objectifies women, reducing them to sexual objects. Watching television programs in which women are objectified increases the likelihood of men engaging in harassing conduct and conforming to violent masculine gender role norms.[53] Since the early 1990s, there has been an epidemic of date rapes on college campuses.[54] Sut Jhally's videos, *Dreamworlds: Desire, Sex and Power in Music Video*, illustrates how music videos and music television content objectifies, sexualizes, and brutalizes girls and women, portraying them as having an insatiable desire to please men and to have sex with them. Such content teaches boys and young men that they are privileged, in control, and have power over women. These music videos teach girls and young women that it is their role to please men.[55]

Violence against women in the media reflects and reinforces sexist and ageist attitudes and misogyny. The following example encapsulates these mainstream media attitudes. In late 2009, Fox channel's *The Best of the Reality Shows* showed a video clip of an old woman repeatedly being hit in the face. Smiling broadly, Daniel Tosh, the male host of the show *Tosh.o*, said: "Although there's nothing I like better than watching an old lady getting repeatedly punched in the face, we have to move on."[56]

History of Media Violence Research

Research investigating television's influence on aggressive and violent behavior began in the early 1950s. Many of the early studies showed a correlation between exposure and increased aggression, and a few showed a direct causal effect. By the early 1980s over 3,000 books and articles had been written about the effects of media, especially television. Now there are probably 6,000 about media effects.

A question discussed in the media-research literature is that of individual differences in susceptibility to violent media effects. These differences include violent program preferences, gender differences, and trait aggressiveness. The research of Carnagey and his colleagues found no such differences, "suggesting that the results are quite robust across individuals."[57]

In the 1970s many researchers continued to believe that media violence was correlated with aggressive and violent behavior. By 1982, the Surgeon General's research concluded that media violence is a contributing factor to the increase in violent crime and antisocial behavior.[58] Since that time most researchers, including those at the American Academy of Pediatrics, agree that there is a causal connection between media violence and aggressive and violent behavior.[59] Three major types of studies, experimental, correlational, longitudinal, and meta-analyses clearly and consistently have linked media violence to aggressive and violent behavior.[60] This finding "is consistent across a multitude of research designs and, most importantly there does not appear to be any identifiable group (e.g., age, sex, personality type) that is immune to these effects."[61] In order to better understand these conclusions, let us review a summary of the research.

Laboratory Experiments

Studies into the effects of violence began in the mid-1950s, not long after television became widespread. For example, researchers in 1956 compared the behavior of twenty-four children watching television. Half of the children watched a violent episode of the cartoon *Woody Woodpecker*, and the other twelve watched a nonviolent cartoon *The Little Red Hen*. During play afterward, the children who watched the violent cartoon were much more likely to hit other children and break toys.[62] Another example occurred six years later. Researchers studied the effect of exposure to real-world violence, television violence, and cartoon violence. They divided one hundred preschool children into four groups. The first group watched a real person shout insults at an inflatable doll while hitting it with a mallet. The second group watched the incident on television. The third watched a cartoon version of the same scene, and the fourth did not watch anything. Later, when all the children were exposed to a frustrating situation, the first three groups responded with more aggression than the control group. The children who watched the incident on television were just as aggressive as the children who watched the real person use the mallet.[63]

Longitudinal Studies

Early on, other scientists outside a laboratory setting established a connection between media and aggression. In 1960, University of Michigan professor Leonard Eron studied 856 third-grade students living in a semi-rural community in Columbia County, New York. He found that the children who watched violent television behaved more aggressively in school. He wanted to track the effect of this exposure over the years, so he revisited

Columbia County in 1971, when the children were nineteen years old. He discovered that boys who watched violent television as children were more likely to get in trouble with the law as teenagers. In 1982, when the study participants were thirty years old, they were found to be more likely to have been convicted of serious crimes, to use violence to discipline their children, and to treat their spouses aggressively. A similar study that included girls arrived at the conclusion that girls who watch more television violence behave more aggressively.[64]

Researchers also have examined communities before and after the introduction of television. In the mid-1970s, University of British Columbia professor Tannis McBeth Williams studied a remote village in British Columbia before and then after television was introduced. She found that two years after television arrived, violent incidents had increased by 160 percent.[65] Three Cree communities in northern Manitoba were studied during the 1970s and early 1980s. Four years after television was introduced, the incidence of fist fights and black eyes among the children had increased significantly.[66]

The murder rate in the United States sharply increased in 1955, eight years after television sets were introduced into homes in the United States.[67] Other research shows that between 1957, the first year the FBI collected such data, and 1992 the murder rate doubled.[68] An examination of the murder rate in South Africa before 1975, the year the government banned television and in 1987, twelve years after the ban was lifted, revealed that murder rates had skyrocketed.[69] The most predominant new influence in the lives of these culturally diverse people was television. A fifteen-year study found that violent television is a stronger influence than parents.[70]

Meta-Analyses

In 2016, a review of the thirty-seven meta-analytic studies was conducted that analyzed the connection between exposure to violent media and hostile appraisals, that is, perceiving ambiguous actions by others as aggressive. Significant correlations were found in experimental, cross-sectional, and longitudinal studies, especially the positive link to exposure and age, indicating that violent media have cumulative effects over time. These findings complement findings from previous meta-analyses that show that violent media can increase aggressive thoughts, angry feelings, physiological arousal, and aggressive behavior. The findings suggest that people who view the world in a hostile manner are more likely to behave aggressively.[71]

Research: Children

Children are now exposed to about eleven hours of screen time a day and are being exposed at increasingly young ages.[72] The assessment of media effects on children needs to take into account individual differences, such as the amount of exposure, gender, violent media preference, and ages of the first exposure. The first two years of growth of a child's brain are vitally important. Children are much more vulnerable to media effects than adults. The brains of infants and toddlers especially grow at a phenomenal rate and are highly responsive to the environment and to the behavior of others. This is a critically important time for children because they need positive interaction with other children and adults to develop good language and social skills. For many children these learning opportunities have been replaced by a mediated world and parasocial interaction.

According to Piaget, the preoperational stage in children's cognitive abilities is between the ages of two and six.[73] During this period something that looks frightening is scary to the preoperational child. A visually grotesque character is more threatening to the young child than evil motives or apparent potential for causing harm. Research has shown that fantasy content, even more than reality content, induces fright more in preoperational children than in older ones.[74] The especially vulnerable period of television influence is probably up to the age of ten.[75]

Over half of the children in the United States have a television in their room.[76] Researchers at Johns Hopkins Bloomberg School of Public Health analyzed data for 2,707 children and found that five-year-olds are more likely to have behavior problems, disturbed sleep, and "less emotional reactivity" if they have a television in their bedroom. The more they watched television the less reactive they were.[77]

As perceptions of the world conform to the depictions they see on television, people may become more passive, anxious, and fearful.[78] Depending on the gender, age, and other personal characteristics of the children, they also may react in fear. Watching media violence frightens children, and the effects may be long-lasting. A survey of 2,000 Ohio children, ages eight to thirteen, showed that the incidences of psychological trauma, including anxiety, depression, and posttraumatic stress increased in proportion to the number of hours they watched television each day.[79] Young children struggle to understand what they see and incorporate it into their worldview and behavior. Many of the messages in the media can undermine their sense of safety and trust and can create the impression that aggression and violence are normal and necessary. Psychologists point out that many children who receive daily doses of television violence eventually feel the need for protection from such a "mean and threatening" world. At times, that protection is offered by guns and gangs.[80]

Academic Performance

While children's television teaches aggression and fear, it actually impedes the learning of academic skills, especially reading, science, and math. Television has a detrimental effect on academic performance, evidenced in an intergenerational "dumbing down of America," which is widely evident in school test scores. As Jane Healy points out in *Endangered Minds*, even moderate television consumption inhibits the ability to think well and critically, and inhibits the ability to read. The widespread and growing problem of inattention among young people is a related result.[81] Many people believe that heavy television involvement may create "passive learners who give up too easily."[82] Dr. Bryant of the University of Alabama notes that television reduces what researchers call "vigilance," the ability to remain actively focused on a task. Over time, with a lot of viewing, children become less vigilant. She writes: "This is especially critical with children—about three to five years seem to be particularly vulnerable times."[83] Media content also is a factor. Adolescents' school success decreases as their exposure to violent and sexual media increases. This negative relationship has been found for boys and girls of all ages.[84] A key part of poor academic performance is the tendency for the brain's right cerebral hemisphere to respond to electronic media. This is of vital importance because the left cerebral hemisphere is responsible for critical thinking and reading, writing, and mathematical skills. Chapter 9, "The Brain's Response to Electronic Media," will discuss this in more detail.

Other Effects

Many people have come to believe that media violence desensitizes people. However, few realize the extent of this effect. A number of studies in the 1970s showed that people who are repeatedly exposed to media violence tend to be less disturbed when they witness real-world violence and have less sympathy for its victims. These findings have been confirmed in the nineties.[85] Research has established that desensitization reduces sympathy for victims and decreases negative attitudes toward violent behavior, helping behavior, and feelings of personal empathy.[86] In the case of violent scenes, the brain region associated with arousal/attention, detection of threat, episodic memory, encoding and retrieval, and motor programing were activated. These scenes are thus likely to be preserved in long-term memory.[87] This finding is replicated in research during this past decade.[88] Desensitization is a survival reaction of the nervous system. In ancient times, children witnessed death and violence at times, as do children nowadays. However, children experience real-world violence at a fraction of a percent of the media violence they experience. Desensitization inhibits the child's natural development and expression of empathy. This means that children who consume an average amount of entertainment media have problems developing empathy.[89] Loss of empathy shows itself as decreased negative feelings toward violence, less helping behavior, and deceased feelings of personal responsibility.[90] Violent media make people numb to the pain and suffering of others.[91] Another negative consequence of desensitization is that children are more likely to seek out more intense levels of violence to achieve the same thrill that lower levels used to give them.[92] This may help to explain the relatively new phenomenon of thrill killings of animals and humans. Also, it is worth noting that Nazi propagandists created films with increasing levels of violence designed to dehumanize their intended victims.

Since the 1950s governmental and nongovernmental health and mental health organizations in the United States have reviewed research and presented reports before Congress that clearly state that media violence has harmful effects. These include the 1954 Kefauver hearings, the 1969 National Commission on the Causes and Prevention of Violence, the 1972 Surgeon General's report, the 1982 National Institute of Mental Health report, and the 1994 American Psychological Association report, among others. Over 1,000 interdisciplinary studies have found conclusively that violent media cause violent behavior.[93] By 1982, the Group for the Advancement of Psychiatry concluded that in terms of positive social development and intellectual development that television "has been of little help and much harm."[94] In 1992, the American Psychological Association Task Force on Television and Society concluded: "High levels of television viewing are correlated with aggressive behavior and the acceptance of aggressive attitudes.... Viewing violence in the mass media is causally related to aggressive behavior.... Viewing of television aggression leads to increases in subsequent aggression and such behavior can become part of a lasting behavioral pattern."[95] In the year 2000, six medical and public health professional organizations submitted a "Joint Statement on the Impact of Entertainment Violence on Children" to the Congressional Public Health Summit. They stated that "entertainment violence can lead to increases in aggressive attitudes, values, and behavior, particularly in children." They added that the research points to a "causal connection between media violence and aggressive behavior in some children."[96] Such reputable professional associations as the American Medical Association, the National Association of School Psychologists, the American Academy of Child and Adolescent Psychiatry, the National Institute of Mental Health, and the American Academy of Pediatrics have separately reviewed over 1,000 studies of media effects. They concur with the research findings and warn about negative effects, especially on children. The American Academy of Pediatrics' review of the literature leads them to conclude that heavy exposure to television can lead to hostility, fear, anxiety, depression, nightmares, and even posttraumatic stress disorder.[97] They believe that research "overwhelmingly" shows a causal connection between media violence and aggressive and violent behavior.[98] The question of whether exposure to violent media causes increased aggression has been "resolved by the research with a resounding 'Yes!'"[99] The American Psychiatric Association concurs by writing: "The debate is over.... The one predominant finding in research on the mass media is that exposure to media portrayals of violence increases aggressive behavior in children." In the words of Jeffrey McIntyre, legislative and federal affairs officer for the American Psychological Association: "To argue against it is like arguing against gravity."[100]

Misinformation and Disinformation

Compelling conclusions about causality have not become part of the public consciousness because of misinformation and disinformation. Misinformation is due to lack of access to valid information and perceived lack of access. Relatively few people among the general public and among news reporters read academic journals, and when they do, at times, journal articles can be faulty and skewed. Misinformation may not be intentional but inadvertently hides the truth. An example is articles in the mainstream press written by people who have little pertinent expertise and who cite a handful of studies while not acknowledging the existence of hundreds of related research articles.

Disinformation is intentional. The purpose of disinformation is to willfully keep pertinent research findings from the public, policy-makers, and legislators. The result is that many people think that, at best, the relationship between exposure and behavior is correlational.

So, why are so many people equivocal about the enormous influence of the entertainment media? Popular media accounts of the research often are misleading and obscure the reality. An example is Terence Smith, moderator of a PBS NewsHour show about entertainment violence, that aired shortly after the Columbine tragedy. Smith introduced the program by saying: "Hundreds of studies over the years have suggested that there indeed may be a link."[101] Actually, there are not hundreds but, rather, thousands of research studies. In addition, this research relentlessly shows a causal connection between violent entertainment media and aggressive and violent behavior. Another example is a 2019 op-ed article in the *New York Times* that discussed the question of a connection between violent media and rampage shootings. The author cited outdated research, only interviewed two media researchers, and concluded that there is "little and often unconvincing evidence." Some researchers make outrageous claims. An example is Christopher Ferguson of Stetson University, who stated that research does not show a causal nor even a correlational relationship between exposure and violent behavior.[102] This statement is patently untrue.

The problem is not limited to ignorance. Some of the obfuscation of research findings is intentional. Public awareness of the nature of the problem and of research findings has been obstructed by the media industry for decades. The media industry has suppressed or misrepresented research findings about the extent of the influence of violent entertainment media. The very fact that the media industry has been able to keep critical information from the public is a testament to its powerful ability to shape worldviews. The scientific evidence about media violence has been culminating for decades so that now there is no scientific doubt that viewing violence increases aggression and violence. However, as scientific evidence has grown stronger, news reports related that the opposite was true.[103]

Advertising

Another feature of the media that warrants our attention is advertising. In his book, *The Politics of Style*, Stuart Ewing points out how the advertising industry, since its inception in 1823, has had such a profound effect on attitudes, values, and lifestyle that there is now much more of an emphasis on style over substance.[104] George Gerbner has pointed out that the advertising industry is so powerful that it has made us consumers before citizens.[105] The purpose of the entertainment media is to sell. As Sut Jhally relates: "Advertising tells us that the way to happiness is through the consumption of objects."[106] The message projected by the advertising industry is that money and material goods bring happiness. However, as with much projected by the advertising industry, the opposite is actually true. Studies show that individuals who strive hardest for wealth develop a lower sense of well-being, a finding that is evident in every culture studied.[107] Other studies have shown that those who instead strive for "intimacy, personal growth, and contribution to the community" experience a higher quality of life.[108] These findings illustrate that some essential elements of being human are a desire for love and self-efficacy and being a responsible and contributing member of the community. The worldview projected by advertisements is that consumption is good and hyper-consumption is even better. As one observer succinctly states it: "The efficacy of advertising in this consumer culture needs no proof."[109]

In 1990, adults were exposed to 1,500 ads a day. Now it is 3,000. Children watch over 40,000 advertisements a year.[110] By eighteen months, babies can recognize logos. By the age of ten, children memorize three hundred to four hundred brands. The average adult can recognize thousands.[111] By the time children reach fifteen, they have been exposed to as many as 500,000 commercial messages. The effects of advertisements, as Jean Kilbourne of Harvard University points out, are "cumulative and unconscious."[112] As such, the content, form, and presentation become more concentrated over time, amplifying their influence.

What are these cumulative and unconscious effects?

Most of children's commercials are for snack food and fast foods.[113] In 2009 the fast food industry spent $4.2 billion on marketing and advertising.[114] A new study from Yale reveals that the ads for fast food restaurants very rarely highlight healthy meal options. At least 30 percent of the calories in the fast food restaurants' menu items are from sugar and saturated fat.[115] These foods—high in sugar, carbohydrates, and fats—are central in the development of childhood obesity and diabetes. These eating habits set the stage for the continuing consumption of bad food, leading to serious consequences for health, learning problems, and aggressive behavior.

Advertising promotes an affluent lifestyle. Advertisements tend to depict an upper-middle class and wealthy world, which mirrors such so-called reality shows as *The Lifestyles of the Rich and Famous*, which was one of the most popular television programs of all time. More recently, wealthy lifestyles have been promoted by such television programs as *The Real Housewives of Beverly Hills*, *Top Chef*, and *The Fashion Show*. Many advertisements for these shows, as well as general programming, portray opulent and rich lifestyles. The advertising media also promote aristocracy and hierarchy. Consider businesses and brands such as Burger King, Dairy Queen, and Budweiser—"the King of Beers."

The culture of violence values revenge, a common theme of crime shows and violent video games, which is also reflected in advertising. A magazine ad for Phys, a nutritional product, features a piece of broccoli in an ice cream cone with the caption, "Get even." Another example is a video game ad in a magazine entitled "Vengeance is his," and a subtitle, "No flesh shall be spared."

Observers are concerned how advertisers create and nurture aggression and a culture of disrespect among young people.[116] Advertising slogans often contain a subscript that is stated as a command—such as Nike's "Just do it!" McDonald's tells the consumer: "What you want is what you get." Not only can you purchase what you want, McDonald's has what you want. Young gamers who play Mortal Kombat are advised by Nintendo to "Be heard! Play it loud!" The least offensive part of this ad is the incorrect use of the word "Loud," which should be "loudly." This gives us a hint about the origins of the denigration of language. This message shows how advertisers benefit from their research, here tapping into the human need to be acknowledged and, therefore, respected and heard.

Advertisers make use of violence and hyperbole based on the premise that some form of arousal is needed for behavior change.[117] In keeping with the media's employment of hyperbole and the extreme language, Dragon Software demands: "Do the impossible!" This trend of hyperbole and exaggeration is coupled with sugared food and caffeinated drinks, resulting in such social phenomena as talk about being "pumped" (excited, enthusiastic) to extreme sports. Other advertising messages blatantly command the consumer to be aggressive and violent. Consider ImmPower, a "front-line defense" for the immune system. Its magazine advertising slogan is "Unleash the Natural Killer in You."[118] Many advertising messages contain violent behavior, and some demand it. An example is a Pepsi-Max television commercial that features a man throwing a can of the no-calorie soda at a woman. Another can of soda is thrown at a man and hits him in his private parts. Ruffles Molten Hot Wings commands: "Punch your mouth in its face." Movie Gallery has a "kick butt" guarantee. OraVet advises "Don't' just freshen your dog's bad breath. Fight it." Bic pens has a "Fight for Your Write" campaign, and Trident Gum not only "fights cavities" but also takes "this cavity fight to the streets." A magazine ad for Progressive Insurance shows a woman pointing her price reducing gun and grimacing, with the message, "Pull the trigger on savings."

Military references are quite plentiful. Hyland's "Defend" cold medicine advises "Your own defenses are your best defenses." A magazine ad by Women Against Osteoporosis, titled "The Fracture Fighters," pictures a woman, labelled "The Warrior," a doctor, labelled "The Ally," and "The Weapon," which is the product. Another example is a magazine ad that urges women to become "action heroes," exclaiming, "We want to join forces with you." Another is an ad for "Flower Bomb" perfume. Redd Remedies has a magazine ad entitled "Introducing Our Warriors," which "help with the battle" against colds and flu. A magazine ad for Syntol AMD candida remedy tells consumers: "Don't surrender to candida. End the war today!" These ads are clear reflections of the ideology of the culture of violence.

The hostile and violent world of media advertising propels young people's hostility and alienation. The Nintendo television campaign, among others, has encouraged young people to vent hostility toward parents and society. They recommend such hostile acts as turning up the volume as far as it goes ("Be heard. Play it loud.") and showing all-around contempt by the ad's command to "Hock a loogie at life." Bob Garfield, a columnist for *Advertising Age*, concludes that Nintendo is positioning itself as "the badge of sullen militancy." He wrote sarcastically: "Pour gasoline on the fire of teenage anger. Encourage kids to be rude.... Assist young people in their often perilous search for identity by suggesting they embrace the most garish kind of self-centered nihilism.... What greater service can an advertiser perform against the background of teen suicide, for example, than to trumpet the meaninglessness of human existence? Bravo."[119]

By the late 1970s, the alcohol industry was spending almost one billion dollars a year on advertising. Beer and wine are among the most advertised products on television. Teenagers are exposed to more than 1,000 ads for beer, wine, and liquor each year. Their exposure was amplified by massive amounts of advertising for alcohol products in such magazines as *Sports Illustrated*, *Playboy*, and *Cosmopolitan*. Drinking is shown to be appropriate in a wide range of situations, and it is done by people who are youthful, physically attractive, healthy, and affluent. Negative consequences, not surprisingly, are never depicted.[120] The internet adds to this mix. There are chat rooms in the form of virtual recipes for "bridge drinks" or "alco-pop," sweet alcohol drinks designed to encourage new drinkers to try hard alcohol. Over 60 percent of these sites are specifically designed to appeal to college and high school students. According to a report by the Center for Media

Education, "These sites exude a joyful attitude about drinking—that it is good, clean, sexy and rebellious fun that doesn't hurt anybody.[121] Teenagers may be particularly receptive to alcohol advertising. Research indicates that advertising is more strongly related to both beer and liquor drinking than is parental influence, age, gender, church attendance, or social status. The teenagers who were already drinking said they would drink more because of high exposure to ads and the nondrinkers who were heavily exposed expressed an intention to drink in the future.[122]

Another negative consequence of relentless, intrusive advertising is reflected in the saying: "When the going gets tough, the tough go shopping." Hyper-consumption in the United States has resulted in an all-time high rate of personal bankruptcies. People in the United States and, to a lesser extent, people in other industrialized countries, have become hyper-consumers. Hyper-consumption is the underlying cause of environmental destruction. Todd Gitlin commented: "The velocity, gaudiness and high-dose stimulus that kids get from TV and the nonstop bombardment with messages equating the good life with consumer splendor . . . is itself a factor leading toward restless dissatisfaction that translates into criminality."[123] Consider an impoverished child who sees the "good life" portrayed on television programs and thousands of commercials for products from fast food to cars, which the child's family cannot afford. To what extent do such commercials fuel thefts and robberies?

Women especially have been targeted by the advertising industry, resulting in a distorted sense of female beauty and body shape.[124] Extreme results are anorexia and plastic surgery. In her educational video *Still Killing Us Softly* (1988), Jean Kilbourne pointed out how the relentlessly denigrating and objectifying depictions of women in advertising have cumulative effects, ranging from low self-esteem among girls and women to anorexia and bulimia to increases in violence against women. A study of college men found that watching sexualized portrayals of women led to moral disengagement and rape myths, such as thinking "She asked for it"[125]

Advertising is becoming more and more sexy. Young people are featured in near nudity and highly provocative poses, some of which suggest sexuality. An example is an ad for Masquerade perfume which shows a man unzipping a woman's dress while they are in the throes of passion. Another is a Schick razor ad, featuring a semi-nude man and woman who are throwing water on each other with the caption "Hydration when you least expect it." As syndicated columnist John Leo tells it: "Calvin Klein is at it again, this time with a series of bus and magazine ads showing young teens poised in what look like opening scenes from a porn movie. . . . It's not just in our face and totally inappropriate on buses. It's decadent."[126]

Furthermore, it is risky. Television exposes children to adult behaviors like sex. It seldom shows the risks and results of sexual activities. Sex is shown as "normal, fun, exciting and without consequences."[127] A current magazine ad for "Bang" cologne for men features, in the center of the full-page ad, a bronze, beautiful nude young man, looking sultrily at the viewer, and holding a large square, gold bottle that proclaims "Bang" over his genitals. Another advertisement that objectifies the female body simply shows a woman's almost nude protruding rear end.

A spokesperson for Calvin Klein told the *Washington Post* that their target population is made up of a generation that's independent and media-savvy. They are "people who do only what they want to do." The *Post* reporter Robin Givhan summed up this analysis as, "Hence, the rule-breaking attitude of the ads."[128] This rule-breaking attitude is evident in such ad slogans as Burger King's "Sometimes you just gotta break the rules." A video game ad features a teacher who admonishes children to: "Stay within the lines. The lines are our friends." Saab's contribution is "Peel off inhibitions. Find your own road," and Nike's is "We are all hedonists and we want what feels good. That's what makes us human."[129] Advertisements exploit the human need for freedom. Even product labels tap into the adolescent desire for rebellion; for example, Rockstar's "Revolt" energy drink contains "killer citrus." The hedonistic message is if it feels good, just do it. In order to feel good, according to the advertisements, we must buy their products.

Taking this a step further, we can acquire freedom and power by buying certain products. Since the 1980s, advertisers have been using the word "power" in ads, especially in ones for cars and technological that target men. The implicit and explicit messages of these ads is that the consumer can acquire power by purchasing the products. Apple Computer's slogan is "The power to be your best." A Gateway Computers ad asked: "Who says you have to be rich to have a lot of power?" Subaru claims that its 2.5 GT "clings to a surface so well you'll swear you have superpowers." Prost-Mate, a male nutritional supplement, has an ad that promises "Power to the prostate!" Advertising slogans are fortified by other media messages. An example is a cover of *Fortune Magazine* that features a man with clenched fists glaring and facing the reader with the captions "Silicon Valley's Stealth Power" and "Ben Horowitz is Schooling Tech's Young Guns." Reminiscent of Marx's concern about "false needs," a Volvo magazine ad claims: "Now you can satisfy your need for power and control." This is an example of another ad that tells consumers what their nature is and what their needs are. A Mastercard magazine ad displays a gold credit card in a man's hand with the message, "We place the power in your hands." GTE's slogan was "The power is on," and featured ads that hyperbolically promised to "give you the power to open any darkness." Similarly, Equitable Insurance promises "Power over tomorrow." Planet Reebok promises that the consumer "can be all-powerful and run the world," and an ad for the *Tiberian Sun* strategy war game promises that playing the game makes the gamer "the most powerful person on earth." "Power" also increasingly is being used with ads aimed at women: Optima Women's Probiotics exclaims: "A probiotic as powerful as you. Super. Strength." Cleaning products now have cleaning power. Arm and Hammer's product, "Crystal Burst," has "powerful cleaning at a fraction of the cost!" and features "Two powerful laundry forces." Clorox advises consumers to buy its products, which have "the power to clean anything," and "Get the power." The effects of repeated images, themes, and words over time, in the words of Jean Kilbourne, are "cumulative and unconscious." The advertising industry has tapped into an element of human nature—the desire to be competent, capable, and effective. The use of these repeated images and words reinforces a cultural ethos, giving it more—in a word—power.

Advertisements depersonalize and objectify people. Human heads often are portrayed as resembling computers or parts of machinery. This dehumanization also is seen in some ads, especially sexual ads, that do not include the person's head in the ad. An Apple computer ad proclaims that "Stacy is state-of-the art" while cartoons show computers behaving in human-like ways. Other examples include a television ad for mayonnaise that shows people embedded in bread to make sandwiches, and an Ultimate Flora probiotics ad superimposes a machine over a woman's stomach and relates: "Your gut is your engine." While ads depersonalize people, they personalize products. An example is a television ad that features cheddar cheese claiming to be smart and telling jokes, or a Kellogg's magazine ad that features "Mini-Wheats" saying "Hey!," "Hi!," and "Supp?" A Pepperidge Farm ad describes Goldfish crackers as "The snack that smiles back." Their magazine ad features Goldfish snacks saying: "We're serious about using real cheddar cheese. Would these faces lie?"

Over time advertisements have become more frightening and more violent. One of the first television ads to use violence was in the mid-1970s, in which a drive-through Jack-in-the-Box exploded. More recent violence in ads includes a television ad in which a man is accidentally shot in the chest by a dart while the characters laughed. A newspaper ad for Security Finance shows a boy face down in a swimming pool, apparently dead. The ad reads: "Are you drowning in debt? Try us!" Such messages and images further desensitize the consumer and help to cultivate the sense of a mean and threatening world. John Leo notes that the advertising industry strikes "at the sense of connectedness that any society needs. . . . They are busy financing our social meltdown."[130]

Advertisements also are more menacing. An example is an ad for a film in which Dennis Hopper, sniffing the shoe of Bruce Willis, tells the audience that Smith "does bad things, man, bad things." This implies that this show carries the threat of "bad things."[131] It also suggests that doing bad things is cool, if not good. Such advertisements reinforce and help to perpetuate a "mean and threatening" worldview. This worldview is reinforced by the names of products, such as sneakers called "Aggression," clothes for young men that proclaim, "No Fear," and clothing for young women called "Cruel Girl." A dangerous world also is projected through camera angles and speed. Advertiser-sponsored studies indicate that the best way to get viewers to pay attention is to capitalize on the brain's instinctive responses to danger. Sudden close-ups, pans, and zooms are effective in alerting the brain because they violate its need to maintain a predictable personal space.[132] Advertisements contribute to the preoccupation with speed in the culture of violence. For example, a recruiting ad for the navy proclaims: "You and the Navy. Full speed ahead." An ad for Citizen watches commands: "Live at the speed of light"; a Power Mac G4 ad advises: "Move over, speed of light."

A key part of advertising effectiveness is branding. To find profit in so many similar items, marketers try to brand a product in the consumer's mind. Branding is the process of imprinting an advertising slogan, logo, or song so that they are remembered and motivate people to buy the product. One way to imprint branding is to repeat the name, message, or image three times in order to make a synaptic connection in the brain. An early example is a 1970s Certs breath mint commercial that said, "Two, two, two mints in one." Print and electronic ads use this device and also repeat images at least three times.

Naomi Klein, in *No Logo*, tracks the birth of "brand marketing" to the mid-1980s, which saw the emergence of a new kind of corporation. Nike, Calvin Klein, and Tommy Hilfiger, to name a few, changed their primary corporate focus from making products to creating a name.[133]

Branding and product recognition become deeply engrained throughout the consumer's life cycle and become part of taken-for-granted everyday reality.[134]

Advertisements illustrate how worldviews are "mutually formed and forming." The images reflect and reinforce the social climate simultaneously. Creators and producers of advertisements themselves have been socialized by the culture of violence and so are exporting what they have learned. To make profit, these exports are based on hyperbole and yet more "pow." The bar is being raised continuously. Advertising images and messages are emblematic of the culture of violence and reinforce that culture. Hyper-consumption of products extends to other arenas and helps to promote a "sex, drugs and rock 'n' roll" mentality among many young people. This is accompanied by messages and images that embody objectification, hyper-sexuality, and violence.

Some people argue that the advertising industry is necessary for the economy. However, consider the following. Since the1950s, people have accumulated more than five times the amount of material wealth. However, personal bankruptcies have been at an all-time high for decades. Politicians use advertising techniques to manipulate voters, and the earth is being destroyed because of hyper-consumption.

Neuromarketing

In his book, *Mechanical Bride*, Marshall McLuhan compares Hollywood and advertising. He writes: "So Hollywood is like the ad agencies in constantly striving to enter and control the unconscious minds of a vast public, not in order to understand it or to present these minds ... but in order to exploit them for profit.... The ad agencies and Hollywood, in their different ways, are always trying to get inside the public mind in order to impose their collective dreams on that inner stage."[135] As with much of McLuhan's thinking, this is prophetic.

Tremendous market forces are at work to increasingly probe and measure brain response to commercial messages. The advertising industry has been conducting such research into brain response for almost fifty years.[136] Since the 1960s, the National Advertising Research Council has been conducting research in how the brain responds to television ads. In the early 1970s, Wilson Bryan Key wrote *Subliminal Seduction*, which pointed out how sexual and violent images are imbedded in print ads in order to arouse emotions to sell products. This process has continued with electronic media.

Since 2002, branding has been taken to a whole new level by the development of neuromarketing. Just as learning to read or practicing the piano can physically alter the brain's cerebral cortex (which is responsible for decision-making), the intense, fast, and repetitive stimulation from screen advertisements may affect the brain circuits involved in making decisions. The new field of neuromarketing monitors brain activity in response to electronic images and messages. Neuromarketing focuses on sensory and cognitive responses, research that enables scientists to uncover subconscious responses as well as the precise point at which a commercial message loses its effectiveness. Attention levels, degree of emotional engagement, and the ability to retain information are examined to assist with marketing.

The BrightHouse Institute for Thought Sciences revolutionized marketing by using the MRI to identify patterns of brain activity that reveal how a consumer evaluates a product. This reveals which parts of the brain react to different types of advertising. Marketing analysts then use this information to more accurately measure consumer preference and then apply this knowledge to help marketers create and design products.[137] Adam Koval of BrightHouse said, "We will enable our clients and partners to design advertising, marketing campaigns and eventually products that will effectively engage and drive their target audiences behavior."[138] The Nielsen marketing enterprise has partnered with NeuroFocus, a company that measures brain waves for marketing. A. K. Pradeep, CEO of NeuroFocus, says, "Literally as a thought or a feeling is forming or coalescing in your mind, we get to catch it."[139]

Neuromarketing epitomizes what Stuart Hills, citing Hannah Arendt, calls "the banality of evil" and demonstrates the principle of profit at any cost. Neuromarketing is a prime example of electronic media's ability to influence behavior. This intrusive method of manipulation is cause for concern because it also can be used to promote political candidates and ideologies.

Cohort Analysis

The escalation of media violence and its effects can be illustrated by a cohort analysis. A cohort analysis looks at significant events in the life of a generation, usually considered to be ten years, and is based on when people are born and what they experience during their lifetimes. A cohort analysis related to exposure to violent entertainment media takes into account the fact that people born in recent decades are exposed to television at an earlier age, watch more television, watch more televised sex and violence, and are exposed to television that is more realistic and engaging. As such, younger generations would be more impacted because of continuous technological development and increased graphic violence.

In 1950, for example, a television was a small box that emitted black and white images and less realistic sound. The progression of more gratuitous and graphic violence can be seen by comparing, the 1952 movie *Shane* with the 1967 film *The Good, Bad, and the Ugly* and with later slasher movies. Similarly, with television, early westerns, for example, were innocuous in terms of violence. Killing rarely occurred. In the 1960s, television became a more realistic and engaging experience. Color was introduced on a wide scale in 1968, in time to provide more realistic coverage of the Vietnam War. Stereo sound heightened the realism as well. Rather than the early twelve-inch diagonal screen of the 1950s, now many people have large plasma wall screens with sharper images in "living color." Samsung now offers a three-dimensional television, the price of which has been cut by two-thirds.[140] Current representations can be more realistic than the real world. An example is the camera zooming in to film the retina of a person's eye. The electronic media now has the ability to project superhuman abilities, in this case, a sense of omnipresence, the ability to be everywhere.

Another aspect of cohort affects is the dynamic of the media's use of hyperbole, which, by its nature, needs to increase over time. This continuously raises the threshold in terms of, for example, the speed and frequency of images and the frequency, severity, and magnitude of violence. The bar, which is market-driven, constantly is being raised and has direct effects. Consider, for example, National Geographic nature shows on television. In the past decade, these shows have begun to focus on predators stalking, chasing, killing, and eating prey. This is new. The content, form, and presentation have become amplified over time, causing the increased use of hyperbole in everyday life and behavior, such as exaggerated body movements and facial expressions. It also shows up in language, such as the commonly used words "absolutely," "great," "awesome," and "perfect." Hyperbole is exemplified in a recent YouTube response: "That dog dances 300,000,000 times better than I do!"

Other Findings

So, what can we conclude about the effects of the media? Media violence in itself is a risk factor for children. Some children have protective factors that reduce or mitigate the effects of media violence, and other children may have risk factors that enhance the effects of media violence.

Violent media reality is not life-affirming, and it eradicates compassion. The values, attitudes, and behaviors projected by the entertainment media represent the antithesis of human nature. The media play a predominant role in the culture of disrespect that exists among young people. The media have fostered "a culture in which disrespectful behavior becomes a legitimate way for people to treat each other."[141] The media erode civility by "demeaning and displacing positive social values."[142]

The media also contributes to youth culture by facilitating the epidemic problems of poor academic performance, poor reading ability, inattention, and loss of language. Media culture creates an addiction to speed and excitement. Some young people are addicted to media violence. The result is boredom with the real world.

The "mean and threatening" world of media has helped to create a culture that is increasingly characterized by mean-spiritedness, a lack of empathy, disrespect, and aggression. This culture also is characterized more by fear, separation, and alienation. The media have contributed greater risks to behavior and to health disorders, ranging from posttraumatic stress disorder to substance abuse to diabetes to suicide. Hyper-consumption ruins personal and national economies and plays a key role in the destruction of the environment.

One of the most insidious outcomes of media socialization is the idea that violence is fun. Fun is the most predominant theme of children's programming, which is also exciting, fast, and violent. Because television is a modal experience for so many children, the importance of fun spills over into other activities. It is very telling that young people tend to describe experiences as either "boring" or "fun."

Consider the following true stories.

A candidate for public office was speaking to a large group of college students. He said something to which a male student responded with a sarcastic and funny statement. The speaker pretended to kick him in the head. With few exceptions, the students responded with smiles and delighted laughter.[143]

For two years, Johnny, a quiet thirteen-year-old, was a human plaything for some of his classmates. The teenagers badgered Johnny for money, forced him to swallow weeds and drink milk mixed with detergent, beat him up in the restroom, tied a string around his neck, and led him around as a "pet." When Johnny's torturers were asked about the bullying, they said they pursued their victim because "it was fun."

Barry Loukaitis, age fourteen, who killed three students and injured another in Moses Lake, Washington, had said that it would be "fun to go on a killing spree."[144] Similarly, a friend of school shooter Kip Kinkel related that Kip "always said that it would be fun to kill someone and do stuff like that."[145]

Media Literacy

The Senate Committee on the Judiciary's media violence report concludes: "Plainly, any solution to the juvenile violence problem that's to address media violence is doomed to failure."[146] They came to such a conclusion because they had not taken into account the need to address the destructive effects of the entertainment media. As citizens and as societies we need to become more media literate and to become aware of the technological functions and political dynamics of the media.[147] Media literacy is a protective factor that can be provided in the classroom and for families. Media literacy gives consumers the tools to respond thoughtfully and critically to media content. It helps people to put media images and messages into perspective, and diffuses some of their power.

The American Academy of Pediatrics recommends that parents teach their children how media influence their values, attitudes, and behavior.[148] The problem is that teachers, parents, and grandparents also have been influenced by media, of course. Parents, on average, watch television about 1,000 minutes a week, and talk, play, and read with their children for about sixty minutes. Adults need to recognize their own dependency on media and start from there. Cathy Wing, codirector of Canada's Media Awareness Network, has commented that a parent also can be "a slave to the screen."[149] The first step is to limit the number of hours the parents and children spend in front of a screen. The academy recommends that children under the age of two watch no television and that older children should watch quality screen time for no more than two hours a day. In order to facilitate this, the academy recommends that parents create an "electronic media-free" environment in all children's rooms.[150] The American Academy of Pediatrics recommends that adults cut screen time by one-third.[151] The resulting free time for children and adults can be used to, as Freire suggests, follow our human vocation to become more fully human.

Media literacy for children and families is necessary to create informed young citizens and peaceful schools. The purpose of media literacy is to help children take charge of the media in their lives by fostering creative play to counteract the negative impact of media culture. Awareness of a negative influence softens its impact. It becomes less pernicious than it might otherwise be. Media literacy brings to light the motivation, structure, and influence of media messages and images. It helps children see the transparency and manipulation of advertising and other images and messages. Media literacy shows that media productions are not windows to reality. Young people's eyes are opened when they realize that the primary reason for media violence is money. Media literacy can help them articulate their feelings and attitudes about violence in real life as well as on the screen. It also teaches young people that they have a role to play as media consumers and that they can become media activists. Because of this, media literacy promotes democracy and informed citizens.

Research has shown that reducing exposure to violent media and changing children's attitudes about media violence and helping them understand it significantly reduce aggression.[152] Media literacy also improves critical thinking and creativity.[153] It also improves body mass index because children learn to spend less time sitting in front of a screen. This also is due to being less exposed to junk food and fast food commercials.[154] Stanford University created the Student Media Awareness to Reduce Television program (SMART) using a research-based curriculum that has demonstrated a reduction in student aggression, a decrease in obesity, and an increase in academic achievement. Because of the program, student aggression decreased, ranging from 25 to 80 percent in eight different school sites.[155] Media literacy also results in improved academic performance because less time is displaced by screen time, because media literacy promotes critical thinking, and because children spend less time involved in this right cerebral hemisphere activity.

How can media literacy be incorporated into classroom curricula? How can a school promote and facilitate family media literacy? First of all, it is good to realize that media literacy costs almost nothing. For example, students can bring magazine advertisements to class and be given homework assignments to record advertisements, which would then be analyzed in class using a variety of deconstruction methods that promote critical thinking. They also could bring videos of their favorite programs that would then be analyzed. Children can be taught how to teach media literacy to their families, an inherently self-empowering activity, such as defining and counting the frequency of aggressive and violent acts. Young people can become empowered by creating their own media. This can range from making a collage of magazine advertisements to a documentary video. Media literacy is an ideal way to teach critical thinking and to encourage reading. Asking the young to dissect their electronic culture and creating a truer media is empowering. It enables young people (and older people), as Freire would say, to "name their world" rather than have it named and created for them.

Discussion

Since the 1950s a massive amount of research has been conducted about media violence. During this time, people have been exposed to more graphic violent media at earlier ages and for longer amounts of time. Also during this time, technological development has rendered the entertainment media more violent and more realistic. With remarkably few exceptions, media researchers now conclude that exposure to violent media increases aggression and violence. The violent media industries are intrinsic to the culture of violence. They promote a culture of mean-spiritedness, sex, drugs, and consumerism. They project an affluent world and promote consumption to the point of many bankruptcies and pollution endangering the planet. The advertising industry's purpose is to sell and to profit. They socialize people to become consumers before citizens. To maximize profits, the advertisers have developed neurologically intrusive methods to manipulate people into buying their products. This has Orwellian implications. Consumers are being manipulated into buying more and are being "entertained to death." This happens at the expense of being active contributors to their communities and their world. The values and ideology projected by violent entertainment media are contrary to human nature. Violent media desensitize people and teach the antithesis of empathy, equality, and respect.

Corporate Responsibility

The core issue is media industry irresponsibility, that is, its placement of profit above social and environmental costs. This has not always been so. The Code of the National Association of Broadcasters (NAB) advised the following: "In selecting program subjects and themes, great care must be exercised to be sure that the treatment and presentation are made in good faith and not for the purpose of sensationalism or to shock or exploit the audience or to appeal to prurient interests or morbid curiosity."[156] The code was abandoned in 1983. Three provisions of the code that restricted the sale of advertising were challenged by the Department of Justice on antitrust grounds. A federal district court issued a summary judgment against the NAB. Since then, programming standards, in the words of the 1999 Juvenile Justice Act, have "deteriorated dramatically."[157]

Similar to the tobacco industry's denial of the smoking–cancer link in favor of its corporate interests, the media industry has denied the connection between viewing and violence.[158] This is compounded by news sources' refusal to cover media violence research findings. Based on its investigation of media violence in 1999, the Senate Committee on the Judiciary requested the industry volunteer to decrease violence and other objectionable content. In a similar vein, the 1999 Juvenile Justice Act asked the industry to volunteer to improve programming. This has not worked. George Lucas, creator of *Star Wars*, warned that films "are extremely violent in a context that violence is fun; hurting other people is a very negative thing. People in the film industry ... should take personal responsibility for what they're saying and what they're doing."[159] In its efforts to do what it wants to do, the entertainment media has relied on First Amendment protection of freedom of expression and labels attempts to regulate censorship. This is ironic, considering that gate-keeping and agenda-setting by the media can itself be construed as censorship.

Legislation

Media violence and industry responsibility has been a public policy issue in a number of Western countries. Central to the debate has been the challenge of accommodating what may appear to be opposing principles—the protection of children from unsuitable media content and upholding the right to freedom of expression.

In the United States where television began as a commercial enterprise, the First Amendment, ensuring free speech and freedom of the press, has been used to argue against any government intervention in the operation of media organizations. The Canadian Constitution also guarantees freedom of expression, but it embodies a more comprehensive understanding of what freedom of expression means. Their constitution acknowledges that reasonable limits can be placed on individual rights for the greater good of society. In Canada, England, Australia, and many European countries, television began with the premise that any enterprise using public airwaves had a social responsibility.[160] The highly touted Children's Television Act of 1990 required television networks to devote time to educational and informative programming, which is currently three hours a week.[161] The act makes no provisions for reducing objectionable content, including violence, but encourages parents to monitor media consumption. The problem is that many parents, as well as grandparents, are "slaves to the screen" and so are not inclined to intervene effectively.[162]

The Telecommunications Act of 1996 requires, among other things, V-chip technology to be included in most television sets sold in the United States. The V-chip is a technological tool that parents can use to control children's exposure to televised violence that was introduced in the United States in 2000. The V-chip is a Canadian invention. It was developed with a classification system that ensured that foreign signals offered by Canadian distributors were encoded with a classification system. Much of this effort was in response to the availability of violent television broadcast from the United States.[163] However, the V-chip has proven to be of limited value in reducing children's exposure to violent programming.[164] The V-chip does not work effectively in the United States because shows are not properly rated or else they lack the proper content indicators. The effectiveness of the V-chip in this country also is confounded because parents have indicated they are not aware of the V-chip, do not believe it is necessary, or do not know how it works. As a result, only about 15 percent of families utilize the V-chip.[165]

Placing responsibility on the parents also does not recognize that the source of the problem is created and broadcast from outside the home. The Federal Trade Commission reports that media industries "promote products they themselves acknowledge warrant parental caution in venues where children make up a substantial percentage of the audience." The report continues that the companies in media industries "still routinely target children under 17 in their marketing of products their own rating systems deem inappropriate or [that] warrant parental caution due to violent content."[166]

Robert McChesney, author of *Corporate Media and the Threat to Democracy*, points out: "The first task for changing the media system is to put control of the media on the political agenda—exactly where it belongs in a democratic society."[167] If enforced, legislation can be an effective way to improve children's programming. Renewed endorsement of the Children's Television Act of 1990 had a positive effect. The possibility of stricter enforcement resulted in broadcasts airing more educational programs and stopping the practice of defining such programs as *The Flintstones* as educational.[168] At the very least, the Federal Communications Commission should strengthen rules implementing the Children's Television Act of 1990.

The National Parent-Teachers' Association, the National Education Association, and the Center for Media Education, as well as other groups, have called on the Federal Communications Commission to: Provide television stations with a clearer definition of educational and informational programming; give broadcasters guidelines clarifying what qualifies as educational and informational programming; and give broadcasters guidelines about how much educational and informational programming is enough.[169] None of these have happened.

Canada has drawn upon the work of other countries, notably Australia, New Zealand, England, and France. The basis for global action is already in place, with the Canadian approach having attracted considerable international attention. France, England, Germany, Sweden, Norway, and Eastern European countries have shown interest in how some of its elements might be adapted to meet their needs.

Producers and broadcasters consistently have concluded that the First Amendment has given them free rein in creating images and messages that are not in the public's best interest.[170] What about the rights of children? The United Nation's 1989 Convention on the Rights of the Child, Article 17, concurred that state parties should "encourage the development of appropriate guidelines for the protection of the child from information and material injurious to his or her well-being."

Canada's Radio-Television and Telecommunications Commission chair Keith Spicer has commented that "the challenge consists of balancing rights: the rights of artists and entrepreneurs and adult viewers to freedom of expression, and the rights of children to be protected from truly harmful violence. And today's children—we should never forget—will define the problems and the health of tomorrow's society."[171]

Censorship is no longer the issue. As the Center for Media Literacy stated it: The issue is "no longer one of protecting free speech but of protecting human life."[172] The rights of citizens and consumers need to be considered within the fullest scale of the intent of the founding documents of the United States, which guarantee the right to "life, liberty, and the pursuit of happiness." The media, as they are now constituted, obstruct these basic rights.

In an increasingly unregulated world, the protection of children cannot rely on the violence industries volunteering to change. Protection relies on the vigilance and activism of media-aware parents, public pressure from consumers and professional groups, and other decision-makers.

The ability of electronic entertainment media to create a virtual reality is epitomized by the virtual world of violent video games. The following two chapters further explore the effects of exposure to violent electronic entertainment media.

CHAPTER 8

FUN AND GAMES: A VIRTUAL REALITY

> We are what we repeatedly do.
> —Aristotle

This chapter brings to light why violent video games have become loved and omnipresent in the lives of hundreds of millions of people around the world. By the year 2000, global video game sales reached $20 billion. By 2017, sales reached $113 billion.[1]

Violent video games are an extension of war toys and war games. Generations of young people have displayed an extraordinary attraction to video games, especially violent games, and have been profoundly influenced by them. Of course, not all video games are violent. They also may be positive teaching tools. Since the early 1980s, research has shown that video games can be useful teaching tools to aid the development of perceptual and motor skills.[2] International research shows that prosocial games increase prosocial cognitions, affect, and helpful behavior.[3] Some video games produce increases in empathy and prosocial behavior.[4] Video games can be very effective in teaching children higher level thinking skills, such as problem-solving, evaluating possible actions, and experimenting with ideas.[5]

Video games for children mimic the genre of children's television cartoons. It is commonly thought that the violence in video games for children is benign. However, one of the most important research findings is that children's violent video games can lead to aggression among children if the games contain a lot of violent action. Research has revealed that the "happy music, cute cartoonish characters and nonhuman enemies characteristic of children's violent video games do not eradicate the aggression-inducing potential of these games."[6] The video games that are regarded as educational, however, also may impede the person's growth because they obstruct involvement and growth in the real world. Video games, like other electronic entertainment media, displace time that can be spent developing and enjoying other leisure-time skills, such as playing the guitar. Video games displace time that could be used to develop positive and productive skills and also allow players to simulate the development of skills. *Guitar Hero* and *Rock Band* allow players to simulate playing the guitar rather than learning to play the guitar.

Since they were first introduced, violent video games have been more popular than nonviolent ones.[7] In a recent study, over half of the children involved preferred games dominated by themes of human violence or fantasy violence.[8] From this, one could conclude that it is the nature of children to be attracted to violence. However, this finding needs to be interpreted within the matrix of influences generated by the culture of violence, in which many children are exposed to war toys and graphic media violence while they are still infants and toddlers.

A Brief History of Video Games

To understand the degree of influence that video games currently exert, we need to look at changes in viewing patterns, content, and technological capability since their introduction. Video games have changed dramatically since 1972 when *Pong*, a simulated ping pong video game, was introduced. The world-creation capability of video games has grown exponentially over time. Video games now are played for longer periods of time and are more engaging, violent, and emotionally gratifying. These factors result in different generations of people being affected differently.

In the 1970s and early 1980s, children played video games in arcades, for at most an hour a day. Games tended to be social events with several participants and onlookers. Nowadays, most children play video games in their homes. It is more likely that the games are solitary activities, often played in the youngster's bedroom. Lone gamers are of particular concern because being a loner predicts violent video game preferences and fuels aggressive inclinations in adolescents.[9]

A 1982 survey found that 24 percent of girls never played video games, and 18 percent of boys were nonplayers. At that time, 93 percent of the children reported sometimes playing video games.[10] In the early 1980s, girls played about an hour a week, and boys played one and one-half hours a week at video arcades.[11] By the late 1980s, children played about four hours a week, and by the 1990s, it was about 4.5 hours a week for fourth grade girls and 7.1 hours a week for fourth grade boys.[12] By the mid-1990s, video game usage increased to 4.5

hours a week for fourth grade girls and 7.1 hours a week for fourth grade boys.[13] By 2004 children aged two to seven played three to five hours a week. Eighth and ninth grade boys reported playing thirteen hours a week, and girls reported playing five hours a week.[14]

As of 2008, 97 percent of children played video games and about 70 percent of the games were violent.[15] The percentage of violent games has increased since that time.

About 45 percent of girls play video games.[16] Boys average sixteen to eighteen hours a week.[17] Some parents report that their children play as many as five hours a day or more.[18] By 2005 about 21 percent of incoming college freshmen played at least six hours per week.[19] Currently, about 3 percent of entering college men play over twenty hours per week.[20] The average age of gamers continues to increase. About 32 percent of the generation that grew up with Atari and Nintendo are playing video games well into adulthood.[21] About two-thirds of surveyed adults indicated they play every day while at work.[22]

Carnagey and Anderson divide the history of video games into three eras.[23] Their first era, from 1977–1985, was what they call the Atari era because Atari consoles dominated the video game market. These games continued to contain little violence. One of the most popular early games, *Pac-Man*, allowed the player to manipulate the character to gobble up little creatures. Nolan Bushnell, the founder of Atari, said, "We have an internal rule that we wouldn't allow violence against people. You could blow up a tank or you could blow up a flying saucer, but you couldn't blow up people."[24] In 1976, the first violent commercial video game to receive attention was *Death Race*, a driving simulator. The goal was to run down stick-figure pedestrians called "gremlins." When struck down, the pedestrians would scream and turn into gravestones. The violent content sparked a public outcry, causing some communities to ban it. Despite the public outcry, the controversy managed to increase sales of the game about tenfold. The public outrage, however, resulted in many game developers having standards for their games, including "no excessive blood and violence."[25]

The second era of the history of video games, 1985–1995, was the Nintendo era. Computers had become more sophisticated and could display more complex graphics. Like Atari before them, Nintendo had game standards. This included "no excessive blood and violence" and "no sex."[26] Despite this, violence appeared more.[27] Even the apparently benign *Mario Bros.* had the capacity to destroy creatures by jumping on them or throwing fireballs at them. It was during this time that video games became common on desktop computers and in hand-held mini-game systems such as Game Boy.

The mid-1980s and early 1990s introduced one-on-one fighting games that pushed the violence envelope and became all-time best-sellers. In 1987 *Double Dragon*, the first hand-to-hand fighter game, was introduced. In this game two martial arts masters fight to defeat the Black Warriors gang in order to rescue a captive woman. Some of the basic characteristics of violent video games emerged during this era. *Mortal Kombat*, introduced in 1992, was a type of fighting game, which allow the gamer to tear out the opponent's vital organs. Such one-on-one fighting games "pushed the boundaries of violence and became all-time best-sellers."[28] Nintendo and Sega then both created versions of *Mortal Kombat* for their competing systems. This violence was still quite stylized for the most part because of technological limitations. Nonetheless, the economic benefits of explicit violence became apparent. Nintendo had toned down the blood and gore in their version of *Mortal Kombat*. However, the Sega Genesis version, which was much more violent, out-sold Nintendo's version three to one. This led to the decline of Nintendo as the market leader and to the conclusion that violence sells.[29]

The year 1992 was a pivotal one in video game technological development because first-person shooter games became widely popular. First-person shooter games that center on military themes, such as *Call of Duty* and *Medal of Honor*, have been especially popular. Since that time, players can look down the gun barrel directly at the intended victims, rendering the killing more intimate and more realistic. With its high-definition relentless action, first-person shooters have an often intensely violent virtual experience.

This innovation dramatically heightened the games' realism and set the stage for increasingly realistic and engaging shooting and war games. First-person shooter games are much more engaging and immersive than third-person shooter games. *Wolfenstein 3D*, introduced in 1992, popularized the first-person game genre. The game was very violent for its era. The player advanced by exploring a maze-like fortress and killing Nazi soldiers. The player would see multiple horrendous murders and hear victims scream and groan. Video game historian Steven Kent noted that "part of *Wolfenstein*'s popularity sprang from its shock value." In previous games, when players shot enemies, the injured targets fell and disappeared. In *Wolfenstein 3D* enemies fell and bled on the floor.[30] *Wolfenstein 3D*, advertised as "Blowing Nazis Away with a Gatling Gun," created the commando style of military war games. "To charge into a building and try to kill as many people as possible is an enactment of video game violence."[31] The first-person shooter games made the players feel not only that they were the ones fighting and killing, but it also gave them opportunities to be killed. Because of this, these dark games are linked to aggressive behavior and also may be linked to the sharp rise in teen suicide since the games' inception.

By 1993, the next major first-person shooter game *Doom* created a new threshold of violence, including even more blood and gore. And, in addition to monsters and demons, it was a death-match game that allowed players to hunt and kill each other. This game was followed by *Quake* the same year. The game featured realistic explosions and immersed the player in a hellish, dungeon-like environment. *Quake* showed the potential for 3D piloting, multiplayer networking, and virtual reality-based training.

The third era of the video game is from 1995 to the present. The Sony PlayStation dominates the console game market. Graphic capabilities have been greatly enhanced because of technological improvements and also because Sony switched from cartridge-based systems to CD-ROM and DVD-ROM-based systems. In addition to PlayStation 4, video game buyers also have the option of buying Nintendo's latest console, Nintendo Switch, or Microsoft's XBox One X. Gaming has grown exponentially because of such technological innovations.[32]

The extraordinary increase in speed and graphic capability has made the violence even more realistic and engaging. In 2000, *Soldier of Fortune* marked a new high in video game realism. In this game, the player explores a city in order to kill terrorists and rescue hostages. This game was designed in collaboration with a retired army colonel, and it identifies twenty-six different "killing zones" on the body. The game characters respond realistically to the shots depending on where in the body they are shot, with what weapons, and from what distance. Shooting a character at close range in the arm, for example, rips the arm from the socket, leaving bone and sinew exposed while blood rushes from the wound.[33]

Other first-person shooter war games include *The World of Warcraft*. Such games allow the player to create a character and to log into a world of warfare that has fully interactive capabilities. The goal, as with all war video game plots, is to kill as many people as possible as quickly as possible in order to win. *The World of Warcraft* has 10 million subscriptions in the United States alone.

In 2002, the ultra-violent *Grand Theft Auto* emerged on the scene and became the most popular game in the world.[34] In *Grand Theft Auto III* the players use cars to run down simulated pedestrians, then beat them with their fists, leaving behind a bloody body. In *Grand Theft Auto: San Andreas* players can carjack vehicles, run down pedestrians, commit drive-by shootings, pick up a prostitute, have sex with her and then kill her. Devin Moore, aged eighteen, spent months playing the game. When he was arrested for stealing a car, he grabbed the police officer's gun and shot three officers in less than a minute.[35]

In 2004 *Doom II* was created, a game in which players advanced by exploring a maze-like environment while killing graphically realistic monsters.[36] *Doom III* expanded these capabilities. In the words of one reviewer, "the illusion the game creates is so realistic... there is a crispness to details, a weight and solidity to objects and figures, a lifelike sheen to surfaces in Doom III that is unlike anything we've seen before."[37]

Between 2000 and 2007 these games were 46 percent more violent, eight times more sexually explicit, and thirty times more likely to contain profane language.[38] Now, video games are even more graphic, immersive, interactive, and violent. Examples include *Hitman: Blood Money*, in which an assassin methodically eliminates targets. The player's missions are to rid the world of drug dealers, child pornographers, and other assassins. It's all in a day's work if innocent bystanders are killed.[39] In *Mortal Kombat II* players advance by inflicting fatal damage to a series of opponents. Players receive extra rewards for using extreme violence, such as ripping out an opponent's spine.[40]

A disturbing and escalating marketing trend is for video games to become more misogynistic: marginalizing and objectifying women by allowing players to assault and kill them. Such violent-sexist video games as *Grand Theft Auto: Vice City* allows players to regularly beat up and kill prostitutes. *BMX XXX* enables players to unlock footage of real-life strippers and deliver nearly nude virtual prostitutes to their pimps. *Dead or Alive Xtreme Beach Volleyball* features barely clad women and includes a control that allows gamers to set the "jiggle factor" for the breasts of women players.[41] A content analysis of thirty-three sampled violent video games shows that 41 percent did not feature female characters, 28 percent portrayed women as sex objects, and 21 percent included violence against women.[42] Another content analysis of 571 video games that featured females between 1983 and 2014 consistently found females to play secondary roles and be more sexualized than male characters.[43]

These trends are particularly troubling because people who view pornography tend to hold misogynistic views. Studies show that exposure to violent-sexist games results in gender stereotyping and more aggressive behavior toward females.[44] As such, it is likely that misogyny among male gamers who watch pornography is reinforced by exposure to these games. It is unknown how many female gamers play violent-sexist games and the extent to which these games socialize them to be more accepting of misogyny and to become more male-defined.

Over 85 percent of video games contain some violence, and about half contain serious violence.[45] Players increasingly experience virtual worlds of heightened and relentless exposure to violent images, killings, brutal deaths, mayhem, and wanton destruction. Not only have they been exposed to this violent world, they live, play, kill, and die in it. One observer has commented that "the smell of virtual death lingers over the entire industry."[46]

Consider the following scenario. The person rips out the throat of an enemy by his teeth like a pop can. The person guts the character with his bare hands and tears his head off. He then rips out the lungs and shoves them up to the heart, and then yanks out the rib cage. This is accompanied by the sound of flesh tearing and bones cracking. Actually, this horrifying scene is not from a violent video game. It is paraphrasing from the diary of Eric Harris, one of the Columbine shooters. He added: "I want to grab some week [sic] little freshman and just want to tear them apart."[47]

Advertising for violent video games often touts the violent conduct as a selling point, the more graphic the better. The copy for the game *Destrega* reads: "Let the slaughter begin." The advertisement for the game *Subspace* reads: "Meet people from all over the world, then kill them." The gamer-hero is a mass murderer. Advertisements in such magazines as *PC Gamer* are very telling. Typical ads include such messages as "Gratuitous Violence is 200 Times Faster with a D-Link Network," "No Cure. No Hope. Only Death;" and "Destroying Your Enemies Isn't Enough. . . . You Must Devour Their Souls."[48]

Gamers experience a kind of ecstasy, stepping out of the mundane into a world where they can be all powerful and feel excited, even euphoric. An eight-year-old boy described the violent game he was playing as "fun" and "exciting" and stated that he feels "pumped." A thirty-one-year-old gamer describes his feeling as "joyful, powerful," and "intensely alive." The issue here is that, as related by John Murray, a professor of child psychology at Kansas State University, "repeated rushes of stimulation to store away ever-more-violent images, to be recalled later as a pose to frustration, producing hair-trigger responses and becoming so desensitized that we behave aggressively." He adds that it is of particular concern that now the player is actively involved in constructing the violence.[49]

A Virtual World

Video games have an extraordinary capacity to construct a virtual reality. Realistic, high-definition, three-dimensional graphic engineering has improved so much since that 1980s that "virtual worlds are now scarcely distinguishable from the real world."[50] Video games increasingly appear to be more real than reality. For example, in some games, the gamer can see characters' eyeballs. These worlds are so realistic that they may spark an experience of resonance in which a real-world scene is reminiscent of a violent scene from a virtual world, catalyzing an aggressive or violent reaction. Resonance may help to explain why at times some people "just snap."

The reality-constructing abilities of video games are further enhanced by the development of simulated worlds and interactive drama. Attraction to these games is evident when one considers that *The Sims*, introduced in 2007, is the most popular computer game of all time.[51]

Also, the electronic-surround is becoming increasingly seamless because of the ability of players to create their own worlds. In these worlds, they interact with other people and beings of their own choosing and can, for example, build their own house or city. In their virtual world, they are tremendously powerful. The maker of *Sims* has also created *Spore*. Instead of just providing a vast and prefabricated virtual world for the player to explore, *Spore* allows the player to design the world. The game is freeform in structure and timescale. This means that it is a perpetual electronic universe in which one can play forever. The player begins with a microbe and helps it evolve into a creature of the player's own design. In other words, the game allows the person to play God. The creature spawns and becomes intelligent, then forms societies and populates the planet. The player can then travel to explore a universe of planets and creatures created by other players, downloading this universe from a central server. *Spore* provides "millions and millions of planets, all the fanciful, scary, inspired, or insipid handiwork of thousands or millions of players."[52]

"Interactive drama" is a recent reality-producing feature of video games. One of Ray Bradbury's books, *Fahrenheit 451*, projected a future world in which attempts were made to burn all books. At specified times, the wife of the main character interacts with characters on a gigantic television screen that comprises a major portion of the living room wall. The gamer not only interacts but, to a great degree, creates and controls social interaction with virtual characters, and becomes even more immersed in a virtual social environment. These games are similar to soap operas and reality shows, featuring stories revolving around virtual "actors" and relationships. Players communicate with the computer characters by speaking, as though having a real-life human conversation. Observers see interactive drama showing "promise for being the new high-tech video games of the future."[53]

These games enable the player to simulate an emotional connection with the game's characters. Andrew Stern, one of the creators of the interactive game, *Façade*, in response to the question of what sort of aesthetic experience they had in mind, said: "Making players feel a true connection to characters on the screen. You'd feel like you're immersed in an actual relationship with these characters."[54] Michael Mateas, the other creator, added his expectation for "having the player actually care about the characters." The interviewer concluded that the goal of interactive drama is "emotional catharsis."[55]

Massive multiplayer online role-playing games (MMORPGs) allow players to create their own character for the game and, through playing the game, increase the skills and power of the character. Characters can kill and be killed by other players. *EverQuest*, one of the largest current MMORPGs, has about 400,000 players worldwide.[56] *World of Warcraft* is the largest MMORPG, with an estimated 10 million subscribers. The average *World of Warcraft* player spends 22.7 hours a week engaged in the game as an avatar.[57]

Some researchers conclude that virtual multiplayer games, such as *World of Warcraft*, do not provide fantasy as much as a "real" relationship between a player and the game as a self-conscious reality for the players.[58] Technological innovations are driven by powerful market forces. In addition, it is in the nature of the development of electronic technological innovations to exhibit exponential growth. Will Wright, the designer of *Spore*, said, "Twenty years from now, games will be as personal to you as your dreams, and as emotionally deep and meaningful to you as your dreams."[59]

Let us hope that Wright's vision is simply fanciful because simulated worlds and interactive drama technology are extremely problematic. For real-world relationships, they substitute a world of virtual friends, virtual situations, and virtual power. In these perpetual universes, any virtual thing is possible.[60] Interactive virtual worlds are evolving to make this prediction come true. Parsa discusses the ways that artificial intelligence and cyberintelligence pose dangers. In terms of video games, for example, artificial intelligence could be developed to take a picture of gamers and more realistically place them in the game. This would result in games that are even more engaging, immersive, and addictive.[61]

Simulated worlds with interactive drama present an ominous future for a person's ability to grow and to deal with and change the world.

Engagement in virtual worlds at a young age wields tremendous influence as children increasingly become immersed in a virtual reality that is synergistically reinforced by other modes of electronic entertainment. The lure of a virtual reality is especially strong during times of fiscal and environmental crises, from which many people seek refuge. Virtual worlds of one's own making and in which one has absolute power are incredibly tantalizing.

The existence of a perpetual electronic universe has some frightening aspects. Heavy consumers of video games, especially if coupled with heavy consumption of other electronic entertainment media, increasingly experience a virtual reality. This reality is created by the synergistic interaction of electronic media, which especially affects children who are heavy consumers. In 2010 *Kinect*, a movement game, emerged on the scene, changing controlled character action to player-prompted action resulting in no separation between the player and the game.[62] Also, because the entire body often is involved, it would seem that these games would be more influential. Research now includes studies about haptic, tactile, and tangible entertainment.[63] This research brings to mind Aldous Huxley's *Brave New World* in which he predicted that movies would become "the feelies."

What are the consequences of players creating virtual friends who they may subsequently harm or kill? What is the possibility of this virtual behavior spilling into the real world? As the technology evolves and immersion becomes easier, this scenario becomes more likely.

There also is a growing interest among film directors in changing their movies into video games and also in creating video games themselves. Peter Jackson, the director of *The Lord of the Rings*, stated that "while a film experience for an audience is over after two or three hours, a successful game experience, if it captures the imagination, can last for days."[64] The virtual world, compared to the real world, is gratifying. And it is easy. This facility denies young people opportunities to develop real-world skills and to express their true, unplugged creativity. This displacement obstructs their innate quest to become more fully human. The antithesis of human nature is to teach children to kill and to enjoy it.

Why are so many game players so involved and even passionate about playing video games? The games allow the player to become all-powerful, which is exhilarating, and the games allow anyone to be a winner. The sole point of the game is to win. As one early gamer said: "When you start to think you're a loser, you come in here and get 4,000 Space Invaders and you ain't a loser anymore."[65] Winning is at the heart of hierarchy, and the competitive drive of the culture of violence. In the virtual video game world, winning is all-important. An example is the player decapitating an opponent, accompanied by the caption, "Barrica wins!" It is fun to win. In violent video games, winning means killing. Violent video games embody killing as fun.

Another incentive to play video games is to be a part of epic stories with classic themes. These games allow the player to be a part of something larger, to be powerful, and to be a hero. Video games glorify violence. Many games allow players to be heroes by killing adversaries who are threats to a free world. Typical games cast players in the role of a shooter, with points scored for each "kill." The nature of video games is a self-reinforcing feedback loop. The more skilled the player, the more violence there is in the game.

Misinformation and Disinformation

The question of the effects of violent video games has been debated for decades. This debate has been confounded by faulty research and also because of disinformation and misinformation. The violent video game industry has a colossal vested interest in keeping negative research findings about violent video games from the public. Because of this, very little news about research findings is aired. In addition, the Electronic Software Ratings Board consistently issues incorrect and misleading information as outlined later in this chapter.

Misinformation also obstructs research findings from reaching public awareness. A comparison of news reports and scientific knowledge about violent media effects reveals "a disturbing discontinuity." The average news report has changed from claims of a weak link to a moderate link and then back to a weak link between electronic entertainment, violence, and aggression. Since 1976, however, the scientific confidence and statistical magnitude of this link has been positive and has consistently increased over time.[66] In fact, as scientific evidence has grown stronger, media reports moved in the opposite direction. This has resulted in the public becoming confused about the issue.[67]

An example of televised misinformation is a Fox News report about school shooters. The report claimed that twenty-five of the twenty-six school shooters were "fatherless."[68] This coverage appears to be an attempt to deflect public attention away from pressure to reform gun laws in the wake of the Marjory Stoneman Douglas High School shooting. The Fox News channel is solidly Republican, and the party that is very supportive of the National Rifle Association (NRA). The fact is that there have been hundreds of rampage school shootings, not twenty-six.

Another form of misinformation is the perhaps well-intentioned but misinformed articles in the popular press. An example is a *New York Times* opinion piece about mass shootings and video games that only cited two researchers. The article relied heavily on *Brown v. Entertainment Merchants* (130 S. Ct. 2398, 2010), a First Amendment challenge to a California law regulating sales of certain violent video games to children.[69] The article failed to note that twenty-seven of the thirty-one amicus curiae briefs filed in the Supreme Court were by people or interests that were financially interested in the outcome of the case.[70] The article also failed to note that the Court was biased in favor of researchers with fewer credentials than the more credible researchers who found a connection between media and real-life violence. For example, the mean number of peer-reviewed articles by researchers who found a connection was 39.2. This compares to the naysayers mean number of 1.49 articles.[71] Similarly, in 2010, a Wikipedia entry reported that "several major studies" show a link between video game violence and violence.[72] There actually are hundreds of such studies.

Another aspect of misinformation and disinformation includes questionable research articles. An example is a research article by a media analyst and his colleagues published in 2011. The article claims that there is considerable evidence to the contrary, whereas in actuality there is little evidence to the contrary that is substantial and from well-established researchers.[73] A small but vocal group of researchers consistently disagree with the majority findings. For example, in a *Chicago Tribune* article, one of these researchers wrote: "Any claims that there is consistent evidence that violent video games encourage aggression are simply false."[74] Another example of disinformation is the violent video game industry claiming that the vast majority of video games are not violent.[75] As related earlier, about 85 percent of video games are violent. The following is a summary of representative articles drawn from the hundreds of studies that investigate the influence of violent video games.

The Research

What do the hundreds of studies reveal about the impact of violent video games? The following summary of research focuses on the most salient and most representative of the studies.

Early thinking about violent video game effects swung between a causal connection with aggressive behavior and the idea that these games are cathartic, providing an outlet for aggressive feelings. Many people believed, like Freud, that violent media act as a catharsis, allowing the person to "vent" negative feelings after watching or playing. This belief is still commonly held even though contemporary research does not support such a conclusion.[76] On the contrary, the research finds that viewing, thinking about, or doing aggressive acts tends to increase later aggressive behavior rather than reduce it.[77]

Social scientific research protocol emphasizes using tentative language when discussing causal relationships in the social world. However, research findings now are so consistently compelling that video game researchers are talking about cause and effect without using tentative language. Nowadays, media violence researchers state with confidence that media violence does cause aggression and violence.[78] An example is Dr. Craig Anderson, a preeminent researcher into video game violence, who concludes: "Over two decades of empirical work using a variety of research methods has found conclusive evidence that violent video game play causes later aggressive behavior."[79] To understand this shift in perspective, it is important to note when the research was conducted. Over time, violent video games have come to wield more influence because of increasing player engagement and the greater realism resulting from technological innovations. Research results vary accordingly.

Concerns about violent video games emerged in the early 1980s. Some researchers thought they were potentially hazardous,[80] and the Surgeon General considered them to be dangerous.[81] In 1984, research findings about violent video games remained somewhat equivocal. The data indicated that "videogame playing was neither the menace that many of its critics have portrayed it to be nor necessarily without possible negative consequence."[82] This was written at a time, however, when video game playing was occasional, its technology more rudimentary, and its content much less violent.

By the late 1990s researchers were actively involved in studying the effects of violent video games. Ballard and Wiest's 1998 study saw a rising level of arousal and feelings of hostility among college men as they played *Mortal Kombat*. They also found that after playing a violent video game people scored higher on hostility measures.[83] Anderson and Dill found that college men who spend the most time playing violent video games tend also to be the most physically aggressive.[84] It has been argued that hostile young people are attracted to these games. However, Gentile and his colleagues found that even the players who scored low in hostility are almost ten times more likely to be involved in fights than nonplayers.[85]

Three experiments were carried out to assess whether the extent of rewards for violent actions affected the player's feelings of hostility. The researchers found that rewarding violent game actions increased hostile emotions, aggressive thinking, and aggressive behavior. And punishing violent actions increased hostile emotion. The research showed that video games that reward violent actions can increase aggressive behavior by increasing aggressive thinking.[86] In other words, aggressive thinking resulted from behavior that was rewarded and also resulted from behavior that was punished. Even short-term exposure to violent video games produces a "hostile bias," which produces a hostile expectation in terms of thoughts, feelings, and behavior. This is similar to that observed in aggressive people.[87] The "hostile attribution bias" in children is the most extensively researched version of this phenomenon.[88] Such findings have been replicated by experimental studies, longitudinal research, and meta-analyses.

Experimental Studies

Experimental studies can yield strong causal answers because they are designed to rule out all alternative explanations. Their primary strength is making causal inferences. This approach randomly assigns participants to the different conditions of the study. Social scientists posit that the independent variable (exposure to video game aggression) causes changes in the dependent variable (aggression). Using this research method, Bushman and Anderson applied the General Aggression Model to the short-term effects of exposure to violent video games. The key question posed by the study is whether short-term exposure to violent video games can temporarily produce a hostile expectation bias similar to that observed among highly aggressive people. The researchers asked 112 male and 112 female college undergraduates to play either violent video games or nonviolent video games. The researchers assessed three types of expectations—thoughts, feelings, and behaviors—and, in the former group studied, found increases in the aggressive content of all three categories.[89]

These players, exposed to a violent video game for just twenty minutes, experienced significant increases in expectations that potential conflict situations would be handled aggressively. This happened even though the players were not provoked nor annoyed in any way in the real-life situation. In one story to which the players responded, Todd's car was rear-ended when he braked quickly at a yellow light. Participants answered the question, "What happened next?" Students who had played the violent video games proposed consistently more aggressive outcomes for the stories. These participants suggested, for example, that Todd would kick out a window, stab, or shoot the other driver, or kick in his head. Another scenario involved Janet's girlfriend, Shannon, who decided not to go on a long-anticipated vacation with Janet. Janet went to Shannon's place to try to convince her to come on the vacation. Aggressive responses included: "You don't want to go? Fuck you then, bitch!"; They get into a fist fight. Then Janet gets into her car, puts the car in drive, and rolls through Shannon's house.[90] Participants' responses included: "This guy's dead meat," "I'm gonna kill him," "I should drive a knife through your eye," and "If I had a hammer I'd beat him with it." Feelings experienced were irritation, fury, viciousness, cruelty, aggression, hatred, anger, and violence because the subject in the study did not get hurt.[91]

A session of violent gaming basically is one more way to learn that the world is dangerous, that aggression is an appropriate way to deal with conflict and anger, and that aggression works. With each repeated exposure, such hostile knowledge structures become "more complex, differentiated, and difficult to change. In this way, repeated exposure to violence can make hostile knowledge structures chronically accessible, essentially creating an aggressive personality."[92]

The General Aggression Model accounts for the fact that severely aggressive and violent acts "rarely occur unless multiple precipitating situational instigators and multiple predisposing personal characteristics converge." According to this model, "habitual aggressive tendencies are most likely to develop in children who grow up in environments that reinforce aggression, provide aggressive models, frustrate and victimize them, and teach them that aggression is acceptable and successful."[93] The virtual environment of violent video games does this. Related research found that children exposed to violent video games are more attracted to guns. Experiments show that children who play violent video games are more likely to pick up a gun and pull the trigger more times and aim the gun at partners or themselves.[94]

Longitudinal Studies

Longitudinal studies measure participant behavior at least twice over time. Such studies can provide solid causal answers because they effectively rule out any alternative explanations. Longitudinal studies that look at video games' influence over time reveal that even children's games with violent content can cause increases in aggression. Another study showed that exposure to violent video games is associated with higher levels of aggression in "the real world" over the long term. And a third study supported these findings by showing that the long-term effects of high exposure to violent video games led to increases in aggressive behavior. A key finding was the negative effect of video game violence on prosocial, helpful behavior. Video game violence not only increases aggressive behavior but also decreases empathic behavior. A related finding measures the direct effect of total screen time on decline in school performance.[95]

Another longitudinal study revealed that exposure results in impulsivity, attention problems, reduced helping behavior, general stereotyping, and video game addiction.[96] German researchers have found that male students exposed to higher rates of media and video game violence are more likely to be involved in later violence. The study showed that this violent behavior typically occurs at age fourteen.[97] It has been found that the long-term effect of video game violence on later aggression and violence is larger than other known risk factors for adolescent violence, such as abusive or antisocial parents and poverty. In fact, only gang involvement presents more of a risk factor than violent video games.[98]

A relevant question is whether video games increase physical aggression over time among people in other cultures. An unprecedented research project looked into long-term effects and comparisons between a high violence culture, the United States, and a low violence culture, Japan. The research found that the amount of exposure to violent video games early in a school year in Japan predicted changes in physical aggressiveness assessed later in the school year, even after statistically controlling for gender and for prior physical aggressiveness.[99] Another longitudinal study compared violent video game effects on aggression, empathy, and prosocial behavior in low-violence Eastern cultures and Western cultures. The study found exposure to violent video games is a causal risk factor for increased aggressive behavior, aggressive affect, and decreased empathy and prosocial behavior. The research also discovered weak evidence of increased cultural or gender differences in susceptibility.[100] A German study found a direct relationship between violent video game exposure and aggressive norms. Violence exposure predicted physical aggression thirty months later and an increase of aggressive norms and hostile attribution bias.[101] A three-day experiment with French university students showed that violent video games increased both hostile expectations and aggression and that the effects increased with each day. The researchers concluded that video games do increase aggression and the effects are cumulative and can be relatively long-lasting.[102] These longitudinal results confirm earlier studies that suggested that playing violent video games is a significant risk factor for later aggressive behavior. These studies show that this violent video game effect on youth generalizes across very different cultures.[103]

Meta-Analyses

The powerful influence of violent video games is supported further by meta-analyses which synthesize and assesses all previous research findings. This form of research is especially valid because it is less susceptible to researcher bias than other forms of research. The first comprehensive meta-analyses of the effects of video games occurred in 2001. These meta-analyses summarized and analyzed the existing research. The findings of the studies, in both laboratory and field settings, support the conclusion that exposure to video game violence increases aggressive behavior in children and young adults. The studies also found that exposure to violent video games increase physiological arousal and aggression-related thoughts and feelings. At the same time, playing violent video games decreases prosocial and empathic behavior.[104]

These findings were supported by meta-analyses in the years following. A recent meta-analysis involves thirty-eight recent studies and 7,000 people. These studies conclude that playing violent video games increases aggressive thoughts, emotions, and behavior.[105] A recent meta-analysis of longitudinal studies found that more exposure results in more aggressive behavior over time.[106] The consistent conclusion of several decades of research is that "there is sufficient research to conclude that violent video game exposure can cause increases in aggressive behavior and that repeated exposure to violent video games is linked to serious forms of aggression and violence."[107]

Meta-analyses of video game effects show that exposure to violent video games is related to heightened aggressive feelings, thoughts and actions, and a decrease in pro-social behavior.[108] These studies reveal that the average effects are great enough to warrant public concern. Bushman and Anderson, for example, found that the size of the effect relating video game violence to aggression was larger than many effects that have led to effective health policies, such as the effect of second-hand smoke on lung cancer, or the effect of lead exposure on reduced IQ in children.[109] These meta-analyses probably underestimated video game effects. Dr. Anderson points out: "Methodologically weaker studies yielded smaller effect sizes than methodologically stronger studies, suggesting that previous meta-analytic studies of violent video games underestimate the true magnitude of observer deleterious effects on behavior, cognition and affect."[110] It could be argued that the entertainment media and video game industries are the most powerful sustaining influences that support the culture of violence. This is a convincing argument when one realizes that aggression in childhood is "the best single childhood predictor of aggression and violence" at later ages.[111]

Violent video games also play a role in gender socialization and gender-role polarity. These games project a virtual world of male hegemony and marginalized, sexualized women. Many male gamers develop a wishful identification with the main character who is usually a warrior-hero.[112] The universal popularity of warrior-hero characters speaks to the human need to be a vital and contributing member of the community. The warrior-hero is the ultimate symbolic representation of this need.

Violent video games provide opportunities to explore traditional concepts of manliness and masculinity. They epitomize what it means to be a man, such as being brave, aggressive or violent, heterosexual and dominant.[113] The most aggressive participants in a study were those who played a violent video game and wished they were like the game character. Although they were not provoked during the experiment, these participants, who had access to loud noisemakers, blasted noise levels that could cause permanent ear damage.[114] Studies also have found that adolescent boys experience joy, even euphoria, when playing violent games,[115] so these games are inherently rewarding and gratifying.

Many violent video games are sexist and contain violence against women. A study of 13,520 French eleven to nineteen-year-old young people showed that violent video game exposure resulted in more sexist beliefs.[116] Playing sexist violent video games increases endorsement of misogynistic beliefs, especially among gamers who highly identify with dominant and aggressive male game characters. Exposure results in reduced empathy toward female victims of violence.[117] Players of violent-sexist video games experienced increased misogynistic beliefs which are negatively related to empathy for female violence victims. The results remained significant even after controlling for age, frequency of game play, and violence ratings.[118] Exposure to sex-stereotyped video games results in gamers being more tolerant of sexual harassment. There also is greater rape myth acceptance.[119]

Research suggests that violent video games influence females less than males.[120] However, of course, female players are affected, as reflected in the rise of cyberbullying. More research is needed about female gamers. It is reasonable to conclude that their self-esteem and self-concept are negative impacted by exposure to sexist violent video games.[121]

Other Effects

Violent video game exposure not only results in aggressive and violent behavior. Other effects include a culture of disrespect, moral disengagement, desensitization, narcissism, attraction to guns, pro-war attitudes, addiction, and reduced academic performance.

The extent to which even the less violent video games promote antisocial attitudes, values, and beliefs is reinforced by video games and video game advertisements. Nintendo and other manufacturers pander to young people by encouraging them to be self-centered and rude and to ridicule authority figures. Additions to the *Diagnostic and Statistical Manual of Mental Disorders* (DSM-5)—used by psychologists and therapists to label troubled behavior—describe negative behaviors of children that now include "conduct disorder" and "oppositional behavior disorder."[122] Diagnostic assessments typically are conducted without acknowledging a connection to violent entertainment media.

Another result of playing violent video games is less self-control and more moral disengagement. A recent study shows that teens who played a violent video game ate more chocolate candy during the game and also cheated eight times more often than did those who played nonviolent games.[123] Other studies found that moral disengagement mitigates the effect of violent video games on self-control and cheating.[124]

Desensitization results from violent video game exposure. Desensitization is the reduction of cognitive, emotional, physiological, and behavioral response to violence. This is a protective response because human beings are not capable of prolonged arousal to a specific act.[125] It is a decrease in normal negative emotional responses, accompanied by decreased prosocial behavior and a lack of moral engagement.[126] Desensitized people are less sensitive to the pain and suffering of others and tolerate increasing levels of violence in society.[127] Many media accounts describe how young murderers in court show no remorse and no emotional response during the trial, even when an unfavorable verdict is announced.

Violent video games cultivate self-centeredness and a sense of entitlement. At one end of the spectrum is self-centeredness and at the other end is extreme narcissism. Eric Harris, of Columbine notoriety, played the most violent video games while he was growing up. For years he relentlessly exercised the power of death over life in his virtual world. In his diary, he wrote: "Ich bin Gott" (I am God), and also related that he wanted to tear "some weak little freshman" apart like a wolf "to show them who is God."[128]

These effects interact with what is called "the weapons effect," which is increased aggressive behavior and attraction to guns among young males after exposure to weapons.[129] A meta-analysis of fifty-six studies confirmed that the sight of weapons increases aggression in both angry and non-angry people.[130] This conclusion also is validated by experimental studies involving exposure to violent video games and virtual guns. For example, a study exposed young males to violent video games and made a handgun available at the site. The study revealed that the children exposed to video game violence were attracted to the gun, held it longer, pointed the gun to themselves and others, and pulled the trigger many more times than children exposed to nonviolent video games.[131] This study affirmed the findings of an earlier experimental study that found similar results.[132]

The dynamic of resonance would apply here, resulting in children, especially those who are heavily exposed, being more at risk of handling and firing a gun in the real world. Another effect related to this fascination with guns is more children carrying weapons. Playing at least some violent video games in the past year was associated with a four-fold increase in children carrying weapons to school.[133]

Globally there are profound interconnections between violent video games, the militarization of society, and politics. There is evidence, for example, that first-person shooter games stimulate and reinforce moral disengagement, pro-war attitudes, and support for military spending.[134]

Many violent video gamers are intensely loyal to their games. Loyalty may become an addiction when gamers become more involved in their virtual world than the real world. Internationally about 1 percent of gamers are addicted.[135] In the United States as many as 10 percent of gamers are addicted.[136]

As many as 40 percent of *World of Warcraft* players are addicted.[137] Extreme addiction becomes obsession. An example is thirteen-year-old Xiao Yi who committed suicide after playing thirty-one consecutive hours of *Warcraft III*, hoping to be "reunited" with his fellow gamers in the afterlife.[138] A few other examples among many include sixteen-year-old, Daniel Petric, who killed his parents because they banned him from *Halo 3*, which he would spend up to eighteen hours daily playing on his Xbox. The Newtown shooter was obsessed with violent video games. His mother said he was "zoned out" when playing and acted "like a zombie."[139]

Some fanatics act out video game plots and scenarios. In Spain, for example, José Rabadán Pardo murdered his mother, father, and sister, proclaiming he was on an "avenging mission" by Squall Leonhart, the main character in *Final Fantasy VIII*. Devin Moore shot and killed two law enforcement officers and a dispatcher, following his arrest for stealing a vehicle. He said he was inspired by *Grand Theft Auto: Vice City*.[140] Crimes resulting from obsession and fanaticism may be heinous. For example, Gary Alcock killed a fifteen-month-old baby because her crying interrupted his Xbox game.

A twenty-two-year-old Florida mother killed her baby because he wouldn't stop crying while she was playing.[141]

The American Psychiatric Association has added internet gaming disorder to the DSM-5 as a condition warranting further research. The World Health Organization included gaming disorder in its eleventh edition of *International Classification of Diseases* (ICD-11). They define gaming disorder as: "Impaired control over gaming, including priority given to gaming over other activities to the extent that gaming takes precedence over other interests and daily activities and continuation or escalation of gaming despite the occurrence of negative consciences"[142] The Center for Internet Behavior in the United States treats addiction, which can be treated medically by such prescription drugs as Naloxone. Several European and Asian countries have opened detox centers, especially China and Japan.

An additional negative effect of violence is diminished academic performance. There is a direct effect between screen time and decline in school performance.[143] Research also shows that exposure to violent video games results in diminished academic performance. There is an inverse relationship between time spent playing video games and performance in school. However, time using computers to do schoolwork results in increased academic performance.[144] This shows that it is the content of screen time and not screen time, per se, that results in poor grades.[145] Most gamers watch television, which reduces intellectual capacity as well, probably resulting in an interactive effect.

Case Studies

The following vignette concerns young men who played violent video games. Both graduated from high school in 1999:

> Seeing that we lived in a very rural area and that there wasn't much to do, we were taken by a game called *Half-Life*. Within a month, we were battling each other for seat time. The graphics in the game were intense, and if you sat in a darkened room with headphones on, you could swear that you were in the game getting "fragged" (first-person shooter term for killed) and instantly respawning. We would shoot each other to pieces. When we played *Half-Life*, our aggressive behavior towards each other increased, with fistfights regularly occurring. When someone on the street or in school made us angry, we would talk about how we wished that real life was like *Half-Life* and we could just frag them into submission.
>
> Within two months of my freshman year I was skipping class to stay in my dorm room to play first-person video games. My studies suffered greatly throughout the year and I was placed on academic probation. I found that the more I played *Half-Life*, the more I used drugs. I became addicted to both. Only at the point that I realized that I would have to drop out of school did I

snap out of it. I knew that I was addicted to violent video games and sought counseling. It was a struggle, but I got rid of my video games—went cold turkey—and again became a good student. Today I am a high school teacher and counsel young people about first-person shooter games.

The following vignette was written by a student who attended college in 2005.

One summer day I took my laptop to a friend's house, Mike, who had not previously been exposed to first-person shooter games. With another friend we set up three different "battle stations." We would all play for hours at a time. One day, after about a week, we played for about five hours and decided to take a break. Mike went outside to shoot a target in the yard with his .22. When the shots stopped I went downstairs to make sure my friend was alright. He was standing on the porch, aiming at something off in the distance. I pulled the sliding glass door open quickly and it made a loud bang. Without hesitation and without thought, my friend of over 10 years swung around, shouldered his rifle, and aimed it right at my face. His eyes were black, the color you see when someone has lost touch with reality, either temporarily or permanently. His face held a scowl that should be reserved for the greatest of enemies. His facial expression and aggressive body language startled me and I froze, not sure if he was joking or if he was about to kill me. I said, "Holy shit," and he snapped out of it . . . literally. He dropped the gun and shook his head and instantly started apologizing to me. "I don't know what came over me," he said. He looked confused, like a duck hit over the head. He walked aimlessly around the porch for a while, seemingly ashamed of what he had done. He came into the house about 10 minutes later and told me he wanted my computer out of the house that afternoon. I didn't protest. After taking my computer home, I uninstalled video games and became an excellent student, focusing all my energies on college and graduating in the next two years.

The players were middle-class young men with no apparent risk factors and no history of delinquent or violent behavior. What would have been the long-term results of Mike playing first person shooter games? How often do such unrecorded scenarios occur?

A Primary Risk Factor

Habitual aggressive tendencies are most likely to develop in young people who grow up in environments that reinforce aggressive behavior, provide aggressive models, victimize them, and teach them that aggression is acceptable, such as the virtual world of video games.[146] Assessing risk factors requires taking into account the social environment in which the child is raised. The violent electronic entertainment environment is so pervasive that it constitutes a primary risk factor. The more time children are exposed to violent video games, the more this virtual world constitutes a risk.

The long-term effect of video game violence on later aggression is larger than most known risk factors for adolescent violence, such as abusive parents and poverty.[147] Research on video effects supports the conclusion that violent video game exposure is a risk factor for everyone who plays, regardless of age, gender, or other factors. Being male, having habitual prior exposure to media violence, having video games in the bedroom, and preferring violent media all lead to significantly higher levels of aggression.[148]

This does not mean that everyone who plays video games will behave aggressively or violently. Rather, this means that people who play violent video games have a higher risk factor for aggressive and violent behavior than nonplayers. The risk is elevated further if the player has other risk factors, such as childhood neglect and social rejection. When the person's risk factors reach critical mass, it becomes highly likely that the person will be involved in aggression or violence.

Protective factors, as discussed earlier, include having a stable family, caring adults, attending a peaceful school. Protective factors also include media literacy training for teachers, families, and students, as well as legislative action.

Why Are Violent Video Games So Engaging?

Researchers conclude that violent video games have more powerful effects than the influence of violent television and movies.[149] This probably is because the games are inherently rewarding and because they tend to require the involvement of the whole body. This research conclusion is echoed by the American Academy of Pediatrics who recognize that preliminary studies about video game violence indicate that "the negative impact may be significantly more severe than that wrought by television, movies or music."[150]

Violent video games incorporate best practices in teaching and are excellent teachers. They provide tangible and steady progress in mastering required knowledge and skills and multiple ways to solve problems. In addition, gamers are rewarded incrementally for achieving success at each level with more advanced tools and higher skill levels. Violent video games are learning reinforcers, They require an acute level of attention, provide active involvement, facilitate identification with violent characters, reinforce violent acts, and frequently display violent scenes.[151] Video gamers are actively involved in enacting the violent acts, which are rewarded and reinforced. In the process gamers become more severely desensitized with the greater frequency of violent acts.[152]

Violent video games have raised the threshold of violent electronic entertainment effects because they make another dimension available, that dimension is interactive. Video games are played with the involvement of the body and hands, rendering the action seemingly even more life-like. The use of the hands is directly linked to the player's ability to, for example, decapitate a character. This creates a direct sensory experience of power. The games require decisions and actions that continuously amplify the player's sense of strength and power.

Violent video games are more influential than other violent media because of the following.

1. The interactive violence is no longer vicarious but direct.
2. Players can become warrior-heroes, a key factor in the warrior-ideal model of socialization.
3. The player's violence is presented as justified and is rewarded.
4. Players experience immediate gratification without real-world fear and with no real-world risks or consequences.
5. They provide an easy way to fulfill the human desire to be effective (powerful) and allow the gamer to become a hero or a rock star with little effort.
6. The player has ultimate power—the power of life or death.

Other Considerations

It is contrary to human nature to kill another human being. After World War II, research looked into why the majority of American soldiers in the past could not kill the enemy face to face.[153] The research of General S. L. A. Marshall found that only 15 to 20 percent of World War II soldiers could bring themselves to fire at an enemy soldier and that only 55 percent of soldiers in the Korean War did so. Many soldiers could not fire their rifles at an enemy they could see or they could not properly aim at them.[154] This points to the natural human quality of empathy.

First-person shooter games overcome the obstacle of empathy because they embody "reflexive fire training." Reflexive fire training becomes muscle training. It does not require thought. The impulse to shoot bypasses the prefrontal cortex, which regulates behavior, so the moral decision to kill a human being is bypassed. Soldiers have reported blanking out or blacking out at the point that they pull the trigger.[155] Many rampage school shooters also report blanking out when firing at their victims.[156] Such reflexive shooting training has resulted in a very high fire ratio in modern battlefields. As one soldier commented, "People are now more lethal than they ever imagined."[157] Dave Grossman concludes that violent video games condition young people to become reflexive shooters. Soldiers who have played video games as children are now easier to train and are more deadly. So are children.[158]

Violent video games wield such a powerful influence because persuasion is deeply embedded in the game itself. "The principles being pushed needn't be presented up front or argued. By playing the game, frantically clicking away and trying to fend off failure, the player realizes, and eventually internalizes, which values work and which don't. Regardless of political stripe, everyone wants to win."[159]

The human mind has a difficult time distinguishing between reality and simulation. This especially occurs when disbelief is suspended and the mind is absorbed in making sense of the game.[160] In addition, the more diverting the game, the more distracted the player. Distraction lowers defenses, resulting in the message's impact being more potent.[161] In addition, violent video games consistently emit positive reinforcement through wins or kills. Because there are no real-world consequences to killing video game entities, there is no negative reinforcement. And, for heavy consumers and addicted players, there is no opportunity for the reinforced behaviors to become extinguished.[162]

Violent video games teach that dominance and winning are the most important values. Young people who are socialized by violent video games not only internalize these values they also repeatedly act on them. Virtual killing is a rewarding experience. And it is fun. As Lt. Colonel Dave Grossman, testifying before the Senate Judiciary Committee on Media Violence, said: "We're not just teaching kids to kill. We're teaching them to like it."[163]

School Violence

What is the relationship between exposure to violent video games and school violence? Video games teach demonstration of power, hierarchy, and domination. Bullies tend to be characterized as lacking empathy and being impulsive. They view violence in a positive light, and they may develop hostile personalities. As the research shows, these qualities are engendered and promoted by violent video games.

Rampage school shooters have been indirectly and directly influenced by violent video games. Indirectly rampage school shooters have been affected because many of them have been bullied chronically, eventually resulting in rage. Shooters also are directly influenced by violent video games. With very few exceptions rampage school shooters are heavily exposed to the most violent video games during formative years of their lives. Risk factors for school shooters include anger, depression, and suicidal ideation.[164] Few have histories of antisocial behavior. However, they are preoccupied by weapons[165] and fantasy.[166] They also display a sense of entitled narcissism, a lack of empathy,[167] and poor impulse control.[168]

Rampage school shooters enact violent video game scenarios in their rampages. They dress in military garb, are heavily armed, and utilize tactical combat strategies during the rampage. Also, the shooters display amazing shooting accuracy. Michael Carneal, who had never shot a handgun fired eight shots and hit eight children. The FBI says that the average, experienced law enforcement officer, at a range of seven yards, hits with less than one bullet in five. As Lt. Colonel Grossman points out, there is no equivalent achievement in the annals of law enforcement or criminal history.[169] This is not to say that video games are the sole cause of school shootings. Other risk factors need to be taken into account. However, these games, especially first-person shooter games, are a primary risk factor and play a decisive role in rampage shootings.

Violent video games are potent socializing agents and reinforce the ideology of the culture of violence because they teach that aggression and conflict is a way of life and preferable to cooperation and peace. Although violent video game research over the decades has become clearer and more conclusive, attempts by various educational groups in the United States to reduce children's exposure to the most violent games have yielded little improvement.[170]

Parental Involvement

The lack of parental or societal oversight of children's involvement with violent video games is a risk factor. Although most parents believe that violent media affect their children, they also tend to believe that the mass media have a greater effect on other children than on their own.[171] In addition, only about 13 percent of parents impose any rules concerning the content their children are allowed to watch on television.[172] About 89 percent of teens surveyed reported that their parents never put limits on how much time they were allowed to play video games.[173] Only 15 percent of middle school children say their parents "always" or "often" check the video game ratings before the children are allowed to buy or rent them. In addition, only about 20 percent of parents have ever kept their children from getting a game because of its rating.[174] This lack of parental involvement reflects the extent to which many parents themselves have been exposed to violent media and game fare and, in the process, have become desensitized to the reality of the actual amount of violence and its effects. Children's access is made easier by many violent games having "demo" versions on the internet that can be downloaded for free by anyone. In addition to parents not being willing to monitor media violence, it also appears that parents' ability to regulate media use is declining.[175]

At the same time the ratings provided by the video game industry do not match those provided by other adults and game-playing children. For example, many cartoon-like characters are classified by the industry as appropriate for general audiences, a classification with which adults and youngsters disagree.[176] About half of teen-rated games include potentially objectionable content that the official content descriptors for the game do not describe.[177]

The Marjory Stoneman Douglas High School rampage shooting in February 2018 was one of the most lethal school shooting in US history. During that time, the violent video game industry released *Active Shooter*, a first-person combat video game that mimicked rampage shootings. This confluence of events outraged and motivated parents and students around the country to oppose such games.

Discussion

Almost seventy years of research has culminated in the conclusion that violent electronic entertainment media, especially violent video games, cause increased aggression and violence. Violent electronic entertainment also contributes to other violent crimes, such as domestic violence and police brutality. Also, it is noteworthy that many of the violent rioters in 2020 were young white men. The crisis provided an opportunity for gamers who played violent video games to assert their power through violent action.

Market-driven competition results in continuous technological development. As a result, violent video games will become more graphically violent, realistic, and immersive, and their effects will be more pronounced.

Rampage shootings have stimulated national debates about guns and gun control. It is necessary to regulate weapons. However, it is not sufficient. It also is necessary to address why many people are extremely attracted to guns. Guns represent and are physical power. To what extent does attachment to guns reflect a personal sense of disempowerment, such as experienced by rampage shooters? The debate needs to acknowledge how violent video games socialize men into the warrior ideal and the role of the heavily armed warrior-hero. Increased aggression and violence is not limited to the school environment but extends to other arenas. Undoubtedly, there is a connection between the growth of violent-sexist games and the rise in violent crimes against women, ranging from dating violence to murder.

It is widely believed that people who engage in rampage shootings are mentally ill. In some cases, this may be true. However what needs to be reckoned with is the connection between this "new and unique" violence and uniquely violent forms of electronic entertainment. Some vulnerable children, who otherwise lead relatively normal lives, become mass murderers because of relentless, long-term, intensive exposure to violent electronic entertainment media, especially violent video games. For these children, this exposure, sparked by a negative catalytic experience, can result in insane ideation and rage.

Many millions of people are involved in violent video games because of the elixir of self-aggrandizement and power. This raises the question of why people are so attracted to feeling powerful in a virtual world. Apparently, what is missing in their real world is a sense of self-empowerment and political efficacy. Widespread involvement in these virtual worlds is an indication of the extent to which people feel disempowered or powerless in their lives. The irony and the tragedy is that heavy exposure results in personal disempowerment. Heavy exposure also displaces time and effort that could be spent in becoming empowered, personally and politically. Millions of people otherwise could become more active in contributing to their communities as well as in assisting the survival of the human race and the planet.

Involvement in a violent virtual world estranges us from our essential human nature. Violent video games embody violence, hierarchy, lack of empathy, gender-role polarization, and other effects that are contrary to human nature. In fact, it seems that the effects are the opposite of the qualities of human nature.

The following illustrates the antithetical relationship between human nature and the results of violent media and video game exposure.

HUMAN NATURE	NONHUMAN NATURE
empathic, compassionate	desensitized
egalitarian	hierarchical
non-sexist	sexist
prosocial	narcissitic
cooperative	competitive
creative	destructive
harmonious	aggressiveness
peaceful	violence
justice through action	mutated justice—revenge

Separating human beings from our essential nature is profoundly violent.

Legislation

Several states and municipalities have passed legislation in order to restrict the sale and rental of the most violent games without parental consent. The video game industry has worked to obstruct the passage of such laws. They have even warned those involved in the legislative process that the industry would "exact a huge price on them if the law under consideration is passed."[178] The threat was not idle. For example, the State of Illinois passed such a law, and the Entertainment Software Association filed a US District Court petition asking the court to order the State to pay them $644,545 in legal fees.[179] The industry has consistently gone to court in order to block enforcement of such laws and has won all the cases.

As part of this campaign, the video game industry denies the validity of the impressive body of video game violence research. An example is the response of the president of the Interactive Entertainment Merchants' Association to California Bill 1793, which would require stores to display signs and brochures explaining the video game ratings to customers. He said: "to date there has been no conclusive research to prove a causal linkage between playing video games and asocial behavior."[180] Industry supporters actively engage in campaigns of disinformation and misinformation. They often cite critics of media violence research who usually have not conducted any scientific research and have at times even been paid by the media industries to write critiques and testify in court. At other times, critics invent tales about researchers, trying to discredit them.[181] These efforts are supported by the more than 500,000 members of the video gaming lobby.[182]

Coupled with this obstruction is the failure of the Federal Communications Commission (FCC) to regulate communications industries adequately. Over the years, the FCC has pressured these violence industries to provide better programming, with some limited success. Many researchers, however, conclude that these limited successes have all but disappeared in recent years because of the FCC's abrogation of responsibility and because of major technological changes in electronic media.[183]

It would be hoped that the ratings system could counteract these campaigns and government failures. The US Senate asked the video game industry to create a rating system. Research has shown, however, that the voluntary rating systems do not accurately reflect the content of the games. The current video game rating system in the United States consists of AO (Adult Only), M (Mature), T (Teen), E+ (Everyone aged six and older), and EC (Everyone aged three and older). It has been found, however, that parents often indicate they would prefer content-based ratings rather than age-appropriate lettering.[184] In response to these research findings, the United States Senate proposed the Family Entertainment Protection Act in 2005 and 2006. This act would have directed the government to examine the quality and ratings of video games. The bill would have imposed financial penalties (up to $5,000) for businesses that sell or distribute to minors video games that have been deemed inappropriate for them to play. The act also would allow the Centers for Disease Control and Prevention to conduct scientific research into the effects that violent media have on children. Neither of these proposals became law.[185]

Efforts to protect children from the harmful effects of violent video games have not kept pace with industry growth. There has been a backslide in ratings awareness and enforcement. Although the Entertainment Software Rating Board (ESRB) continues to educate the public about its video game rating system, too many children continue to play inappropriate video games that can harm their health and development. The National Institute on Media and the Family concluded "right now families and retailers have put too much faith in the current ratings system, the ESRB has put too much trust in the gaming industry, and some in the gaming industry have not done enough to monitor themselves."[186] The United States, unlike other governments, has not funded large-scale public education programs. There are numerous parent and advocacy groups that are doing so, but their limited funding inhibits their success.[187]

The predominant approach in the United States consists of the so-called voluntary rating systems of the entertainment industries. "Voluntary" is a misnomer because in each case the ratings systems for television, films, music, and video games were created only after Congress threatened the industries with government regulation. The ratings approach has failed. The ratings are based on invalid conclusions about what is safe for different age groups; the criteria are often misapplied and have become more lenient over time, and age-based systems often encourage underage consumption.[188] The United States does not require these industries to provide and enforce their own rating systems. The 1996 Telecommunications Act required that television ratings be created, but it did not specify how or by whom. The government could create its own ratings systems and agencies, requiring that all entertainment media products be rated by the agency prior to distribution and sale. Many countries, including England and Australia, have such systems in place. The government could enact legislation requiring the entertainment industries to create one universal rating system, and the legislation could mandate that the ratings be administered independent of the industries.[189]

Violent video game researchers suggest warning labels much like those used on tobacco products that warn consumers of the product's negative effects. The warning could be something like the following: "Warning: This video game contains violence. Playing violent video games increases the likelihood of aggressive behavior in the immediate situation. Repeatedly playing violent video games increases the likelihood of aggressive behavior across longer periods of time."[190]

Government-enforced age-based ratings and restrictions are fairly common in industrialized societies. However, these do not exist in the United States. This approach is feasible in this country, moreover, because media industries do acknowledge that some products are not appropriate for children and give them an R rating. Also, legal precedent has established that the government has an appropriate role in limiting the influences to which children are exposed. For example, state and local authorities routinely restrict children's access to tobacco, guns, pornography, and gambling.[191]

Heavy violent media involvement partially was blamed for the 1999 Columbine High School shootings. President Bill Clinton asked the Federal Trade Commission to investigate who was purchasing and renting violent video games. They found that most of the M-rated (Mature, seventeen years and older) were explicitly marketed to children. They also found that 83 percent of the time teenagers, ages thirteen to sixteen, could purchase these games.[192] In 2000, the US Senate Committee on Commerce, Science, and Transportation held a hearing on violent video game effects. Media violence experts reported on the current state of the research, and video game industry representatives denied that there was any credible evidence of harm.[193]

In 2011, the US Supreme Court ruled that the video game industry should "enjoy full, free speech." They based their decision on an insufficient review of the scientific literature.[194] They also ignored the 1934 Federal Communications Act that requires broadcasters to "serve the public interest, convenience and necessity."[195] The First Amendment of the US Constitution sates that "Congress shall pass no law respecting the establishment of religion or prohibits the free exercise thereof or abridging the freedom of speech or the press, or the right of people peaceably to assemble and petition the government." Ironically, the violent electronic entertainment industries have used the First Amendment to stifle criticism of their industries.

European governments ensure freedom of speech while being responsive to the threats posed by violent video games. England, Italy, France, Germany, the Netherlands, Spain, and Finland have been concerned about violent media and have taken steps to implement a workable public policy to restrict or ban sales of violent video games to children.[196] The European Union created a new rating system adopted by the Interactive Software Federation of Europe, called the Pan European Games Information (PEGI). The goal is to create a unified rating system across the majority of the countries in the European Union. Unlike the ESRB system in the United States, the PEGI has eight categories with easily understood symbols for parents, children, and retailers. The game ratings include age-level appropriateness (3+, 7+ and 16+) for violence, bad language, fear, sex, drugs, discrimination, and gambling.[197]

Germany has the most restrictive public policy initiative. Germany has begun public policy debates to ban violent video games from all children. The governments of Bavaria and Lower Saxony have begun to draft a bill, which would sentence video game producers to fines and a maximum of one year in jail for making video games that emphasize "cruel violence on humans or human-looking characters." The bill was created in response to a 2006 school shooting in Emsdetten by Sebastian Bosse, who was a heavy violent video game player.[198] Asian countries also are responding. Even low-violence countries like South Korea and Japan are experiencing the negative effects of violent video games. China has blocked importing "hostile" games.[199] Multinational efforts are underway to shape public policy regarding media and video game violence. These efforts are motivated by the United Nations Convention on the Rights of the Child. The convention produced Article 17, which is concerned with developing guidelines for protecting children from material that may be harmful to their well-being.[200]

Market-driven technological development will continue to make violent video games more engaging, immersive, addictive, and influential. The violent video game industry and its advertisers need to be accountable for the forces they encourage in a youth culture that is increasingly on the edge. The spirit of our children as well as their future are being sacrificed at the altar of profit.

CHAPTER 9

THE BRAIN'S RESPONSE TO ELECTRONIC ENTERTAINMENT MEDIA

> A democratic civilization will save itself only if it makes the language of the image into a stimulus for critical reflection—not an invitation for hypnosis.
> —Umberto Eco

The human brain, composed of many billions of cells, is the most complex object in the universe. The essential purpose of the human brain and the nervous system is to ensure the body's survival. The nervous system and the brain comprise the structures that allow us to perceive, feel, think, remember, move, and respond.

This chapter does not pretend to fully describe the functioning of the brain. It does, however, provide basic information about how the brain functions in order to better understand the research about brain response to electronic media. This chapter describes the brain structures that are most responsive to these media.

The central nervous system consists of the brain and spinal cord. The autonomic nervous system is a subdivision of the nervous system and, to some extent, is independent or autonomous from the central nervous system. So it is not readily under voluntary control. The major functions of the autonomic nervous system include cardiac, vascular, regulatory, respiratory, and electrodermal. As such, it is involved in regulating visceral functions, such as breathing, heart rate, blood pressure, intestinal movements, and hormone secretions.[1]

The Autonomic Nervous System

The autonomic nervous system consists of the sympathetic nervous system and the parasympathetic nervous system. The body is prepared for emotional responses through the action of both its sympathetic and parasympathetic divisions.[2] The parasympathetic nervous system maintains bodily functions, and the sympathetic nervous system is involved with arousal functions.[3]

The parasympathetic nervous system conserves energy and resources during relaxed states and usually is associated with periods of rest. Through the action of its sympathetic and parasympathetic division, the autonomic nervous system prepares the body for emotional responses.[4]

The sympathetic nervous system mobilizes energy and resources during times of stress and arousal. Physiologically strong emotions such as fear or anger activate the body's emergency reaction system, which then prepares the body for potential danger. The sympathetic nervous system directs the release of hormones from the adrenal glands, which in turn, leads the internal organs to release blood sugar, raise blood pressure, and increase sweating and salivation.[5]

With mild, unpleasant stimulation, the sympathetic division is more active and with mild, pleasant stimulation, the parasympathetic division is more active. With more intense stimulation of either kind, both divisions are increasingly involved.[6] To calm the person after the emergency has passed, the parasympathetic nervous system inhibits the release of the activating hormones.[7]

The autonomic nervous system's capacity for learning has been well established. Autonomic nervous system responses, starting with Pavlov, have been associated with a broad range of stimulus conditions by means of classical conditioning.[8] The autonomic nervous system helps to process emotions, such as anger, distrust, fear, happiness, and sadness. Emotional experience is associated with greater emotion-specific autonomic nervous system activity.[9] How excitable one is relates to the functioning of the autonomic nervous system.

Emotional experience is associated with greater autonomic nervous system activity across cultures. For example, a high similarity of emotions and autonomic activity has been demonstrated across the cultures of the United States and West Sumatra, a culture in which people are socialized to not display negative emotions. Researchers conclude that patterns of autonomic activity are "an important part of our common evolved biological heritage."[10]

The Cerebral Hemispheres

The human brain seems to have finished its evolution 40,000 years ago.[11] The forebrain is the highest and most prominent portion of the brain that has undergone the greatest evolutionary development of any region in the nervous system. The major subdivisions of the forebrain include the cerebral cortex, the limbic system, the thalamus, and the hypothalamus.

The cerebral cortex of the brain is what distinguishes us as human. The dominant status of humans "in large part must rest upon ... tremendous cortical endowment, rivaled only by the whales and dolphins."[12] The cerebral cortex is the highest, most recently evolved part of the brain. It is responsible for all our conscious thoughts, feelings, memories, and voluntary actions.

The two cerebral hemispheres comprise the outermost portion of the forebrain, consisting of the cerebral cortex, corpus callosum, basal ganglia, and limbic system. Because these parts are each found separated from one another on both right and left sides of the brain, each half is called a cerebral hemisphere.[13] Each cerebral hemisphere is composed of four distinct lobes, and connected by a highway of fibers called the corpus callosum. The corpus callosum is a huge structure, consisting of 200 million cells that connect the left and the right cerebral hemispheres and allow them to communicate with each other.[14]

The four lobes located in the hemispheres are the frontal, parietal, temporal, and occipital lobes, each having somewhat different functions. The lobes are either sensory or motor, areas for bodily sensations such as touch and temperature. Or the lobes are association, areas with neurons whose axons influence the musculature to produce movement. The frontal lobe is responsible for motor areas for all of the skeletal muscles in the body. Frontal lobes plan for the future, control movement, produce speech, and consider consequences. They focus attention and are involved in decision-making, inhibition, and self-control. The temporal lobes hear and interpret language and music, receiving information indirectly from the cochlea of the ear. Parietal lobes are bodily sense areas receiving axon projections from other brain areas whose function are to process and to pass on body sense information such as touch, pressure, and position, gained from receptors located in the skin, joints, and other tissue.[15]

The occipital lobes specialize in vision. They are cortical sensory analyzers for information from the retina of the eye. This region consists largely of the cerebral cortex most directly in receipt of visual (light) information.[16] Vision is the most studied of the senses. About one-fourth of the brain is involved in visual processing, more than for all other senses. The visual process begins with a comparison of the amount of light striking any small region of the retina and the amount of light around it.[17] The neural system for vision includes extensive networks in which millions of nerve cells are packed in the retina rather than in the brain. These are involved in such complex neural analysis that the retina might legitimately be considered as a brain lying outside the cranial cavity.[18]

The functioning of the right and the left cerebral hemispheres is described as bilateral symmetry. Although they appear to be mirror images of each other, the hemispheres exhibit differences or asymmetries in both physical and functional characteristics.[19] The hemispheres are specialized for specific tasks, which tend to be complementary. The most distinguishing characteristic of the left hemisphere is its ability to order a linear concept of time.[20] The left hemisphere is responsible for linear reasoning that involves processing speech, writing, language, calculation, organization, and time.

The left hemisphere comprises the executive system. It is more involved in voluntary behavior than the right hemisphere.[21] Voluntary responses are evaluated by the left hemisphere. The left hemisphere is "the one that does the heavy duty thinking," according to Michael Gazzaniga, a neuroscientific pioneer.[22]

Generally speaking, the left hemisphere specializes in identifying, organizing, and categorizing pieces of information. It specializes in identifying discrete units of information. In processing language, for example, the left hemisphere goes through and sequentially transforms each letter into an internal code (i.e., names them).[23]

Several regions in the left hemisphere are especially adapted to process language. Broca's area is an area in the frontal cortex of the left hemisphere that has been closely linked to language function. Wernicke's area, located in the left cerebral hemisphere between the temporal and parietal lobes, is critical to language comprehension.[24] Left hemisphere dominant people tend to score higher on the SAT mathematics subtest, are faster in concept identification tasks, and tend to major in science and other quantitative areas.[25]

The right hemisphere has functions that complement the left hemisphere. The left hemisphere describes or names, and the right hemisphere points.[26] The right hemisphere cannot process information in a linear manner. As such, it relies more on imagery than language.[27] The right hemisphere provides the neural basis for the ability to take fragmentary sensory information and construct from it a coherent concept of the spatial organization of the outside world. This constitutes a kind of cognitive spatial map by which we plan our actions.[28] The right hemisphere's specialty in perceiving spatial relationships is complemented by high involvement with vision. The right hemisphere is more synthetic and holistic than analytic and sequential in processing information. It is superior for part-whole relationships, described as gestalt formation of closure.[29] One might say that the left hemisphere identifies each tree in the forest while the right hemisphere perceives the whole forest. This contrasts with the left hemisphere's focus on features or abstracting essentials from a field.[30]

Early studies noted that the drawings made by patients with right hemispheric damage, and having an intact left hemisphere, tended to be full of details but details that were disarticulated, having no coherent organization. On the other hand, patients with left hemispheric damage and an intact right hemisphere had the correct overall configuration, but the drawings were greatly oversimplified and had few details. This shows that the right hemisphere is more specialized in the interrelationships of the parts of the whole than it is in the parts or details themselves. Neuroscientists refer to this as a "holistic bias."[31]

In addition to spatial abilities, the right hemisphere specializes in face recognition, certain aspects of musical perception, and other nonverbal sounds.[32] The right hemisphere is involved with processing sounds, color, facial recognition, drama, fun, and movement in the immediate milieu. This indicates that television content and format are ideally suited to the capabilities of the right cerebral hemisphere.

There is a lot of evidence that the right hemisphere is superior in tasks using tactile, kinesthetic, and auditory modalities.[33] That is, the right hemisphere is more involved in processing sound and bodily sensation. In keeping with this, the right hemisphere focuses on the immediate milieu and is involved in manipulation of objects in the immediate environment.[34]

The right hemisphere is the seat of emotion, especially negative emotion.[35] Brain scans show greater activity in the brain's left hemisphere for positive pictures and in the right hemisphere for negative pictures.[36] This indicates that the right cerebral hemisphere is more closely involved with processing information related to fear.

People who are right hemisphere dominant tend to be "relational" thinkers while left hemisphere dominant people appear to be "analytic" thinkers.[37] Relational thinkers consider themselves to be more musical and more artistic.[38] The right hemisphere also is specialized for understanding the relative position of objects in space and mentally turning around three-dimensional figures.[39]

Hartnett found that successful foreign language students who succeeded in being taught by an analytic, heavily deductive method of learning Spanish—which consist of explicit rules that preceded practice—were predominantly left hemisphere dominant. Right hemisphere language students were more successful at a more direct, conversational inductive approach. This suggests that the learning demonstrated by right hemisphere dominant people can be achieved through either hemisphere or a combination of both. In other words, these people tend to be bilateralized in their thinking and also have more access to the right hemisphere than left hemisphere dominant people.[40]

Optimal functioning of the brain occurs when both hemispheres are communicating with each other. Whole brain functioning facilitates the "aha!" moments, the times when we literally have brainstorms. Millions of nerve cells light up with the creative genius that occurs when both cerebral hemispheres are interacting optimally. These brainstorms are more likely to occur with men and women who are the most bilateralized.

The type of hemisphere required for a task determines which hemisphere is the dominant one for that task.[41] Over time, if one hemisphere is used more predominantly than the other, that hemisphere becomes more dominant in use. People tend to appeal to one hemisphere and its mode of thought more than the other hemisphere. This is referred to by various terms, such as cerebral hemisphere dominance and hemisphericity.[42] Right hemisphere dominant people report more vivid imagery that is related to specialization for visual-spatial functions. Left hemisphere dominant people describe themselves as analytic and very capable in organizing details.

Neurosociology

The field of neurosociology investigates how the society and the culture in which people are raised tend to encourage left or right hemispheric dominance. Neurosociology investigates how people use their hemispheres in ways that are responsive to the social and cultural environment. Warren TenHouten's work with Australian Aborigines, for example, demonstrates how cultural attitudes and values shape the ways and the extent to which groups of people tend to rely on one hemisphere more than the other. The Aboriginal people are highly cooperative, sharing, congenial, and sensitive to the feelings of others in the group.[43]

Many people try to ascribe philosophical and spiritual dualism that has intrigued human beings to the right cerebral hemisphere. Robert Nebes, a neuroscientist, comments that "it seems natural to many researchers in related fields that the scientific and technological aspects of our civilization are products of the left hemisphere, while the mystical and humanistic aspects are products of the right."[44] Some terms describing the dichotomous theory of intelligence include *buddi* and *manas* (Akhilnanda), *digital* and *analogic* (Bateson and Jackson), *intellectual* and *sensuous* (Blackburn), *deductive* and *imaginative* (Bronowski), *rational* and *metaphoric* (Bronowski), *secondary* and *primary* (Freud), *analytic* and *gestalt* (Levy and Sperry), *positive* and *mythic* (Levi-Strauss), *rational* and *intuitive* (Maslow), *analytic* and *holistic* (Ornstein), *second signaling* and *first signaling* (Pavlov), and *objective* and *subjective* (Schopenhauer).[45]

The extent to which capabilities of the hemispheres are developed depends upon the social environment in which the person lives. Paolo Freire writes of a "submerged consciousness," which appears to be linked to right hemispheric functioning. He also writes about "critical consciousness," which apparently is connected to left hemispheric functioning.[46]

People in industrialized countries, especially white males, tend to be socialized to become right-cerebral hemisphere dominant. "Our own society . . . seems to be, in some respects, a good example: a scholastized, post-Guttenberg-industrialized, computer-happy exaggeration of the Graeco-Roman penchant for propositionizing."[47] Sperry has noted "our educational system, as well as science in general, tends to neglect the non-verbal form of intellect. What it comes down to is that modern society discriminates against the right hemisphere."[48]

A key factor in left hemispheric dominance is the ability to read and write. Nonliterate people tend to be more right hemispheric dominant. This does not mean that people are born with a tendency to become left cerebral hemisphere dominant or right cerebral hemisphere dominant. Rather, as neurosociology has illustrated, this is a socially learned response. The most left cerebral dominant people in the world tend to be white, educated men in industrialized countries. The most right cerebral hemisphere people in the world tend to be nonliterate women in the most impoverished countries in Africa. This can be explained by the society or culture eliciting cerebral hemisphere responses that are consonant with cultural norms and values.

The Limbic System

In order to better understand the research that investigates brain response to electronic media, we need to see how the functioning of the brain is rooted in the limbic system. It is necessary to look at the limbic system because it controls emotions and stores emotions linked to action, especially aggression.[49] The limbic system is an evolutionarily ancient region of the brain that is a physically widespread yet closely interconnected group of brain structures. As far back as 1939, the limbic system was identified as the seat of emotion.[50] The limbic system is a complex, linked set of structures that include the hippocampus, amygdala, hypothalamus, and the posterior gyrus cingulated.[51] It receives input from and directs output to the thalamus, hypothalamus, and the brainstem. Limbic system structures modulate motivational (eating and drinking), emotional (aggression), and sexual behavior.[52]

A key part of the limbic system is the amygdala, an ancient structure deep inside the forebrain that is hardwired for survival. The amygdala, located in each cerebral hemisphere, is a mass of nerve cells found to be related to emotions, especially fear, rage, and aggression. It is a key brain structure for mediating violence.[53] Electrical stimulation of the amygdala can incite fury. One patient with a long history of violence and spells of rage screamed that he was "going wild" when doctors stimulated his amygdala.[54] Charles Whitman, who killed people from the University of Texas's tower in Austin, in 1966, left a note that asked that his brain be examined for possible dysfunction. His autopsy revealed he had a tumor pressing into his amygdala.[55]

The amygdala plays an important role in the limbic system because it is a gateway for emotion and also acts as a filter for memory, storing emotional aspects of memory.[56] It generates emotions from perceptions and thoughts, attaching significance to the information it receives from the senses.

The amygdala plays an especially significant role by attaching meaning to negative experiences.[57] When people look at fearful facial expressions, for example, the right amygdala shows increasing activity as the intensity of the expression increases. Happy facial expressions produce less activity in the same structure the more intensely happy the face becomes.[58] Patients with their left amygdala removed, however, showed no preference for the emotional words over neutral words.[59] The amygdala may be abnormally activated in anxiety disorder.[60] This further demonstrates that the right hemisphere is more involved in processing emotion.

Fear is an emotion that is evoked to deal with danger and threats to survival. The amygdala controls the body's fear response, as demonstrated in a person's fight or flight reaction.[61] Fear causes an automatic, protective response that occurs without the need for conscious thought.[62] If people experience high levels of activation in the amygdala, they may not be able to inhibit the emotions that lead to aggressive behavior.[63]

The amygdala is closely associated with what is stored and how strongly it is stored. The amygdala plays an important role in remembering an action in terms of whether it is followed by rewarding consequences.[64] This is a significant principle in determining what behaviors the person will learn and remember. The inbuilt reward and punishment mechanisms in violent video games is a key factor to remember when assessing the role of the response of the amygdala.

The hippocampus is intimately involved with learning and plays an important role in emotion-laden memories.[65] Human beings deprived of the hippocampus cannot store events into permanent memory.[66] It consolidates recently acquired information, somehow turning short-term memory into long-term memory. It is necessary for forming and retrieving memories of facts and events. The hippocampus plays a role in a long-lasting increase in the strength of a synaptic response following stimulation.[67]

The cingulated gyrus is an evolutionary new addition to the brain.[68] The gyrus consists of tissue expansion between sulci in the mammalian cerebral cortex. Sulci are infoldings or grooves in the surface of the mammalian cerebral cortex. The large number and complicated pattern of sulci are a distinguishing feature of primate brains and those of marine animals, including whales, dolphins, and porpoises.[69] The cingulated gyrus is an evolutionarily recent region that controls complex expressions of emotions, such as disapproving looks rather than physical aggression.[70]

The anterior cingulated gyrus is located in the front middle portion of the brain. It is a recent evolutionary feature of the brain. This region plays a critical role in a variety of cognitive and emotional tasks. It functions to monitor and correct ongoing behavior. It is suited for various functions, including inhibition, performance monitoring, and error correction. It becomes active following errors in cognitive tasks. It serves as an interface between cognition and emotion, between response and arousal.[71] It plays a central role in linking emotions (such as the emotional responses to making errors) and cognitions (such as formulating new task strategies).[72] The relatively recent emergence of this brain structure suggests that it developed when human beings found it necessary to live in an extended group beyond the family.

The posterior cingulate is involved in processing negative emotions. This area is implicated in posttraumatic stress disorder and may be abnormally activated in anxiety disorder.[73] As such, the posterior cingulated is involved in long-term storage of negative emotions.

The thalamus, hypothalamus, and the brainstem give input to the limbic system, which, in turn, directs output to these structures. The thalamus is the major sensory relay in the brain. Located at the center of the forebrain, it is a large structure, composed of many different collections of neurons. It relays sensory, motor, and limbic information to the cerebral cortex and basal ganglia.[74] It possesses other neurons specialized for other tasks, such as widespread activation of the cortical association areas, a function presumably linked to arousal processes.[75]

If a case could be made for one "brain center," it would be the hypothalamus. The hypothalamus is a complex brain structure at the base of the forebrain, right below the thalamus, and has widespread connections with many other brain areas. It is essential in coordinating central nervous system functions, including the regulation of body temperature, sex drive, thirst, and hunger.[76] It has been found to be involved in a wide variety of behaviors and processes and plays an important role in emotions of pain and pleasure. It plays a key role in aggressive behavior and also coordinates the "fight or flight" reaction.[77]

Stress activates the hypothalamus, which stimulates other glands.[78] The hypothalamus has a reciprocal relationship with the endocrine system. It is composed of many neurons with various functions and works in concert with the master endocrine gland, the pituitary. The pituitary gland, in humans, is composed of two lobes and secretes a number of hormones that regulate the activity of other endocrine organs in the body.[79] The hypothalamus triggers the pituitary gland to release adrenocorticotropic hormones (ACTH), a stress hormone, through the bloodstream.[80]

The brainstem is the brain structure that has least changed across species. The brainstem is the junction between the brain and spine and is the major route by which the forebrain sends information to and receives information from the spinal cord and peripheral nerves. Although not considered to be a brainstem structure, the cerebellum communicates with the rest of the brain via the brainstem and is involved in the control and cooperation of muscles.[81]

In processing information, there are close relationships between the cortex and the brainstem. The reticular formation is a net of neurons occupying much of the core of the brainstem. The ascending axons of this system terminate primarily in the thalamus, controlling arousal.[82] Changes come about in patterns of brain activity that reflect the involvement of the cortex and the brain according to the nature of the problems confronted.[83]

The brainstem also contains neurons of the autonomic nervous system. Locus coeruleus, a small neuron located in the upper portion of the brainstem, appears to play a role in dreaming and in brain mechanisms of reward.[84] Axons of the locus coeruleus use norepinephrine as a neurotransmitter, which innervates the spinal cord, raphe nuclei, cerebellum, hypothalamus, thalamus, limbic system, and the cerebral cortex.

A neurotransmitter is a chemical substance released by a neuron's axon terminal which diffuses across the synaptic gap to influence the electrical activity of the receiving neuron.[85] It is possible that the various brain circuits each have a unique neurotransmitter.[86] The brain manufactures dopamine, a neurotransmitter that is central to reward-based learning. The brain also manufactures serotonin, which plays a key role in mediating aggressive and violent behavior. Medication that augments serotonergic efficacy has been shown to reduce hostile feelings and violent outbursts in aggressive psychiatric patients. In addition, some people with a history of impulsively violent behavior show low levels of serotonin in their cerebral spinal fluid.[87] Although these findings present an interesting correlation, it is important to remember that the direction of effect is unclear. It may be that aggressive behavior induces low serotonin levels rather than vice versa.[88] Social circumstances, such as living in poverty or living in a violent environment, may trigger violent behavior in people who are genetically at risk.

As we see, the brain has many structures and processes involved with memory and learning. Memory and learning are dispersed throughout the brain and are amazingly complex. The human brain has an infinite capacity for memory, although it is not always possible to retrieve certain memories. No single brain center stores memory. There are distinct locations where memory is stored. Each part of the brain appears to contribute differently to permanent memory storage.[89] Memory poses an apparent paradox. Experiments with animals with portions of the brain surgically removed show that specific memories are not deleted. Rather, the memory deficit is related to the amount of tissue removed rather than its specific location. As such, on the one hand, memories are localized. On the other hand, they appear to be diffuse.[90] An engram, which is a memory trace, possibly has no specific location but is represented by a "diffuse and perhaps redundant network of altered neurons."[91]

Movement control and motor learning, like memory and learning, is diffused throughout the brain. It involves the interaction of many brain regions, including the basal ganglia, the thalamus, the cerebellum, and many neuron groups located in the midbrain and brainstem, regions that connect the cerebral hemispheres with the spinal cord.[92] The cerebellum is a large and highly convoluted brain structure, located immediately behind the brainstem, with which it is intimately connected. It is involved in aspects of motor learning, and it plays an important role in coordinating movements.[93] The cerebellum governs muscle coordination, the learning of rote movements and all skilled movement.[94] It acts to integrate all this information to ensure smooth coordination of muscle action, enabling us to perform skilled movements more or less automatically. As we learn to walk or speak, or to play video games, for example, the necessary control information is stored within the cerebellum where it can be called upon by commands from the cerebral cortex.[95]

The Child's Brain

The brains of children, particularly the frontal cortex, are not fully developed. As such, children's social scripts are more malleable.[96] Although all of the neurons in the cortex are produced before birth, they are poorly connected. In contrast to the brainstem and spinal cord, the cerebral cortex produces most of its synaptic connections after birth in a massive burst of synapse formation known as the exuberant period. At its peak, the cerebral cortex creates an astonishing two million new synapses every second. These connections bring on a baby's many mental milestones, such as color vision, a pincer grasp, and a strong attachment to parents.[97]

By two years of age, a toddler's cerebral cortex contains well over a hundred trillion synapses. This period of exuberance begins earlier in primary sensory regions, like the visual cortex. It takes off somewhat later in the temporal and frontal lobes, which are involved in higher cognitive and emotional functions. Nonetheless, the number of synapses remains at this peak, over-abundant level in all areas of the cerebral cortex throughout middle childhood, from four to eight years of age. It is theorized that between infancy and the early grade school years, the brain over produces connections—some 50 percent more than will be preserved in adulthood.[98]

The information that is initially transmitted to the frontal lobes for processing and interpretation, then the frontal lobes transmit messages back to the limbic system to modify emotion signals and to the sensory-motor cortex to influence potential actions. The frontal lobes are heavily involved in decision-making, integrating data involving emotions with knowledge-based information. In early childhood, there are few interconnections between the limbic system and the frontal lobes. What results is the "terrible twos" in which children frequently hit, bite, or kick when they feel angry. As children mature, increasing neuronal interconnections evolve between the frontal lobes and the limbic system. This is important regarding self-control because the frontal cortex becomes increasingly able to regulate impulses from the limbic areas and modify actions.[99]

Between the ages of five and seven, a shift occurs in which the frontal areas achieve significant dominance in exerting emotional self-regulation and self-control. However, these developments do not automatically occur, but are heavily influenced by environmental input throughout early childhood. If these networks do not develop in an optimal manner, children do not have the neuronal structure necessary to control their actions in response to strong emotional signals.[100] Very early involvement with electronic entertainment, especially violent video games, thus interfere with a child developing self-control. This appears to be a key contributing factor to childhood conduct disorders and other aggressive and violent behavior.

During this critical period, a child's sensory, motor, emotional, and intellectual experience determines which of these synapses will be preserved, through pruning of the least useful connections. When the brain is in the midst of major rewiring, it is extremely susceptible to outside influences. The experiences children have when their brains are developing have a profound impact on the way they think and perceive as adults.[101] Learning itself may create critical periods in a child's brain. That is, the longer a child has been exposed to one type of experience or environment, the less likely s/he will be able to reverse the synaptic learning that has already taken place.[102] Beginning in the middle elementary school years and continuing until the end of adolescence, the number of synapses gradually declines down to adult levels.[103] During this time, however, the adolescent brain continues to develop.

The ages from two to six comprise Piaget's pre-operational state. Pre-operational thought is characterized by centration and concreteness. Centration is the ability to fix attention on a single, striking feature of an object. Concentration is reacting to things as they appear in immediate, egocentric perception. Readily apparent visual cues dominate the pre-operational child's perception.[104] The pre-operational child is affected by what s/he sees more than by what s/he hears. As such, something what looks frightening is especially scary to the pre-operational child. The fear response in young children results from an inability to distinguish between play and reality.[105]

The development of language skills depends critically on verbal input in the first few years of childhood or certain skills, especially grammar and pronunciation, may be permanently impacted. The critical period of language learning begins to close around five years of age and ends around puberty.[106]

The concrete operational stage is from around seven to eleven years of age. The child is less concretely oriented to the "here and now," to the immediacy of the situation. This is also a time of social development when the child is beginning to develop the notion of self-identity and the process of mastery. The concrete operational child is less frightened.

As Cantor and Sparks point out: "To the extent that fear is a function of perceived or potential threat or danger, unrealistic, impossible or fantastic happenings should diminish in their potential to frighten as children grow and develop cognitively."[107]

Young children have incompletely developed corpora callosa and so have language present in both hemispheres.[108] Eventually, around the age of twelve or thirteen the corpus callosum matures and interconnects the two hemispheres more completely.[109] The maturation of the child's corpus callosum corresponds with Piaget's "symbolic age," the age at which the child is able to think less concretely and more abstractly. Before this maturation children are less able to draw upon the decision-making capability of the left cerebral hemisphere. Also during this time, children learn to utilize their cerebral hemispheres for specific tasks, such as writing or watching television.

Women and Men

Electrical measurements reveal differences in boys' and girls' brain function from the moment of birth. By three months of age, boys' brains and girls' brains respond differently to the sound of human speech. Such differences are presumably a product of sex-related genes or hormones because they appear so early in life.[110]

It is known that testosterone levels rise in male fetuses as early as seven weeks of gestation, and that testosterone affects the growth and survival of neurons in many parts of the brain. Female sex hormones may also play a role in shaping brain development. However, their functions currently are not well understood.[111]

Through growth and from experience with the social environment, the left hemisphere tends to gradually become dominant for sequential, verbal semantic, of propositional functions. At the same time the right hemisphere becomes adept for simultaneous, spatial-imaginal, appositional functions.[112]

Girls and boys have somewhat different developmental timetables, which are reflected by sex differences in the brain. Girls are slightly more advanced by most measures of sensory and cognitive development, including vision, hearing, memory, smell and touch. In addition, they generally lead boys in the emergence of fine motor and language skills.[113]

Boys eventually catch up in many of these areas. By age three, they tend to outperform girls in visual-spatial integration, which is involved in navigation, assembling jigsaw puzzles, and in certain types of hand-eye coordination. Males of all ages tend to perform better on tasks like mental rotation, imagining how an object would look if it were turned 90 degrees. Females of all ages tend to perform better at certain verbal tasks.[114]

Girls' brains seem to be more attuned to social responses. For example, they are more capable of identifying emotional expression in another person's face.[115] Girl babies also tend to respond more readily to human faces and cry more vigorously in response to another infant's cry.[116]

It is important to note that hormones and genes set the stage. However, they do not fully account for sex differences in children's brains. Experience also plays a fundamental role. For example, consider a boy, with his more advanced spatial skills. He may prefer activities like pushing trucks around or climbing, activities, which further develop his visual-spatial skills. A girl, by contrast, may gravitate toward games with dolls and siblings, which further reinforce her verbal and social skills. As such, initial abilities of the brain are magnified into significant differences because of the remarkable plasticity of young's children's brains. This adaptability is facilitated and reinforced by social norms and settings that encourage girls and boys to conform to expectations to behave and play like girls and like boys.

Men tend to have more activity in their temporal-limbic system, which controls emotions linked to action, especially aggression.[117] In one study, subjects were asked to "think of nothing." In men's idling brains, the action was in the temporal-limbic system. This primitive region controls extreme expressions of emotion, such as fighting. "If the pilot light is always on in men in neurons that control aggression and action," it may explain, in part, why men are more prone to violent behavior than women."[118]

Men's brains tend to more lateralized. That is, men tend to rely more on left hemisphere processing. In addition, the two hemispheres operate more independently during certain mental tasks like speaking or navigating around one's environment. The corpora callosa of men take up less volume suggesting that the two hemispheres communicate less.[119] Women tend to be bilaterized for the same kinds of tasks. That this, they tend to use both hemispheres more equally. Women's brains are "a paragon of holism, while men's are a house divided."[120]

Women also tend to utilize the capabilities of the right hemisphere, including the right hemisphere's capacity for language, more than men. This means that women tend to have more communication between the hemispheres and use both hemispheres more fully. This is demonstrated by research of volunteers doing math problems. The women who excelled in performing the problems were apparently using their brain more efficiently than women who did average work.[121] This suggests that these women were using both hemispheres to solve the problems.

The difference between the functioning of the cerebral hemispheres of men and women is illustrated by an experiment by Cecile Naylor of the Bowman Gray School of Medicine. She asked men and women who had brains marked with radioactive tracers to sing, "Row, row, row your boat," and to life their finger when they heard a four-letter word. For men, only one side of the brain lit up. For women, tiny spots on both sides of the brain lit up. As one writer states it, "Women's mental acrobatics were all over the brain;

men's were compartmentalized." This study also showed that with the women, but not the men, some areas associated with vision lit up, indicating that women use more of a visual strategy than men.[122] This may be facilitated by the fact that the corpora callosa of women is 23 percent larger than those of men.[123]

The research also found that women did not have to work as hard as men's brains in judging emotion and emotional expression in faces. Women had more activity in the cingulated gyrus, the evolutionarily recent region that controls complex expressions of emotions, such as showing anger by looks rather than punches. This area in the women's limbic system glowed eight times more than those of men.[124] Women are much more adept in identifying sadness in faces. PET scans showed their brains use less energy to identify the emotion than the men's. Such access to negative emotion may be the reason why women are more prone to depression than men.[125]

Early Research

Research into brain response to electronic media began in the 1960s, using the electroencephalogram, or EEG. In the early 1930s, Hans Berger developed this technique for recording "brain waves" of electrical activity from the surface of the scalp.

The billions of neurons in the brain produce electrochemical changes that can be recorded with highly sensitive instruments that measure small amounts of electrical activity. The EEG has been used widely to measure changes in electrical activity of large areas of the brain, such as the cortex. It has been a valuable tool for investigating many aspects of brain function, such as the mental and cognitive processes associated with sensory stimulation and attention, and the daily sleep-waking cycle.

The EEG is comprised of several different electrical frequencies, two of which are observed in a person who is awake. The alpha rhythm, at 8–12 cycles/second, indicates a resting, inattentive mental state, appearing mainly in the parietal and occipital regions. Alpha rhythms are present when the person is awake, resting, or has her/his eyes closed. When the person is instructed to pay attention to a stimulus or when engaged in active mental activity, a beta rhythm, 15–30 cycles/second is evident.[126]

The EEG has demonstrated correlations between brain activity and television viewing in adults, particularly in advertising industry research.[127] Early research that attempted to ascertain different brain responses to activity measured the EEG of a person who browsed through a magazine immediately prior to viewing television commercials. The researcher found that the person's EEG response to print was different from the EEG response to television. The response to print was described as "active," composed primarily of beta waves, and the response to television was comprised of slow alpha waves.[128] This research finding was later replicated. Weinstein and his associates also found higher levels of alpha activity for television commercials. They also found more beta wave activity for magazine advertising than for television commercials.[129]

Shagass and his colleagues, studying psychiatric patients, found that most showed a reduction in EEG response amplitude, characteristic of beta activity, during television viewing.[130] Mulholland studied the response of children to television using an alpha-biofeedback technique.[131] He also found that children's brains emit alpha waves when watching television. He concluded that children are spending a lot of time learning how to be inattentive or how to operate at a low level of attention while watching television before they begin to go to school.

Television viewing dramatically calls forth alpha waves in the right hemisphere, especially among women and children. This is exhibited by a tendency toward mental passivity, demonstrated by a shortened attention span, a relative inability to think critically, and difficulty in reading. They theorized that television has the tendency to create alpha waves because of the entertaining, dramatized, colorful, and noisy characteristics of television program, qualities that call for processing by the right cerebral hemisphere. They also surmised that the television screen technology of fifty to sixty half-frames per second engaged the left hemisphere's ability to track and identify discrete units of information, thus keeping the left hemisphere occupied. As such, the left hemisphere is not available to process television program content.

Rothschild and his associates found that verbal components of television commercials are more likely to be processed in the left hemisphere, while the right hemisphere showed more involvement in the nonverbal aspects of the commercial.[132] This indicates that the content and form of television programming to some extent and in some circumstances may mitigate right hemisphere involvement.

The research of Yoshida and Kaneko exposed boys, ages six to thirteen, to an animation video. They concluded that there was more right hemisphere activity in the alpha range while watching the video.[133] This is the case because the right hemisphere specializes in visual configurations rather than printed language and also specializes in processing nonverbal sounds, music, and color.

Schellberg and his colleagues found that emotional processing was activated in the right hemisphere.[134] The right hemisphere, particularly the frontal lobe, showed greater activation during negative emotions, while the left was more active during positive emotions.[135] Several other researchers have reported hemispheric differences in relation to negative versus positive television scenes, with greater right hemisphere involvement in negative scenes.[136]

This research showed that television content, especially when portraying negative emotions, is processed by the right hemisphere. A number of these studies revealed that right hemisphere involvement might be mitigated by the content of the programming, the gender of the viewer, and the age of the viewer.

Considering that women tend to rely more on right cerebral hemisphere functioning than men, it is reasonable to conclude that women are more affected by electronic entertainment media and video games that elicit more of a right hemisphere response. It also could be surmised that before the corpus callosum is completely formed, children process television in the right hemisphere because there is incomplete communication between hemispheres.

Now, forty years after this original research, television tends to be more realistic and more violent. There also is more music, and images flash on the screen more quickly. Programming is louder and contains more dangerous sounds, such as gunshots and explosions. All these features, to an even greater degree, trigger right hemisphere activity.

Recent Research

Since the turn of the twenty-first century, neuroscientific research about violent electronic entertainment media has yielded compelling evidence supporting a causal relationship between violent media and aggressive and violent behavior. This recent research also has vindicated the conclusions of early researchers about predominant right hemisphere involvement in television viewing. This newer research utilizes more sophisticated and precise technology, such as magnetic resonance imaging (MRI), which shows a right cerebral hemisphere response to violent video games.

The MRI provides a high-quality, three-dimensional image of organs and structures inside the body without x-rays or other radiation. The MRI uses blood-borne, oxygenated hemoglobin in high magnetic fields to create brain maps with high resolution that allows the tracking of changes in oxygen exchange associated with blood flow in the brain. These images are unsurpassed in detail and may reveal small changes that occur with time. The MRI is particularly helpful in studying the brain and the spinal cord.[137]

The fMRI is a yet more recent development. It provides more detailed maps of brain activities, using noninvasive scanning techniques that measure brain activity under resting and active conditions. It combines high spatial resolution, noninvasive imaging, and a strategy for detecting changes in blood oxygenation levels driven by neuronal activity. The success of this measurement tool is documented in numerous studies.[138] This technologically based research shows that virtual violence activates the same brain patterns of people who are having negative thoughts or who tend to behave aggressively.[139]

Recent fMRI research has lent more credence to earlier research. In 2006 Murray and his colleagues found that violent excerpts predominantly are activated in the right hemisphere, especially the amygdala.[140] In 2006, fMRI research revealed that most of the seventeen distinct brain areas that were activated when a person watches "coherent, interpretable" action sequences were in the right cerebral hemisphere, with activation of the amygdala, the anterior gyrus cingulated, and the posterior gyrus cingulated. It showed deactivation of the anterior gyrus cingulate.[141]

The neuroimaging research validates the earlier research about a right hemisphere response to electronic media. This ability to watch brain responses demonstrates the biological bases for decades of research findings about media exposure. The researchers, however, did not find any activation of left hemisphere language areas by the visual action sequences. This strongly suggests that, while viewing, these sequences are not verbally encoded. Rather, there is a specialized, nonverbal predominantly right hemisphere network that is activated to comprehend film action.[142]

Murray and his colleagues, using the fMRI, asked if brain structures were selectively activated by violent content compared to nonviolent content. They showed violent boxing excerpts to eight to ten-year-old children, as well as nonviolent excerpts from a children's educational television program. They found that violent film excerpts activated children's right hemisphere in areas involved in emotional processing, similar to when children witness real violence.[143] Researchers also found that the perception of threat was evident in activation of the right amygdala.[144] This makes sense because of the amygdala's key role in processing and storing negative emotions.

The posterior cingulated is an area of the brain that serves as a "ready file" for memories that return in a flash. Research shows that this area is activated during violent scenes. This area is implicated in activating aggressive scripts and posttraumatic stress disorder.[145] This suggests that these young children were actively processing the video violence and storing the aggressive scripts in an area of the brain that is reserved for long-term memory of traumatic events. These aggressive scripts facilitate rapid recall and serve as a guide for behavior. Because these scripts are readily available, the child is more likely to behave more aggressively and more swiftly when provoked.[146] This helps to explain why children who are exposed to violent electronic media and games are more likely to be physically aggressive.

A key research study discovered that although the children were viewing violence that they knew was fantasy violence, their brains did not distinguish between fantasy violence and real violence.[147] This is in keeping with earlier research that discovered this inability to differentiate between mediated violence and real violence. Other initial research shows that although video game players are aware that they are playing a fantasy game, "preconscious neural mechanisms" might not differentiate between fantasy and reality.[148]

Desensitization

A key issue in studies of media effects has been desensitization. Neuroscientific research has begun to identify the regions of the brain that are associated with desensitization and aggression. Neuroscientists define desensitization as "a reduction in emotion-related physiological reactivity to real violence."[149] Desensitization includes a flattening of affect reactions to violence, a reduced likelihood of helping a victim, and reduction in sympathy for the victim.[150] The General Aggression Model is useful in understanding desensitization processes. Affective and cognitive components of the General Aggression Model have been examined at a neural level. They help to investigate how neurocognitive systems are shaped, perhaps permanently, by repeated exposure to violent media.[151] Aggressive behavior is based on the learning, activation, and application of aggression-related brain structures stored in memory. This learning takes place through encounters with the social world. Much of this learning occurs by observing real and fictional characters.[152]

The first response of children and many adults to violent media is fear and anxiety.[153] When violent stimuli are repeatedly presented in a positive emotional context, such as alongside exciting background music, sound effects, visual effects, and rewards for violence, these initial distressing reactions are reduced, as evidenced in lowered physiological arousal. Desensitized people are less likely to notice aggressive events, perceive fewer injuries, feel less empathy, and have fewer negative attitudes about violence. People who play violent video games become habituated or get used to all the violence, eventually becoming physically numb to it.[154] As one neuroscientist states it, "In short, the modern entertainment media landscape could accurately be described as an effective systemic violence desensitization tool."[155]

Recent evidence suggests that exposure to violent media is linked to decreases in the activity of brain structures that are needed for regulation of aggressive behavior and to increases in the activity of structures needed to carry out aggressive plans.[156] Desensitization is linked to the anterior cingulated cortex, which has the executive function of monitoring and correcting ongoing behavior. The anterior cingulated cortex is also associated with antisocial behaviors and aggression. Activity in this region is chronically low in aggressive people.[157]

Activity in the anterior cingulated cortex is reduced during imagined aggressive interaction.[158] Researchers have found a negative relationship between activation in the anterior cingulated cortex and the amount of violent media exposure in adolescents in the previous twelve months.[159] They discovered that specific brain areas that process emotion are deactivated while playing violent video games. They examined activation in the anterior cingulated gyrus as young adults played the violent games. They were able to determine whether activity in the anterior cingulated cortex was different during specific types of play within the game, which ranged from passive observation to active fighting and killing. They discovered that violent game play substantially reduced activation in the portion of the anterior cingulated cortex that is most involved in processing emotions. This and other research show that activation is reduced for neural mechanisms important for self-control and evaluation.[160] If chronic violent game play reduces emotional processing in these brain structures, then it is possible that this reduced emotional processing underlies the effects of chronic violent video games on aggression and desensitization.[161] The observed patterns of brain activity were not very different from those observed in chronically violent individuals or from the patterns observed when witnessing real violence.[162]

Research with children has shown that violent scenes activate a network of brain regions, including the posterior cingulated cortex and the hippocampus, that are involved in processing emotional stimuli, episodic memory retrieval, detecting threats in the environment, memory encoding, and motor programming. The resultant linking of memory and emotion to motor activation shows how viewing media violence can integrate existing aggression-related thoughts and feelings, and thereby facilitate aggressive behavior.[163]

Executive Functioning

The prefrontal cortex is responsible for executive functioning, which involves the ability to inhibit, regulate, direct, plan, and execute behavior. A deficit in executive functioning is likely to underlie impulsive, poorly planned, and aggressive behavior, cognitive function, and emotional control.[164] Researchers have found that even short-term exposure to violent video games inhibits frontal lobe functioning that is involved in suppressing uninvited thoughts and behavior.[165] Researchers also found moderate to strong relationships between higher amounts of media violence exposure and executive functioning They also found a stronger relationship for adolescents who had disruptive behavior disorder diagnoses.[166]

Another study found that young adult males with low past exposure to violent video games showed less activation in the left inferior frontal lobe while playing violent video games for one week. Researchers concluded that their findings indicate that violent video games have a long-term negative effect on brain functioning. They also found that these effects were reduced after one week of not playing violent video games.[167] Research also has revealed that changes in frontal lobe activity during extended video game exposure may be similar to those observed during the early stages of addiction.[168]

Violent video game play involves the right hemisphere for many of the same reasons that television elicits the right hemisphere's response. Violent video games involve processing negative emotions, color, and motion. They also require other right hemispheric functions, such as cognitive mapping and manipulating objects in the immediate environment. The left cerebral hemisphere may be involved somewhat because of the need for decision-making, but the right hemisphere has much more involvement than the left cerebral hemisphere.

It is likely that children who watch television before their brains are fully developed are more susceptible to media violence and video game violence. Women and people who live in cultures that reinforce right hemisphere dominance also would be more receptive.

Violent electronic entertainment and video games influence learning, emotions, and behavior. They elicit survival and appetite responses from the most ancient parts of the nervous system. With exposure, especially repeated exposure, brain mechanisms activate aggressive behavioral scripts and suppress executive structures that normally inhibit aggressive and violent actions. In addition, neuroscientists suggest that brain structures may be modified over time with repeated exposure, especially exposure to violent video games.

The behavior resulting from the brain's response to electronic media and games is contrary to human nature. What are some of the long-term behavioral consequences of these deeply rooted influences on brain functioning? To answer this question, look at the behavior of children nowadays. Many children have become excitement addicts, with short attention spans, a low boredom threshold, an often sullen or indifferent attitude, and sarcastic and aggressive social interaction. Many children have developed a "hostile bias" and tend to have a worldview that is dark.

An increasing number of children exhibit characteristics of conduct disorders, such as oppositional defiant disorder. Research indicates that this disorder is not genetically based and appears across the income spectrum.[169] So why has this disorder become more prevalent in recent years? A key factor that that is overlooked is the influence of violent electronic entertainment media.

Academic Performance

In addition to aggressive behavior, electronic media and games influence academic performance. How does the preponderance of right cerebral hemisphere involvement caused by electronic media affect children's academic performance, especially in terms of the three Rs?

The Flynn effect documents increases in IQ scores of people in industrialized countries in the twentieth century.[170] Flynn reports that gains in IQ test scores have been about 0.30 points per year from 1947 to 2007.[171] At first glance, the Flynn effect seems to fly in the face of the argument that electronic media consumption tends to require right cerebral hemisphere skills. However, Neisser pointed out that the Flynn effect is largely due to increased performance in nonverbal items, especially those that draw on spatial visualization,[172] a right cerebral hemisphere function. Flynn reports that Americans gained twenty-four points on identifying similarities in figures between 1947 and 2002. At the same time, they showed only a four-point gain in vocabulary and two points on arithmetic and information.[173] The large point gains relate to visual-spatial reasoning (right hemisphere skills) and the small gains relate to computational reasoning (left hemisphere skills). Neisser rightly concludes that the Flynn effect might be due to the great increase in the use of electronic media by children. This conclusion is supported by electronic media being newly introduced in the twentieth century. Also, the Flynn effect is evident in industrialized countries, countries in which electronic media are prevalent.

What is the current state of young people's academic ability in the United States? There are severe deficits in subjects that require left cerebral hemisphere involvement. Only 3 percent of fourth, eighth, and twelfth graders can write above a "minimal" or "adequate" level. Less than 10 percent of seventeen-year-olds can do "rigorous" academic work in "basic" subjects. Only 20 percent of nine-year-olds can perform even basic mathematical operations. Among thirteen-year-olds, only 10 percent find, understand, and summarize complicated information. Only one in eight thirteen-year-olds can understand and apply intermediate scientific knowledge and principles. This is among the lowest of many countries in the developed world. A 1993 study by the United States Department of Education found that 90 million adults, 47 percent of the population, demonstrate low levels of literacy.[174]

What about children for whom television viewing is a modal activity? The tendency is to become right hemisphere dominant.[175] This conclusion is evident in research and also in our everyday world. Activities that require left hemisphere activities, such as reading, writing, and arithmetic, are more difficult for right hemisphere dominant people. This conclusion has been consistently supported by research for decades. In the early 1980s, Fetler correlated the results of the California Assessment Program, a study of over 10,000 sixth graders. He found that heavy television viewing affects school achievement. Not surprisingly, he found that the students most affected were the most socially disadvantaged.[176] Similarly, Salomon and Leigh found that reading requires more cognitive capacity, that is, more left hemisphere involvement, than television.[177] Forty-seven percent of high school graduates in 1950 could name the largest lake in North America compared to 38 percent in 2002. In 2001, 52 percent identified Germany, Japan, or Italy, not the Soviet Union as a United States' World War II ally. One-quarter of eighteen to twenty-four-year-olds in a 2004 survey drew a blank on Dick Cheney.[178] Some investigators conclude that extensive television viewing results in an inability to think critically.[179] Generations of children increasingly have exhibited an inability to pay attention, persevere with problems, read, and use language effectively. As Healey concludes, children have "endangered minds."

Research that investigates brain response to electronic media demonstrates that the ability of violent entertainment media and games to compromise critical thinking and to teach violence is deeply rooted within the nervous system. These compelling research findings reinforce and add another level of validation to the previous research that shows that violent media, especially violent video games, have profoundly negative effects. These findings lay to rest the argument that violent electronic entertainment media do not have a significant influence on thinking and behavior.

CHAPTER 10

THE FUTURE OF VIOLENCE

> What would our children be like if it were not for the movies?
> —Walter Lippman, 1930

What is the future of violence? History is prologue to the present and to the future. To predict future violence, the history of violence needs to be scrutinized within larger social, economic, and political contexts. This allows a cohort analysis, an assessment of the socializing influences that affect different generations of people.

At the beginning of the twentieth century, youth violent crime was a rare phenomenon. The century's massive, prolonged wars fortified an ideology that considered violence an acceptable, if not a preferable way, to settle conflict. Continuous wars also have amplified the warrior-ideal as the model for boys and men. Juvenile delinquency first was recognized as a social problem during World War II when young men were committing "acts against common decency."[1] In addition to world wars, the twentieth century witnessed the advent of increasingly violent electronic entertainment media on a massive scale. The last decade of the twentieth century also experienced the most brutal youth violence up to that period of time.

In the midst of what may appear to be widespread material abundance, the culture of violence has been complicit in severe and widespread poverty, resulting in more disenfranchised young people who have little hope for the future. At the same time the culture of violence, fueled by capitalism, has allowed violence industries to become renegade.

The culture of violence and its industries have created a social climate that has become incendiary. Between 1960 and 1991, the United States population increased by 40 percent. However, violent crime increased 500 percent. In 1957, the assault rate was 60 per 100,000, and by 1995, it was 440.[2] During the early 1990s, homicide was the leading cause of death for adolescent and older males.[3] Youth violence outside of school peaked in 1993. By 1994, the rate of children twelve years and younger who committed violent crimes increased by 32 percent. By 1997, the juvenile homicide rate escalated, increasing 49 percent.[4]

Observers expressed great concern, projecting dramatic increases in juvenile violent crime.[5] Professor Alan Fox warned of an even greater "impending youth crime wave" in the early decades of the twenty-first century, as did the US House of Representatives.[6] The magnitude of these predictions was mitigated by tremendous government and community efforts. Massive energy and resources were directed to reduce youth violence and school violence in the 1990s. These efforts included the formation of the new Office of Juvenile Justice and Delinquency Prevention, the Community-Oriented Policing program, and community-based movements, such as the Million Man March. Other influences include a relatively robust economy in the 1990s, a large youth cohort graduating into adulthood, and a "get tough" policy on sentencing.[7] In addition, some advances were made in gun legislation that, although weak and partial, may account for some of the reductions in homicide.[8] The "best guess" of some criminologists about the drop in the homicide rate was the decline in the market for crack cocaine. The related murder rate had fallen off and deals became more secretive and less combative.[9]

In 1985 1.3 million juveniles were arrested for violent crimes. By the late 1990s, it appeared that that youth violent crime rate had declined. However, juvenile violent crime arrests still exceeded the 1988 level by 49 percent.[10] Although the level of violence was still very high, observers breathed a sigh of relief. There were 1.86 million young people arrested for violent crime in 1998, but this rate declined in the next few years. By 2002, crime increased again.[11] Between 2013 and 2017 property crimes committed by juveniles had decreased, but murders by juveniles had increased 23 percent.[12]

School Violence

The 1990s also were an extraordinarily troubled time for schools. The decade experienced a marked increase in bullying, school-associated violent deaths, and the introduction of a "new and unique" violence, rampage school shootings. Bullying increased precipitously, with estimates of one-quarter of school children being victimized by bullying. Nowadays as many as half of students report being bullied.

The 1992–1993 school year experienced an unprecedented spike in school violence.

That school year experienced the highest peak of school-associated violent deaths that were ever recorded. In 1993, youth homicide outside of school also peaked. The year 1994 also was the year in which rampage school shootings became more frequent and more lethal, shocking the national consciousness. By 1994, violence was identified as the biggest problem experienced in public schools.

Between 1992 and 2006, school-associated violent deaths increased by almost 235 percent.[13] Between 1994 and 1998, there were a yearly average of forty-two school-associated violent deaths.[14] Between 2000 and 2008, the annual average dropped to thirty-two violent deaths annually. By 2009, the number increased to thirty-eight violent deaths on school campuses.

Rampage school shootings also increased in frequency and lethality. In the seventeen-year period between 1974 and 1991, the United States experienced ten rampage school shootings in which forty people were killed or injured. This is about 0.6 shootings a year with about 2.4 victims a year. In the fifteen-year period between 1992 and 2007, there were thirty-seven school rampage shootings in which 236 people were killed or injured. This is an annual average of 2.5 rampage school shootings and sixteen victims. This represents a 417 percent increase in rampage school shootings during that time and a 267 percent increase in victims.[15] Between 2000 and 2009, there were approximately twenty-five rampage school shootings. Between 2010 and 2017, there were forty-seven, almost double the number of the previous nine years.[16] By 2018, there were dozens of rampage school shootings and public rampage shootings. In 2019, there were over four hundred rampage shootings.

A Cohort Analysis

A cohort analysis of the effects of violent electronic entertainment media takes into account the year the person was born, the age of first exposure to media and video game violence, the amount of time spent consuming media, the kind of violence and the degree of realism in the material. These factors are assessed within the culture.

The aggression and violence depicted in cartoons was reinforced in the early 1980s by the introduction of action figures in children's programming in 1983. In 1984, the National Association of Broadcasters deregulated its guidelines. These changes resulted in even more violent content and more program alignment with war toys.

Children in the culture of violence grew up in the 1990s with a heightened consciousness of war. They witnessed the onslaught of Operation Desert Storm, "the forever war." This was been the most extensively and intensely televised war since the advent of the electronic media. The war was accompanied by remarkable changes in the entertainment media landscape.

The year 1992 was pivotal. Violent television content doubled to ten violent acts an hour and again increased to fourteen per hour in 1994. A powerful new factor was the sudden and widespread popularity of first-person shooter games. This new technology was literally a game-changer. Games like *Castle Wolfenstein* allowed gamers to look down the gun barrel and directly shoot people. This was closely followed by *Doom*, which raised the bar on graphic and realistic violence even higher. This new landscape of violence was reinforced by the *Mortal Kombat* series, another incredibly violent game.

The Primary Causal Factor

Rampage school shootings are a new and unique form of violence that can be understood by analyzing new and unique events that engendered them. These events include the escalation of war in the 1990s, unprecedentedly high entertainment media violence, and first-person shooter games, a new and unique entertainment technology. These monumental events raised the threshold of the influence of violent electronic entertainment to new heights. The intensity of this synergistic interaction has been sustained by perpetually higher rates of entertainment media violence and the continuous development of increasingly realistic, immersive, and graphically violent video games. These new and unique innovations constitute the primary causal factor in the escalation of bullying and in the genesis of the new and unique rampage school shootings.

Rampage school shooters, with few exceptions, have played ultra-violent video games for years that embody wishful identification with warrior-heroes. Many are heavily exposed to or addicted to violent video games, especially first-person shooter combat games. Rampage shootings are enactments of first-person shooter combat games. These shootings are characterized by charging into a space and killing as many people as possible in a short period of time. Rampage shooters mimic military tactics and strategies they learned from first-person shooter combat games. The shooters realize their wishful identification with video game warrior-heroes by replicating and playing out the scenarios they learned so well. They often wear military combat garb, including body armor at times. They usually are heavily armed, often with automatic weapons, and they often have extraordinarily high hit rates. The military garb, equipment, appearance, and maneuvers of rampage school shooters are very similar to the first-person shooter, warrior-hero games that were their teachers. Many shooters black out and do not remember the actual rampage. This is an indication that the shooting is reflexive, a neurological reaction taught so well by first-person shooter games.

So, what is the primary causal factor in rampage school shootings, this "new and unique violence"? The primary causal factor consists of two nearly simultaneous events that interact synergistically. In 1992 entertainment media violence doubled to unprecedently high rates. Also, in 1992 first-person shooter games, a new and unique form of video game technology, became widely available. A compelling connection between these two new events and rampage school shootings becomes evident when realizing that this extraordinary new violence emerged very shortly after these innovations were introduced.

Identifying the primary causal factor lays to rest the argument that violent electronic media do not play a decisive role in this new and unique violence. Progressively more violent electronic entertainment media are being developed continuously. Research and development are driven by market competition. These developments strengthen and perpetuate the effects of the primary causal factor. There seems to be no end in sight.

What Is the Future of Violence?

Violence in the future will worsen if the root cause of violence is not addressed—social and economic injustice. As the quality of life in the culture of violence continues to deteriorate, more people will find refuge in an electronic virtual world. It will become even more enticing to escape to a world in which one is heroic and extraordinarily powerful. Without intervention, future generations of children will retreat even more into violent virtual worlds. They will become more desensitized and more prone to aggressive and violent behavior. At the same time, they will be less able to think critically and less likely to become involved in civic life.

The violent content and resulting desensitization will be raised continuously. The more people become immersed in violent virtual worlds, the more industries will raise the threshold with more technological innovations in order to hold the consumers' interest. It is like the dragon eating its own tail. If not stopped, it can only escalate.

Pervasive poverty and lack of public resources will produce more violence in the family, school, and community. The family will experience more domestic violence, and if not sufficiently addressed, bullying will become even more commonplace, motivating future criminal behavior as well as school shootings.

The violence industries are motivated solely by profit at any cost. These industries continue to develop programs and games that are increasingly violent and realistic. The consequences will continue to be deadly. If uncheck, these violence industries will continue to shape the future.

Schools are the crucibles of the future. Schools are powerful forces that produce violence. They also are mighty forces that can transform the culture of violence.

CHAPTER 11

WHAT WE CAN DO: THE OPPORTUNITY

> Washing one's hands of the conflict between the powerful and the powerless means to side with the powerful, not to be neutral.
>
> —Paolo Freire

The culture of violence does not respect life. It promotes violence and death. The crisis of school violence gives us the opportunity to change the culture of violence. This is an opportunity to act on the human need for more peaceful schools and a more peaceful world. Our ability to transform the future depends on our willingness to change the present. Religious leaders have acknowledged the need for "a moral revolution that begins with a fundamental respect for life, recovers a sense of right and wrong, and rejects vengeance in the face of violence."[1]

Our essential human nature is contrary to the culture of violence and the violence industries. The interrelated qualities of acceptance, respect, compassion, personal efficacy, democracy, and justice are embedded in our nature. We need to ensure that our children honor and embody the qualities of compassion, empathy, and the human desire to be of service. These qualities are essential for democracy and peace. They also are necessary for human survival.

Martin Luther King Jr. reminds us that "there can be no peace without justice." This means justice in the family, the school, the workplace, the community, the country, and the world.

Human nature requires that the individual be capable and effective in the world. Human beings are most gratified when making a contribution to the world. We resonate with working to safeguard our nature. The history of the human struggle for justice and for freedom is testament to this. People still make tremendous sacrifices, at times giving their lives for justice and freedom.

Mutual respect among men and women is part of our nature. Boys and men need to be given emotional, intellectual, and social support for nonviolence and respect for women.

Schools are the crucibles of democracy and we are its guardians. We can change the future by taking action in our intertwined roles as individuals, parents, teachers, and citizens. Resources for change are included in this book's appendix.

Individuals

Change starts by making the decision to act. Carl Rogers concluded that when we make a decision that we know is the right decision, we always become stronger.[2] The most fundamental way to begin to change the present and the future is to change ourselves. Gandhi advised us to be the change that we want to see in the world. Archbishop Shuen advises us to "speak the truth, be peacemakers and take positive steps to rid our local community and society of violence."[3] Pope Paul VI succinctly said that if you want peace, work for justice. The venerable Thich Nhat Hanh points out that by cultivating "the seeds of compassion, we nourish peace within us and around us."[4] Desiring peace is simply a sentiment if this desire is not put into action. The sage advises us that compassion that is not put into practice is "like beautiful flowers that are colorful but have no fragrance."[5]

We all have been socialized since birth in the culture of violence. We have become desensitized while thinking that others are more influenced by violent media. In order to embody change, we need to assess the extent to which we have been affected by the culture and its industries. To what extent has the culture of violence stolen our humanity?

Working to free ourselves from the shackles of the culture of violence is a move toward greater humanization and freedom. The Dalai Lama writes: "We are all on this planet together. We are all brothers and sisters with the same physical and mental faculties, the same problems, and the same needs. We must all contribute to the fulfillment of the human potential and the improvement of life as much as we are able.... Ours is a desperate time. Those who have something to offer should come forward."[6] It may be that true peace can come to us as individuals only if we work for peace.

Parents

Young people are exposed to an increasingly violent culture. Parents can encourage creative and cooperative play rather than play that is competitive and simulates killing.

Parents can spark the creation of media literacy at home and in school and advocate for this proven method and educate the educators about its effectiveness and necessity. Mothers and fathers can provide children with more opportunities to develop positive leisure-time skills. Limiting screen time allows families to spend more quality time together.

Parents can help to empower their children by encouraging them to become involved in issues that affect their lives and their future. Young people's banner is the desire for efficacy and freedom. Children want opportunities to make a difference in the world. Parents can become empowered and so help their children become empowered. However, there is no empowerment without action. Become involved in your schools. Support the staff and become involved in the Parent Teacher Association. As a parent at a meeting recently said: "Everything seems to be out of control until you act."

Teachers

Teachers can be the world's most powerful change agents because they can teach democracy, peace, and justice. Teachers and schools can better meet the needs of human nature through liberatory principles and practices. Democracy is fostered by facilitating democratic classrooms in which students have a chance to express themselves and have a voice in decision-making. Such practices can be intertwined with the curriculum in any discipline, especially history, government, and the social sciences.

Teach democracy, compassion, and justice by modeling democracy, compassion, and justice. To do this, the warrior-ideal and the Barbie-ideal need to be countered because they promote polarization, hierarchy, disrespect, and violence.

As Paolo Freire has shown us, we cannot support democracy and the humanization of students through the banking education method. "True humanists" work for the humanization of students as well as for their own humanization. Banking methods negate the pursuit of humanization and liberation.

Liberatory education centers on the needs of human nature. The values of acceptance, respect, compassion, efficacy, democracy, and justice can be nurtured in the classroom. This can take a variety of forms, such as democratic decision-making, student-centered learning, empathy training, gender sensitivity, and service learning. Media literacy is a key component in safeguarding human needs and in teaching critical thinking which is necessary for an effective citizenry.

Young people want to be of service and contribute to the world. Incorporate opportunities for their involvement in your teaching. Young people love to create alternative media and to teach media literacy to their families and peers. Media literacy can help them to directly address the causes of their own oppression and become effective leaders. Media literacy is a catalyst for understanding and for action. Media literacy prompts critical thinking and inspires young people to act. The deconstruction of media messages and themes that constitute their culture is a natural tool to spark critical thinking and positive social change. Media literacy challenges children and adults to understand how human culture is shaped by commercial interests. It provides opportunities to create a life-affirming culture rather than one that promotes death.

Teachers can play a key role in helping to empower young people to become involved in improving their schools, communities, and world. Provide teachers with support and guidance so that they can make more meaningful contributions. Teachers can play a decisive role in helping children to, in Freire's words, "name their world."

In addition, teacher organizations and teacher unions can join efforts with such advocacy organizations as T.R.U.C.E. (Teachers Resisting Unhealthy Children's Education) to bring about positive changes in policies and legislation that regulate the violence industries, especially the violent entertainment media industries.

Schools

There is no hope for peace in our communities and world if we do not have peace in our schools. School culture can teach violence or it can evolve into a culture that creates peace and justice. Schools can institute a school-wide violence prevention program that embraces and establishes policies, programs, and curricula that acknowledge and celebrate the human need for respect, acceptance, compassion, efficacy, democracy, and justice. Schools can address the problem of excessive hierarchy in schools, from student cliques to the school board room. Schools can reduce and prevent school violence by creating school-wide and district-wide media literacy training and implementation. As a corollary, schools can place less emphasis on competitive sports, especially violent ones. Schools are in a unique position to provide opportunities for young people to learn new roles and positive leisure-time activities, including volunteerism.

School boards and school board associations can yield tremendous influence on industry regulation, policy, and legislation, especially when joining efforts with likeminded organizations.

Citizens

These recommendations are necessary. However, they are not sufficient. In order for our actions to be sufficient, elected representatives need to be held accountable. Our government needs to fulfill its responsibility "to create a more perfect union" by reining in and regulating the renegade violence industries.

There truly is power in numbers. We can restore ourselves by joining the many other good-hearted people working to improve schools, communities, country, and world. Many organizations are dedicated to protecting democracy and working for peace. Citizens can work with likeminded organizations to bring pressure to bear on elected representatives to enact and enforce laws that regulate the violence industries. Legislators can hold the electronic entertainment industry accountable.

We cannot afford to have our children and future sacrificed at the altar of profit. We are powerful because our votes and our money sustain government and corporations. And they know it. Let us hold them accountable. Let us reclaim our power.

APPENDIX

SCHOOL VIOLENCE PREVENTION RESOURCES

American Academy of Pediatrics. "Media Matters." www.aap.org. The national media education campaign of the AAP. This page has links to helpful articles about children and media violence, as well as action alerts and policy statements.

Bushman, Brad. J. "Teaching Students about Violent Media Effects." *Teaching of Psychology* 45, no. 2 (March 2018): 200–206.

Center for Internet Behavior. www.virtual-addiction.com. Psychological help for internet and video game addiction.

Center for Media Literacy. www.medialit.org. A comprehensive Web site of media literacy information and resources. Emphasis on critical thinking skills in accessing, analyzing, evaluating, and creating media. Teaching resources include "Beyond Blame: Challenging Violence in the Media."

Center on Media and Child Health, Children's Hospital, Boston, Harvard Medical School. www.cmch.tv. Its mission is to help children use media in safe and healthy ways. "Smart searches" are available for research.

Coalition for Quality Children's Media. www.kidsfirst.org. Their newsletter, *Kids First*, reviews and rates children's movies and videos.

Commonsense Media. www.commonsensemedia.org. Reviews children's media in terms of age appropriateness and rates media based on developmental criteria, including role models, commercialism, violence, and stereotyping.

Engaging Schools (formerly Educators for Social Responsibility). https://engagingschools.org. Promotes equity, community, and democracy. Its Early

Childhood Peaceable Classroom Project was described in Dr. Diane E. Levin's book *Teaching Young Children in Violent Times: Building a Peaceable Classroom*.

International Children's Media Center. https://icmediacenter.org. Advocacy and resources for media literacy.

International Clearinghouse on Children, Youth and Media. Nordicom, University of Gothenburg, Sweden. http://www.nordicom.gu/se/en/clearinghouse. An international knowledge center.

Media Education Foundation. www.mediaed.org. Produces and distributes award-winning resources, such as *The Killing Screens: Media and the Culture of Violence*, *Consuming Kids: The Commercialization of Children*, *Media Violence and the Culture of Fear*, and *Dreamworlds 3*, which addresses violence against women. It is funded, in part, by the Canadian Radio-Television Telecommunications Commission and provides resources for teachers and parents, such as "Deconstructing Online Hate," "Exploring Media and Race," "Talking to Kids About Advertising: How Marketers Target Kids."

Media Wise. https://www.poynter.org/mediawise. Educates about violence in the media through public awareness, education, and community action. They help children, youth, and adults to become discriminating media consumers by learning how to analyze, evaluate, and interpret media messages and images. *MediaSmarts* is a video-based media literacy and antiviolence curriculum for middle schools and youth-serving agencies.

Moore, Michael. *Bowling for Columbine*. Documentary. 2002. The Cannes award-winning video about the Columbine tragedy.

National Coalition on Television Violence. www.nctvv.org. Since 1980, the NCTV has been providing useful information regarding the amount of television violence, the accuracy of rating systems, and practical ideas for citizen advocacy.

Peace Action. www.peaceaction.org. The nation's largest grassroots peace network with chapters and affiliates across the country. Its purpose is to advocate for a lower, more reasonable military budget.

Teachers Resisting Unhealthy Children's Education (TRUCE). www.truceteachers.org. A national group of educators who are deeply concerned about how children's entertainment and toys affect the play and behavior of children in the classroom. They promote awareness with such resources as "Toys, Play and Young Children Action Guide." TRUCE also publishes a helpful newsletter.

Turn Off the TV. www.turnoffthetv.com. Its mission is to bring people together by encouraging families and friends to turn off the television and spend time playing, learning, and communicating.

Veterans for Peace. htps://www.vereransforpeace.org. A global organization of military veterans and allied dedicated to creating a culture of peace by using their unique experiences as veterans. Over 140 chapters worldwide.

War Resisters League. www.warresistersleague.org. The oldest peace organization in the United States. Promotes peace and advocates for a reasonable US Department of Defense budget.

Wired Safety. https://wiresafety.com. Information about internet safety.

NOTES

■ **Introduction: The Crisis**

1. Kathleen Maguire and Ann L. Pastore, *Sourcebook of Criminal Justice, 1995* (Washington, DC: US Department of Justice, 1996).
2. Lauren Musu-Gillette, Anlan Zhang, Ke Wang, Zizhi Zhang, and Barbara A. Oudekerk, *Indicators of School Crime and Safety: 2018* (Washington, DC: Bureau of Justice Statistics and National Center for Education Statistics, 2019), iii, https://nces.ed.gov/pubs2019/2019047.pdf.
3. Ira Pollack and Carlos Sundermann, "Creating Safe Schools: A Comprehensive Approach," *Juvenile Justice: School Violence, An Overview* 8, no. 1 (2001): 13.
4. Mark H. Moore, Carol V. Petrie, Anthony A. Braga, and Brendan L. McLaughlin, eds., *Deadly Lessons: Understanding Lethal School Violence* (Washington, DC: National Academies Press, 2003), 9.
5. Resources for change are included in the appendix.

■ **Chapter 1. The Causes of Violence: Standard Explanations**

1. N. A. Weiner, M. A. Zahn, and R. J. Sagi, eds., introduction to *Violence: Patterns, Causes, Public Policy* (San Diego: Harcourt, Brace, Jovanovich, 1990), xiii.
2. Isabella Granic, Adam Lobel, and C. M. E. Engels Rutger, "The Benefits of Playing Video Games," *American Psychologist* 69, no. 1 (2014): 1–66.

3. World Health Organization, *World Report on Violence and Health* (Geneva: WHO, 2019), 1.
4. Margaret Seawell, ed., *National Television Violence Study*, vol. 1 (Thousand Oaks, CA: Sage, 1997). Graeme Newman, *Understanding Violence* (New York: J.B. Lippincott, 1979), 1.
5. Patrick Tolan and Nancy Guerra, *What Works in Reducing Adolescent Violence: An Empirical Review of Field* (Boulder: The Center for the Study of Violence and Violence Prevention, 1994), 1.
6. Tolan and Guerra, *What Works in Reducing Adolescent Violence*, 1.
7. M. A. Straus and R. J. Gelles, "Societal Changes in Family Violence from 1975 to 1985 as Revealed by Two National Surveys," *Journal of Marriage and Family* 48 (1986): 465–79.
8. Osgood, O'Malley, Bachman, and Johnston, 1989, in Tolan and Guerra, *What Works in Reducing Adolescent Violence*, 3.
9. Margaret A. Zahn, Henry J. Brownstein, and Shelly L. Jackson, eds., *Violence: From Theory to Research* (Cincinnati, OH: Anderson, 2004), 181.
10. Phillip J. Cook and John H. Laub, "After the Epidemic: Recent Trends in Youth Violence in the United States," *From Crime and Justice: A Review of Research*, edited by Michael Tonry (University of Chicago Press, 2002), cited in Weiner et al., *Violence*, 181.
11. Weiner et al., *Violence*, 181.
12. Darrell J. Steffensmeier, Emilie Anderson Allan, Miles D. Harer, and Cathy Streifel, "Age and the Distribution of Crime," *Journal of Sociology* 94, no. 4 (1989): 803–31; P. E. Tracy, M. E. Wolfgang, and R. M. Figlio, *Delinquency Careers in Two Birth Cohorts* (New York: Plenum Press, 1990).
13. National Criminal Justice Research Service, *Serving High Risk Youth: Lessons from Research and Programming* (Washington, DC: U.S. Department of Justice, 2009).
14. Margaret Seawell, ed., *National Television Violence Study*, vol. 2 (Thousand Oaks, CA: Sage Publications, 1998).
15. *McNeil-Lehrer Report*, "Youth Violence," aired December 29, 1994, on PBS.
16. Joanna Schaffhausen, "The Biological Basis of Aggression," Brain Connection, November 26, 2006, https://brainconnection.brainhq.com/2006/11/26/the-biological-basis-of-aggression/.
17. Richard J. Gerrig and Philip G. Zimbardo, *Psychology and Life* (Boston: Pearson/Allyn and Bacon, 2005), 588.
18. Gerrig and Zimbardo, *Psychology and Life*, 589.
19. Schaffhausen, "The Biological Basis of Aggression."
20. Richard J. Davidson, David .C. Jackson, and Nancy.H. Kalin, "Emotion, Plasticity, Context and Regulation: Perspectives for Neuroscience," *Psychological Bulletin* 126 (2000): 890–909.
21. Schaffhausen, "The Biological Basis of Aggression."
22. Cara Santa Maria, "The Mind of a Mass Murderer: Charles Whitman, Bain Damage and Violence," *Science* (March 28, 2012).
23. Anthony A. Mazur and Andrew Booth, "Testosterone and Dominance in Men," *Behavioral and Brain Sciences* 21 (1998), 353–63.
24. Schaffhausen, "The Biological Basis of Aggression."

25. Berman et al. (1993) and Olweus et al. (1988), as cited in David G. Myers, *Exploring Psychology* (New York: Worth, 2007), 552.
26. James M Dabbs Jr., Frank J. Bernieri, Rebecca K. Strong, Rebecca Campo, and Rhonda Milan, "Going on Stage: Testosterone in Greetings and Meetings," *Journal on Research in Personality* 35 (2001): 27–40.
27. Schaffhausen, "The Biological Basis of Aggression."
28. Reiss and Roth, as cited in Stephen E. Brown, Esbensen Finn-Aage, and Gilbert Geis, *Criminology: Explaining Crime and Its Context,* 6th ed. (Cincinnati, OH: Anderson, 2007), 256.
29. Mazur and Booth, "Testosterone and Dominance in Men."
30. Paul C. Bernhardt, James M. Dabbs, Jr., James Fielden, Julies A. Lutter, and Candice D. Lutter, "Testosterone Changes during Vicarious Experiences of Winning and Losing among Fans at Sporting Events," *Physiology and Behavior* 65 (1998): 59–62.
31. Steven Stolberg, "Fear Clouds Search for Genetic Roots of Violence," *Los Angeles Times*, December 30, 1993.
32. D. P. Farrington, "Implications of Biological Findings for Criminological Research," *The Causes of Crime: New Biological Approaches,*" edited by Sarnoff A. Mednick, Terrie E. Moffitt, and Susan A. Stack (New York: Cambridge University Press, 1987), 42–61.
33. Charles Q. Choi, "Steroids Fuel Crime," *Live Science*, November 6, 2006.
34. Richard B. Felson, "A Rational-Choice Approach to Violence," *Violence: From Theory to Research*, edited by Margaret A. Zahn, Henry J. Brownstein, and Shelly L. Jackson (Cincinnati, OH: Anderson, 2004), 78.
35. Frank H. Gawin, "Cocaine Addiction: Psychology and Neurophysiology," *Science* 251, no. 5001 (1991): 1580–86.
36. Brad J. Bushman, "Human Aggression While under the Influence of Alcohol and Other Drugs: An Integrative Research Review," *Current Directions in Psychological Science* 2 (1993): 148–52.
37. Greenfeld (1998), cited in Myers, *Exploring Psychology*, 553.
38. American Academy of Child and Adolescent Psychiatry, "Teens: Alcohol and Other Drugs," *Facts for Families*, no. 3 (2008), updated March 2018, https://www.aacap.org/AACAP/Families_and_Youth/Facts_for_Families/FFF-Guide/Teens-Alcohol-And-Other-Drugs-003.aspx.
39. Eric Schlosser, *Fast Food Nation: The Dark Side of the All-American Meal* (New York: Penguin, 2001), 56.
40. Morgan Spurlock, *Super Size Me* (TheCon, 2004). People are becoming more aware of the important role of nutrition and also complementary forms of health care, such as acupuncture and herbal remedies. EBSCO Publishing has an enormous database of studies that demonstrate that alternative health care is effective in making people healthier.
41. Gibson and Tibbetts (2000), cited in Stephen E. Brown, Esbensen Finn-Aage, and Gilbert Geis, *Criminology: Explaining Crime and Its Context*, 6th ed. (Cincinnati, OH: Anderson, 2007), 259.
42. Roger D. Masters, "Acetylcholines, Toxins and Human Behavior," *Journal of Clinical Toxicology*

(May 5, 2012), doi:10.4172/2161-0495.S6-004.
43. Schaffhausen, "The Biological Basis of Aggression."
44. Robert O. Wright, Jay Schutz, R. J. Wright, Virginia Bollati, Inger Tarantini, Susan K. Park, Henry Hu, Diane Sparrow, and Paul Vokonas, "Biomarkers of Lead Exposure and DNA Manipulation within Retrotransposins," *Environmental Health Perspectives* 118, no. 6 (June 2010): 790–95.
45. Sharon Begley, Andrew Murr, and Adams Rogers, "Gray Matters," *Newsweek*. March 27, 1995, 53; Brown et al., *Criminology*, 261.
46. Gerrig and Zimbardo, *Psychology and Life*, 588
47. Niehoff (1999), cited in Christopher J. Ferguson and Keith W. Beaver, "Natural Born Killers: The Genetics of Extreme Violence," *Aggression and Violent Behavior* 14, no. 5 (2009): 288.
48. Steven Stolberg, "Fear Clouds Search for Genetic Roots of Violence," *Los Angeles Times*, December 30, 1993, A18.
49. Myers, *Exploring Psychology*, 551.
50. Paul Billings, "Comments on the Social, Legal and Policy Issues Arising From the Genetic Revolution," testimony before the Senate Select Committee on Genetics and Public Policy, April 8, 1996.
51. Myers, *Exploring Psychology*, 551.
52. Brad J. Bushman, "Violent Media and Hostile Appraisals: A Meta-Analytic Review." *Aggressive Behavior*. 42, no. 6 (November 2016): 605–13.
53. Johannes Breuer and Malte Elson. "Frustration-Aggression Theory," in *The Wiley Handbook of Violence and Aggression*.
54. Craig A. Anderson and Daniel C. Anderson, "Ambient Temperature and Violent Crime: Tests of the Linear and Curvilinear Hypotheses," *Journal of Personality and Social Psychology* 46 (1984): 91–97. Also see Craig A. Anderson, "Heat and Violence: Current Directions," *Psychological Science* 10 (2001): 33–38.
55. Marc Posner, "Research Raises Troubling Questions About Violence Prevention Programs," *The Fourth R* 52 (August/September 1994): 12.
56. Deborah Prothrow-Smith, "Assimilating Prevention Techniques into the Curriculum," *The Fourth R* 52 (August/September 1994): 1.
57. McCord (1979), cited in Rebecca Atnafou, "Ensuring the Safety of Our Future Generations: Parent Education as a Preventive Strategy for Youth Violence," *Options* 4 (Summer 1996): 2.
58. Atnafou, "Ensuring the Safety," 2.
59. Maguire and Pastore (1995), cited in Delbert S. Elliott, Beatrix A. Hamburg, and Kirk R. Williams, *Violence in American Schools: A New Perspective* (Cambridge, UK: Cambridge University Press, 1998), 10.
60. Price in Everett (1997), cited in Elliott et al., *Violence in American Schools*, 10.
61. Jeri LaBahn, "Education and Parental Involvement in Secondary Schools: Problems, Solutions and Effects," *Educational Psychology Interactive* (Valdosta, GA: Valdosta State University 1995), http://

www.edpsycinteractive.org/files/parinvol.html.

62. California Attorney General's Office's Policy Council on Violence Prevention, "Violence Prevention: A Vision of Hope; Final Report" (Sacramento: Policy Council on Violence Prevention, 1995).

63. California Attorney General's Office's Policy Council on Violence Prevention, "Violence Prevention."

64. Myrna B. Shure, "Preventing Violence the Problem-Solving Way," *Juvenile Justice Bulletin* (Washington, DC: US Department of Justice, Office of Juvenile Justice and Delinquency Prevention, 1999).

65. Triandis (1994) in Myers, *Exploring Psychology*, 554.

66. National Criminal Justice Research Service, *Serving High Risk Youth: Lessons from Research and Programming* (Washington, DC: US Department of Justice, 2009), 1988.

67. Marcus and Betzer (1996), cited in Atnafou, "Ensuring the Safety," 2.

68. David G. Myers, *The American Paradox: Spiritual Hunger in an Age of Plenty* (New Haven, CT: Yale University Press, 2000).

69. Lugaila (1998), cited in Terence P. Thornberry, Carolyn A. Smith, Craig Rivera, David Huizinga, and Magda Stouthamer-Loeber. "Family Disruption and Delinquency," *Juvenile Justice Bulletin* (Washington, DC: US Department of Justice, 1999), 1.

70. David Finkelhor and Richard Ormrod, "Homicides of Children and Youth," *Juvenile Justice Bulletin* (Washington, DC: US Department of Justice, 2001), 4.

71. Center for the Study and Prevention of Violence, *Blueprints for Healthy Youth Development— Olweus Bullying Prevention Program* (Boulder: University of Colorado, 2004).

72. Donna K. Crawford and Richard J. Bodine, "Conflict Resolution Education: Preparing Youth for the Future," *Juvenile Justice: School Violence; An Overview* 8, no. 1 (2001): 21.

73. Joan Ferrante, *Sociology: A Global Perspective* (Belmont, CA: Wadsworth, 1995), 431.

74. Finn-Aage Esbensen, Dana Peterson, Terrance J. Taylor, and Adrienne Feng, *Differences in Offending, Victimization and Gang Membership* (Philadelphia: Temple University Press, 2010), 87.

75. Ira Pollack and Carlos Sundermann, "Creating Safe Schools: A Comprehensive Approach," *Juvenile Justice: School Violence, An Overview* 8, no. 1 (2001): 13.

76. Mark H. Moore, Carol V. Petrie, Anthony A. Braga, and Brendan L. McLaughlin, eds., *Deadly Lessons: Understanding Lethal School Violence* (Washington, DC: The National Academies Press, 2003), 9; Peter Langman, *Why Kids Kill: Inside the Minds of School Shooters* (New York: Palgrave Macmillan, 2009).

77. Bryan Vossekuil, Robert A. Fein, Marissa Ready, Randy Borum, William Modzelski, *The Final Report and Findings of the Safe School Initiative: Implications for the Prevention of School Attacks in the United States* (Washington, DC: US Secret Service and US Department of Education, 2002).

78. Robert Merton (1967), cited in Joan Ferrante, *Sociology: A Global Perspective* (Belmont, CA: Wadsworth, 1995), 36.

79. David Weinstein, "Herbert Spencer," *The Stanford Encyclopedia of Philosophy*, edited by Edward N. Zalta (Stanford University, 2019), https://plato.stanford.edu/archives/fall2019/entries/spencer/.
80. Karl Marx, *Selected Writings on Society and Social Philosophy*, edited by Thomas Bottoms (London: McGraw-Hill, 1964), 51.
81. Joe R. Feagin and Clairece Booher Feagin, *Social Problems: A Critical Power-Conflict Perspective* (Upper Saddle River, NJ: Prentice Hall, 1990), 15.
82. Feagin and Feagin, *Social Problems*, 17–18.
83. C. Wright Mills, *The Power Elite* (New York: Oxford University Press, 1956).
84. Mills, *The Power Elite*. Also see Maurice Zeitlin, "Is There a Ruling Class?" *New York Review of Books*, July 17, 1975; Edward S. Herman and Noam Chomsky, *Manufacturing Consent: The Political Economy of the Mass Media* (New York: Pantheon, 1988); G. William Domhoff, *The Power Elite and the State: How Policy is Made in America* (Berlin: Aldine deGruyter, 1990).
85. Marx, *Selected Writings*, 115.
86. Marx, *Selected Writings*.
87. Zahn, et.al., *Violence*, 19–30.
88. Zahn et al., *Violence*, 37–42.
89. Zahn et al., *Violence*, 43–46.
90. Zahn et al., *Violence*, 43–47.
91. Zahn et al., *Violence*, 43–44.
92. Zahn et al., *Violence*, 31–32.
93. Zahn et al., *Violence*, 91–97.
94. Zahn et al., *Violence*, 95–97.
95. Zahn et al., *Violence*, 121–129.
96. Zahn et al., *Violence*, 125–129.
97. Zahn et al., *Violence*, 151, 258.
98. Sarah V. Hart, "Violence Theory Workshop," National Institute of Justice, 2002.
99. National Commission on the Causes and Prevention of Violence, introduction to *Violence in America: Final Report of the National Commission on the Causes and Prevention of Violence* (New York: Chelsea House, 1983), xxii.
100. Barbara Ehrenreich, *Blood Rites: Origin, History and the Passions of War* (New York: Henry Holt), 1998.
101. US National Commission on the Causes and Prevention of Violence, "Final Report of the National Commission on the Causes and Prevention of Violence" (Washington, DC: US Government Printing Office, 1969).
102. Triandis (1994), in Myers, *Exploring Psychology*, 554.
103. Bennett Harrison, *Education, Training and the Urban Ghetto* (Baltimore: Johns Hopkins University Press, 1972), 143–44.

Chapter 2. Standard Practices: Necessary but Not Sufficient

1. Quoted by Keean Davis, a student in the author's School Violence class.
2. Patrick Tolan and Nancy Guerra, *What Works in Reducing Adolescent Violence: An Empirical Review of the Field* (Boulder: Center for the Study of Violence and Violence Prevention, 1994), 29.
3. Karol L. Kumpfer and Rose Alvarado, "Effective Family Strengthening Interventions," *Juvenile Justice Bulletin* (Washington DC: US Department of Justice, 1998), 6; Scott Decker, "Increasing School Safety through Juvenile Accountability Programs," *Juvenile Accountability Incentive Block Grants Program Bulletin* (Washington, DC: US Department of Justice, 2000), 4–5.
4. Suyapa Siluva, Jonathon Blutstein, Jason Williams, Chris Ringwalt, Linda Dusenbury, and William Hansen, *Impacts of a Violence Prevention Program for Middle Schools* (Washington, DC: US Department of Education, National Center for Education Evaluation and Regional Assistance, 2010).
5. US Department of Justice, *2000 Annual Report on School Safety* (Washington, DC: US Department of Justice, 2000).
6. Marc Posner, "Research Raises Troubling Questions about Violence Prevention Programs," *The Fourth R* 52 (August/September 1994): 4.
7. Posner, "Research Raises Troubling Questions," 4.
8. Jarrod Hindman, *Child and Adolescent Violence in Colorado: A 2005 Status Report* (Denver: Colorado Department of Public Health and Environment, 2005), 1.
9. Lynn McDonald and Heather E. Frey, *Families and Schools Together: Building Relationships* (Washington, DC: US Department of Justice, 1999), 2.
10. Pollard, Hawkins, and Arthur (1999), cited in McDonald and Frey, *Families and Schools Together*, 6–7.
11. McDonald and Frey, *Families and Schools Together*, 7.
12. Virginia K. Molgaard, Richard L. Spoth, and Cleve Redmond, "Competency Training: The Strengthening Families Program for Parents and Youth 10–14," *Juvenile Justice Bulletin* (Washington, DC: US Department of Justice, 2000), 4.
13. Farrington (1997), cited in J. David Hawkins, Todd. I. Herrenkohl, David P. Farrington, Devon Brewer, Richard F. Catalano, Tracy W. Harachi, and Lynn Cothern, "Predictors of Youth Violence," *Juvenile Justice Bulletin* (Washington, DC: US Department of Justice, 2000), 7.
14. Bonnie Benard, *Fostering Resiliency in Kids: Protective Factors in the Family, School and Community* (Portland, OR: Western Regional Center for Drug-Free Schools and Communities, 1992), 15.
15. Hawkins et al., "Predictors of Youth Violence," 1–6; Hindman, *Child and Adolescent Violence in Colorado*, 5.
16. Hawkins et al., "Predictors of Youth Violence," 1–6.
17. Hindman, *Child and Adolescent Violence in Colorado*, 5.

18. Hindman, *Child and Adolescent Violence in Colorado*, 1.
19. Hindman, *Child and Adolescent Violence in Colorado*, 5.
20. McDonald and Frey, *Families and Schools Together*, 7.
21. Bernard, *Fostering Resiliency in Kids*, 3–5.
22. Bernard, *Fostering Resiliency in Kids*, 3.
23. Perry Preschool Program, "Curriculum," www.highscope.org.
24. Lily-Ann Gauthier, David Hicks, Daniel Sanfacon, and Leanne Salel, *100 Promising Crime Prevention Programs from across the World* (Washington, DC: International Centre for the Prevention of Crime and the US Department of Justice, 1999), 71.
25. Gauthier et al., *100 Promising Crime Prevention Programs*, 71.
26. Stephen J. Bavolek, *Nurturing Programs for Parents and Children*, 4th ed. (Denver, CO: Family Development Resources, 1999), 1.
27. Hawkins et al., "Predictors of Youth Violence," 1–6.
28. Posner, "Research Raises Troubling Questions," 13.
29. McDonald and Frey, *Families and Schools Together*, 7.
30. McDonald and Frey, *Families and Schools Together*, 7.
31. Bernard, *Fostering Resiliency in Kids*, 9–10.
32. Virginia K. Molgaard, Richard L. Spoth, and Cleve Redmond, "Competency Training: The Strengthening Families Program for Parents and Youth 10–14," *Juvenile Justice Bulletin* (Washington, DC: US Department of Justice, 2000), 2–3.
33. Bernard, *Fostering Resiliency in Kids*, 9–10.
34. Donna K. Crawford and Richard J. Bodine, "Conflict Resolution Education: Preparing Youth for the Future," *Juvenile Justice: School Violence; An Overview* 8, no. 1 (2001): 25.
35. Maton (1990), cited in Bernard, *Fostering Resiliency in Kids*, 13.
36. Hunt and Sullivan (1974) and Siegel (2001), cited in Jacqueline G. Brooks and Eustace G. Thompson, "Social Justice in the Classroom," *Educational Leadership* (Association for Supervision and Curriculum Development, 2005).
37. Sarason (1990), cited in Bernard, *Fostering Resiliency in Kids*, 13.
38. Hawkins et al., "Predictors of Youth Violence," 1–6.
39. Karol L. Kumpfer, *Strengthening America's Families: Promising Parenting Strategies for Delinquency Prevention; User's Guide* (Washington, DC: Office of Juvenile Justice and Delinquency Prevention, US Department of Justice, 1993).
40. Kumpfer and Alvarado, "Effective Family Strengthening Interventions," 6.
41. Karol L. Kumpfer and Connie M. Tait, "Family Skills Training for Parents," *Juvenile Justice Bulletin* (Washington, DC: US Department of Justice, 2002).
42. Kumpfer and Tait, "Family Skills Training for Parents," 5–6.
43. Bavolek, *Fostering Resiliency in Kids*, 3
44. Bavolek, *Nurturing Programs*, 5

45. Bavolek, *Nurturing Programs*, 9
46. Kumpfer and Alvarado, "Effective Family Strengthening Interventions," 6.
47. Taylor and Biglan (1998) and Norman and Turner (1993), cited in Kumpfer and Alvarado, "Effective Family Strengthening Interventions," 3–4.
48. Gauthier et al., *100 Promising Crime Prevention Programs*, 100.
49. William DeJong, "Preventing Interpersonal Violence among Youth: An Introduction to School, Community, and Mass Media Strategies," *Issues and Practices in Criminal Justice* (Washington, DC: US Department of Justice, 1994), 35, 38.
50. Scott Decker, "Increasing School Safety through Juvenile Accountability Programs," *Juvenile Accountability Incentive Block Grants Program Bulletin* (Washington, DC: US Department of Justice, 2000), 1.
51. Decker, "Increasing School Safety," 3.
52. Tolan and Guerra, *What Works in Reducing Adolescent Violence*, 6.
53. Mary Terzian, Katherine Henth, and Thomson Linney, "What Works for Acting-Out (Externalizing) Behavior: Lessons from Experimental Evaluations of Social Interventions," *Fact Sheet* (Washington, DC: Child Trends, 2011): 1–6.
54. California Child Development CORPS, "Prevention and Early Intervention Cost Less, Work Better," *Children's Advocate* (2000).
55. Eileen M. Garry, "A Compendium of Programs That Work for Youth," *OJJDP Fact Sheet* (Washington, DC: US Department of Justice, 1999), 1.
56. Thomas N. Thornton, Carole A. Craft, Linda L. Dahlberg, Barbara S. Lynch, and Katie Baer, eds., *Best Practices of Youth Violence Prevention: A Sourcebook for Community Action*, rev. ed. (Atlanta: Centers for Disease Control and Prevention, 2002).
57. Center for the Study and Prevention of Violence, *Blueprints Model Programs—Functional Family Therapy* (Boulder: University of Colorado, 2004).
58. Myrna B. Shure, "Preventing Violence the Problem-Solving Way," *Juvenile Justice Bulletin* (Washington, DC: US Department of Justice, 1999), 1.
59. Shure, "Preventing Violence the Problem-Solving Way," 1.
60. Shure (1992), cited in Shure, "Preventing Violence the Problem-Solving Way," 4–9.
61. Werner and Smith (1974, 1991, 1982), Rutter and Garmezy (1984, 1983), cited in Bernard, *Fostering Resiliency in Kids*, 4.
62. Brook et al. (1989), cited in Bernard, *Fostering Resiliency in Kids*, 5.
63. Center for the Study and Prevention of Violence, *Blueprints Model Programs—Big Brothers Big Sisters of America* (Boulder: University of Colorado, 2004); Gauthier et al., *100 Promising Crime Prevention Programs*.
64. Center for the Study and Prevention of Violence, *Blueprints Model Programs—Promoting Alternative Thinking Strategies (PATHS)* (Boulder: University of Colorado, 2004).
65. Sharon Mihalic, Katherine Irwin, Delbert Elliott, Abigail Fagan, and Diane Hansen. "Blueprints

for Violence Prevention," *Juvenile Justice Bulletin* (Washington, DC: US Department of Justice, 2001), 3.
66. Center for the Study and Prevention of Violence, *Blueprints Model Programs—Nurse-Family Partnerships* (Boulder: University of Colorado, 2004).
67. Mihalic et al., "Blueprints for Violence Prevention," 5.
68. University of Utah Health Center, Families Therapy Program, http://www.healthcare.Utah.edu/programs. 2020.
69. Gauthier et al., *100 Promising Crime Prevention Programs*, 74–75.
70. Center for the Study and Prevention of Violence, *Promoting Alternative Thinking Strategies*.
71. Kusche (1984), cited in the Center for the Study and Prevention of Violence, *Promoting Alternative Thinking Strategies*, 3.
72. Center for the Study and Prevention of Violence, *Promoting Alternative Thinking Strategies*, 1.
73. Center for the Study and Prevention of Violence, *Promoting Alternative Thinking Strategies*, 3.
74. Center for the Study and Prevention of Violence, *Promoting Alternative Thinking Strategies*, 5.
75. Center for the Study and Prevention of Violence, *Promoting Alternative Thinking Strategies*.
76. John C. Howell, ed. *Guide for Implementing the Comprehensive Strategy for Serious, Violent, and Chronic Juvenile Offenders* (Washington, DC: Office of Juvenile Justice and Delinquency Prevention, 1995).
77. Coordinating Council on Juvenile Justice and Delinquency Prevention, *Combating Violence and Delinquency: The National Juvenile Justice Action Plan* (Washington, DC: US Department of Justice, 1996), F-30.
78. Stephen E. Brock, Philip J. Lazarus, and Shane R. Jimerson, *Best Practices in School Crisis Prevention and Intervention* (Bethesda, MD: National Association of School Psychologists, 2006).
79. Decker, "Increasing School Safety," 8.
80. Martin L. Gross, *The Psychological Society* (New York: Touchstone, 1978).
81. Decker, "Increasing School Safety," 4.
82. Susan P. Limber, "Addressing Youth Bullying Behaviors," *Educational Forum on Adolescent Health: Youth Bullying*, edited by Missy Fleming and Kelley Towey (Chicago: American Medical Association, 2002), 13.
83. Roger Fisher, William Ury, and Bruce Patton, *Getting to Yes: Negotiating Agreement without Giving In* (New York: Penguin Books, 1991), 1.
84. Crawford and Bodine, "Conflict Resolution Education," 24.
85. Crawford and Bodine, "Conflict Resolution Education," 24–25.
86. Crawford and Bodine, "Conflict Resolution Education," 23.
87. Crawford and Bodine, "Conflict Resolution Education," 23.
88. Coordinating Council on Juvenile Justice and Delinquency Prevention, *Combating Violence and Delinquency*, 57.
89. Crawford and Bodine, "Conflict Resolution Education," 22.

90. Crawford and Bodine, "Conflict Resolution Education," 22.
91. Webster (1993), in Gail A. Wasserman, Laurie S. Miller, and Lynn Cothern, "Prevention of Serious and Violent Juvenile Offending," *Juvenile Justice Bulletin* (Washington, DC: Office of Juvenile Justice and Delinquency Prevention, 2000): 4.
92. Missy Fleming and Kelley Towey, eds., "Youth Bullying: An Overview," *Educational Forum on Adolescent Health* (Chicago: American Medical Association, 2002), 1; Tolan and Guerra, *What Works In Reducing Adolescent Violence*, 30.
93. Brewer et al., cited in Wasserman et al., "Prevention of Serious and Violent Juvenile Offending," 4.
94. Lam (1989), cited in Wasserman et al., "Prevention of Serious and Violent Juvenile Offending," 4; Tolan and Guerra, *What Works in Reducing Adolescent Violence*, 30.
95. Fleming and Towey, "Youth Bullying: An Overview," 1.
96. Cohen (2002), cited in Limber, "Addressing Youth Bullying Behaviors," 13.
97. Limber, "Addressing Youth Bullying Behaviors," 13.
98. Delbert S. Elliott, *Safe Communities—Safe Schools: Some Emerging Lessons and Recommendations* (Boulder: Center for the Study and Prevention of Violence, University of Colorado, 2000).
99. Gottfredson (1997), cited in Decker, "Increasing School Safety," 4.
100. Fleming and Towey, *Educational Forum on Adolescent Health*, 15.
101. Dan Olweus, *Bullying at School* (Boston: Blackwell, 2006), 2.
102. Center for the Study and Prevention of Violence, *Promoting Alternative Thinking Strategies*, 6.
103. Center for the Study and Prevention of Violence, *Promoting Alternative Thinking Strategies*, 1; Gauthier et al., *Promising Crime Prevention Programs*, 98.
104. Center for the Study and Prevention of Violence, *Promoting Alternative Thinking Strategies*, 8.
105. National Center for School Engagement, "Bully-Proofing Your School," http://schoolengagement.org/school-engagement-services/bully-proofing-your-school/.
106. Christopher D. Bell, Kathryn Raczynski, and Arthur M. Horne, "Bully Busters: Evaluation of a Group-Based Bully Intervention and Prevention Program," *Group Dynamics: Theory, Research, and Practice* 14, no. 3 (2010): 257–67.
107. Stop Bullying Now! www.stopbullyingnow.com.
108. Hawkins et al. (1992), cited in Tolan and Guerra, *What Works in Reducing Adolescent Violence*, 22.
109. Dennis Kenney, "Crime in the Schools: A Problem-Solving Approach." *National Institute of Justice Research Preview* (Washington, DC: National Institute of Justice, US Department of Justice, 1998), 1.
110. Brooks and Thompson, "Social Justice in the Classroom," 52.
111. Bry (1982), cited in Tolan and Guerra, *What Works in Reducing Adolescent Violence*, 22.
112. Shure, "Preventing Violence the Problem-Solving Way."
113. McDonald, Pugh, and Alexander (1996), cited in McDonald and Frey, *Families and Schools Together*, 14.
114. US Department of Education, *Turning around Low-Performing Schools: A Guide for State and*

Local Leaders (Washington, DC: US Department of Education, 1998), https://www2.ed.gov/pubs/turning/index.html.
115. Posner, "Research Raises Troubling Questions," 13.
116. Olweus, Limber, and Mihalic (1999), cited in Fleming and Towey, *Educational Forum on Adolescent Health*, 12.
117. Payne (1991), cited in Tolan and Guerra, *What Works in Reducing Adolescent Violence*, 21; 23.
118. Coordinating Council on Juvenile Justice and Delinquency Prevention, *Combating Violence and Delinquency*, 57.
119. Children's Safety Network, *Taking Action to Prevent Adolescent Violence* (Newton, MA: Education Development Center, 1995), xv.
120. DeJong, "Preventing Interpersonal Violence among Youth," 12.
121. DeJong, "Preventing Interpersonal Violence among Youth," 12.
122. Mihalic et al., "Bluprints for Violence Prevention," 6; National Criminal Justice Research Service, *Serving High Risk Youth: Lessons from Research and Programming* (Washington, DC: US Department of Justice, 2009).
123. William DeJong, "Building the Peace: The Resolving Conflict Creatively Program (RCCP)," *National Institute of Justice Program Focus* (Washington, DC: US Department of Justice, 1995), 12.
124. Lorion et al. (1987), McCord (1978), and Miller (1962), cited in Tolan and Guerra, *What Works in Reducing Adolescent Violence*, 34.
125. American Academy of Pediatrics, "Joint Statement on the Impact of Entertainment Violence on Children," Congressional Public Health Summit, July 26, 2000, http://www.aap.org/advocacy/releases/jstmtevc.htm.
126. Decker, "Increasing School Safety," 9.
127. Brooks and Thompson, "Social Justice in the Classroom," 52.
128. Katherine Hanson and Anne McAuliffe, "Gender and Violence: Implications for Peaceful Schools," *The Fourth R* 52 (1994): 11.
129. Hanson and McAuliffe, "Gender and Violence: Implications for Peaceful Schools," 11.

■ Chapter 3. Paolo Freire and the Question of Human Nature

1. Paolo Freire, *Education for Critical Consciousness* (New York: Continuum, 1990); Paolo Freire, *Pedagogy of the Oppressed* (New York: Continuum, 1989).
2. Freire, *Education for Critical Consciousness*, 56.
3. Freire, *Education for Critical Consciousness*, 57.
4. Freire, *Education for Critical Consciousness*, 58.
5. Freire, *Pedagogy of the Oppressed*, 65.
6. Freire, *Education for Critical Consciousness*, 59.

7. Freire, *Education for Critical Consciousness*, 67.
8. Freire, *Education for Critical Consciousness*, 73.
9. Freire, *Education for Critical Consciousness*, 4.
10. Carolyn Edwards, Lella Gandini, and George Forman, *The Hundred Languages of Children: The Reggio Emilia Approach—Advanced Reflections* (New York: Ablex, 1998), 94.
11. Stephen E. Brown, Esbensen Finn-Aage, and Gilbert Geis, *Criminology: Explaining Crime and Its Context*, 6th ed. (Cincinnati, OH: Anderson, 2007), 458; C. R. Block, "Lethal Violence in the Chicago Latino Community," *Homicide: The Victim/Offender Connection*, edited by A.V. Wilson (Cincinnati: Anderson, 1993), cited in Margaret A. Zahn, Henry J. Brownstein, and Shelly L. Jackson, eds., *Violence: From Theory to Research* (Cincinnati, OH: Anderson, 2004), 182.
12. Freire, *Pedagogy of the Oppressed*, 60.
13. Richard J. Gerrig and Philip G. Zimbardo, *Psychology and Life* (Boston: Pearson/Allyn and Bacon, 2005), 588.
14. Charles Darwin, *On the Origin of Species by Means of Natural Selection* (New York: Pantheon Press, 1977).
15. Konrad Lorenz, *On Aggression* (New York: Harcourt, Brace and World, 1966).
16. Stanley Milgram, "Some Conditions of Obedience and Disobedience to Authority," *Human Relations* 18 (1965): 57–76; Stanley Milgram, *Obedience to Authority* (New York: Harper and Row, 1974).
17. S. L. A. Marshall, *Men against Fire: The Problem of Battle Command* (New York: William Morrow, 1947).
18. Dave Grossman and Gloria DeGaetano, *Stop Teaching Our Kids to Kill: A Call to Action Against TV, Movie and Video Game Violence* (New York: Crown, 1999) 48.
19. Dave Grossman, *On Killing: The Psychological Cost of Learning to Kill in War and Society* (Boston: Little, Brown, 1996).
20. Grossman, *On Killing*.
21. Terry L. Schell and Terri Tanielian, eds., *A Needs Assessment of New York State Veterans: Final Report to the New York State Health Foundation* (New York: Rand Corporation and the New York State Health Foundation. 2011).
22. Richard A. Goddard, interview with the author, November 21, 2008, and March 3, 2009.
23. Richard E. Leakey and Roger Lewin, *People of the Lake* (New York: Anchor Press, 1978).
24. Hinde (1970), cited in Roy F. Baumeister and Brad J. Bushman, *Social Psychology and Human Nature* (Boston: Wadsworth Cengage Learning, 2016), 294–95.
25. Goddard, interview with author.
26. Goddard, interview with author.
27. Pat Shipman, "Scavenger Hunt," *Natural History*, April 1984; Rachel T. Boaz and Renard L. Ciochan, "The Scavenging of Peking Man," *Natural History*, March 2001.
28. Donna K. Crawford and Richard J. Bodine, "Conflict Resolution Education: Preparing Youth for

the Future," *Juvenile Justice: School Violence; An Overview* 8, no. 1 (2001): 21.
29. Hinde (1970), in Baumeister and Bushman, *Social Psychology and Human Nature*, 294–95.
30. Merlin Stone, *When God Was a Woman* (New York: Harcourt Brace Jovanovich, 1976), 15.
31. Stone, *When God Was a Woman*, 4; Marija Gimbutas, *The Language of the Goddess* (New York: Harper Collins, 1989).
32. Erich Neumann, *The Great Mother* (Princeton, NJ: Princeton University Press, 1991).
33. Gimbutas, *The Language of the Goddess*; Neumann, *The Great Mother*.
34. Stone, *When God Was a Woman*, 4; Gimbutas, *The Language of the Goddess*; Neumann, *The Great Mother*.
35. Wikipedia, "Mother Goddess."
36. Gerda Lerner, *The Creation of Patriarchy* (New York: Oxford University Press, 1986).
37. Goddard, interview with author.
38. Lerner, *The Creation of Patriarchy*, 29.
39. Eleanor Leacock, *Myths of Male Dominance* (New York: Monthly Review, 1981).
40. Leacock, *Myths of Male Dominance*.
41. Lerner, *The Creation of Patriarchy*, 32–35.
42. Fry (2006), cited in Melissa M. McDonald, Carlos David Navarrette, and Mark Van Vugt. "Evolution and the Psychology of Intergroup Conflict: The Male Warrior Hypothesis," *Philosophical Transactions of the Royal Society B* 367 (March 5, 2012), doi:10.1098/rstb.2011.0301.
43. James Mellaart, *Catal Huyuk: A Neolithic Town in Anatolia* (New York: Thames and Hudson, 1967).
44. Fry (2006), cited in McDonald, et al., "Evolution and the Psychology of Intergroup Conflict."
45. Fry (2006), cited in McDonald, et al., "Evolution and the Psychology of Intergroup Conflict."
46. Goddard, interview with author.
47. Lerner, *The Creation of Patriarchy*, 46.
48. Roy F. Baumeister, *The Cultural Animal: Human Nature, Meaning, and Social Life* (New York: Oxford University Press, 2005).
49. DeWaal, cited in Geoffrey Cowley, "The Roots of Good and Evil," *Newsweek*, February 26, 1996, 53.
50. Twenge et al. (2001, 2002), cited in David G. Myers, *Exploring Psychology* (New York: Worth, 2007), 365.
51. Margaret Mead, *Coming of Age in Samoa* (New York: Morrow, 1929).
52. *Meet the Natives: USA*, produced by Charlie Parsons, aired November 29–December 20, 2009, on Travel Channel.
53. Roger Fisher, William Ury, and Bruce Patton, *Getting to Yes: Negotiating Agreement without Giving In* (New York: Penguin, 1991).
54. Fisher, et al., *Getting to Yes*.
55. Abraham Maslow, "A Theory of Human Motivation," *Psychological Review* 50 (1943): 370–96.
56. Carl R. Rogers, *On Personal Power: Inner Strength and Its Revolutionary Impact* (New York: Delacourte, 1977).

57. Karen Horney, *Neurosis and Human Growth* (New York: Norton, 1991).
58. Carolyn Edwards, Lella Gandini, and George Forman, *The Hundred Languages of Children: The Reggio Emilia Approach* (New York: Ablex, 1998), 95.
59. Kurt Lewin, *Principles of Topological Psychology* (New York: McGraw-Hill, 1936).
60. John B. Rotter, *Social Learning and Clinical Psychology* (Englewood Cliffs, NJ: Prentice-Hall, 1954).
61. Albert Bandura, *Social Learning Theory* (Englewood Cliffs, NJ: Prentice-Hall, 1972).
62. Bandura, *Social Learning Theory*.
63. Matthew Fox, *Creation Spirituality: Liberating Gifts for the Peoples of the Earth* (San Francisco: Harper, 1991), 31.
64. Carlson et al. (1988), cited in Myers, *Exploring Psychology*, 566
65. See, for example, Levy (2003) and Chamberlain and Haaga (2001), cited in Alfie Kohn, "Unconditional Teaching," *Educational Leadership* 63, no. 1 (2005): 24; Carlson et al. (1988) in Myers, *Exploring Psychology*, 566
66. Kohn, "Unconditional Teaching," 20.
67. Mark R. Leary, Robin M. Kowalski, Laura Smith, and Stephen Phillips, "Teasing, Rejection, and Violence: Case Studies of the School Shootings," *Aggressive Behavior* 29, no. 3 (2003): 212.
68. Bryan Vossekuil, Marisa Reddy, and Robert Fein, *Safe School Initiative: An Interim Report on the Prevention of Targeted Violence in Schools* (Washington, DC: US Secret Service, National Threat Assessment Center, US Department of Education, and the National Institute of Justice, 2000), 3.
69. Charles Thompson, "Student Jailed in a Bomb Plot," *Arizona Republic*, April 1, 2005, p. 20.

■ Chapter 4. The Culture of Violence

1. Lily-Ann Gauthier, David Hicks, Daniel Sanfacon, and Leanne Salel, *100 Promising Crime Prevention Programs from Across the World* (Washington, DC: International Centre for the Prevention of Crime and the US Department of Justice, 1999).
2. Richard Deats, "The Culture of Violence," *Fellowship*, Fellowship of Reconciliation. Also see Francis Barker, *The Culture of Violence: Essays of Tragedy and History* (University of Chicago Press, 1993), and Elizabeth Thurman, "Making Connections: Media's Role in Our Culture of Violence," Center for Media Literacy, http://www.medialit.org/reading_room/article379.html.
3. Deats, "The Culture of Violence."
4. Michael J. Shuen, "Confronting a Culture of Violence." *People of God* 13, no. 2 (1995).
5. Raymond D. Gastil, "Homicide and a Regional Culture of Violence," *American Sociological Review* 36, no. 3 (1971): 412.
6. Fox and Zawitz (2001), cited in David Finkelhor and Richard Ormrod, "Homicides of Children and Youth," *Juvenile Justice Bulletin* (Washington, DC: US Department of Justice, 2001), 2.
7. Patrick A. Langan and David P. Farrington, "Crime and Justice in the United States and in England

and Wales, 1981–1996," *Bureau of Justice Statistics Executive Summary* (Washington, DC: US Department of Justice, 1997), ii.; also see Federal Bureau of Investigation, "Violent Crime Offenses Reported, 1996," *Crime in the United States, 1996*, Uniform Crime Reports, https://ucr.fbi.gov/crime-in-the-u.s/1996.

8. Federal Bureau of Investigation, *Crime in the United States, 2016*, Uniform Crime Reports, https://ucr.fbi.gov/crime-in-the-u.s/2016/crime-in-the-u.s.-2016.
9. Dave Grossman and Gloria DeGaetano, *Stop Teaching Our Kids to Kill: A Call to Action Against TV, Movie, and Video Game Violence* (New York: Crown, 1999), 15.
10. Children's Safety Network, *Taking Action to Prevent Adolescent Violence* (Newton, MA: Education Development Center, 1995), x.
11. Daniel E. Lungren, *Violence Prevention: A Vision of Hope* (Crime and Violence Prevention Center, 1995).
12. William DeJong, "Preventing Interpersonal Violence among Youth: An Introduction to School, Community, and Mass Media Strategies," *Issues and Practices in Criminal Justice* (Washington, DC: US Department of Justice, 1994), 1.
13. Lungren, *Violence Prevention*.
14. Chris Kahn, "Documents Tell of Shootings," *Denver Post*, August 7, 2006, 10A.
15. Kahn, "Documents Tell of Shootings."
16. Beldon West, "The Death Penalty: A National Disgrace," *The Nonviolent Activist*, November/December 1993, p. 16.
17. West, "The Death Penalty," 16.
18. Tracy L. Snell, "Capital Punishment 1997," *Bureau of Justice Statistics Bulletin* (Washington, DC: US Department of Justice, Bureau of Justice Statistics, 1998), 1.
19. Tracy L. Snell, "Capital Punishment 2000," *Bureau of Justice Statistics Bulletin* (Washington, DC: US Department of Justice, Bureau of Justice Statistics, 2002), 4.
20. West, "The Death Penalty," 1.
21. West, "The Death Penalty," 13.
22. West, "The Death Penalty," 13.
23. Center for Economic and Social Rights, "From Disparity to Dignity" (New York: CESR, 2016), http://www.cesr.org.
24. Deats, "The Culture of Violence."
25. Finn-Aage Esbensen, "Youth Violence: An Overview," *Violence: From Theory to Research*, edited by Margaret A. Zahn, Henry J. Brownstein, and Shelly L. Jackson (Cincinnati, OH: Anderson, 2004), 177.
26. Dave Grossman, "Teaching Kids to Kill," *Phi Kappa Phi National Forum* (Fall 2000).
27. James Alan Fox, *Trends in Juvenile Violence: A Report to the United States Attorney General on Current and Future Rates* (Washington, DC: Bureau of Justice Statistics, US Department of Justice, 1996).

28. The Disaster Center, "United States Crime Rates 1960–2018," www.disastercenter.com/crime/uscrime.htm.
29. Karen Colvard, "Crime Is Down? Don't Confuse Us with the Facts," *Crimes of Violence* 2 (Fall 1997): 1.
30. The Disaster Center, "United States Crime Rates 1960–2018."
31. Esbensen, "Youth Violence," 177–78.
32. Esbensen, "Youth Violence," 178.
33. Howard N. Snyder, "Juvenile Arrests 1997," *Juvenile Justice Bulletin* (Washington, DC: US Department of Justice, Office of Juvenile Justice and Delinquency Prevention, 1998), 1.
34. Howard N. Snyder, "Juvenile Arrests 1995," *Juvenile Justice Bulletin* (Washington, DC: US Department of Justice, Office of Juvenile Justice and Delinquency Prevention, 1997), 1.
35. Huff (2004), cited in Finn-Aage Esbensen, Dana Peterson, Terence J. Taylor, Adrienne Feng, D. Wayne Osgood, and Dena C. Carton, "Evaluation and Evolution of the Gang Resistance Education and Training (G.R.E.A.T.) Program," *Journal of School Violence* 10, no. 1 (2011). Also see Cheyenne Morales Harty, "The Causes and Effects of Get-Tough: A Look at How Tough-on-Crime Policies Rose to the Agenda and an Evaluation of Their Effects on Prison Populations and Crime" (master's thesis, University of Southern Florida, 2012), https://scholarcommons.usf.edu, and Nation of Islam, "About the Million Man March: A Glimpse of Heaven," https://www.noi.org/about-million-man-march.
36. Children's Safety Network, *Taking Action to Prevent Adolescent Violence*.
37. Snyder et al. (1996), cited in Barbara Tatem Kelley, David Huizinga, Terence P. Thornberry, and Rolf Loeber, "Epidemiology of Serious Violence," *Juvenile Justice Bulletin* (Washington, DC: US Department of Justice, 1997), 2.
38. Esbensen et al., "Evaluation and Evolution."
39. Fox, *Trends in Juvenile Violence*, 1.
40. Centers for Disease Control and Prevention, "Youth Violence," https://www.cdc.gov/violenceprevention/youthviolence/index.html.
41. National Center for Injury Prevention and Control, "WISQARS Injury Mortality Reports, 1999–2007," http://webappa.cdc.gov/Sasweb/ncipc/mortrate10_sy.html.
42. American Academy of Child and Adolescent Psychiatry, "Suicide in Children and Teens," *Facts for Families*, no. 10, 2008, updated June 2018, https://www.aacap.org/AACAP/Families_and_Youth/Facts_for_Families/FFF-Guide/Teen-Suicide-010.aspx.
43. Marcia Purse, "An Overview of Suicidal Ideation," Very Well Mind, December 2019, https://www.verywellmind.com.
44. Doctors Against Handgun Injury, *Our Position* (New York: DAHI, 2006). Source available at the time of writing.
45. American Academy of Pediatrics, "Television—How It Affects Children," http://patiented.aap.org/television.html."

46. Wintemute et al. (1988), cited in Doctors Against Handgun Injury, *Our Position*.
47. Allen-Hagen et al. (1994), cited in Stuart Greenbaum, "Kids and Guns: From Playgrounds to Battlegrounds," *Journal of the Office of Juvenile Justice and Delinquency Prevention* 3, no. 2 (1997): 4.
48. Centers for Disease Control and Prevention (1996), cited in Greenbaum, "Kids and Guns," 5.
49. American Academy of Pediatrics, Committee on Adolescents, "Suicide and Suicide Attempts in Adolescents," *Pediatrics* 105, no. 4 (April 2000): 871.
50. American Academy of Child and Adolescent Psychiatry, "Suicide in Children and Teens," *Facts for Families*, no. 10, 2008, updated June 2018, https://www.aacap.org/AACAP/Families_and_Youth/Facts_for_Families/FFF-Guide/Teen-Suicide-010.aspx.
51. Koop and Lundberg (1992), cited in Margaret A. Hamburg, "Youth Violence Is a Public Health Concern," in *Violence in American Schools: A New Perspective*, edited by Delbert S. Elliott, Beatrix A. Hamburg, and Kirk R. Williams (Cambridge, UK: Cambridge University Press, 1998), 37
52. Children's Safety Network, *Taking Action to Prevent Adolescent Violence*, x.
53. American Medical Association, "Proceedings of the Educational Forum on Adolescent Health: Youth Bullying," http://www.amaassn.org/ama1/pub/upload/mm/39/youthbullying.pdf. Source available at the time of writing.
54. Centers for Disease Control, cited in DeJong, "Preventing Interpersonal Violence among Youth," 2.
55. DeJong, "Preventing Interpersonal Violence among Youth," 2–3.
56. DeJong, "Preventing Interpersonal Violence among Youth," 3.
57. Krug, Dahlberg, and Powell (1996), cited in Finkelhor and Ormrod, "Homicides of Children and Youth," 2.
58. Silverman and Kennedy (1993), cited in Kelley et al., "Epidemiology of Serious Violence," 1.
59. Peters, Kochanek, and Murphy (1998), cited in David Sheppard, "Strategies to Reduce Gun Violence," *OJJDP Fact Sheet* (Washington, DC: US Department of Justice, Office of Juvenile Justice and Delinquency Prevention, 1999), 1.
60. Krug, Dahlberg, and Powell (1996), cited in Finkelhor and Ormrod, "Homicides of Children and Youth," 2.
61. Katherine Hanson and Anne McAuliffe, "Gender and Violence: Implications for Peaceful Schools," *The Fourth R* 52 (1994).
62. Katherine Browning and David Huizinga, "Highlights of Findings from the Denver Youth Survey," *OJJDP Fact Sheet* (Washington, DC: US Department of Justice, 1999), 1.
63. Robert Greenwald, Larry V. Hedges, and Richard D. Laine, "The Effects of School Resources on Student Achievement," *Review of Educational Research* 61, no. 3 (1996): 361–96.
64. Jeffrey A. Butts and Howard N. Snyder, "The Youngest Delinquents: Offenders under Age 15," *Juvenile Justice Bulletin* (Washington, DC: US Department of Justice, 1997).
65. Butts and Snyder, "The Youngest Delinquents," 1.

NOTES

66. Kelley et al., "Epidemiology of Serious Violence," 5.
67. Adam Lankford, "Mass Shootings in the U.S.: 1966–2010," *Justice Quarterly* 32, no. 2 (2015): 360–79.
68. Lankford, "Mass Shootings in the U.S."
69. Shay Bilchik, *Promising Strategies to Reduce Gun Violence* (Washington, DC: US Department of Justice, Office of Juvenile Justice and Delinquency Prevention, 1999), 6; June L. Arnette and Marjorie C. Walsenben, "Combating Fear and Restoring Safety in Schools," *Juvenile Justice Bulletin* (Washington, DC: US Department of Justice, 1998), https://ojjdp.ojp.gov/sites/g/files/xyckuh176/files/jjbulletin/9804/gangs.html.
70. Arnette and Walsenben, "Combating Fear and Restoring Safety in Schools," 6.
71. Egley, Howell, and Major, cited in Esbensen, "Youth Violence," 184.
72. Arnette and Walsenben, "Combating Fear and Restoring Safety in Schools," 6.
73. Klein, cited in Esbensen et al., "Evaluation of Evolution."
74. Alexander C. Lichenstein and Michael A. Kroll, "The Fortress Economy: The Economic Role of the U.S. Prison System," *Criminal Injustice: Confronting the Prison Crisis*, edited by Elihu Rosenblatt (New York: South End Press, 1996).
75. Cohen, cited in Arnette and Walsenben, "Combating Fear and Restoring Safety in Schools," 6.
76. Grant Duwe, *A History: Mass Murder in the United States* (Jefferson, NC: McFarland, 2007).
77. "Mass Shooting," Wikipedia, https://en.wikipedia.org/wiki/Mass_shooting.
78. Adam Lankford, "Mass Shooters and Firearms: A Comprehensive National Study of 171 Countries," *Violence and Victims* 31, no. 2 (2016): 187–99.
79. Mark Follman, Gaven Arsonsen, and Deanna Pan, "U.S. Mass Shooters: 1982–2019: Data from *Mother Jones*' Investigation," Mother Jones, August 4, 2019, 2, https://www.motherjones.com/politics/2012/12/mass-shootings-mother-jones-full-data/.
80. David Finkelhor, Heather Turner, Richard Ormrod, Sherry Hamby, and Kristen Kracke, "Children's Exposure to Violence: A Comprehensive National Survey," *Juvenile Justice Bulletin* (Washington, DC: US Department of Justice, 2009), 1–2.
81. Finkelhor et al., "Children's Exposure to Violence," 1–2.
82. David Finkelhor, *Childhood Victimization: Violence, Crime, and Abuse in the Lives of Young People* (New York: Oxford University Press, 2008).
83. Finkelhor et al., "Children's Exposure to Violence," 1–2.
84. Finkelhor et al., "Children's Exposure to Violence," 1–2.
85. Catherine Widom and M. G. Maxfield, "An Update on the 'Cycle of Violence,'" *Research in Brief* (Washington, DC: US Department of Justice, 2001).
86. Finkelhor and Ormrod, "Homicides of Children and Youth," 6.
87. Butts and Snyder, "The Youngest Delinquents," 7
88. Steffensmeier, Alan, Haren, and Striefel; Tracy, Wolfang, and Figlio, cited in Patrick Tolan and Nancy Guerra, *What Works in Reducing Adolescent Violence: An Empirical Review of the Field*

(Boulder: Center for the Study of Violence and Violence Prevention, 2002).

89. Kelley et al., "Epidemiology of Serious Violence," 8.
90. Kelley et al., "Epidemiology of Serious Violence," 5.
91. Tonya Fischio, "Mean Girls Start in Preschool, BYU Study Shows," *Brigham Young University News*, May 5, 2005, https://news.byu.edu/news/mean-girls-start-preschool-byu-study-shows; Annie Murphy Paul, "Safety First," *Time*, October 11, 2010, p. 56.
92. Anderson, Kochanek, and Murphy (1997), cited in Babette Gutmann, dir., *Trends in the Well-Being of America's Children and Youth* (Washington, DC: US Department of Health and Human Services, Office of the Assistant Secretary for Planning and Evaluation, 2001), 164–68.
93. Kate Smith, "U.S. Homicide Rate: Female Victims Rose by 21 Percent," CBS News, December 6, 2017.
94. US Department of Justice, *Intimate Partner Violence: Attributes of Victimization* (US Department of Justice, Bureau of Justice Statistics, 1993), 96.
95. Orrin Hatch and Senate Committee on the Judiciary, "Children, Violence, and the Media: A Report for Parents and Policy Makers" (1999), http://judiciary.senate.gov/oldsite/mediavio.htm. Website available at the time of writing.
96. Hanson and McAuliffe, "Gender and Violence"; Lungren, *Violence Prevention*.
97. Hanson and McAuliffe, "Gender and Violence."
98. Federal Bureau of Investigation, "2016 Crime Statistics Released," September 25, 2017, https://www.fbi.gov/news/stories/2016-crime-statistics-released.
99. Cathy Schoen, Melinda K. Abrams, and Karen Davis, "The Commonwealth Fund Survey of the Health of Adolescent Girls," Commonwealth Fund, November 1, 1997.
100. Cook and Laub (2002), cited in Esbensen, "Youth Violence," 181.
101. Howard H. Snyder and Melissa Sickmund, *Juvenile Offenders and Victims: 2006 National Report* (Washington, DC: US Department of Justice, 2006).
102. Esbensen et al., "Evaluation and Evolution."
103. Esbensen et al., "Evaluation and Evolution."
104. Patrice Opplinger, *Girls Gone Skank: The Sexualization of Girls in American Culture* (Jefferson, NC: McFarland, 2008).
105. Kike Arnal, *In the Shadow of Power* (Milan, Italy: Charta, 2010).
106. Peter Schrag, "Bailing Out of Public Education," *The Nation*, October 4, 1993, p. 351.
107. Steven H. Woolf, Robert E. Johnson, and H. Jack Geiger, "The Rising Prevalence of Severe Poverty in America: A Growing Threat to Public Health," *American Journal of Preventive Medicine* 31, no. 4 (2006): 1.
108. Woolf et al., "The Rising Prevalence of Severe Poverty in America."
109. Woolf et al., "The Rising Prevalence of Severe Poverty in America."
110. Snyder et al. (1996), cited in Kelley et al., "Epidemiology of Serious Violence," 2.
111. Jeff John Roberts, "The Big Economy Squeeze on Workers," *Fortune*, January 2019, p. 68.

112. Roberts, "The Big Economy Squeeze on Workers," 71.
113. Jason DeParle, "Hunger in United States at 14-Year High," *New York Times*, November 16, 2009.
114. Bernadette D. Proctor, Jessica L. Semega, and Melissa A. Kollar, "Income and Poverty in the United States: 2015," US Census Bureau, report no. P60–256, September 13, 2016.
115. Jessica Semega, Melissa Kollar, John Creamer, and Abinash Mohanty, "Income and Poverty in the United States: 2018," US Census Bureau, report no. P60–266, September 10, 2019.
116. Elise Gould and Jessica Schieder, "Poverty Persists 50 Years after the Poor People's Campaign," Economic Policy Institute, May 17, 2018.
117. Peter S. Goodman, "Millions of Unemployed Face Year without Jobs," *New York Times*, February 23, 2010.
118. Robert W. Fuller, *Somebodies and Nobodies: Overcoming the Abuse of Rank* (Gabriola Island, BC: New Society, 2004).
119. David Denby, *Snark: A Polemic in Seven Fits* (New York: Simon and Schuster, 2010).
120. Denby, *Snark*.
121. *Energy Times*, http://energytimes.com, 33.
122. James R. Healy, "Jazzy New Little Suzuki SX4 SportBack Packs a Nice Punch," *USA Today*, May 21, 2010.
123. *Delicious Living*, April 2011.
124. Dave Krantzler, "The Fed is Running Out of Bullets," *The Daily Coin*, June 19, 2019.
125. Greenbaum, "Kids and Guns," 3.
126. DeJong, "Preventing Interpersonal Violence among Youth," xi.
127. American Academy of Child and Adolescent Psychiatry, "Children and Firearms," *Facts for Families*, no. 37, 2008, http://www.aacap.org.
128. American Academy of Child and Adolescent Psychiatry, "Suicide in Children and Teens," *Facts for Families*, no. 10, 2008, updated June 2018, https://www.aacap.org/AACAP/Families_and_Youth/Facts_for_Families/FFF-Guide/Teen-Suicide-010.aspx.
129. George W. Dowdall, *College Drinking* (Santa Barbara, CA: Praeger, 2008).
130. Howard N. Snyder, "Juvenile Arrests 1995," *Juvenile Justice Bulletin* (February 1997), 1; Howard N. Snyder, "Juvenile Arrests 1997," *Juvenile Justice Bulletin* (December 1998), 1.
131. American Academy of Child and Adolescent Psychiatry, "Teens: Alcohol and Other Drugs," *Facts for Families*, no. 3 (2008), updated March 2018, https://www.aacap.org/AACAP/Families_and_Youth/Facts_for_Families/FFF-Guide/Teens-Alcohol-And-Other-Drugs-003.aspx.
132. Mohkiber, cited in Winslow, in Tara Herival and Paul Wright, *Prison Nation: The Warehousing of America's Poor* (New York: Routledge, 2003), 42.
133. John F. Helliwell, Richard Layard, and Jeffrey D. Sachs, eds., *World Happiness Report 2019* (New York: United Nations Sustainable Development Solutions Network, 2019).
134. William Dufty, *Sugar Blues* (New York: Grand Central, 1986).
135. Dufty, *Sugar Blues*.

136. Ad Council, *Healthy Lifestyles and Disease Prevention: Media Campaign Report* (Washington, DC: US Department of Health and Human Services, 2004).
137. Commonwealth Fund, "2013 Commonwealth Fund Health Policy Survey," November 13, 2013.
138. Eric Schlosser, *Fast Food Nation: The Dark Side of the All-American Meal* (New York: Penguin, 2001), 4–5.
139. Schlosser, *Fast Food Nation*, 4–5.
140. Carl Lowe, "The Blood Sugar Blues," *Energy Times* (July/August 2003): 20.
141. Annie Graves, "Diabetes without the Sugar Coating," *Remedies: The Best Nutrition for Health and Renewal* 1, no. 1 (2005).
142. "New Studies" (2004), cited in Roy F. Baumeister and Brad J. Bushman, *Social Psychology and Human Nature* (Boston: Wadsworth Cengage Learning, 2016), 309.
143. Lowe, "The Blood Sugar Blues," 20.
144. Lowe, "The Blood Sugar Blues," 26.
145. Glenda Olsen, "Foods," *Energy Times* (July/August2003): 44. Source was available at the time of writing.
146. Olsen, "Foods," 44.
147. Olsen, "Foods," 47.
148. Rob Gifford, "U.S. on List of UNICEF's Worst Countries for Kids," National Public Radio, February 14, 2007.
149. The Foundation Center, "Child Poverty Rate Up Since 2007," *Philanthropic News Digest*, http://foundationcenter.org. Source available at the time of writing.
150. *Sicko*, produced and directed by Michael Moore (New York: Weinstein, 2007).
151. Matthew Robinson and Daniel Murphy, *Greed is Good: Maximization and Elite Deviance in America* (Lanham, MD: Rowman and Littlefield, 2008).
152. Stuart L. Hills, ed., *Corporate Violence: Injury and Death for Profit* (New York: Rowman and Littlefield, 1987), 8.
153. Letha A. (Lee) See, and Nancy Khashan, "Violence in the Suites: The Corporate Paradigm" *Journal of Human Behavior in the Social Environment* 4, no. 2/3 (2001).
154. George Winslow, "Capital Crimes," *Prison Nation: The Warehousing of America's Poor*, edited by Tara Herival and Paul Wright (New York: Routledge, 2003), 43.
155. See and Khashan, "Violence in the Suites," 63.
156. Baron, cited in See and Khashan, "Violence in the Suites," 62.
157. Francis T. Cullen, Gray Cavender, William J. Maakestad, and Michael L. Benson, *Corporate Crime under Attack: The Fight to Criminalize Business Violence* (Cincinnati, OH: Anderson, 2006); Joe R. Feagin and Clairece Booher Feagin, *Social Problems: A Critical Power-Conflict Perspective* (Upper Saddle River, NJ: Prentice Hall, 1990); Hills, *Corporate Violence*.
158. Cullen et al., *Corporate Crime under Attack*, 25.
159. Winslow, "Capital Crimes," 54.

160. "Corporate Profits: Breaking Records," *The Economist*, February 12, 2005.
161. Nancy Carlsson and Diane E. Levin, *Calling the Shots: How to Respond Effectively to Children's Fascination with War Play and War Toys* (Gabriola Island, BC: New Society, 1990), 89.
162. "Harper's Index," *Harper's Bazaar*, December 1991.
163. Karen Hall, "For Real Life?: War Toys in the Peace-Loving Household," Syracuse Peace Council, http://www.peacecouncil.net. Source available at the time of writing.
164. Athens Herald Banner, December 11, 1982, cited in Craig A. Anderson, "An Update on the Effects of Playing Violent Video Games," *Journal of Adolescence* 27, no. 1 (2004): 141.
165. Grossman and DeGaetano, *Stop Teaching Our Kids to Kill*, 23.
166. "Harper's Index," *Harper's Bazaar*, December 1991.
167. "Harper's Index," *Harper's Bazaar*, December 1991.
168. "Harper's Index," *Harper's Bazaar*, December 1991.
169. CSN National Injury and Violence Prevention Resource Center, *Do You Know These Facts about Violence?* (Newton, MA: Education Development Center, 1997).
170. Christopher J. Mumola, "Substance Abuse and Treatment, State and Federal Prisoners, 1997," *Special Report* (Washington, DC: US Department of Justice, 1999).
171. American Academy of Child and Adolescent Psychiatry, "Children and Firearms," *Facts for Families*, no. 37, 2008, http://www.aacap.org.psychiatry
172. Patricia Horn, "Caging America: The U.S. Imprisonment Binge," *Dollars and Sense* (September 1991): 12.
173. Horn, "Caging America," 12.
174. Pew Charitable Trusts, "Public Safety, Public Spending: Forecasting America's Prison Population 2007–2011" (Washington, DC: Public Safety Performance Project, 2005), ii.
175. Ken Silverstein, introduction to *Prison Nation: The Warehousing of America's Poor*, edited by Tara Herival and Paul Wright (New York: Routledge, 2003), 1.
176. Horn, "Caging America," 13.
177. Allen J. Beck and Paige Harrison, "Prisoners in 2000," *Bureau of Justice Statistics Bulletin* (Washington, DC: Bureau of Justice Statistics, 2001).
178. Lichenstein and Kroll, "The Fortress Economy," 17.
179. Horn, "Caging America," 15.
180. Lichenstein and Kroll, "The Fortress Economy," Lichenstein and Kroll, cited in Rosenblatt, *Criminal Injustice*, 57.
181. Silverstein, introduction to *Prison Nation*, 2.
182. Judith Greene, "Bailing Out Private Jails," *American Prospect*, December 19, 2001, cited here in Herivel and Wright, *Prison Nation*, 139.
183. *William P. vs. Corrections Corporation of America* C/A No.: 3:98–290-17, "Verdict, Phase 1" document, filed December 14, 2000, in Judith Greene, "Bailing Out Private Jails," cited in Herival and Wright, *Prison Nation*, 139.

184. Mark H. Moore, Carol V. Petrie, Anthony A. Braga, and Brendan L. McLaughlin, eds., *Deadly Lessons: Understanding Lethal School Violence* (Washington, DC: The National Academies Press, 2003), 249.

185. American Academy of Pediatrics, Committee on Injury and Poison Prevention, "Policy Statement: Firearm-Related Injuries Affecting the Pediatric Population," *Pediatrics* 130, no. 5 (2012): 2–3, https://doi.org/10.1542/peds.2012-2481.

186. "List of Countries by Firearm-Related Death Rate," Wikipedia, https://en.wikipedia.org/wiki/List_of_countries_by_firearm-related_death_rate.

187. Abigail Abrams and Melissa Chan, "Special Report: Guns in America," *Time*, November 5, 2018, p. 29.

188. Centers for Disease Control and Prevention, "Trends in Rates of Homicides—United States, 1985–1995," *Morbidity and Mortality Weekly Report*, June 7, 1996.

189. James A. Mercy and Mark L. Rosenberg, "Preventing Firearm Violence in and around Schools," *Violence in American Schools*, edited by Delbert S. Elliott, Beatrix A. Hamburg, and Kirk R. Williams (Cambridge, UK: Cambridge University Press, 1998), 161.

190. Mercy and Rosenberg, "Preventing Firearm Violence."

191. Richard W. Riley and Janet Reno, *1998 Annual Report on School Safety* (Washington, DC: US Department of Justice and US Department of Education, 1999), 193.

192. Mercy and Rosenberg, "Preventing Firearm Violence," 168.

193. Bilchik, *Promising Strategies to Reduce Gun Violence*, 4.

194. James A. Roth, *Firearms and Violence: Research in Brief* (Washington, DC: US Department of Justice, National Institute of Justice, 1994).

195. Associated Press, "Congress Lets Assault Weapons Ban Expire," NBC News, September 19, 2004, www.nbcnews.com.

196. Roth, *Firearms and Violence*.

197. Bilchik, *Promising Strategies to Reduce Gun Violence*, 3.

198. Center to Prevent Handgun Violence, *Gun Industry Experts Predict Far-Reaching Reforms: Point to Tobacco and Other Industries as Precedent* (Washington, DC: Center to Prevent Handgun Violence, 1997).

199. *Bill Moyers Journal*, "Gun Violence," aired March 10, 1995, on PBS.

200. Fox Butterfield, "To Rejuvenate Gun Sales, Critics Say, Industry Started Making More Powerful Pistols," *New York Times*, February 14, 1999

201. David Gonzales, "Gunmakers and a Culture on Trial," *New York Times*, February 3, 1999.

202. Center to Prevent Handgun Violence, *Gun Industry Experts Predict Far-Reaching Reforms*.

203. Center to Prevent Handgun Violence, *Gun Industry Experts Predict Far-Reaching Reforms*.

204. Center to Prevent Handgun Violence, *Gun Industry Experts Predict Far-Reaching Reforms*.

205. Center to Prevent Handgun Violence, *Gun Industry Experts Predict Far-Reaching Reforms*.

206. Roy E. Larsen, prod., *March of Time* newsreel, "The Youth Problem," released 1942, aired

December 2013, on Turner Classic Movies.
207. Deats, "The Culture of Violence."
208. Chalmers Johnson, "We Have the Money If Only We Didn't Waste It on the Defense Budget," Tom Dispatch, September 29, 2008, http://www.TomDispatch.com.
209. Robert L. Borosage, "Disinvesting in America," *The Nation*, October 4, 1993, p. 346.
210. War Resisters League, "Where Your Income Tax Money Really Goes—2017," https://www.warresisters.org.
211. War Resisters League, "Where Your Income Tax Money Really Goes—2003."
212. War Resisters League, "Where Your Income Tax Money Really Goes—2010."
213. John Hillkirk, "It's Time to Put a Hold on the Pentagon's Blank Check," *USA Today*, May 21, 2010, p. 8A.
214. War Resisters League, "Where Your Income Tax Money Really Goes—2021."
215. Hilkirk, "It's Time to Put a Hold on the Pentagon's Blank Check."
216. War Resisters League, "Where Your Income Tax Money Really Goes—2021."
217. Hilkirk, "It's Time to Put a Hold on the Pentagon's Blank Check."
218. War Tax Resisters League, "Where Your Income Tax Money Really Goes—2019."
219. David Jolly, "Credit Agency Warns U.S. and Others of Risk to Top Rating," *New York Times*, March 15, 2010.
220. Paul Kawika Martin, "InSane," *Peace Action Peace Blog*, February 18, 2010, http://peaceblog.wordpress.com.
221. Peace Action, National Center for Peace Action, "Common Dreams," http://www.peaceaction.org. Source available at the time of writing.
222. *Bowling for Columbine*, directed by Michael Moore (2002; Beverley Hills, CA: MGM Home Entertainment, 2003).

■ Chapter 5. The Culture of School Violence: The School Environment

1. June L. Arnette and Marjorie C. Walsenben, "Combating Fear and Restoring Safety in Schools," *Juvenile Justice Bulletin* (Washington, DC: US Department of Justice, 1998), 8.
2. US Department of Justice, *Sourcebook of Criminal Justice Statistics, 2002* (Washington, DC: Bureau of Justice Statistics, 2003), 1.
3. Mark Anderson, Joanne Kaufman, Thomas R. Simon, et al, "School-Associated Violent Deaths in the United States, 1994–1999," *JAMA* 286, no. 21 (December 2001): 2695–2702, doi:10.1001/jama.286.21.2695.
4. Rachel Dinkes, Jana Kemp, Katrina Baum, and Thomas D. Snyder, *Indicators of School Crime and Safety: 2009* (Washington, DC: Bureau of Justice Statistics and National Center for Education Statistics, 2009), 1, https://nces.ed.gov/pubs2010/2010012.pdf.

5. Dinkes et al., *Indicators of School Crime and Safety: 2009*, 1.
6. Dinkes et al., *Indicators of School Crime and Safety: 2009*, 1.
7. National Institute of Education, *Violent Schools—Safe Schools: The Safe School Study Report to Congress* (Washington, DC: US Government Printing Office, 1978.)
8. Rachel Dinkes, Jana Kemp, Katrina Baum, and Thomas D. Snyder, *Indicators of School Crime and Safety: 2008* (Washington, DC: Bureau of Justice Statistics and National Center for Education Statistics, 2009), https://nces.ed.gov/pubs2009/2009022REV.pdf.
9. National Institute of Education, *Violent Schools—Safe Schools*.
10. William DeJong, "Preventing Interpersonal Violence among Youth: An Introduction to School, Community, and Mass Media Strategies," *Issues and Practices in Criminal Justice* (Washington, DC: US Department of Justice, 1994), 4.
11. Children's Institute International, *Armed and Ready for School* (Los Angeles: Pacific Visions Communication, 1996).
12. Centers for Disease Control and Prevention (1993), cited in DeJong, "Preventing Interpersonal Violence among Youth," 4.
13. DeJong, "Preventing Interpersonal Violence among Youth," 2.
14. DeJong, "Preventing Interpersonal Violence among Youth," 2.
15. Children's Institute International, *Armed and Ready for School*.
16. Arnette and Walsenben, "Combating Fear and Restoring Safety in Schools," 2.
17. Arnette and Walsenben, "Combating Fear and Restoring Safety in Schools," 2.
18. "NBC News Special," *New York Times*, July 1994.
19. "NBC News Special," *New York Times*, July 1994.
20. Arnette and Walsenben, "Combating Fear and Restoring Safety in Schools," 2.
21. Jarrod Hindman, *Child and Adolescent Violence in Colorado: A 2005 Status Report* (Denver: Colorado Department of Public Health and Environment, 2005), 12–13.
22. American Psychological Association, "Child Violence" (2000), cited in Mark R. Leary, Robin M. Kowalski, Laura Smith, and Stephen Phillips, "Teasing, Rejection, and Violence: Case Studies of the School Shootings," *Aggressive Behavior* 29, no. 3 (2003): 213.
23. American Psychological Association, "Child Violence," 213.
24. Delbert S. Elliott, Beatrix A. Hamburg, and Kirk R. Williams, *Violence in American Schools: A New Perspective* (Cambridge, UK: Cambridge University Press, 1998), 8.
25. Children's Institute International, *Armed and Ready for School*.
26. Centers for Disease Control and Prevention (1991), cited in DeJong, "Preventing Interpersonal Violence among Youth," 2.
27. Maguire and Pastore, cited in Elliott et al., *Violence in American Schools*, 9.
28. Dinkes et al., *Indicators of School Crime and Safety: 2008*.
29. Dinkes et al., *Indicators of School Crime and Safety: 2008*.
30. Simone Robers, Jana Kemp, Amy Rathbun, Rachel E. Morgan, and Thomas D. Snyder, *Indicators of*

NOTES 257

School Crime and Safety: 2013 (Washington, DC: Bureau of Justice Statistics and National Center for Education Statistics, 2014), https://nces.ed.gov/pubs2014/2014042.pdf.
31. Elliott et al., *Violence in American Schools*.
32. Lauren Musu-Gillette, Anlan Zhang, Ke Wang, Zizhi Zhang, and Barbara A. Oudekerk, *Indicators of School Crime and Safety: 2016* (Washington, DC: Bureau of Justice Statistics and National Center for Education Statistics, 2017), iv, https://nces.ed.gov/pubs2017/2017064.pdf.
33. Kirsten Olsen, *Wounded by School: Recapturing the Joy in Learning and Standing Up to Old School Culture* (New York: Teachers College Press, 2009), 203.
34. Paolo Freire, *Pedagogy of the Oppressed* (New York: Continuum, 1989).
35. Mark H. Moore, Carol V. Petrie, Anthony A. Braga, and Brendan L. McLaughlin, eds., *Deadly Lessons: Understanding Lethal School Violence* (Washington, DC: The National Academies Press, 2003), 1.
36. Moore et al., *Deadly Lessons*, 6.
37. Richard A. Goddard, personal communication with author, November 21, 2008 and March 3, 2009.
38. Laura Kann, Tim McManus, William A. Harris, et al., "Youth Risk Surveillance—United States, 2017," *Morbidity and Mortality Weekly Report Surveillance Summaries* 67, no. 8 (2018), http://dx.doi.org/10.15585/mmwr.ss6708a1.
39. Musu-Gillette et al., *Indicators of School Crime and Safety: 2016*, viii.
40. American Educational Research Association. www.agra.nea/publications; Cheryl Lero Jonson, "Preventing School Shootings: The Effectiveness of Security Measures," *Victims and Offenders* 12, no. 6 (2017): 956–73.
41. Tim Walker, "Cameras in the Class: Is Big Brother Evaluating You?," *NEA Today*, January 23, 2015.
42. Dave Grossman and Gloria DeGaetano, *Stop Teaching Our Kids to Kill: A Call to Action Against TV, Movie and Video Game Violence* (New York: Crown, 1999), 18.
43. Jill DeVoe, Katharin Peter, Margaret Noonan, Thomas Snyder, and Katrina Baum, *Indicators of School Crime and Safety: 2005* (Washington, DC: Bureau of Justice Statistics and National Center for Education Statistics, 2005), https://nces.ed.gov/pubs2006/2006001.pdf.
44. DeVoe et al., *Indicators of School Crime and Safety: 2005*.
45. DeVoe et al., *Indicators of School Crime and Safety: 2005*.
46. Glenda Olsen, "Foods." *Energy Times*, July/August 2003, p. 25.
47. DeVoe et al., *Indicators of School Crime and Safety: 2005*.
48. DeVoe et al., *Indicators of School Crime and Safety: 2005*.
49. Physicians for Safe Technology, "Wi-Fi in Schools" and "Scientific Literature," updated November 24, 2019, www.mdsafetech.org.
50. Arnette and Walsenben, "Combating Fear and Restoring Safety in Schools."
51. Anlan Zhang, Lauren Musu-Gillette, and Barbara A. Oudekerk, *Indicators of School Crime and Safety: 2015* (Washington, DC: Bureau of Justice Statistics and National Center for Education

Statistics, 2016), https://www.bjs.gov/content/pub/pdf/iscs15.pdf.
52. Arnette and Walsenben, "Combating Fear and Restoring Safety in Schools."
53. Sara Neufeld, "Seeking to Curb School Violence," *Baltimore Sun*, April 10, 2008.
54. Louis Rosen, "Violence Prevention: School's Newest Challenge," *School Safety News Journal* (Spring 1993).
55. Rosen, "Violence Prevention."
56. "Bullying: No Escape," *Anderson Cooper 360 Degrees*, aired October 10, 2010, on CNN.
57. Dan Olweus, Susan Limber, and Steven Mihalic, *The Bullying Prevention Program: Blueprints for Violence Prevention* (Boulder, CO: Center for the Study and Prevention of Violence, 1999).
58. S. Harris, G. Petrie, and W. Willoughby, "Bullying among 9th Graders: An Exploratory Study," *NASSP Bulletin* 86 (2002): 630.
59. "Bullying: No Escape," *Anderson Cooper 360 Degrees*.
60. Hoover et al. (1992), cited in Fleming and Towey, *Educational Forum on Adolescent Health*, 11.
61. Leary et al., "Teasing, Rejection, and Violence: Case Studies of the School Shootings," 213.
62. DeJong, "Preventing Interpersonal Violence among Youth," 4.
63. DeJong, "Preventing Interpersonal Violence among Youth," 3.
64. DeJong, "Preventing Interpersonal Violence among Youth," 12.
65. Margaret A. Hamburg, "Youth Violence Is a Public Health Concern," *Violence in American Schools*, edited by Delbert S. Elliott, Beatrix A. Hamburg, and Kirk R, Williams (Cambridge, UK: Cambridge University Press, 1998), 36.
66. Grossman and DeGaetano, *Stop Teaching Our Kids to Kill*, 18.
67. Thanks to Erynn Bourdo, a student in the author's class, fall 2010.
68. Hamburg, "Youth Violence Is a Public Health Concern," 47.
69. American Medical Association, "Youth Bullying," 9.
70. Lowry et al. (1995), Hamburg, "Youth Violence Is a Public Health Concern," 36.
71. Anderson et al., "School-Associated Violent Deaths in the United States, 1994–1999."
72. Lauren Musu, Anlan Zhang, Ke Wang, Jizhi Zhang, and Barbara A. Oudekerk, *Indicators of School Crime and Safety: 2018* (Washington, DC: Bureau of Justice Statistics and National Center for Education Statistics, 2019), https://nces.ed.gov/pubs2019/2019047.pdf.
73. National School Safety Center, "NSSC Review of School Safety Research" (Washington, DC: US Department of Education, 2006).
74. Musu-Gillette et al., *Indicators of School Crime and Safety: 2016*.
75. Musu-Gillette et al., *Indicators of School Crime and Safety: 2016*.
76. Phillip Kaufman, Chen Xianglei, Susan P. Chou, Sally A. Ruddy, Amanda K. Miller, Jill K. Fleury, Kathryn A. Chandler, Michael R. Rand, Patsy Klaus, and Michael G. Planty, *Indicators of School Crime and Safety, 2000* (Washington, DC: US Department of Education and US Department of Justice, 2000), https://nces.ed.gov/pubs2001/2001017a.pdf.
77. DeVoe et al., *Indicators of School Crime and Safety: 2005*.

78. Arnette and Walsenben, "Combating Fear and Restoring Safety in Schools," 2.
79. Arnette and Walsenben, "Combating Fear and Restoring Safety in Schools," 2.
80. David Finkelhor, *Childhood Victimization: Violence, Crime and Abuse in the Lives of Young People* (New York: Oxford University Press, 2008).
81. J. Baxter Oliphant, "Women and Men in Both Parties Say Sexual Harassment Allegations Reflect 'Widespread Problem' in Society," *Factank—News in the Numbers*, Pew Research Center, December 7, 2017.
82. Timothy W. Lineberry and Stephen S. O'Connor, "Suicide in the U.S. and the U.S. Army," *Mayo Clinic Proceedings* 87, no. 9 (September 2012).
83. Noemi E. Olsen, "Bullying Levels and Reporting Preferences in Urban, Suburban and Rural Schools" (education specialist thesis, Brigham Young University, 2010), https://scholarshipsarchieve_BYU.edu/edt/2418.
84. Shane R. Jimerson, Susan M. Swearer, and Dorothy L. Espelage, eds., *Handbook of Bullying in Schools: An International Perspective* (New York: Routledge, 2010).
85. Virginia Youth Violence Project, "Middle School Bullying," School of Education, University of Virginia, http://youthviolence.edschool.virginia.edu/bullying/bullying-middle-school-research.html.
86. Fleming and Towey, *Educational Forum on Adolescent Health*, 44.
87. American Medical Association, "Proceedings of the Educational Forum on Adolescent Health: Youth Bullying," 21, http://www.amaassn.org/ama1/pub/upload/mm/39/youthbullying.pdf.
88. Center for the Study and Prevention of Violence, *Blueprints for Healthy Youth Development—Olweus Bullying Prevention Program* (Boulder: University of Colorado, 2004).
89. Thanks to Keean Davis, a student in the author's class, fall 2010.
90. Thanks to Keean Davis.
91. Jill Smolowe and Moira Bailey, "Confessions of a Bully," *People*, October 18, 2010, p. 70.
92. Richard B. Felson, "A Rational-Choice Approach to Violence," *Violence: From Theory to Research*, edited by Margaret A. Zahn, Henry J. Brownstein, and Shelly L. Jackson (Cincinnati, OH: Anderson, 2004), 79.
93. Maguire and Pastore, cited in Elliott et al., *Violence in American Schools*, 9.
94. Alex Tresniowski, Nicole Weisensee, Diane Herbst Egan, Charlotte Triggs, Lesley Messer, Joanne Flower, Daniel S. Levy, and Nadine Shabeeb, "Tormented to Death?" *People*, October 18, 2010, p. 57.
95. Kaufman et al., *Indicators of School Crime and Safety, 2000*, 82.
96. Ramin Setoodeh, "Young, Gay and Murdered," *Newsweek*, July 28, 2008, p. 41.
97. Olweus, cited in Fleming and Towey, *Educational Forum on Adolescent Health*, 7.
98. David Finkelhor, Heather Turner, Richard Ormrod, Sherry Hamby, and Kristen Kracke, "Children's Exposure to Violence: A Comprehensive National Survey," *Juvenile Justice Bulletin* (Washington, DC: US Department of Justice, 2009), 5.

99. Finkelhor et al., "Children's Exposure to Violence," 5.
100. Maguire and Pastore, cited in Elliott et al., *Violence in American Schools*, 9.
101. Hindman, *Child and Adolescent Violence in Colorado*, 13.
102. Nansel et al., cited in Fleming and Towey, *Educational Forum on Adolescent Health*.
103. Fleming and Towey, *Educational Forum on Adolescent Health*, 12.
104. Fleming and Towey, *Educational Forum on Adolescent Health*, 12.
105. Fleming and Towey, *Educational Forum on Adolescent Health*, 12.
106. DeJong "Preventing Interpersonal Violence among Youth," 4.
107. DeJong "Preventing Interpersonal Violence among Youth," 5.
108. DeJong "Preventing Interpersonal Violence among Youth," 4.
109. Finkelhor et al., "Children's Exposure to Violence," 5.
110. Wired Safety Group, "Stop Cyberbullying," http://www.stopcyberbullying.org.
111. Wired Safety Group, "Stop Cyberbullying."
112. Musu-Gillette et al., *Indicators of School Crime and Safety: 2016*, vi.
113. Monica Anderson, "A Majority of Teens Have Experienced Some Form of Cyberbullying," Pew Research Center, September 27, 2018.
114. Virginia Dalla Pozza, Anna Di Pietro, Sophie Morel, and Emma Psaila, "Cyberbullying among Young People," report for the European Parliament, Policy Department C: Citizens' Rights and Constitutional Affairs, 2016.
115. Wired Safety Group, "Stop Cyberbullying."
116. Wired Safety Group, "Stop Cyberbullying."
117. Wired Safety Group, "Stop Cyberbullying."
118. Wired Safety Group, "Stop Cyberbullying."
119. Michelle Morgan Bolton, "Anti-Bully Pulpit," *Boston Globe*, April 16, 2009.
120. Shari Keller Schneider, Lydia O'Donnell, Ann Stueve, and Robert W. S. Coulter, "Cyberbullying, School Bullying and Psychological Distress: A Regional Census of High School Students," *American Journal of Public Health* 102, no. 1 (January 2012): 171–77.
121. Wired Safety Group, "Stop Bullying."
122. Wired Safety Group, "Stop Bullying."
123. Wired Safety Group, "Stop Bullying."
124. Wired Safety Group, "Stop Bullying."
125. Wired Safety Group, "Stop Bullying."
126. Robert Leitman and Katherine Binns, project directors, *The Metropolitan Life Survey of the American Teacher, 1993: Violence in America's Public Schools* (New York: Metropolitan Life Insurance, 1993).
127. Center for the Study and Prevention of Violence, *Blueprints—Olweus Bullying Prevention*.
128. Hamburg, "Youth Violence Is a Public Health Concern," 35
129. Lowry et al. (1995), cited in Hamburg, "Youth Violence Is a Public Health Concern," 35.

130. "NBC News Special," *New York Times*.
131. Susan P. Limber and Maury M. Nation, "Bullying among Children and Youth," *Juvenile Justice Bulletin* (Washington, DC: US Department of Justice, 1998), 4.
132. Limber and Nation, "Bullying among Children and Youth," 4.
133. Dennis Kenney, "Crime in the Schools: A Problem-Solving Approach," *National Institute of Justice Research Preview* (Washington, DC: National Institute of Justice, US Department of Justice, 1998), 1.
134. Nansel et al. (2001), cited in Virginia Youth Violence Project, "Bullying," School of Education, University of Virginia, https://curry.virginia.edu/faculty-research/centers-labs-projects/research-labs/youth-violence-project/bullying.
135. DeVoe et al., *Indicators of School Crime and Safety: 2005*.
136. Virginia Youth Violence Project, "Bullying."
137. Nansel et al. (2001), cited in Virginia Youth Violence Project, "Bullying."
138. DeVoe et al., *Indicators of School Crime and Safety: 2005*.
139. Zhang et al., *Indicators of School Crime and Safety: 2015*.
140. Musu-Gillette et al., *Indicators of School Crime and Safety: 2016*.
141. Musu-Gillette et al., *Indicators of School Crime and Safety: 2016*.
142. Musu-Gillette et al., *Indicators of School Crime and Safety: 2016*.
143. National Commission on Excellence in Education, *A Nation at Risk: The Imperative for Educational Reform* (Washington, DC: National Commission on Excellence in Education, 1983), 9.
144. Arnette and Walsenben, "Combating Fear and Restoring Safety in Schools," 2.
145. Hamburg, "Youth Violence Is a Public Health Concern," 36.
146. Olweus, cited in Fleming and Towey, *Educational Forum on Adolescent Health*, 8.
147. Fleming and Towey, *Educational Forum on Adolescent Health*, 1.
148. American Medical Association, "Youth Bullying," 21.
149. DeJong, "Preventing Interpersonal Violence among Youth."
150. Cunningham et al. (2000), cited in Fleming and Towey, *Educational Forum on Adolescent Health*, 9.
151. Fleming and Towey, *Educational Forum on Adolescent Health*, 9.
152. Arnette and Walsenben, "Combating Fear and Restoring Safety in Schools," 3.
153. Olweus (1993a), cited in Sharon Mihalic, Katherine Irwin, Delbert Elliott, Abigail Fagan, and Diane Hansen, "Blueprints for Violence Prevention," *Juvenile Justice Bulletin* (Washington, DC: US Department of Justice, 2001), 7.
154. Fleming and Towey, *Educational Forum on Adolescent Health*, 1, 4, 9.
155. Tonya Fischio, "Mean Girls Start in Preschool, BYU Study Shows." *Brigham Young University News*, May 3, 2005, https://news.byu.edu/news/mean-girls-start-preschool-byu-study-shows.
156. Annie Murphy Paul, "Safety First," *Time*, October 11, 2010, p. 56.
157. Fischio, "Mean Girls Start in Preschool."

158. Nansel et al. (2001), cited in Dan Olweus, *Bullying at School* (Boston: Blackwell, 2006).
159. Fischio, "Mean Girls Start in Preschool."
160. American Medical Association, "Youth Bullying," 2.
161. Fleming and Towey, *Educational Forum on Adolescent Health*, 7.
162. Kaufman et al., *Indicators of School Crime and Safety, 2000*, 83.
163. DeVoe et al., *Indicators of School Crime and Safety: 2005*.
164. DeVoe et al., *Indicators of School Crime and Safety: 2005*.
165. Arnette and Walsenben, "Combating Fear and Restoring Safety in Schools," 3.
166. Cohen, cited in Arnette and Walsenben, "Combating Fear and Restoring Safety in Schools," 11.
167. Susan P. Limber and Maury M. Nation, "Bullying among Children and Youth," *Juvenile Justice Bulletin* (Washington, DC: US Department of Justice, 1998).
168. Parks, cited in National Criminal Justice Research Service, *Serving High Risk Youth: Lessons from Research and Programming* (Washington, DC: U.S. Department of Justice, 2009).
169. Smolowe and Bailey, "Confessions of a Bully," 70–71.
170. Jimerson et al., Handbook of Bullying in Schools.
171. Ann Shields and Dante Cicchetti, "Emotion Regulation Among School-Age Children: The Development and Validation of a New Criterion Q-Sort Scale," *Developmental Psychology* 33, no. 6 (November 1997): 906–16.
172. Kowalski (2003), cited in Leary et al., "Teasing, Rejection, and Violence," 213; Rigby (1996), cited in Fleming and Towey, *Educational Forum on Adolescent Health*, 11.
173. Fleming and Towey, *Educational Forum on Adolescent Health*, 9–10.
174. Fleming and Towey, *Educational Forum on Adolescent Health*, 9–10.
175. Shields and Cicchetti (2001), cited in Fleming and Towey, *Educational Forum on Adolescent Health*, 9.
176. Shields and Cicchetti, "Emotion Regulation Among School-Age Children."
177. Fleming and Towey, *Educational Forum on Adolescent Health*, 9–10.
178. Kann, et al. (2000), cited in Center for the Study and Prevention of Violence, *Blueprints*.
179. Lowry, cited in Hamburg, "Youth Violence Is a Public Health Concern," 36.
180. Olweus (1993a), cited in Fleming and Towey, *Educational Forum on Adolescent Health*, 11.
181. Thomas N. Thornton, Carole A. Craft, Linda L. Dahlberg, Barbara S. Lynch, and Katie Baer, eds., *Best Practices of Youth Violence Prevention: A Sourcebook for Community Action,* rev. ed. (Atlanta: Centers for Disease Control and Prevention, 2002).
182. Rigby (1996), cited in Fleming and Towey, *Educational Forum on Adolescent Health*, 11.
183. Tresniowski et al., "Tormented to Death?," p. 58.
184. Thanks to Lindsey Cherry, a student in the author's fall 2010 class.
185. Tresniowski et al., "Tormented to Death?," 58.
186. American Medical Association, "Youth Bullying," 10.
187. Kumppulainen and Rasanen (2000), cited in Fleming and Towey, *Educational Forum on*

Adolescent Health, 10.

188. Olweus (1993), cited in Fleming and Towey, *Educational Forum on Adolescent Health*, 10.
189. Quoted by Keean Davis, a student in the author's class.
190. Anderson et al., "School-Associated Violent Deaths in the United States, 1994–1999."
191. Dedman (2000), cited in American Medical Association, "Youth Bullying."
192. Matt Apuzzo and Sharon Cohen, "VA Tech Shooter: A Textbook Case," *Pueblo Chieftain* (Associated Press), April 20, 2007, 1.
193. Fleming and Towey, *Educational Forum on Adolescent Health*, 44.
194. Center for the Prevention and Study of Violence, *Blueprints*.
195. Arnette and Walsenben, "Combating Fear and Restoring Safety in Schools."
196. Ira Pollack and Carlos Sundermann, "Creating Safe Schools: A Comprehensive Approach," *Juvenile Justice: School Violence; An Overview* 8, no. 1 (2001): 14.
197. International Safe Schools, "International Safe Schools: A Project in Collaboration with the World Health Organization Collaborating Centre on Community Safety Practices," 2002.
198. US Department of Justice, *2000 Annual Report on School Safety*, https://www.ncjrs.gov/pdffiles1/ojjdp/193163.pdf.
199. Kenney, "Crime in the Schools," 1.
200. Freire, *Pedagogy of the Oppressed*.

■ Chapter 6. School Rampage Shooters: More Lethal Than Ever

1. Adam Lankford, "Mass Shootings in the U.S.: 1966–2010," *Justice Quarterly* 32, no. 2 (2015): 360–379.
2. Lankford, "Mass Shootings in the U.S."
3. Mark H. Moore, Carol V. Petrie, Anthony A. Braga, and Brendan L. McLaughlin, eds., *Deadly Lessons: Understanding Lethal School Violence* (Washington, DC: National Academies Press, 2003), 295.
4. Moore et al., *Deadly Lessons*, 11.
5. Moore et al., *Deadly Lessons*, 252.
6. Moore et al., *Deadly Lessons*, 9.
7. CBS News, "Boy Behind Columbine-Style Plot," December 19, 2007.
8. Peter Langman, *Why Kids Kill: Inside the Minds of School Shooters* (New York: Palgrave Macmillan, 2009), 3.
9. Dewey G. Cornell, "Psychology of the School Shootings: Testimony presented at the House Judiciary Committee Oversight Hearing to Examine Youth Culture and Violence," US House Judiciary Committee, May 13, 1999.
10. Cornell, "Psychology of the School Shootings."

11. Langman, *Why Kids Kill*, 79.
12. Moore et al., *Deadly Lessons*, 108.
13. Moore et al., *Deadly Lessons*.
14. Moore et al., *Deadly Lessons*, 108.
15. Bryan Vossekuil, Marisa Reddy, and Robert Fein, *Safe School Initiative: An Interim Report on the Prevention of Targeted Violence in Schools* (Washington, DC: US Secret Service National Threat Assessment Center, US Department of Education, and the National Institute of Justice, 2000).
16. Langman, *Why Kids Kill*, 3; Moore et al., *Deadly Lessons*, 108.
17. Cara Santa Maria, "The Mind of a Mass Murderer: Charles Whitman, Brain Damage, and Violence," *Huffington Post*, March 28, 2012, https://www.huffpostr.com/entry/mind-murderer.
18. Moore et al., *Deadly Lessons*
19. *The First Columbine*, aired April 20, 2009, on WeTV.
20. Katherine Ramsland, "School Killers," Crime Library on truTV.com, https://web.archive.org/web/20090307073643/http://www.trutv.com:80/library/crime/serial_killers/weird/kids1/index_1.html?print=yes. Also see Katherine Ramsland, *Inside the Minds of Mass Murderers: Why They Kill* (Praeger, 2005).
21. Mark R. Leary, Robin M. Kowalski, Laura Smith, and Stephen Phillips, "Teasing, Rejection, and Violence: Case Studies of the School Shootings," *Aggressive Behavior* 29, no. 3 (2003): 202–14.
22. Katie Serena, "Brenda Ann Spencer Shot Up a School. Her Reason? 'I Don't Like Mondays,'" February 7, 2018, www.allthatsinteresting.com/brenda-ann-spencer.
23. Langman, *Why Kids Kill*, 79.
24. Christopher J. Ferguson, Mark Coulson, and Jane Barnett, "Psychological Profiles of School Shooters: Positive Directions and One Big Wrong Turn," *Journal of Police Crisis Negotiations* 11, no. 2 (2011).
25. Ramsland, "School Shooters." Also see Ramsland, *Inside the Minds of Mass Murderers*.
26. Langman, *Why Kids Kill,* 3.
27. Timothy Egan, "Where Rampages Begin: A Special Report; From Adolescent Angst to Shooting Up Schools," *New York Times*, June 14, 1998.
28. June L. Arnette and Marjorie C. Walsenben, "Combating Fear and Restoring Safety in Schools," *Juvenile Justice Bulletin* (Washington, DC: US Department of Justice, 1998), 8.
29. Leary et al., "Teasing, Rejection, and Violence," 1, 202.
30. "List of School Shootings in the United States by Death Toll," Wikipedia, https://en.wikipedia.org/wiki/List_of_school_shootings_in_the_United_States_by_death_toll.
31. "Timeline of Worldwide School and Mass Shootings," https://www.infoplease.com/history/world/timeline-of-worldwide-school-and-mass-shootings.
32. Leary et al., "Teasing, Rejection, and Violence," 300.
33. Leary et al., "Teasing, Rejection, and Violence," 301.
34. Leary et al., "Teasing, Rejection, and Violence," 204.

NOTES

35. Leary et al., "Teasing, Rejection, and Violence," 293.
36. Michael Rocque, "Exploring School Rampage Shootings: Research, Theory and Policy," *Social Science Journal* 47, no. 3 (September 2012): 304–13.
37. Leary et al., "Teasing, Rejection, and Violence," 206.
38. Leary et al., "Teasing, Rejection, and Violence," 208.
39. Devoe et al., cited in Finn-Aage Esbensen, "Youth Violence: An Overview," *Violence: From Theory to Research*, edited by Margaret A. Zahn, Henry J. Brownstein, and Shelly L. Jackson (Cincinnati, OH: Anderson, 2004), 188.
40. "List of School Shootings in the United States by Death Toll," Wikipedia.
41. Leary, et al., "Teasing, Rejection, and Violence," 207.
42. Leary, et al., "Teasing, Rejection, and Violence," 295–96.
43. Phillip Kaufman, Xianglei Chen, Suan P. Choy, Sally A. Ruddy, Jill K. Fleury, Kathryn A. Chandler, Michael R. Rand, Patsy Klaus, and Michael G. Planty, *Indicators of School Crime and Safety, 2000* (Washington, DC: US Department of Education and US Department of Justice, 2000), https://nces.ed.gov/pubs2001/2001017a.pdf.
44. Leary, et al., "Teasing, Rejection, and Violence," 207.
45. Leary, et al., "Teasing, Rejection, and Violence," 207.
46. Leary, et al., "Teasing, Rejection, and Violence."
47. Ramsland, "School Shooters." Also see Ramsland, *Inside the Minds of Mass Murderers*.
48. Wikipedia, "List of Mass Shootings in the United States," https://en.wikipedia.org/wiki/Mass_shootings_in_the_United_States. This is the most comprehensive list of mass shootings currently available.
49. Wikipedia, "List of Mass Shootings in the United States."
50. Leary et al., "Teasing, Rejection, and Violence," 207.
51. Ferguson et al., "Psychological Profiles of School Shooters."
52. Langman, *Why Kids Kill*, 26.
53. Langman, *Why Kids Kill*, 16.
54. Rachel Kalish and Michael Kimmel, "Suicide by Mass Murder: Masculinity, Aggrieved Entitlement, and Rampage School Shootings," *Health Sociology Review* 19, no. 4 (December 2010): 451–64.
55. Meary, Kemper, Mohandle, Shiva, and Gray, cited in Langman, *Why Kids Kill*, 80.
56. Leary et al., "Teasing, Rejection, and Violence," 210.
57. Kalish and Kimmel, "Suicide by Mass Murder," 451–64.
58. Vossekuil et al., *Safe School Initiative*, 5.
59. Meary et al., cited in Langman, *Why Kids Kill*, 80.
60. Ramsland, "School Killers." Also see Ramsland, *Inside the Minds of Mass Murderers*.
61. Kalish and Kimmel, "Suicide by Mass Murder."
62. Leary et al., "Teasing, Rejection, and Violence," 208.
63. Langman, *Why Kids Kill*, 92.

64. Langman, *Why Kids Kill,* 17.
65. Langman, *Why Kids Kill,* 26.
66. Langman, *Why Kids Kill,* 16.
67. Kalish and Knoll, "Suicide by Mass Murder."
68. "School Shooters," aired February 7, 2010, on Discovery Channel.
69. Moore et al., *Deadly Lessons,* 114.
70. Leary et al., "Teasing, Rejection, and Violence."
71. Leary et al., "Teasing, Rejection, and Violence," 210.
72. Langman, *Why Kids Kill,* 141.
73. Verlinde et al. (2000), cited in Langman, *Why Kids Kill,* 80.
74. Craig A. Anderson, Douglas A. Gentile, and Kathrine E. Buckley, *Violent Video Game Effects on Children and Adolescents: Theory, Research, and Public Policy* (Oxford: Oxford University Press, 2007), 48.
75. Masten (2001), cited in Anderson et al., *Violent Video Game Effects,* 40.
76. Cornell, "Psychology of the School Shootings."
77. Moore et al., *Deadly Lessons,* 8.
78. John Cloud, "Of Arms and the Boy," *Time,* July 6, 1998, p. 58.
79. John King, "Violent Crime Rising in U.S. Schools," *CNN,* April 12, 1998.
80. Langman, *Why Kids Kill,* 26.
81. Moore et al., *Deadly Lessons.*
82. Moore et al., *Deadly Lessons.*
83. Kalish and Kimmel, "Suicide by Mass Murder."
84. Eric Madfis, "Triple Entitlement and Homicidal Anger: An Exploration of Intersectional Identifies of American Mass Murderers," *Men and Masculinities* (March 24, 2014): 67–86.
85. Vossekuil et al., *Safe School Initiative,* 5.
86. Moore et al., *Deadly Lessons.*
87. Vossekuil et al., *Safe School Initiative,* 5.
88. Cornell, "Psychology of the School Shootings."
89. Leary et al., "Teasing, Rejection, and Violence," 213.
90. David F. Luckenbill and Daniel Doyle, "Structural Position and Violence: Developing a Cultural Explanation," *Criminology* 27 (1989): 419–36.
91. Vossekuil et al., *Safe School Initiative,* 5.
92. Dedman (2000), quoted in American Medical Association, "Proceedings of the Educational Forum on Adolescent Health: Youth Bullying," 4, http://www.amaassn.org.
93. Leary et al., "Teasing, Rejection, and Violence," 212.
94. Leary et al., "Teasing, Rejection, and Violence," 10.
95. Moore et al., *Deadly Lessons,* 6.
96. Leary et al., "Teasing, Rejection, and Violence," 251.

97. Ramsland, "School Shooters," 2. Also see Ramsland, *Inside the Minds of Mass Murderers*.
98. Cornell, "Psychology of the School Shootings," 23.
99. Vossekuil et al., *Safe School Initiative*, 3.
100. CNN News, "Parents of Shooting Suspect among Those Asking 'Why?,'" March 27, 1998, http://www.cnn.com.
101. Vossekuil et al., *Safe School Initiative*.
102. Ramsland, "School Killers." Also see Ramsland, *Inside the Minds of Mass Murderers*.
103. Vossekuil et al., *Safe School Initiative*, 5.
104. Leary et al, "Teasing, Rejection, and Violence," 293–294.
105. Ramsland, "School Killers." Also see Ramsland, *Inside the Minds of Mass Murderers*.
106. Ramsland, "School Killers." Also see Ramsland, *Inside the Minds of Mass Murderers*.
107. CNN News, "Parents of Shooting Suspect among Those Asking 'Why?,'" March 27, 1998, http://www.cnn.com/US/9803/27/shooting.investigation.2/index.html.
108. Ramsland, "School Killers." Also see Ramsland, *Inside the Minds of Mass Murderers*.
109. Dave Grossman and Gloria DeGaetano, *Stop Teaching Our Kids to Kill: A Call to Action Against TV, Movie and Video Game Violence* (New York: Crown, 1999), 61.
110. Martin Savidge, "Accused Oregon School Shooter Shows No Emotion in Court," CNN Interactive, May 22, 1998, http://www.cnn.com/US/9805/22/oregon.shooting.pm/.
111. Ramsland, "School Killers." Also see Ramsland, *Inside the Minds of Mass Murderers*.
112. Ramsland, "School Killers." Also see Ramsland, *Inside the Minds of Mass Murderers*.
113. James L. Knoll, "Pseudo-Commandos Mass Murder: Part I, The Psychology of Revenge and Obliteration," *Journal of the American Academy of Psychiatry and the Law* 38, no. 1 (March 2010): 87–94.
114. Langman, *Why Kids Kill*, 1.
115. Michele Steinberg, "Programmed to Kill: Video Games, Drugs and 'The New Violence.'" *21st Century* 13, no. 3 (Fall 2000), https://21sci-tech.com/articles/New_violence.html.
116. John P. McGee and Cecile R. de Bernardo, "Classroom Avenger: A Behavioral Profile of School Based Shootings," *Forensic Examiner* 8, nos. 5/6 (May/June 1999): 16–18.
117. Moore et al., *Deadly Lessons*, 136.
118. Langman, *Why Kids Kill,* 16.
119. McGee and de Bernardo, "Classroom Avenger."
120. Moore et al., *Deadly Lessons*, 137.
121. Moore et al., *Deadly Lessons*, 138.
122. Moore et al., *Deadly Lessons*, 151.
123. Steinberg, "Programmed to Kill."
124. Grossman and DeGaetano, *Stop Teaching Our Kids to Kill*, 4.
125. Steinberg, "Programmed to Kill."
126. Moore et al., *Deadly Lessons*, 146.

127. Moore et al., *Deadly Lessons*.
128. Moore et al., *Deadly Lessons*, 146.
129. Moore et al., *Deadly Lessons*, 147.
130. Leary et al., "Teasing, Rejection, and Violence," 212.
131. Moore et al., *Deadly Lessons*, 142.
132. Moore et al., *Deadly Lessons*, 150–51.
133. Moore et al., *Deadly Lessons*.
134. Leary et al., "Teasing, Rejection, and Violence," 206.
135. Langman, *Why Kids Kill*, 17.
136. Moore et al., *Deadly Lessons*, 108–9.
137. Moore et al., *Deadly Lessons*, 108–9.
138. Leary et al., "Teasing, Rejection, and Violence," 206.
139. Moore et al., *Deadly Lessons*, 105
140. Leary et al., "Teasing, Rejection, and Violence," 206.
141. Leary et al., "Teasing, Rejection, and Violence," 206.
142. Moore et al., *Deadly Lessons*, 116, 118.
143. Julie Grace, Sylvester Monroe, and Timothy Roche, "Campus Shooters," *Time*. July 6, 1998.
144. Moore et al., *Deadly Lessons*, 118.
145. Moore et al., *Deadly Lessons*, 118.
146. Moore et al., *Deadly Lessons*, 107–8.
147. Moore et al., *Deadly Lessons*, 118.
148. Langman, *Why Kids Kill*, 83.
149. Moore et al., *Deadly Lessons*, 116.
150. Moore et al., *Deadly Lessons*, 118.
151. Moore et al., *Deadly Lessons*, 108.
152. Michele Steinberg, "Programmed to Kill: Video Games, Drugs and 'The New Violence,'" *21st Century* 13, no. 3 (Fall 2000), https://21sci-tech.com/articles/New_violence.html.
153. Moore et al., *Deadly Lessons*, 76.
154. "Andrew Wurst," Criminal Justice Research, 2010, http://criminal-justice.iresearchnet.com/crime/school-violence/andrew-wurst/.
155. Moore et al., *Deadly Lessons*, 73.
156. Moore et al., *Deadly Lessons*, 77–79.
157. Moore et al., *Deadly Lessons*, 77–79.
158. Langman, *Why Kids Kill*, 17.
159. Jonathon Fast, *Ceremonial Violence: A Psychological Explanation of School Shootings* (Woodstock: Overlook, 2008), 51.
160. Fast, *Ceremonial Violence*, 51–58.
161. Erica Erwin, "Unanswered: Why?," *Workplace Violence News*, April 24, 2008, http://

workplaceviolencenews.com/2008/04/24/answered-why/.
162. Erwin, "Unanswered: Why?."
163. Steinberg, "Programmed to Kill."
164. Langman, *Why Kids Kill*, 17.
165. Langman, *Why Kids Kill*, 14.
166. Leary et al., "Teasing, Rejection, and Violence," 207.
167. Leary et al., "Teasing, Rejection, and Violence," 207.
168. Leary et al., "Teasing, Rejection, and Violence," 207.
169. Langman, *Why Kids Kill*, 8.
170. Langman, *Why Kids Kill*, 121.
171. Nancy Gibbs and Anton Chaikin, "The Columbine Tapes," *Time*, December 20, 1999, 40–51.
172. State of Colorado, *The Report of Governor Bill Owens' Columbine Review Commission* (May 2001).
173. Ramsland, "School Shooters." Also see Ramsland, *Inside the Minds of Mass Murderers*.
174. Vossekuil et al., *Safe School Initiative*.
175. Moore et al., *Deadly Lessons*, 25.
176. Leary et al., "Teasing, Rejection, and Violence," 207.
177. "Metal/Hip Hop Sales in the U.S.," *SoundScan*, March 3, 2014, Blabbermouth.com.
178. Moore et al., *Deadly Lessons*, 38–39.
179. Moore et al., *Deadly Lessons*, 50.
180. Moore et al., *Deadly Lessons*, 57.
181. Moore et al., *Deadly Lessons*, 41.
182. Quoted in Robert Weller, "Columbine: Questions Still Remain," *The Pueblo Chieftain* (Associated Press), April 20, 2007, p. 8C.
183. Langman, *Why Kids Kill*, 92–93.
184. Langman, *Why Kids Kill*, 93.
185. Vosssekuil et al., *Safe School Initiative*.
186. Langman, *Why Kids Kill*, 17.
187. William Wan, Kevin Sullivan, David Weingrad, and Mark Berman, "Florida Shooting Suspect Nikolas Cruz: Guns, Depression and a Life in Trouble," *Washington Post*, February 15, 2018, pp. 1–4.
188. Wan et al., "Florida Shooting Suspect Nikolas Cruz," 5.
189. Katherine Lam, "Florida School Shooting Suspect Nikolas Cruz' Cryptic Love Letters from Jail to UK Woman Revealed," Fox News, April 9, 2018, https://www.foxnews.com/.
190. Matthew Vann and Corky Siemoszco, "Nikolas Cruz, Accused Parkland Shooter, 'Restless' in Solitary, Reports Say," NBC News, March 7, 2018, https://www.nbcnews.com/.
191. Lani Seelinger, "Survivors Are Standing Up to Politics and the NRA," *Bustle*, February 19, 2018, https://www.bustle.com/.
192. Mark Gillespie, "School Violence Still a Worry for American Parents," Gallup News Service,

September 7, 1999, https://news.gallup.com/poll/3613/school-violence-still-worry-american-parents.aspx.

■ Chapter 7. Media Reality

1. Donald E. Cook, Clarence Kestenbaum, L. Michael Honiker, and E. Ratcliffe Anderson, Jr. *Joint Statement on the Impact of Entertainment Violence on Children Congressional Public Health Summit,* July 26, 2000, https://iianthropology.org/psychology_childrenviolence.html.
2. Michael W. Salwen and Michele DePagne, "The Third-Person Effect: Perceptions of the Media's Influence and Immoral Consequences," *Communication Research* 26, no. 5 (January 10, 1999): 523–49.
3. Gunther and Hwa, cited in Ulla Carlsson and Cecilia von Feilitzen, eds., *Children and Media Violence: Yearbook for the UNESCO International Clearinghouse on Children and Violence on the Screen,* 1998.
4. American Academy of Pediatrics, "Impact of Entertainment Violence on Children."
5. Orrin Hatch, and US Senate Committee on the Judiciary, "Children, Violence, and the Media: A Report for Parents and Policy Makers," September 14, 1999, 16, http://judiciary.senate.gov/oldsite/mediavio.htm. Website available at the time of writing.
6. Sut Jhally, *Dreamworlds: Desire, Sex and Power in Music Video* (Media Education Foundation, 1997; 2007), DVD.
7. Hatch and Senate Committee on the Judiciary, "Children, Violence, and the Media."
8. Jhally, *Dreamworlds*.
9. Jhally, *Dreamworlds*.
10. Hatch and Senate Committee on the Judiciary, "Children, Violence, and the Media," 8.
11. Media Awareness Network, "Media Education and Media Violence," http://www.media-awareness.ca/english/isses/role_media.html. Source was available at the time of writing.
12. Nicholas L. Carnagey, Craig A. Anderson, and Brad J. Bushman, "The Effect of Video Game Violence on Physiological Desensitization to Real-Life Violence," *Journal of Experimental Social Psychology* 43, no. 3 (2007): 494.
13. Media Education Foundation, "Research on the Effects of Media Violence." Source available at the time of writing.
14. Media Education Foundation, "Research on the Effects of Media Violence."
15. David L. Altheide and Roger Snow, *Media Reality* (Boston: Beacon, 1976).
16. George Gerbner, Larry Gross, Mary Morgan, and Nancy Signorelli, *Television's Mean World: Violence Profile* (Philadelphia: Annenberg School of Communications, University of Pennsylvania, 1986).
17. Robert Horton and Egin Wohl, "Para-Social Interaction," *Journal of the American Medical*

Association 201, no. 14 (1958).

18. Alfred Schutz, *On Phenomenology and Social Relations*, edited and with an introduction by Helmut R. Wagner (University of Chicago Press, 1970), 1–11.
19. Harold Garfinkel lectures, "Ethnomethodolgy," graduate seminar, Sociology Department, University of California–Los Angeles, Fall 1979.
20. BYJU's Learning App, "Definition of Resonance," www.byjus.com/physics/resonance.
21. Todd Gitlin, *Inside Prime Time* (New York: Pantheon, 1983).
22. Brad J. Bushman, "Violent Media and Hostile Appraisals: A Meta-Analytic Review," *Aggressive Behavior* 42, no. 6 (2016): 605–613.
23. Ben H. Bagdikian, *The Media Monopoly* (Boston: Beacon, 1983).
24. Herbert I. Schiller, *Mass Communication and American Empire* (Boston: Beacon, 1971).
25. Neil Postman and Steve Powers, *How to Watch TV News* (New York: Penguin, 1992), 147–48.
26. David L. Altheide, *Creating Reality: How TV News Distorts Events* (Thousand Oaks, CA: Sage, 1976), 9.
27. Craig A. Anderson, Leonard Berkowitz, Edward Donnetstein, L. Rowell Huesmann, James D. Jason, David Linz, Neil M. Malamuth, and Ellen Wartella, "The Influence of Media Violence in Youth," *Psychological Science* 4, no. 3 (2012): 81–110.
28. Brandon S. Centerwall, "Television and Violence: The Scale of the Problem and Where to Go from Here," *Journal of the American Medical Association* 267, no. 22 (June 10, 1992): 3059.
29. US National Library of Medicine, "Children and Screen Time," *MediLine Plus*, https://medlineplus.gov/ency/patientinstructions/000355.htm.
30. Victoria J. Rideout, Elizabeth Vandewater, and Ellen A. Wartella, *Zero to Six: Electronic Media in the Lives of Infants, Toddlers and Preschoolers* (Washington, DC: Henry J. Kaiser Foundation, 2003).
31. Centerwall, "Television and Violence," 3059.
32. Robert Weller, "Columbine: Questions Still Remain," *The Pueblo Chieftain* (Associated Press), April 20, 2007, p. 8C.
33. Centerwall, "Television and Violence," 3059.
34. Center on Media and Child Health, Harvard Medical School, 2005, 10, http://www.cmch.tv.
35. G. Tina Wolridge, "Too Sexy Too Soon: A Mother's Battle Against the Sexualization of Girls," *In the Public Interest Newsletter*, American Psychological Association, September 2013, https://www.apa.org/pi/about/newsletter/2013/09/sexualization-girls.
36. Greenberg et al. (1980), cited in Canadian Radio-Television and Telecommunications Commission, "Selected Bibliography of Studies on the Effects of Media Violence," http://www.crtc.gc.ca/Eng/Social/Bblio.htm.
37. UCLA Center for Communication Policy, *UCLA Television Violence Monitoring Report* (Los Angeles: UCLA Center for Communication Policy, 1995).
38. Jenny Radesky and Dimitri Christakis, "Media and Young Minds," *Pediatrics* 138, no. 5 (November 2016), https://doi.org/10.1542/peds.2016-2591.

39. American Academy of Pediatrics, "Impact of Entertainment Violence on Children."
40. Dave Grossman and Gloria DeGaetano, *Stop Teaching Our Kids to Kill: A Call to Action Against TV, Movie and Video Game Violence* (New York: Crown, 1999), 40.
41. Weller, "Columbine," 8C.
42. Hatch and Senate Committee on the Judiciary, "Children, Violence, and the Media," 16.
43. Eugene V. Beresin, "The Impact of Media Violence on Children and Adolescents: Opportunities for Clinical Interventions," National Network Opposing Militarization of Youth, 2009, http://www.aacap.or/cs/root/developmentor/www.nmomy.net.
44. Grossman and DeGaetano, *Stop Teaching Our Kids to Kill*, 40.
45. Diane Levin and Carol Copple, *Remote Control Childhood? Combating the Hazards of Media Culture* (Washington, DC: National Association for the Education of Young Children, 1998), 15.
46. Altheide and Snow, *Media Reality* (Boston: Beacon, 1976).
47. Robert Ferris, "American Kids See About 2 Alcohol Ads Each Day: Rand Study," CNBC, May 20, 2011, https://www.cnbc.com/2016/05/18/american-kids-see-about-3-ads-for-alcohol-each-day-rand-study.html.
48. Hatch and Senate Committee on the Judiciary, "Children, Violence, and the Media," 16.
49. Courtney N. Plante, Douglas A. Gentile, Christopher T. Gross, Adam Modlin, and Jorge Blanco-Herrera, "Video Games as Coping Mechanism in the Etiology of Video Game Addiction," *Psychology of Popular Media Culture* 8, no. 4 (2019): 385–94.
50. Media Awareness Network, "Television Violence: A Review of the Effects on Children," www.media-wareness.ca/english/issues/violence.
51. Kevin Jackson, "Senators, Pro-Family Activists Rally against 'Disturbing' TV Trends," *Christian Post*, June 27, 2007.
52. Barbara Israel, *Beauty Mark: Body Imaging and the Race for Perfection* (Media Education Foundation, 2009), DVD.
53. Sut Jhally, *The Date Rape Backlash: Media and the Denial of Rape* (Media Education Foundation, 2006), DVD.
54. Emily Reynolds, "Universities are Home to a Rape Epidemic," *The Guardian*, March 2, 2018.
55. Jhally, *Dreamworlds*.
56. "The Best of the Reality Shows," *Tosh.0*, aired November 2, 2008, on Fox.
57. Carnagey, Anderson, and Bushman, "The Effect of Video Game Violence," 494.
58. Christopher P. Bartlett and Craig Anderson, "Violent Video Games and Public Policy," in *Handbuch Computerspiele, Politik und Gesellschaft (Handbook of Video Games, Politics and Society)*, ed. Tobias Beve and Holger Zapf (Konstanz: UVK Verlagsgesellschaft, 2009), 6.
59. Media Awareness Network, "Media Education and Media Violence."
60. Media Awareness Network, "Media Education and Media Violence."
61. Bartlett and Anderson, "Violent Video Games and Public Policy," 6.
62. Media Awareness Network, "Media Education and Media Violence."

63. Media Awareness Network, "Media Education and Media Violence."
64. Hatch and the Senate Committee on the Judiciary, "Children, Violence, and the Media, " 6.
65. Media Awareness Network, "Media Education and Media Violence."
66. Media Awareness Network, "Media Education and Media Violence."
67. Media Awareness Network, "Media Education and Media Violence."
68. Grossman and DeGaetano, *Stop Teaching Our Kids to Kill*.
69. Media Awareness Network, "Media Education and Media Violence."
70. L. Rowell Huesmann, Jessica Moise, Cheryl Lynn Podolski, and Leonard E. Eron, "Longitudinal Relations Between Children's Exposure to TV Violence and Their Aggressive and Violent Behavior in Young Adulthood: 1977–1992," *Developmental Psychology* 39, no. 2 (2003): 201–21.
71. Brad J. Bushman, "Teaching Students About Violent Media Effects," *Teaching of Psychology* 45, no. 2 (2018): 200–206.
72. Dan Tynan, "Screen Wars: How to Win the Screen Time Battle without Alienating Your Teens," *Family Circle*, February 2019, p. 47.
73. Jean Piaget, *The Child's Conception of the World* (London: Routledge, 1929).
74. Joanne Cantor and Glenn G. Sparks, "Children's Fear Reponses to Mass Media: Testing Some Piagetian Predictions," *Journal of Communications* 34, no. 2 (1984): 90–105.
75. Eron et al. (1983), cited in Canadian Radio-Television and Telecommunications Commission, "Selected Bibliography of Studies on the Effects of Media Violence."
76. Hatch and the Senate Committee on the Judiciary, "Children, Violence, and the Media."
77. Brad J. Bushman and Craig A. Anderson, "Comfortably Numb: Desensitization Effects of Violent Media on Helper Roles," *Psychological Science* 20, no. 3 (March 2009): 273–77.
78. Gerbner et al., *Television's Mean World*.
79. Media Awareness Network, "Media Education and Media Violence."
80. American Humane Society's Children Division, "Tell Congress to Vote for the Keeping All Students Safe Act," http://www.americanhumanesociety.com. Source available at the time of writing.
81. Jane M. Healy, *Endangered Minds: Why Our Children Don't Think* (New York: Simon and Schuster, 1990), 201.
82. Media Awareness Network, "Media Education and Media Violence."
83. Eron (1982), cited in Canadian Radio-Television and Telecommunications Commission, "Selected Bibliography of Studies on the Effects of Media Violence."
84. "Joint Statement" (2000), cited in Bartlett and Anderson, "Violent Video Games and Public Policy," 7.
85. Committee on Public Education, "Media Violence," *Pediatrics* 108, no. 5 (Nov. 2001): 1222–26.
86. Brad J. Bushman and Craig A. Anderson, "Violent Video Games and Hostile Expectations: A Test of the General Aggression Model," *Personality and Social Psychology Bulletin* 28, no. 2 (2002): 1679.
87. Cited by Hatch and Senate Committee on the Judiciary, "Children, Violence, and the Media," 6.

88. "Powerful Influences," *NewsHour*, aired May 10, 1999, on PBS, http://www.pbs.org/.
89. Bushman and Anderson, "Violent Video Games and Hostile Expectation"; Author interview with Ron Slaby, senior scientist at the Center on Media and Child Health, Harvard Medical School, April 25, 2007.
90. Stuart Ewing, *All Consuming Images: The Politics of Style in Contemporary Culture* (New York: Basic, 1999).
91. Gerbner et al., *Television's Mean World*.
92. Joanne Cantor, *Mommy, I'm Scared: How TV and Movies Frighten Children and What We Can Do to Protect Them* (New York: Harcourt Brace, 1998), 169.
93. A smart search database of effects of media can be found at Center for Media and Child Health, http://www.cmch.tv.
94. Group for the Advancement of Psychiatry, *The Child and Television Drama: The Psychosocial Impact of Cumulative Viewing* (New York: Mental Health Materials Center, 1982).
95. American Psychological Association, "Report of the APA Task Force on Television and Society," http://www.apa.org. Source available at the time of writing. Also see Brian L. Wilcox, Dale Kunkel, Joanne Cantor, Peter Dowrick, Susan Linn, Edward Palmer, "Report of the APA Task Force on Advertising and Children" (American Psychological Association, 2004), https://www.apa.org/pi/families/resources/advertising-children.pdf.
96. "Joint Statement" (2000), cited in Bartlett and Anderson, "Violent Video Games and Public Policy," 7.
97. Committee on Injury and Poison Prevention, "Firearm-Related Injuries Affecting the Pediatric Population," *Pediatrics* 105, no. 4 (April 2000): 888–895.
98. Committee on Injury and Poison Prevention, "Firearm-Related Injuries Affecting the Pediatric Population."
99. Committee on Injury and Poison Prevention, "Firearm-Related Injuries Affecting the Pediatric Population."
100. American Psychiatric Association, cited by Hatch and Senate Committee on the Judiciary, "Children, Violence, and the Media," 6.
101. Terence Smith, *NewsHour*, "Powerful Influences," aired May 10, 1999, on PBS, http://www.pbs.org/.
102. Kevin Draper, "Video Games Aren't Why Shootings Happen: Politicians Still Blame Them," *New York Times*, August 5, 2019.
103. Bushman and Anderson, "Violent Video Games and Hostile Expectations."
104. Ewing, *All Consuming Images*.
105. Gerbner et al., *Television's Mean World*.
106. Jhally, *Dreamworlds*.
107. Ryan (1999), cited in David G. Myers, *Exploring Psychology* (New York: Worth, 2007), 392.
108. Kasser (2002), cited in Myers, *Exploring Psychology*, 392.

109. Ann DeVaney, "Reading the Ads: The Bacchanalian Adolescence," *The State of Media Education* (Albuquerque: New Mexico Media Literacy Project, 1995), 137.
110. Gary Ruskin, "Commercial Alert Asks Senate Commerce Committee to Investigate Neuromarketing," *Commercial Alert*, July 12, 2004.
111. Ruskin, "Commercial Alert."
112. Jean Kilbourne, "Still Killing Us Softly: Advertising and the Obsession with Thinness," *Feminist Perspectives on Eating Disorders*, edited by P. Fallon, M. A. Katzman, and S. C. Wooley (New York: Guilford, 1994), 395–418.
113. Gentile and Walsh (2002), cited in Stephen Kline, "Media Consumption as a Health and Safety Risk Factor," Simon Frasier University, Media Analysis Lab, 2003.
114. The Foundation Center, 2010.
115. The Foundation Center, 2010.
116. Garfield, quoted in John Leo, "Modern Ads Thrive on Porn, Aggression," Associated Press, April 2, 1996.
117. Henthorne et al. (1993), in Tim Jones, Peggy A. Cunningham, and Kathrine Gallagher, "Violence in Advertising: A Multilayered Content Analysis," *Journal of Advertising* 39, no. 4 (November 2010): 25.
118. *Energy Times*, October 2006, 34.
119. Leo, "Modern Ads Thrive on Porn, Aggression."
120. Charles Atkin, John Hocking, and Martin Block, "Teenage Drinking: Does Advertising Make a Difference?," *Journal of Communication* 34, no. 2 (1984): 157–64.
121. Media Awareness Network, "How Marketers Target Kids," www.media-awareness.ca/english/issues/violence/gov/industry. Source available at the time of writing.
122. Atkin, Hocking, and Block, "Teenage Drinking."
123. Gitlin, *Inside Prime Time*, 92.
124. Shelly Grabe, L. Monique Ward, and Janet Shibley Hyde, "The Role of the Media in Body Image Concerns of Young Women: A Meta-Analysis," *Psychological Bulletin* 134, no. 3 (2008): 460–476, https://doi.org/10.1037/0033-2909.134.3.460; Amanda Holstrum, "The Effects of the Media on Body Image: A Meta-Analysis," *Journal of Broadcasting and Electronic Media* 48, no. 2 (2004): 196–217.
125. Kaycee Vance, Megan Sutter, Paul B. Perrin, and Martin Heesacker, "The Media's Sexual Objectification of Women, Rape Myth Acceptance, and Interpersonal Violence," *Journal of Aggression, Maltreatment and Trauma* 24, no. 5 (June 10, 2015): 569–587, https://doi.org/10.1080/10926771.2015.1029179.
126. Leo, "Modern Ads Thrive on Porn, Aggression."
127. Leo, "Modern Ads Thrive on Porn, Aggression."
128. Quoted by Leo, "Modern Ads Thrive on Porn, Aggression."
129. Leo, "Modern Ads Thrive on Porn, Aggression."

130. Leo, "Modern Ads Thrive on Porn, Aggression."
131. Leo, "Modern Ads Thrive on Porn, Aggression."
132. Cited in Media Awareness Network, "How Marketers Target Kids."
133. Naomi Klein, *No Logo: Taking Aim at the Brand Bullies* (New York: Knopf Canada, 1999).
134. New Dream, http://www.newdream.org.
135. McLuhan (1967), cited in Arthur Asa Berger, *Media Analysis Techniques* (Thousand Oaks, CA: Sage, 1982), 58–59.
136. Harold D. Krugman, "The Impact of Television Advertising: Learning without Involvement," *Public Opinion Quarterly* 29 (1965): 349–56; Harold D. Krugman, "Brainwave Measures of Media Involvement," *Journal of Advertising Research* 11 (1971): 3–9.
137. BrightHouse Institute for Thought Sciences, "BrightHouse Institute for Thought Sciences Launches First 'Neuromarketing' Research Company: Company Uses Neuroimaging to Unlock the Consumer Mind," news release, June 22, 2002, http://www.prweb.com/releases/2002/6/prweb40936.php.
138. BrightHouse Institute for Thought, "Brighthouse Institute for Thought Sciences Launches First 'Neuromarketing' Research Company." Also see Roger Dooley, *Brainfluence: 100 Ways to Persuade and Convince Consumers with Neuromarketing* (Wiley, 2011), and Gail Schiller, "Nielsen Making Brain Waves," *Commercial Alert*, 2009, http://www.commercialalert.org/issues/culture/neuromarketing.
139. Roger Dooley, "Focus on NeuroFocus: Interview with A. K. Pradeep," *Neuromarketing*, www.neuromarketing.com.
140. *Nightly Business Report*, aired January 6, 2010, on PBS.
141. Missy Fleming and Kelley Towey, eds., "Youth Bullying: An Overview," *Educational Forum on Adolescent Health* (Chicago: American Medical Association, 2002).
142. Media Awareness Network, "Media Education and Media Violence."
143. *Al Frankel: God Spoke*, directed by Nick Doob and Chris Hegedus (Balcony Releasing, 2006), DVD, 90 min.
144. Katherine Ramsland, "School Killers," Crime Library, TruTV, https://web.archive.org/web/20090307073643/http://www.trutv.com:80/library/crime/serial_killers/weird/kids1/index_1.html?print=yes.
145. Martin Savidge, "Accused Oregon School Shooter Shows No Emotion in Court," CNN Interactive, May 22, 1998, http://www.cnn.com/US/9805/22/oregon.shooting.pm/.
146. Hatch and Senate Committee on the Judiciary, "Children, Violence, and the Media," 5; Media Awareness Network, "Media Education and Media Violence."
147. Brad J. Bushman, "Teaching Students About Violent Media Effects," *Teaching of Psychology* 45, no. 2 (2018): 200–206.
148. American Academy of Pediatrics, "Impact of Entertainment Violence on Children," 1072. Robert McCannon, "New Mexico Media Literacy Project," University of New Mexico.

149. Cathy Wing, codirector of Media Awareness Network, telephone conversation with author, November 3, 2014.
150. American Academic of Pediatrics, "Television—How It Affects Children," http://patientd.aaap.org. Source available at the time of writing.
151. American Academic of Pediatrics, "Television—How It Affects Children."
152. Bushman, "Teaching Students About Violent Media Effects."
153. Huesmann (1988), cited in Brad J. Bushman, "Does Venting Anger Feed or Extinguish the Flame? Catharsis, Rumination, Distraction, Anger, and Aggressive Responding," *Personality and Social Psychology Bulletin* 28, no. 6 (2002): 724–31.
154. Elizabeth Thoman, "Beyond Blame: Media Literacy as Violence Prevention," *Media and Values* 62 (Spring 1993), http://www.medialit.org/reading-room/beyond-blame-media-literacy-violence-prevention.
155. Thomas N. Robinson and Dina L. G. Borzekowski, "Effects of the SMART Classroom Curriculum to Reduce Child and Family Screen Time," *Journal of Communication* 56, no. 1 (February 2006): 1–26.
156. Cited in Violent and Repeat Juvenile Offender Accountability and Rehabilitation Act of 1999, H.R. Resolution 1501, 106th Cong. (1999), 318–19.
157. H.R. Resolution 1501, 106th Cong. (1999), 320.
158. Hatch and Senate Committee on the Judiciary, "Children, Violence, and the Media," 11.
159. "Interview with George Lucas," *Daily Show with Jon Stewart*, aired January 5, 2010, on Comedy Central.
160. Peter J. Humphrey, *Mass Media and Media Policy in Western Europe* (New York: St. Martin's, 1996).
161. Humphrey, *Mass Media*.
162. Humphrey, *Mass Media*.
163. Media Awareness Network, "Media Education and Media Violence."
164. Paul McElligott, "V-Chip Is Not the Answer for TV," *Los Angeles Times*, March 18, 1996.
165. Hatch and Senate Committee on the Judiciary, "Children, Violence, and the Media," 10.
166. Media Awareness Network, "Media Education and Media Violence."
167. Robert McChesney, *Corporate Media and the Threat to Democracy* (New York: Seven Stories, 1998), 1.
168. Patricia Aufderheide, "Why Kids Hate Educational TV," *Children and the Media*, edited by Everette E. Dennis and Edward C. Pease (New Brunswick, NJ: Transaction, 1996).
169. Federal Communications Commission, "Before the FCC: 'Revision of Programming Policies for Television Broadcast Stations,'" August 8, 1996. Source available at the time of writing.
170. Craig A. Anderson, Douglas A. Gentile, and Katherine E. Buckley, *Violent Video Game Effects on Children and Adolescents: Theory, Research, and Public Policy* (Oxford: Oxford University Press, 2007).
171. Canada Radio-Television and Telecommunications Commission, "Canada and TV Violence:

Cooperation and Consensus," http://www.crtc.gc.ca.
172. Cited in Media Awareness Network, "Media Education and Media Violence."

■ Chapter 8. Fun and Games: A Virtual Reality

1. Coburn (2000), cited in Douglas A. Gentile and Craig A. Anderson, "Violent Video Games: The Effects on Youth, and Public Policy Implications," *Handbook of Children, Culture and Violence*, edited by N. Dowd, D. G. Singer, and R. F. Wilson (Thousand Oaks, CA: Sage, 2006), 135.
2. Jones (1981), in Kendy (1981), in Joseph R. Dominick, "Videogames, Television Violence and Aggression in Teenagers," *Journal of Communication* 34, no. 2 (1984): 137.
3. Jodi Whitaker and Brad J. Bushman, "'Boom, Headshot': Effect of Video Game Play and Controller Type on Firing, Aim and Action," *Communication Research* 41, no 7 (2012): 879–91.
4. Douglas A. Gentile, Craig A. Anderson, Shintaro Yukawa, Nobuko Ihori, Muniba Saleem, Lim Kam Ming, Akiko Shibuya, Albert K. Liau, Angeline Khoo, Brad J. Bushman, L. Rowell Huesmann, and Akira Sakamoto, "The Effects of Prosocial Video Games on Prosocial Behavior: International Evidence for Correlational, Longitudinal and Experimental Studies," *Personality and Social Psychology Bulletin* 35, no. 6 (June 2009): 752–63.
5. Gentile and Anderson, "Violent Video Games," 2.
6. Craig A. Anderson, Douglas A. Gentile, and Katherine E. Buckley, *Violent Video Game Effects on Children and Adolescents: Theory, Research, and Public Policy* (Oxford: Oxford University Press, 2007), 76.
7. Jones (1981), in Kendy (1981), in Dominick, "Videogames, Television Violence and Aggression in Teenagers," 137.
8. Anderson et al., *Violent Video Game Effects*, 3.
9. Alessandro Gabbadini and Paolo Riva, "The Lone Gamer: Social Exclusion Predicts Violent Video Game Preferences and Fuels Aggressive Inclinations in Adolescent Players," *Aggressive Behavior* 44, no. 2 (2018): 113–24.
10. *Athens Herald Banner*, November 11, 1982, cited in Alessandro Gabbiadini, Brad J. Bushman, Paolo Riva, Luca Andrighetto, and Chiara Volpato, "Grand Theft Auto Is a 'Sandbox' Game, but There are Weapons, Criminals, and Prostitutes in the Sandbox: Response to Ferguson and Donnellan (2017),'" *Journal of Youth and Adolescence* 46 (2017): 141.
11. Gabbiadini et al. "Grand Theft Auto Is a 'Sandbox Game,'" 146.
12. Nicholas L. Carnagey and Craig A. Anderson, "Violent Video Game Exposure and Aggression: A Literature Review," *Minerva Pediatrica* 45 (March 2004): 4.
13. Carnagey and Anderson, "Violent Video Game Exposure and Aggression," 4.
14. Mary Jane Irwin, "Classic Rock Rising—Thanks to Video Games," NBC News, March 11, 2008, http://www.nbcnews.com/.

15. Anderson et al., *Violent Video Game Effects*, 15–17. Also see Amanda Lenhart, Joseph Kahne, Ellen Middaugh, Alexandra Rankin MacGill, Chris Evans, and Jessica Vitak, "Teens, Video Games, and Civics: Teens' Gaming Experiences are Diverse and Include Significant Social Interaction and Civic Engagement," Pew Internet and American Life Project, September 16, 2008, https://www.pewresearch.org/internet/2008/09/16/teens-video-games-and-civics/.
16. Mediakix, "11 Female Gamer Statistics Marketers Must Know," January 9, 2018, https://mediakix.com/blog/female-gamer-statistics-demographics/.
17. Ingrid Möller and Barbara Krahe, "Exposure to Violent Video Games and Aggression in German Adolescents: A Longitudinal Analysis," *Aggressive Behavior* 35, no. 1 (January/February 2009): 75–89.
18. Youssef Hasan, Laurent Bègue, and Brad J. Bushman, "Viewing the World Though Blood-Red Glasses: The Hostile Expectation Bias Mediates the Link between Violent Video Game Exposure and Aggression," *Journal of Experimental Psychology* 48, no. 4 (July 2012): 953–56.
19. Anderson et al., *Violent Video Game Effects*, 7.
20. Elmer, cited in Kathleen Nader, *Rampage School Shootings and Other Youth Disturbances: Early Preventative Interventions* (London: Routledge, 2013), 14.
21. Carnagey and Anderson, "Violent Video Game Exposure and Aggression," 2.
22. John, L. Sherry, "The Effects of Violent Video Games on Aggression: A Meta-Analysis," *Human Communication Research* 27 (2001): 4309–19.
23. Carnagey and Anderson, "Violent Video Game Exposure and Aggression," 4.
24. Carnagey and Anderson, "Violent Video Game Exposure and Aggression," 4.
25. Carnagey and Anderson, "Violent Video Game Exposure and Aggression," 1.
26. Carnagey and Anderson, "Violent Video Game Exposure and Aggression," 1.
27. Carnagey and Anderson, "Violent Video Game Exposure and Aggression," 1.
28. Steven Kent, *The Ultimate History of Video Games* (Roseville, CA: Prima, 2001), 465.
29. Kent, *The Ultimate History of Video Games*, 1127.
30. Anderson et al., *Violent Video Game Effects*, 6.
31. Grossman (2004), cited in Anderson et al., *Violent Video Game Effects*.
32. Carnagey and Anderson, "Violent Video Game Exposure and Aggression," 2G.
33. Grossman (2004), cited in Anderson et al., *Violent Video Game Effects*.
34. Brad J. Bushman and Craig A. Anderson, "Comfortably Numb: Desensitization Effects of Violent Media on Helper Roles," *Psychological Science* 20, no. 3 (March 2009): 273–77.
35. Gabbiadini et al. (2014), in Bushman and Anderson, "Comfortably Numb."
36. "Doom II," Doom Wiki, www.doomwiki.org/wiki/Doom_II.
37. "Doom III," Doom Wiki, https://doom.fandom.com.
38. Anderson et al., *Violent Video Game Effects*, 6.
39. Daniel Terdiman, "Will Wright on the Origins of 'Spore,'" February 2, 2009, https://www.cnet.com/news/will-wright-on-the-origins-of-spore/.

40. "Expert," in Wikipedia.org, December 6, 2008.
41. Lauren Sandler, "Popular Video Games Are Often Misogynistic," *At Issue: Video Games*, edited by David M. Haugen (Detroit: Greenhaven, 2008), 61–65.
42. Sandler, "Popular Video Games Are Often Misogynistic," 61.
43. Teresa Lynch, Jessica E. Tompkins, Irene I. Van Driel, and Niki Fritz, "Sexy, Strong and Secondary: A Content Analysis of Female Characters in Video Games across 31 Years," *Journal of Communication* 66, no. 4 (June 2016): 564–84.
44. "Children Now," in Nicholas L. Carnagey, Craig A. Anderson, and Brad J. Bushman, "The Effect of Video Game Violence on Physiological Desensitization to Real-Life Violence," *Journal of Experimental Social Psychology* 43, no. 3 (2007): 489–496.
45. David Thomas, "Players Grapple with Killing, Not Killing and Morality," *Denver Post*, July 4, 2006.
46. Brad J. Bushman and Craig A. Anderson, "Violent Video Games and Hostile Expectations: A Test of the General Aggression Model," *Personality and Social Psychology Bulletin* 28, no. 2 (2002): 1684–85.
47. Peter Langman, *Why Kids Kill: Inside the Minds of School Shooters* (New York: Palgrave Macmillan, 2009), 84.
48. *PC Gamer Magazine* (US Edition), https://www.pcgamer.com/magazine/.
49. Murray, quoted in Paul Kegan, "Quake," *Mother Jones*, November/December 1999, http://www.motherjones.com/news/feature/1999/11/quake.html.
50. Gentile et al. (2004), in Carnagey et al., "The Effect of Video Game Violence, 2.
51. Carnagey et al., "The Effect of Video Game Violence, 2.
52. Carnagey and Anderson, "Violent Video Game Exposure and Aggression," 2.
53. Nicholas Szilas, "The Future of Interactive Drama," *Proceedings of the Second Australasian Conference on Interactive Entertainment*, edited by Yusuf Pisan (Sydney: University of Technology, Sydney), 193–99.
54. Jonathan Raunch, "Video Games Will Become More Artistically and Emotionally Satisfying," *At Issue: Video Games*, edited by David M. Haugen (Detroit: Greenhaven, 2002), 91.
55. Raunch, "Video Games Will Become More Artistically and Emotionally Satisfying."
56. "EverQuest," Wikipedia, https://en.wikipedia.org/wiki/EverQuest.
57. Elizabeth Erkenberg, "Discursive Engagements in World of Warcraft: A Semiotic Analysis of Player Relationships," *Social Exclusion, Power, and Video Game Play: New Research in Digital Media and Technology*, edited by David G. Embrick, J. Talmadge Wright, and Andrus Lukacs (Lanham, MD: Lexington Books, 2012), 13–165.
58. David Dietrich, "Worlds of Whiteness: Race and Character Creation in Online Games," *Social Exclusion, Power, and Video Game Play: New Research in Digital Media and Technology*, edited by David G. Embrick, J. Talmadge Wright, and Andrus Lukacs (Lanham, MD: Lexington Books, 2012), 107–12.
59. Daniel Terdiman, "Will Wright on the Origins of 'Spore,'" February 2, 2009, https://www.cnet.

com/news/will-wright-on-the-origins-of-spore/.
60. Douglas Potter, Joachim Stader, and Roman Teessler, "PKDGRAV 3: Beyond Billion Particle Cosmological Simulations to the Next Generation of Galaxy Simulations," *Computational Astrophysics and Cosmology* 4, no. 11 (2017).
61. Cyrus A. Parsa, *Artificial Intelligence: Dangers to Humanity* (AI Organization, 2019).
62. John Sutherland, "Why Kinect Is the Future of Game Story," *Gamasutra: John Sutherland's Blog*, November 3, 2010, http://www.gamasutra.com/blogs.
63. Tetsuaki Baba, Kumiko Kushiyama, and Kouki Doi, "ThermoGame: Video Game Interaction System That Offers Dynamic Temperature Sensation to Users" (poster presented at the International Conference on Computer Graphics and Interactive Techniques, Los Angeles, CA, July 26–30, 2010). "Negative Effects of Video Game Play," Wikipedia, accessed August 30, 2019.
64. Raunch, "Video Games Will Become More Artistically and Emotionally Satisfying," 87.
65. "Tele-Immersion," *Visions of the Future: The Computer Revolution*, hosted by Michio Kaku, aired January 4, 2009, on *Science Channel*.
66. Brad J. Bushman and Deana Pollard-Sacks, "Supreme Court Decision Based on the First Amendment, Not Scientific Evidence," *American Psychologist* 69 (2014): 306–7.
67. Bushman and Pollard-Sacks, "Supreme Court Decision."
68. Suzanne Venker, "Missing Fathers and America's Broken Boys—The Vast Majority of Mass Shooters Come from Broken Homes," Fox News Report, February 18, 2018, www.fox.com.
69. Maya Salam and Liam Stack, "Do Video Games Lead to Mass Shootings? Researchers Say No," *New York Times*, February 23, 2018.
70. Deana Pollard-Sacks, Brad J. Bushman, and Craig A. Anderson, "Do Violent Video Games Harm Children? Comparing the Scientific Amicus Curiae 'Experts,' in *Brown v. Entertainment Merchants Association*," *Northwestern University Law Review* (2011): 2.
71. Pollard-Sacks et al., "Do Violent Video Games Harm Children?."
72. "Video Game Controversies," Wikipedia, https://en.wikipedia.org/wiki/Video_game_controversies.
73. Christopher J. Ferguson, Mark Coulson, and Jane Barnett, "Psychological Profiles of School Shooters: Positive Directions and One Big Wrong Turn," *Journal of Police Crisis Negotiations* 11, no. 2 (2011).
74. Christopher J. Ferguson, "It's Time to End the Debate About Video Games and Violence," *Chicago Tribune*, February 16, 2018.
75. "Video Game Controversies," Wikipedia.
76. Brad J. Bushman, "Does Venting Anger Feed or Extinguish the Flame? Catharsis, Rumination, Distraction, Anger and Aggressive Responding," *Personality and Social Psychology Bulletin* 28, no. 6 (2002): 200.
77. Anderson et al., *Violent Video Game Effects*, 144.
78. Anderson et al., *Violent Video Game Effects*, 144.

79. Craig A. Anderson and Christine R. Murphy, "Violent Video Games and Aggressive Behavior in Young Women," *Aggressive Behavior* 29 (2003): 423–29.
80. Christopher P. Bartlett and Craig Anderson, "Violent Video Games and Public Policy," *Handbuch Computerspiele, Politik und Gesellschaft (Handbook of Video Games, Politics and Society)*, edited by Tobias Beve and Holger Zapf (Konstanz: UVK Verlagsgesellschaft, 2009), 2. Dominick, "Videogames, Television Violence and Aggression in Teenagers,"146.
81. Craig A. Anderson and Karen E. Dill-Shackleford, "Video Games and Aggressive Thoughts, Feelings and Behavior in the Laboratory and in Life," *Journal of Personality and Social Psychology* 78 (2000): 772–90.
82. Dominick, "Videogames, Television Violence and Aggression in Teenagers."
83. Mary E. Ballard and J. Rose Wiest, "Mortal Kombat: The Effects of Violent Videogame Play on Males' Hostility and Cardiovascular Responding," *Journal of Applied Social Psychology* 26 (1995): 717–55.
84. Anderson and Dill-Shackleford, "Video Games and Aggressive Thoughts."
85. Gentile et al., "Violent Video Games."
86. Gentile et al., "Violent Video Games," 495.
87. Gentile et al., "Violent Video Games," 494.
88. Nicholas L. Carnagey and Craig A. Anderson, "The Effects of Reward and Punishment in Violent Video Games on Aggressive Affect, Cognition, and Behavior," *Psychological Science* 16 (2005): 882.
89. Bushman and Anderson, "Violent Video Games," 1679–1686.
90. Bushman and Anderson, "Violent Video Games," 1684–1685
91. Bushman and Anderson, "Violent Video Games," 1680.
92. Anderson et al., *Violent Video Game Effects*, 46–47.
93. Anderson et al., *Violent Video Game Effects*.
94. Brad J. Bushman, "The Weapons Effect," *Journal of the American Medical Association* 167, no. 2 (2013): 1094–95.
95. Anderson et al., *Violent Video Game Effects*, 46–47.
96. Douglas A. Gentile, Hyeyung Choo, Albert Liau, Timothy Sim, Dongkong Li, Daniel Fung, and Angeline Khoo, "Pathological Video Game Use among Youths: A Two-Year Longitudinal Study," *Pediatrics* (October 29, 2010).
97. Werner H. Hopf, Günter L. Huber, and Rudolf H. Weiss, "Media Violence and Youth Violence: A 2-Year Longitudinal Study," *Journal of Media Psychology: Theories, Methods and Applications* 20, no. 3 (2008): 79–96.
98. Anderson et al., *Violent Video Game Effects*.
99. Craig A. Anderson, Akira Sakamoto, Douglas A. Gentile, Nobuko Iori, Akiko Shibuya, Shintaro Yukawa, Mayume Naito, and Kumiko Kobayashi, "Longitudinal Effects of Violent Video Games on Aggression in Japan and the United States," *Pediatrics* 122, no. 5 (2008).
100. Anderson et al., "Longitudinal Effects."

101. Möller and Krahe, "Exposure to Violent Video Games and Aggression in German Adolescents."
102. Möller and Krahe, "Exposure to Violent Video Games and Aggression in German Adolescents."
103. Möller and Krahe, "Exposure to Violent Video Games and Aggression in German Adolescents."
104. Craig A. Anderson and Brad J. Bushman, "Effects of Violent Video Games on Aggressive Behavior, Aggressive Cognition, Aggressive Affect, Physiological Arousal, and Prosocial Behavior: A Meta-Analytic Review of the Scientific Literature," *Psychological Science* 12, no. 5 (2001): 353–59. John L. Sherry, "The Effects of Violent Video Games on Aggression: A Meta-Analysis," *Human Communication Research* 27 (2001).
105. Anderson and Bushman, "Effects of Violent Video Games on Aggressive Behavior, Aggressive Cognition, Aggressive Affect, Physiological Arousal, and Prosocial Behavior," 353–59.
106. Youssef Hasan, Laurent Bègue, Michael Scharkow, and Brad J. Bushman, "The More You Play, the More Aggressive You Become: A Long-Term Experimental Study of Cumulative Violent Video Game Effects on Hostile Expectations and Aggressive Behavior," *Journal of Experimental Social Psychology* 49 (March 2017): 224–27.
107. Anderson and Dill-Shackleford (2000), in Bushman and Anderson, "Violent Video Games and Hostile Expectations," 1679.
108. Craig A. Anderson, "An Update on the Effects of Playing Violent Video Games," *Journal of Adolescence* 27, no. 1 (2004): 113–22.
109. Bushman and Anderson, "Violent Video Games and Hostile Expectations."
110. Anderson, "An Update on the Effects of Playing Violent Video Games," 113.
111. Anderson and Huesmann (2003), cited in Anderson et al., *Violent Video Game Effects*, 24.
112. Elly Konijn, Marie Nije Bijvank, and Brad J. Bushman, "I Wish I Were a Warrior: The Role of Wishful Identification in the Effects of Violent Video Games on Aggression in Adolescent Boys," *Developmental Psychology* 43 (2007): 1038–44.
113. David G. Embrick, J. Talmadge Wright, and Andrus Lukacs, *Social Exclusion, Power, and Video Game Play: New Research in Digital Media and Technology* (Lanham, MD: Lexington Books, 2012), 8–12.
114. Konijn, Brjvank, and Bushman, "I Wish I Were a Warrior."
115. Jereen Jansz, "The Emotional Appeal of Violent Video Games for Adolescent Males," *Communications Theory*. 15, no. 3 (2006): 218–41.
116. Laurent Bègue, Douglas A. Gentile, Elisa Sardo, Clementine Bry, and Sebastian Roche, "Video Game Exposure and Sexism in a Representative Sample of Adolescents," *Frontiers in Psychology* 8 (March 2017): 1–5, https://doi.org/10.3389/fpsyg.2017.00466.
117. Gabbiadini et al. "Grand Theft Auto Is a 'Sandbox Game,'" 3.
118. Gabbadini et al., "Grand Theft Auto is a 'Sandbox Game.'"
119. Karen E. Dill, Brian P. Brown, and Michael A. Collins, "Effects of Exposure to Sex Stereotyped Video Game Characters," *Journal of Experimental Social Psychology* 44, no. 5 (2008): 1402–8.
120. Craig A. Anderson and Christine R. Murphy, "Violent Video Games and Aggressive Behavior in

Young Women," *Aggressive Behavior* 29 (2003).
121. Gabbadini et al., "Grand Theft Auto Is a 'Sandbox Game,'" 4.
122. American Psychiatric Association, *Diagnostic and Statistical Manual of Mental Disorders*, 5th ed. (Washington, DC: APA, 2013).
123. Anderson, Gentile, and Buckley, *Video Game Effects on Children and Adolescents*.
124. Anderson et al., *Violent Video Game Effects*,76. Carnagey and Anderson, "Violent Video Game Exposure and Aggression," 5–6.
125. Anderson and Bushman, "Effects of Violent Video Games on Aggressive Behavior, Aggressive Cognition, Aggressive Affect, Physiological Arousal, and Prosocial Behavior."
126. Carnagey et al., "The Effect of Video Game Violence," 495.
127. Carnagey et al., "The Effects of Video Game Violence," 494.
128. JSCO (1999), cited in Peter Langman, *Why Kids Kill: Inside the Minds of School Shooters* (New York: Palgrave Macmillan, 2009), 84.
129. Bushman, "The Weapons Effect."
130. Marcus-Newhall and Miller (1990), cited in Roy F. Baumeister and Brad J. Bushman, *Social Psychology and Human Nature* (Boston: Wadsworth Cenage Learning, 2016), 304.
131. Justin H. Chang and Brad J. Bushman, "Effects of Exposure to Gun Violence in Video Games on Children's Dangerous Behavior With Real Games: A Randomized Clinical Trial," *JAMA Network* 2, no. 5 (May 2019), doi:10.1001/jamanetworkopen.2019.4319.
132. Dillon and Bushman (2017), cited in Chang and Bushman, "Effects of Exposure to Gun Violence."
133. Michele L. Ybarra, L. Rowell Huesmann, Josephine P. Korchmaros, and Sari L. Reisner, "Cross-Sectional Association between Violent Video and Computer Game Playing on Weapon Carrying in a National Cohort of Children," *Aggressive Behavior* 40, no. 4 (July–Aug 2014): 345–58.
134. Toby Hopp, Scott Parrott, and Yuan Wang, "Use of Military-Themed First-Person Shooter Games and Militarism: An Investigation of Two Potential Facilitating Mechanisms," *Computers in Human Behavior* 78 (2018): 192–99. Nick Robinson, *Video Games, Popular Culture and World Politics* (London: Routledge, 2015).
135. Center for Internet and Technological Addiction, http://www.virtual-addiction.com.
136. Samantha Bresnahan and Will Worley, "When Video Games Become an Addiction," *Vital Signs*, CNN Health, January 6, 2016, https://www.cnn.com/2016/01/06/health/video-games-addiction-gentile-feat/index.html.
137. Clara Moscowitz, "How to Tell If You Are Addicted to Technology," *Live Science*, https://www.livescience.com.
138. "Video Game Controversy," Wikipedia, http://en.wikipedia.org/wiki/Video_game_controversy.
139. Edecio Martinez, "Game Over for Teen Who Killed Mother Over Video Game," CBS News, June 17, 2009, https://www.cbsnews.com/news/game-over-for-teen-who-killed-mother-over-video-game/.
140. CNN News, "18-Year-Old Charged with Police Station Killings," June 7, 2003, http://www.cnn.com/2003/US/South/06/07/alabama.shooting/index.html.

141. *Daily Mail* reporter, "Jailed for Life: 'Sadist' Who Murdered 15-Month-Old Toddler Because Her Crying Interrupted Him Playing on His X-Box," *Daily Mail*, April 13, 2010.
142. World Health Organization, "Gaming Disorder: Predominantly Online (6C51.0)," *International Classification of Disorders*, 11th ed. (Geneva: WHO, 2018).
143. Nancy Carlsson and Diane E. Levin, *Calling the Shots: How to Respond Effectively to Children's Fascination with War Play and War Toys* (Gabriola Island, BC: New Society, 1990), 16.
144. Douglas A. Gentile, Paul J. Lynch, Jennifer Ruth Linder, and David A. Walsh, "The Effect of Violent Video Game Habits on Adolescent Hostility, Aggressive Behavior, and School Performance," *Journal of Adolescence* 27, no. 1 (February 2004): 6–22. Anderson et al., *Violent Video Game Effects*, 46–47.
145. Anderson et al., *Violent Video Game Effects*, 46–47.
146. Anderson et al., *Violent Video Game Effects*, 46–47.
147. Anderson et al., *Violent Video Game Effects*.
148. Anderson et al., *Violent Video Game Effects*.
149. L. Rowell Huesmann, "Nailing the Coffin Shut on Debates That Violent Video Games Stimulate Aggression: Comment on Anderson et al.," *Psychological Bulletin* 136, no. 2 (February 2010): 179–81.
150. Anderson et al., *Violent Video Game Effects*, 48.
151. American Academy of Pediatrics Council of Communications and Media, "Media and the Young Mind," *Pediatrics* 138, no. 50 (November 2016): e20162591.
152. Carnagey and Anderson, "Violent Video Game Exposure and Aggression," 5–6.
153. Carnagey and Anderson, "Violent Video Game Exposure and Aggression."
154. S. L. A. Marshall, *Men against Fire: The Problem of Battle Command* (New York: William Morrow, 1947).
155. Marshall, *Men against Fire*.
156. Dave Grossman and Gloria DeGaetano, *Stop Teaching Our Kids to Kill: A Call to Action Against TV, Movie and Video Game Violence* (New York: Crown, 1999), 48.
157. Grossman and DeGaetano, *Stop Teaching Our Kids to Kill*.
158. Grossman and DeGaetano, *Stop Teaching Our Kids to Kill*.
159. Grossman and DeGaetano, *Stop Teaching Our Kids to Kill*.
160. B. J. Fogg, *Expert Guide: The Elements of Human Behavior* (self-pub., 2017).
161. Fogg, *Expert Guide*.
162. See B. F. Skinner, *Science and Human Behavior* (New York: MacMillan, 1953).
163. Grossman and DeGaetano, *Stop Teaching Our Kids to Kill*, 4
164. Verlande et al. (2000), cited in Langman, *Why Kids Kill*, 80.
165. Meary, Hemper, Mohandle, Shiva, and Gray (2001), cited in Langman, *Why Kids Kill*.
166. Meary, Hemper, Mohandle, Shiva, and Gray (2001), cited in Langman, *Why Kids Kill*.
167. Toole (2000), cited in Langman, *Why Kids Kill*, 80.

168. Levy, Kavalski, Smith, and Phillips (2003), cited in Langman, *Why Kids Kill*, 80.
169. Orrin Hatch and Senate Committee on the Judiciary, "Children, Violence, and the Media: A Report for Parents and Policy Makers" (1999), http://judiciary.senate.gov/oldsite/mediavio.htm. Website available at the time of writing.
170. Grossman and DeGaetano, *Stop Teaching Our Kids to Kill*, 4.
171. Gentile and Walsh (2002), cited in Bartlett and Anderson, "Violent Video Games and Public Policy," 12.
172. Roberts, Foehr, and Rideout (2005), cited in Bartlett and Anderson, "Violent Video Games and Public Policy," 12.
173. Walsh (2000), cited in Anderson et al., *Violent Video Game Effects*, 8.
174. Gentile and Anderson, "Violent Video Games."
175. Larson (2001: 1250), cited in Anderson et al., *Violent Video Game Effects*, 8.
176. Funk, Flores, Buchman, and Germann (1999), cited in Anderson et al., *Violent Video Game Effects*, 8.
177. Kimberly Haninger and Kevin Thompson, "Violence in E-Rated Video Games," *JAMA* 286 (2001): 561.
178. Haninger and Thompson (2004), cited in Anderson et al., *Violent Video Game Effects*, 154–55.
179. Gamasutra (2006), cited in Anderson et al. *Violent Video Game Effects*, 155.
180. Halpin, cited in Anderson et al., *Violent Video Game Effects*, 155.
181. Anderson et al., *Violent Video Game Effects*,155.
182. Jeff Grubb, "Gaming Lobby Video Game Voters Network Surpasses 500k Members," *Venture Beat*, March 18, 2013, https://venturebeat.com/2013/03/18/vgvn-500k-members/.
183. Anderson et al., *Violent Video Game Effects*,157–58.
184. Bushman and Cantor (2003), and Gentile, Humphrey, and Walsh (2005), cited in Bartlett and Anderson, "Violent Video Games and Public Policy."
185. Daniel R. Anderson, "A Neuroscience of Media and Children," *Journal of Children and Media*, no. 1 (2007): 8.
186. National Institute on Media and the Family, "Raising Media Wise Kids." Note that the institute was closed at the time of printing.
187. National Institute on Media and the Family, "Raising Media Wise Kids."
188. Anderson et al., *Violent Video Game Effects*, 156.
189. Gentile et al. (2005), cited in Anderson et al., *Violent Video Game Effects*, 156–57.
190. Anderson et al., *Violent Video Game Effects*,158.
191. Anderson et al., *Violent Video Game Effects*, 157.
192. Anderson et al., *Violent Video Game Effects*, 158.
193. Anderson et al., *Violent Video Game Effects*, 159.
194. Pollard-Sacks et al., "Do Violent Video Games Harm Children?."
195. Author interview with Ron Slaby, senior scientist at the Center on Media and Child Health,

Harvard Medical School, April 25, 2007.
196. Pinsent Masons, "Europe to Ban Sales of Violent Video Games to Kids," *Out-Law News*, January 18, 2007.
197. Dewey G. Cornell, "Psychology of the School Shootings: Testimony presented at the House Judiciary Committee Oversight Hearing to Examine Youth Culture and Violence," US House Judiciary Committee, May 13, 1999, http://www.apa.org/ppo/pi/cornell.html.
198. Cornell, "Psychology of the School Shootings."
199. Tom Phillips, "As Console Ban Lifts, China Reveals 'Hostile' Games Block," *Eurogamers*, January 13, 2014.
200. UN General Assembly, Resolution 44/25, Convention on the Rights of the Child, Article 17, https://www.ohchr.org/en/professionalinterest/pages/crc.aspx.

■ Chapter 9. The Brain's Response to Electronic Entertainment Media

1. M. C. Wittrock, Jackson Beatty, Joseph E. Bogen, Michael S. Gazzaniga, Harry J. Jerison, Stephen D. Krashen, Robert D. Nebes, and Timothy J. Teyler, *The Human Brain* (Englewood Cliffs, NJ: Prentice-Hall, 1977), 187.
2. Wittrock et al., *The Human Brain*, 187–88.
3. Richard M. Restak, *The Mind* (New York: Bantam, 1988), 317.
4. Robert W. Levenson, Karl Heider, Paul Ekman, and Wallace V. Friesen, "Emotion and Autonomic Nervous System Activity in the Minankabau of West Sumatra," *Journal of Personality and Social Psychology* 62, no. 6 (1992): 972.
5. Richard J. Gerrig and Philip G. Zimbardo, *Psychology and Life* (Boston: Pearson/Allyn and Bacon, 2005), 398.
6. Gerrig and Zimbardo, *Psychology and Life*.
7. Gerrig and Zimbardo, *Psychology and Life*.
8. Levenson et al, "Emotion and Autonomic Nervous System in the Minankabau of West Sumatra," 972.
9. Levenson et al, "Emotion and Autonomic Nervous System in the Minankabau of West Sumatra," 975–79.
10. Levenson et al, "Emotion and Autonomic Nervous System in the Minankabau of West Sumatra," 986.
11. Diane Connors, "Interview: Michael Gazzaniga," *Omni: Special Issue—Science and the Soul* (October 1993): 110.
12. Wittrock et al., *The Human Brain*, 16.
13. Wittrock et al., *The Human Brain*, 190.
14. Wittrock et al., *The Human Brain*, 191.

15. Wittrock et al., *The Human Brain*, 7–9.
16. Wittrock et al., *The Human Brain*, 200–201.
17. Joseph Carey, *Brain Facts: A Primer on the Brain and Nervous System* (Washington, DC: The Society for Neuroscience, 2002), 12–14.
18. Wittrock et al., *The Human Brain*, 51.
19. Wittrock et al., *The Human Brain*, 188.
20. Wittrock et al., *The Human Brain*, 141.
21. Connors, "Interview: Michael Gazzaniga,"106.
22. Connors, "Interview: Michael Gazzaniga."
23. Wittrock et al., *The Human Brain*,103.
24. Wittrock et al., *The Human Brain*, 189, 207.
25. Bakan (1969, 1971); Weitan and Etaugh (1973), cited in in Wittrock et al., *The Human Brain*, 121–22.
26. Wittrock et al., *The Human Brain*, 101–2.
27. Michael S. Gazzaniga, "Organization of the Human Brain," *Science* 245, no. 4921 (1989).
28. Wittrock et al., *The Human Brain*, 104.
29. Wittrock et al., *The Human Brain*, 140–41.
30. Wittrock et al., *The Human Brain*.
31. Wittrock et al., *The Human Brain*, 102.
32. Wittrock et al., *The Human Brain*, 101, 140; Carey, *Brain Facts*, 48.
33. Wittrock et al., *The Human Brain*, 138–39.
34. Wittrock et al., *The Human Brain*, 116.
35. Sharon Begley, Andrew Murr, and Adams Rogers, "Gray Matters," *Newsweek*, March 27, 1995, p. 54.
36. Davidson and Fox (1988, 1989), cited in Katherine V. Fite, "Television and the Brain" (paper commissioned by Children's Television Workshop, June 15, 1993), 16; Canli et al. (1998), cited in Gerrig and Zimbardo, *Psychology and Life*, 399.
37. Cohen (1969), cited in Wittrock et al., *The Human Brain*, 122.
38. Bakan (1969); Harnad (1972), cited in Wittrock et al., *The Human Brain*, 122.
39. Bakan (1969), cited in Wittrock et al., *The Human Brain*, 122.
40. Wittrock et al., *The Human Brain*,122–23.
41. Wittrock et al., *The Human Brain*, 137.
42. Wittrock et al., *The Human Brain*, 121.
43. Warren TenHouten, "Neurosociology," graduate seminar, University of California, Los Angeles, Spring 1980.
44. Wittrock, et. al., *The Human Brain*, 104.
45. Wittrock et al., *The Human Brain*, 135.
46. Paolo Freire, *Education for Critical Consciousness* (New York: Continuum, 1990).
47. Wittrock et al., *The Human Brain*, 145.

48. Sperry (1973), cited in Wittrock et al., *The Human Brain*, 145.
49. Begley et al., "Gray Matters," 50.
50. Richard M. Restak, *The Mind* (New York: Bantam, 1988), 79.
51. Restak, *The Mind*, 319.
52. Gerrig and Zimbardo, *Psychology and Life*, 50.
53. Jack Fincher, *The Brain: Mystery of Matter and Mind* (Washington, DC: U.S. News Books, 1981), 94.
54. Fincher, *The Brain*.
55. Joanna Schaffhausen, "The Biological Basis of Aggression," *Brain Connection*, November 26, 2006, https://brainconnection.brainhq.com/2006/11/26/the-biological-basis-of-aggression/.
56. Gerrig and Zimbardo, *Psychology and Life*, 403.
57. Morris et al. (1996), cited in Gerrig and Zimbardo, *Psychology and Life*, 399.
58. Morris et al. (1996), cited in Gerrig and Zimbardo, *Psychology and Life*.
59. Gerrig and Zimbardo, *Psychology and Life*, 403.
60. Daniel R. Anderson, Jennings Bryant, John P. Murray, Michael Rich, Michael J. Rivkin, and Dolf Zillmann, "Brain Imaging: An Introduction to a New Approach to Studying Media Processes and Effects," *Media Psychology* 8 (2006): 4.
61. Anderson et al., "Brain Imaging."
62. Yehuda (1999), cited in Irwin G. Sarason and Barbara R. Sarason, *Abnormal Psychology: The Problem of Maladaptive Behavior* (Small River, NJ: Prentice-Hall, 2002), 239.
63. Davidson et al. (2000), cited in Gerrig and Zimbardo, *Psychology and Life*, 589.
64. Carey, *Brain Facts*, 18.
65. Yehuda (1999), cited in Sarason and Sarason, *Abnormal Psychology*, 239.
66. Wittrock et al., *The Human Brain*, 11.
67. Carey, *Brain Facts*, 18.
68. Begley et al., "Gray Matters," 51.
69. Wittrock et al., *The Human Brain*, 194, 204.
70. Begley et al., "Gray Matters," 50.
71. John P. Murray, "TV Violence and Children," *Psychiatric Times* 18, no. 10 (2001): 181.
72. Daniel R. Anderson, "A Neuroscience of Media and Children?" *Journal of Children and Media* 1, no. 1 (2007).
73. Anderson et al., "Brain Imaging," 4–6.
74. Wittrock et al., *The Human Brain*, 206.
75. Wittrock et al., *The Human Brain*, 10.
76. Fincher, *The Brain*, 153.
77. Fincher, *The Brain*, 98.
78. Fincher, *The Brain*, 98–99.
79. Carey, *Brain Facts*, 51.
80. Fincher, *The Brain*, 99.

81. Wittrock et al., *The Human Brain*, 14.
82. Wittrock et al., *The Human Brain*, 203.
83. Wittrock et al., *The Human Brain*, 63.
84. Wittrock et al., *The Human Brain*, 189, 199.
85. Wittrock et al., *The Human Brain*, 199.
86. Wittrock et al., *The Human Brain*, 25.
87. Begley et al., "Gray Matters," 53.
88. Schaffhausen, "The Biological Basis of Aggression."
89. Carey, *Brain Facts*, 18–19.
90. Wittrock et al., *The Human Brain*, 29.
91. Wittrock et al., *The Human Brain*.
92. Carey, *Brain Facts*, 21.
93. Wittrock et al., *The Human Brain*, 190.
94. Wittrock et al., *The Human Brain*, 14.
95. Carey, *Brain Facts*, 21.
96. Nicholas L. Carnagey, Craig A. Anderson, and Brad J. Bushman, "The Effect of Video Game Violence on Physiological Desensitization to Real-Life Violence," *Journal of Experimental Social Psychology* 43, no. 3 (2007): 489–96.
97. Zero to Three, "Brain Wonders: Nurturing Healthy Brain Development," February 16, 2016. www.zerotothree.org/resourcess/156-brain-wonders.
98. Zero to Three, "Brain Wonders."
99. Zero to Three, "Brain Wonders."
100. Sharon Mihalic, Abigail Fagan, Katherine Irwin, Diane Ballard, and Delbert Elliot, "Blueprints for Violence Prevention," *Office of Juvenile Justice and Delinquency Prevention Report* (Washington, DC: US Department of Justice, Office of Justice Programs, 2004).
101. National Institute on Media and the Family, "Brain Development," Media Family, http://www.mediafamily.org/hot-topics/brain_development.shtml. Note: This research was retrieved in 2008 and the institute closed in 2009.
102. Zero to Three, "Brain Wonders." See also Natalie Angier, "We Are Six: The Hormone Surge of Middle Childhood," *New York Times*, December 2, 2011.
103. Zero to Three, "Brain Wonders."
104. Joanne Cantor and Glenn G. Sparks, "Children's Fear Responses to Mass Media: Testing Some Piagetian Predictions," *Journal of Communications* 34, no. 2 (1984): 93.
105. Singer and Singer (1981), cited in Cantor and Sparks, "Children's Fear Responses to Mass Media," 93–94.
106. Zero to Three, "Brain Wonders."
107. Cantor and Sparks, "Children's Fear Responses to Mass Media," 94.
108. Wittrock et al., *The Human Brain*, 178.

109. Wittrock et al., *The Human Brain*.
110. Zero to Three, "Brain Wonders."
111. Zero to Three, "Brain Wonders."
112. Wittrock et al., *The Human Brain*, 178.
113. Zero to Three, "Brain Wonders."
114. Zero to Three, "Brain Wonders."
115. Zero to Three, "Brain Wonders."
116. Zero to Three, "Brain Wonders."
117. Begley et al., "Gray Matters," 51.
118. Begley et al., "Gray Matters."
119. Begley et al., "Gray Matters," 51.
120. Begley et al., "Gray Matters."
121. Begley et al., "Gray Matters," 50.
122. Begley et al., "Gray Matters," 70.
123. Begley et al., "Gray Matters," 51.
124. Begley et al., "Gray Matters," 50.
125. Begley et al., "Gray Matters," 51, 54.
126. Wittrock et al., *The Human Brain*, 34.
127. Fite, "Television and the Brain," 4–5
128. Harold D. Krugman, "The Impact of Television Advertising: Learning without Involvement," *Public Opinion Quarterly* 29 (1965): 349–56; Harold D. Krugman, "Brainwave Measures of Media Involvement," *Journal of Advertising Research* 11 (1971): 3–9.
129. Fite, "Television and the Brain," 10
130. Shagass et al. (1971), cited in Fite, "Television and the Brain," 8–9.
131. Thomas Mulholland, "Training Visual Attention," *Academic Therapy* 10, no. 1 (1974): 5–17.
132. Rothschild et al. (1988), cited in Fite, "Television and the Brain," 14–15.
133. Yoshida and Kaneko (1989), cited in Fite, "Television and the Brain," 17–18.
134. Schellberg et al. (1990), cited in Fite, "Television and the Brain," 18.
135. Springer and Deutsch (1989), cited in Fite, "Television and the Brain," 16
136. Reeves et al. (1987) and Schellberg et al. (1990), cited in Fite, "Television and the Brain," 17.
137. Carey, *Brain Facts*, 43–44.
138. Carey, *Brain Facts*, 44.
139. Craig A. Anderson, Nicholas L. Carnagey, Mindy Flanagan, Arlin J. Benjamin Jr., Janie Eubanks, and Jeffrey C. Valentine, "Violent Video Games: Specific Effects of Violent Content in Aggressive Thoughts and Behavior," *Advances in Experimental Social Psychology* 36 (2004): 199–249.
140. John P. Murray, Mario M. Liotti, Paul T. Ingmundson, Helen S. Mayberg, Yu Pu, and Frank Zamarripa, "Children's Brain Activation while Viewing Televised Violence Research by fMRI," *Media Psychology* 8 (2006): 25–38.

141. Anderson et al., "Brain Imaging," 5.
142. Daniel R. Anderson, "A Neuroscience of Children and Media?," *Journal of Children and Media* 1, no. 1 (2007): 80.
143. Murray, "TV Violence and Children."
144. Anderson, "A Neuroscience of Media and Children," 84.
145. Anderson et al., "Brain Imaging," 5–6.
146. Anderson et al., "Brain Imaging," 6.
147. Anderson et al., "Brain Imaging."
148. Carnagey et al., "The Effect of Video Game Violence," 181.
149. Carnagey et al., "The Effects of Video Game Violence,"490.
150. Carnagey et al., "The Effects of Video Game Violence."
151. Carnagey et al., "The Effects of Video Game Violence."
152. Carnagey et al., "The Effects of Video Game Violence," 491
153. Joanne Cantor, *Mommy, I'm Scared: How TV and Movies Frighten Children and What We Can Do to Protect Them* (New York: Harcourt, Brace, 1998), 491–95.
154. Cantor, *Mommy, I'm Scared*, 491–95.
155. Carnagey et al., "The Effects of Video Game Violence," 495.
156. Nicholas L. Carnagey, Craig A. Anderson, and Bruce D. Bartholow, "Media Violence and Social Neuroscience: New Questions and New Opportunities," *Current Directions in Psychological Science* 16, no. 4 (2007): 180.
157. Anderson, "A Neuroscience of Media and Children,"81.
158. Anderson, "A Neuroscience of Media and Children."
159. Matthews et al. (2005), cited in Anderson et al., "Brain Imaging," 81.
160. Carnagey et al., "Media Violence and Social Neuroscience."
161. Anderson et al., "Brain Imaging," 81.
162. Murray, "TV Violence and Children."
163. Murray, "TV Violence and Children."
164. Sarason and Sarason, *Abnormal Psychology*, 482.
165. William G. Kronenberger, Vincent P. Matthews, David W. Dunn, Yang Wang, Elisabeth A. Wood, Ann L. Giauque, Joelle J. Larsen, Mary E. Rembusch, Mark J. Lowe, and Tie-Quiang Li, "Media Violence Exposure and Executive Functioning in Aggressive and Control Adolescents," *Journal of Clinical Psychology* 61, no. 6 (2005): 725–37.
166. Kronenberger et al., "Media Violence Exposure."
167. Dale Archer, "Violence, the Media and Your Brain: How Media Violence from Movies to TV to Video Games Adversely Affect the Brain," *Psychology Today*, March 9, 2013.
168. American Psychiatric Association, "Internet Gaming: Internet Gaming in DSM 5," Patients and Families Series, reviewed June 2018, https://www.psychiatry.org/patients-families/internet-gaming.

169. Sarason and Sarason, *Abnormal Psychology*, 482.
170. James R. Flynn, *What is Intelligence?* (Cambridge, UK: Cambridge University Press, 2007), 2–3.
171. Flynn, *What is Intelligence?*, 187.
172. Neisser (1997), cited in Anderson, "A Neuroscience of Media and Children," 82.
173. Anderson, "A Neuroscience of Media and Children," 9.
174. Charles J. Sykes, *Dumbing Down Our Kids* (New York: St. Martin's, 1995), 20–21.
175. Fred Emery and Merrelyn Emery, *A Choice of Futures: To Enlighten or Inform* (Leiden, Netherlands: Martinus Nijhoff Social Sciences Division, 1976); Marianna King, "A Neurosociological Assessment of Television Viewing" (master's thesis, University of California, 1983).
176. Mark Fetler, "Television Viewing and School Achievement," *Journal of Communication* 34, no. 2 (1984): 104–6.
177. Gabriel Salomon and Tamar Leigh, "Predisposition about Learning from Print and Television," *Journal of Communication* 34, no 2 (1984): 120–21.
178. Sharon Begley and Jeneen Interlandi, "The Dumbest Generation? Don't Be Dumb," *Newsweek*, June 2, 2008, p. 43.
179. Jane M. Healy, *Endangered Minds: Why Our Children Don't Think* (New York: Simon and Schuster, 1990), 216.

■ Chapter 10. The Future of Violence

1. Roy E. Larsen, prod., *March of Time* newsreel, "The Youth Problem," released 1942, aired December 2013, on Turner Classic Movies.
2. Dave Grossman and Gloria DeGaetano, *Stop Teaching Our Kids to Kill: A Call to Action Against TV, Movie, and Video Game Violence* (New York: Crown, 1999), 13.
3. Huff (2004), cited in Margaret A. Zahn, Henry J. Brownstein, and Shelly L. Jackson, eds., *Violence: From Theory to Research* (Cincinnati, OH: Anderson, 2004), 182.
4. Snyder (1996), cited in Barbara Tatem Kelley, David Huizinga, Terence P. Thornberry, and Rolf Loeber, "Epidemiology of Serious Violence," *Juvenile Justice Bulletin* (Washington, DC: US Department of Justice, 1997).
5. Karen Colvard, "Crime is Down? Don't Confuse Us with the Facts," *Crimes of Violence* 2 (Fall 1997): 1.
6. James Alan Fox, "The Impending Crime Wave Can Be Averted" (unpublished paper presented at Northeastern University, 1996); Violent and Repeat Juvenile Offender Accountability and Rehabilitation Act of 1999, H.R. Resolution 1501, 106th Cong. (1999), 8–9.
7. Colvard, "Crime is Down?," 1.
8. Orrin Hatch and US Senate Committee on the Judiciary, "Children, Violence, and the Media: A

Report for Parents and Policy Makers" (September 14, 1999), http://judiciary.senate.gov/oldsite/mediavio.htm. Website available at the time of writing.

9. Mark H. Moore, Carol V. Petrie, Anthony A. Braga, and Brendan L. McLaughlin, eds., *Deadly Lessons: Understanding Lethal School Violence* (Washington, DC: National Academies Press, 2003), 249.
10. Ames Grawert, Matthew Friedman, and James Cullen, "Crime Trends: 1990–2016," *Brennan Center Report*, Brennan Center for Justice, April 18, 2017.
11. Centers for Disease Control Injury Center, "School Associated Violent Deaths," http://www.cdc.gov/ncipc/dvp/sch-shooting.htm.
12. Charles Puzzanchera, "Juvenile Arrests, 2017," *Juvenile Justice Statistics National Report Series* (Washington, DC: US Department of Justice, Office of Justice Programs, 2019), 1–3.
13. Rachel Dinkes, Jana Kemp, Katrina Baum, and Thomas D. Snyder, *Indicators of School Crime and Safety: 2009* (Washington, DC: Bureau of Justice Statistics and National Center for Education Statistics, 2009), 1, https://nces.ed.gov/pubs2010/2010012.pdf.
14. David Sheppard, "Strategies to Reduce Gun Violence," *OJJDP Fact Sheet* (Washington, DC: US Department of Justice, Office of Juvenile Justice and Delinquency Prevention, 1999), 1.
15. Finn-Aage Esbensen, "Youth Violence: An Overview," *Violence: From Theory to Research*, edited by Margaret A. Zahn, Henry J. Brownstein, and Shelly L. Jackson (Cincinnati, OH: Anderson, 2004), 180; Mark H. Moore, Carol V. Petrie, Anthony A. Braga, and Brendan L. McLaughlin, eds., *Deadly Lessons: Understanding Lethal School Violence* (Washington, DC: National Academies Press, 2003), 249.
16. Lauren Musu-Gillette, Anlan Zhang, Ke Wang, Zizhi Zhang, and Barbara A. Coudekerk, *Indicators of School Crime and Safety: 2016* (Washington, DC: Bureau of Justice Statistics and National Center for Education Statistics, 2017), vi, https://nces.ed.gov/pubs2017/2017064.pdf.

■ Chapter 11. What We Can Do: The Opportunity

1. Michael J. Shuen, "Confronting a Culture of Violence," *People of God* 13, no. 2 (1995): 1.
2. Carl R. Rogers, *On Personal Power: Inner Strength and Its Revolutionary Impact* (New York: Delacorte, 1977).
3. Shuen, "Confronting a Culture of Violence," 1.
4. Thich Nhat Hanh, *Creating True Peace: Ending Violence in Yourself, Your Family, Your Community, and the World* (New York: Free Press, 2003), 9.
5. Nhat Hanh, *Creating True Peace*, 9.
6. Dalai Lama, *The Path to Tranquility: Daily Wisdom*, edited by Renuka Singh (New York: Penguin, 2002), 2.

BIBLIOGRAPHY

Abrams, Abigail, and Melissa Chan. "Special Report: Guns in America." *Time*. November 5, 2018.

Ad Council. *Healthy Lifestyles and Disease Prevention: Media Campaign Report*. Washington, DC: US Department of Health and Human Services, 2004.

Altheide, David L. *Creating Reality: How TV News Distorts Events*. Thousand Oaks, CA: Sage, 1976.

Altheide, David L., and Roger Snow. *Media Reality*. Boston: Beacon, 1976.

American Academy of Child and Adolescent Psychiatry. "Children and Firearms." *Facts for Families*, no. 37 (2008). http://www.aacap.org.

———. "The Influence of Music and Music Videos." *Facts for Families*, no. 40 (2008). http://www.aacap.org.

———. "Suicide in Children and Teens." *Facts for Families*, no. 10 (2008). Updated June 2018. https://www.aacap.org/AACAP/Families_and_Youth/Facts_for_Families/FFF-Guide/Teen-Suicide-010.aspx.

———. "Teens: Alcohol and Other Drugs." *Facts for Families*, no. 3 (2008). Updated March 2018. https://www.aacap.org/AACAP/Families_and_Youth/Facts_for_Families/FFF-Guide/Teens-Alcohol-And-Other-Drugs-003.aspx.

American Academy of Family Physicians. "Violence, the Media and Entertainment." Position Paper. http://www.aafp.org.

American Academy of Pediatrics. "Joint Statement on the Impact of Entertainment Violence on Children." Congressional Public Health Summit, July 26, 2000. http://www.aap.org.

———. "Media Violence." *American Academy of Pediatrics* 124, no. 5 (2009): 1495–1503.

———. "Television—How It Affects Children." http://patiented.aap.org.

American Academy of Pediatrics, Committee on Adolescents. "Suicide and Suicide Attempts in Adolescents." *Pediatrics* 105, no. 4 (April 2000): 871–74.

American Academy of Pediatrics, Committee on Injury and Poison Prevention. "Policy Statement: Firearm-Related Injuries Affecting the Pediatric Population." *Pediatrics* 130, no. 5 (2012): 2–3. https://doi.org/10.1542/peds.2012-2481.

American Academy of Pediatrics, Council of Communications and Media. "Media and the Young Mind." *Pediatrics* 138, no. 50 (November 2016).

American Association of University Women. "Three-Fourths of Schools Report Zero Incidents of Sexual Harassment in Grades 7–12." October 24, 2017.

American Association of University Women and Wellesley College Center for Research on Women. *How Schools Shortchange Girls*. AAUW Education Foundation, 1992.

American Diabetes Association. "Diabetes Statistics." http://www.diabetes.org/diabetes-basic/disbetes-statistics.

American Educational Research Association. http://www.agra.nea/publications.

American Humane Society, Children's Division. "Tell Congress to Vote for the Keeping All Students Safe Act." http://www.americanhumanesociety.com.

American Medical Association. "Proceedings of the Educational Forum on Adolescent Health: Youth Bullying." http://www.amaassn.org.

American Psychiatric Association. *Diagnostic and Statistical Manual of Mental Disorders*. 5th ed. Washington, DC: APA, 2013.

American Psychiatric Association. "Internet Gaming: Internet Gaming in DSM 5." Patients and Families Series. Reviewed June 2018. https://www.psychiatry.org/patients-families/internet-gaming.

American Psychological Association. "Resolution on Violent Video Games." 2015. http://www.apa.org/about/policy/violent-video-games.aspx.

———. "Report of the APA Task Force on Television and Society." http://www.apa.org.

Anderson, Craig A. "Heat and Violence: Current Directions." *Psychological Science* 10 (2001): 33–38.

———. "Temperature and Aggression." *Advances in Experimental Social Psychology*. Edited by M.P. Zanna. San Diego: Academic Press, 2010.

———. "An Update on the Effects of Playing Violent Video Games." *Journal of Adolescence* 27, no. 1 (2004): 113–22.

Anderson, Craig A., and Daniel C. Anderson. "Ambient Temperature and Violent Crime: Tests of the Linear and Curvilinear Hypotheses." *Journal of Personality and Social Psychology* 46 (1984): 91–97.

Anderson, Craig A., Leonard Berkowitz, Edward Donnetstein, L. Rowell Huesmann, James D. Jason, David Linz, Neil M. Malamuth, and Ellen Wartella. "The Influence of Media Violence in Youth." *Psychological Science: Public Interest*. 4, no. 3 (2013).

Anderson, Craig A., and Brad J. Bushman. "Effects of Violent Video Games on Aggressive Behavior, Aggressive Cognition, Aggressive Affect, Physiological Arousal, and Prosocial Behavior: A Meta-Analytic Review of the Scientific Literature." *Psychological Science* 12, no. 5 (September 2001):

353–59.

———. "Media Violence and the American Public: Scientific Facts Versus Media Misinformation." *American Psychologist* 56, nos. 6–7 (2001): 477–89.

———. "Media Violence and the American Public Revisited." *American Psychologist* 57, nos. 6–7 (2002): 448–50.

Anderson, Craig A., and Nicholas I. Carnagey. "Violent Evil and the General Aggression Model." *Social Psychology of Good and Evil*. Edited by A. Miller. New York: Guilford, 2004.

Anderson, Craig A., Nicholas L. Carnagey, and Janie Eubanks. "Exposure to Violent Media: The Effects of Songs With Violent Lyrics on Aggressive Thoughts and Feelings." *Personality and Social Psychology* 84, no. 5 (2003).

Anderson, Craig A., N. L. Carnagey, M. Flanagan, A. J. Benjamin Jr., J. Eubanks, and J. C. Valentine. "Violent Video Games: Specific Effects of Violent Content in Aggressive Thoughts and Behavior." *Advances in Experimental Social Psychology* 36 (2004): 199–249.

Anderson, Craig A., and Karen E. Dill-Shackleford. "Video Games and Aggressive Thoughts, Feelings and Behavior in the Laboratory and in Life." *Journal of Personality and Social Psychology* 78 (2000): 772–90.

Anderson, Craig A., Douglas A. Gentile, and Katherine E. Buckley. *Violent Video Game Effects on Children and Adolescents: Theory, Research, and Public Policy*. Oxford: Oxford University Press, 2007.

Anderson, Craig A., Nobuko Ihori, Edward S. Swill, Brad J. Bushman, Akira Sakamoto, Hannah R. Rothstein, and Maniba Sazeem. "Violent Video Game Effects on Aggression, Empathy, and Personal Behavior in Eastern and Western Countries: A Meta-Analytic Review." *Psychological Bulletin* 136, no. 2 (March 2010): 151–73.

Anderson, Craig A., and Christine R. Murphy. "Violent Video Games and Aggressive Behavior in Young Women." *Aggressive Behavior* 29 (2003): 423–29.

Anderson, Craig A., Akira Sakamoto, Douglas A. Gentile, Nobuko Ihori, Akiko Shibuya, Shintaro Yukawa, Mayume Naito, and Kumiko Kobayashi. "Longitudinal Effects of Violent Video Games on Aggression in Japan and the United States." *Pediatrics* 122, no. 5 (2008).

Anderson, Daniel R. "A Neuroscience of Children and Media?." *Journal of Children and Media* 1, no. 1 (2007): 77–85.

Anderson, Daniel R., Jennings Bryant, John P. Murray, Michael Rich, Michael J. Rivkin, and Dolf Zillmann. "Brain Imaging: An Introduction to a New Approach to Studying Media Processes and Effects." *Media Psychology* 8 (2006): 1–6.

Anderson, Mark, Joanne Kaufman, Thomas R. Simon, et al. "School-Associated Violent Deaths in the United States, 1994–1999." *JAMA* 286, no. 21 (December 2001): 2695–2702. doi:10.1001/jama.286.21.2695.

Anderson, Monica. "A Majority of Teens Have Experienced Some Form of Cyberbullying." Pew Research Center. September 27, 2018.

"Andrew Wurst." Criminal Justice Research, 2010. http://criminal-justice.iresearchnet.com/crime/school-violence/andrew-wurst/.

Angier, Natalie. "We Are Six: The Hormone Surge of Middle Childhood." *New York Times*. December 2, 2011.

Anscheim, Joan. "The Children's Community Bridge Project: A Demonstration Child Abuse Prevention Project." *Options*. Education Development Center, 1997.

Apuzzo, Matt, and Sharon Cohen. "V.A. Tech Shooter: A Textbook Case." *Pueblo Chieftain* (Associated Press). April 20, 2007.

Archer, Dale. "Violence, the Media and Your Brain: How Media Violence from Movies to TV to Video Games Adversely Affect the Brain." *Psychology Today*. March 9, 2013.

Arnal, Kike. *In The Shadow of Power*. Milan, Italy: Charta, 2010.

Arnette, June L., and Marjorie C. Walsenben. "Combating Fear and Restoring Safety in Schools." *Juvenile Justice Bulletin*. Washington, DC: US Department of Justice, 1998.

Associated Press. "Congress Lets Assault Weapons Ban Expire." NBC News. September 19, 2004. www.nbcnews.com.

Atkin, Charles, John Hocking, and Martin Block. "Teenage Drinking: Does Advertising Make a Difference?." *Journal of Communication* 34, no. 2 (1984): 157–67.

Atnafou, Rebecca. "Ensuring the Safety of Our Future Generations: Parent Education as a Preventive Strategy for Youth Violence." *Options* 4 (Summer 1996).

Aufderheide, Patricia. "Why Kids Hate Educational TV." *Children and the Media*. Edited by Everette E. Dennis and Edward C. Pease. New Brunswick, NJ: Transaction, 1996.

Baba, Tetsuaki, Kumiko Kushiyama, and Kouki Doi. "ThermoGame: Video Game Interaction System That Offers Dynamic Temperature Sensation to Users." Poster presented as the International Conference on Computer Graphics and Interactive Techniques, Los Angeles, CA, July 26–30, 2010.

Bagdikian, Ben H. *The Media Monopoly*. Boston: Beacon, 1983.

Ballard, Mary E., and J. Rose Wiest. "Mortal Kombat: The Effects of Violent Videogame Play on Males' Hostility and Cardiovascular Responding." *Journal of Applied Social Psychology* 26 (1995): 717–55.

Bandura, Albert. *Social Learning Theory*. Englewood Cliffs, NJ: Prentice-Hall, 1972.

Barker, Francis. *The Culture of Violence: Essays on Tragedy and History*. University of Chicago Press, 1993.

Bartlett, Christopher P., and Craig Anderson. "Violent Video Games and Public Policy." *Handbuch Computerspiele, Politik und Gesellschaft (Handbook of Video Games, Politics and Society)*. Edited by Tobias Beve and Holger Zapf. Konstanz: UVK Verlagsgesellschaft, 2009.

Baumeister, Roy F. *The Cultural Animal: Human Nature, Meaning, and Social Life*. New York: Oxford University Press, 2005.

Baumeister, Roy F., and Brad J. Bushman. *Social Psychology and Human Nature*. Boston: Wadsworth Cengage Learning, 2016.

Bavolek, Stephen J. *Nurturing Programs for Parents and Children*. 4th ed. Denver, CO: Family Development Resources, 1999.

Begley, Sharon, and Jeneen Interlandi. "The Dumbest Generation? Don't Be Dumb." *Newsweek*. June 2, 2008.

Begley, Sharon, Andrew Murr, and Adams Rogers. "Gray Matters." *Newsweek*. March 27, 1995.

Bègue, Laurent, Douglas A. Gentile, Elisa Sardo, Clementine Bry, and Sebastian Roche. "Video Game Exposure and Sexism in a Representative Sample of Adolescents." *Frontiers in Psychology* 8 (March 2017): 1–5. https://doi.org/10.3389/fpsyg.2017.00466.

Bell, Christopher D., Kathryn Raczynski, and Arthur M. Horne. "Bully Busters: Evaluation of a Group-Based Bully Intervention and Prevention Program." *Group Dynamics: Theory, Research, and Practice* 14, no. 3 (2010): 257–67.

Benard, Bonnie. *Fostering Resiliency in Kids: Protective Factors in the Family, School and Community*. Portland, OR: Western Regional Center for Drug-Free Schools and Communities, 1992.

Beresin, Eugene V. "The Impact of Media Violence on Children and Adolescents: Opportunities for Clinical Interventions." National Network Opposing Militarization of Youth. 2009. http://www.aacap.or/cs/root/developmentor/www.nmomy.net.

Berger, Arthur Asa. *Media Analysis Techniques*. Thousand Oaks, CA: Sage, 1982.

Bernhardt, Paul C., James M. Dabbs Jr., Julie A. Fielden, and Candice D. Lutter. "Testosterone Changes during Vicarious Experiences of Winning and Losing among Fans at Sporting Events." *Physiology and Behavior* 65, no. 1 (August 1998): 59–62.

Berrigan, Frida. "Then, This Is the Year: Imaging Our Way to the Peace Economy." *Off Our Backs* 38, no. 1 (2008): 34–36.

Best, Raphaela. *We've All Got Scars: What Boys and Girls Learn in Elementary School*. Bloomington: Indiana University Press, 2003.

Bhattachaya, Shaoni. "Lyrics Increase Aggression." *New Science*. May 4, 2003.

Bilchik, Shay. *Promising Strategies to Reduce Gun Violence*. Washington, DC: US Department of Justice, Office of Juvenile Justice and Delinquency Prevention, 1999.

———. *Report to Congress on Juvenile Violence Research*. Washington, DC: US Department of Justice, 1999.

Bill Moyers Journal. "Gun Violence." Aired March 10, 1995, on PBS.

Billings, Paul. "Comments on the Social, Legal, and Policy Issues Arising From the Genetic Revolution." Testimony before the Senate Select Committee on Genetics and Public Policy, April 8, 1996.

Block, C. R. "Lethal Violence in the Chicago Latino Community." *Homicide: The Victim/Offender Connection*. Edited by A.V. Wilson. Cincinnati: Anderson, 1993.

Boaz, Rachel T., and Renard L. Ciochan. "The Scavenging of Peking Man." *Natural History*. March 2001.

Bolton, Michelle Morgan. "Anti-Bully Pulpit." *Boston Globe*. April 16, 2009.

Borosage, Robert L. "Disinvesting in America." *The Nation*. October 4, 1993.

Bresnahan, Samantha, and Will Worley. "When Video Games Become an Addiction." *Vital Signs*. CNN

Health. January 6, 2016. https://www.cnn.com/2016/01/06/health/video-games-addiction-gentile-feat/index.html.

Breuer, Johannes, and Malte Elson. "Frustration-Aggression Theory." *The Wiley Handbook of Violence and Aggression*. Edited by Peter Sturmey. Hoboken, NJ: Wiley-Blackwell, 2017.

Brewer, N. D., T. P. San, B. G. King, and R. Lowry. "Recent Trends in Violence Related Behaviors among High School Students in the United States." *Journal of the American Medical Association* 282 (1999): 440–46.

BrightHouse Institute for Thought. "Brighthouse Institute for Thought Sciences Launches First 'Neuromarketing' Research Company: Company Uses Neuroimaging to Unlock the Consumer Mind." News release. June 22, 2002. http://www.prweb.com.

Brock, Stephen E., Philip J. Lazarus, and Shane R. Jimerson. *Best Practices in School Crisis Prevention and Intervention*. Bethesda, MD: National Association of School Psychologists, 2006.

Brooks, Jacqueline G., and Eustace G. Thompson. "Social Justice in the Classroom." *Educational Leadership*. Association for Supervision and Curriculum Development, 2005.

Brown, Stephen E., Esbensen Finn-Aage, and Gilbert Geis. *Criminology: Explaining Crime and Its Context*. 6th ed. Cincinnati, OH: Anderson, 2007.

Browning, Katherine, and David Huizinga. "Highlights of Findings from the Denver Youth Survey." *OJJDP Fact Sheet*. Washington, DC: US Department of Justice, 1999.

Bullying Statistics. www.bullyingstatistics.org.

Bureau of Justice Statistics. *Indicators of School Crime and Safety*. Washington, DC: US Department of Justice, 2003.

Bushman, Brad J. "Does Venting Anger Feed or Extinguish the Flame? Catharsis, Rumination, Distraction, Anger and Aggressive Responding." *Personality and Social Psychology Bulletin* 28, no. 6 (2002): 724–31.

———. "Human Aggression While Under the Influence of Alcohol and Other Drugs: An Integrative Research Review." *Current Directions in Psychological Science* 2 (1993): 148–52.

———. "Teaching Students About Violent Media Effects." *Teaching of Psychology* 45, no.2 (2018): 200–206.

———. "Violent Media and Hostile Appraisals: A Meta-Analytic Review." *Aggressive Behavior*. 42, no. 6 (November 2016): 605–13.

———. "The Weapons Effect." *Journal of the American Medical Association*. 167, no. 2 (2013): 1094–95.

Bushman, Brad J., and Craig A. Anderson. "Media Violence and the American Public: Scientific Facts Versus Media Misinformation." *American Psychologist* 56 (2001): 477–89.

———. "Violent Video Games and Hostile Expectations: A Test of the General Aggression Model." *Personality and Social Psychology Bulletin* 28, no. 2 (2002): 1679–86.

———. "Comfortably Numb: Desensitization Effects of Violent Media on Helper Roles." *Psychological Science*. 20 no. 3 (March 2009): 273–77.

Bushman, Brad J., Thomas Kerwin, Tyler Whitlock, Janet M. Weisenberger. "The Weapons Effect on

Wheels: Motorists Drive More Aggressively When There Is a Gun in the Vehicle." *Journal of Experimental Social Psychology* 73 (November 2017): 82–85. doi.org/10.1016/j.jesp.2017.06.007.

Bushman, Brad J., and Deana Pollard-Sacks. "Supreme Court Decision Based on the First Amendment, Not Scientific Evidence." *The American Psychologist* 69 (2014): 306–7.

Butterfield, Fox. "Grim Forecast Offered on Rising Juvenile Crime." *New York Times.* September 8, 1995.

———. "To Rejuvenate Gun Sales, Critics Say, Industry Started Making More Powerful Pistols." *New York Times.* February 14, 1999.

Butts, Jeffrey A., and Howard N. Snyder. "The Youngest Delinquents: Offenders under Age 15." *Juvenile Justice Bulletin.* Washington, DC: US Department of Justice, 1997.

BYJU's Learning App. "Definition of Resonance." www.byjus.com/physics/resonance.

California Attorney General's Office's Policy Council on Violence Prevention. "Violence Prevention: A Vision of Hope; Final Report." Sacramento: Policy Council on Violence Prevention, 1995.

California Child Development CORPS. "Prevention and Early Intervention Cost Less, Work Better." *Children's Advocate.* 2000.

"Campus Killer." Aired 2007, on Investigative Discovery.

Canada Radio-Television and Telecommunications Commission. "Canada and TV Violence: Cooperation and Consensus." http://www.crtc.gc.ca.

———. "Selected Bibliography of Studies on the Effects of Media Violence." http://www.crtc.gc.ca/Eng/Social/Bblio.htm.

Cantor, Joanne. *Mommy, I'm Scared: How TV and Movies Frighten Children and What We Can Do to Protect Them.* New York: Harcourt, Brace, 1998.

Cantor, Joanne, and Glenn G. Sparks. "Children's Fear Responses to Mass Media: Testing Some Piagetian Predictions." *Journal of Communications* 34, no. 2 (1984): 90–103.

Carey, Joseph. *Brain Facts: A Primer on the Brain and Nervous System.* Washington, DC: The Society for Neuroscience, 2002.

Carlsson, Ulla, and Cecelia von Feilitzen, eds. *Children and Media Violence: Yearbook for the UNESCO International Clearinghouse on Children and Violence on the Screen.* 1998.

Carlsson, Nancy, and Diane E. Levin. *Calling the Shots: How to Respond Effectively to Children's Fascination with War Play and War Toys.* Gabriola Island, BC: New Society, 1990.

Carnagey, Nicholas L., and Craig A. Anderson. "The Effects of Reward and Punishment in Violent Video Games on Aggressive Affect, Cognition, and Behavior." *Psychological Science* 16, no. 11 (2005): 882–89.

Carnagey, Nicholas L., and Craig A. Anderson. "Violent Video Game Exposure and Aggression: A Literature Review." *Minerva Pediatrica* 45 (March 2004): 1–18.

Carnagey, Nicholas L., Craig A. Anderson, and Bruce D. Bartholow. "Media Violence and Social Neuroscience: New Questions and New Opportunities." *Current Directions in Psychological Science* 16, no. 4 (2007): 178–82.

Carnagey, Nicholas L., Craig A. Anderson, and Brad J. Bushman. "The Effect of Video Game Violence on

Physiological Desensitization to Real-Life Violence." *Journal of Experimental Social Psychology* 43, no. 3 (2007): 489–96.

Carnagey, Nicholas L., and Brad J. Bushman. "Music and Aggression." *Encyclopedia of Children, Adolescents, and the Media*. Vol. 2. Edited by in J.J. Arnett, 846–47. Thousand Oaks, CA: Sage, 2006.

Center for Economic and Social Rights. "U.S. Faces Rare International Scrutiny on Economic and Social Rights." http://www.cesr.org/article.

———. "From Disparity to Dignity." New York: CESR, 2016. http://www.cesr.org.

Center for Media Literacy. "Beyond Blame: Challenging Violence in the Media." 2010. https://www.medialit.org/beyond-blame-challenging-violence-media.

Center for the Study and Prevention of Violence. *Blueprints Model Programs—Big Brothers Big Sisters of America*. Boulder: University of Colorado, 2004.

———. *Blueprints for Healthy Youth Development—Olweus Bullying Prevention Program*. Boulder: University of Colorado, 2004.

———. *Blueprints Model Programs—Functional Family Therapy*. Boulder: University of Colorado, 2004.

———. *Blueprints Model Programs—The Incredible Years Series*. Boulder: University of Colorado, 2004.

———. *Blueprints Model Programs—Nurse-Family Partnerships*. Boulder: University of Colorado, 2004.

———. *Blueprints Model Programs—Promoting Alternative Thinking Strategies (PATHS)*. Boulder: University of Colorado, 2004.

Center on Media and Child Health TV. "Media Literacy: A Potent Antidote to Media Violence." Harvard Medical School. https://cmch.tv.

Centers for Disease Control and Prevention. "Trends in Rates of Homicides—United States, 1985–1995." *Morbidity and Mortality Weekly Report*. June 7, 1996.

———. "Youth Violence." Updated March 2, 2020. https://www.cdc.gov/violenceprevention/youthviolence/.

———. "Youth Risk Behavior Surveillance System (YRBSS) Reports." https://www.cdc.gov/healthyschools/data/yrbss.htm.

Centers for Disease Control and Prevention, US Department of Education, US Department of Justice, and National School Safety Center. "The School-Associated Violent Death Study 1992–1999." 1999. https://www.cdc.gov/violenceprevention/youthviolence/schoolviolence/SAVD.html.

Center to Prevent Handgun Violence. *Gun Industry Experts Predict Far-Reaching Reforms: Point to Tobacco and Other Industries as Precedent*. Washington, DC: Center to Prevent Handgun Violence, 1997.

Centerwall, Brandon S. "Television and Violence: The Scale of the Problem and Where to Go From Here." *Journal of the American Medical Association* 267, no. 22 (June 10, 1992): 3059–63.

Chang, Justin H., and Brad J. Bushman. "Effects of Exposure to Gun Violence in Video Games on Children's Dangerous Behavior with Real Games: A Randomized Clinical Trial." *JAMA Network* 2, no. 5 (May 31, 2019). doi:10.1001/jamanetworkopen.2019.4319.

Chase, Jennifer. "Best Practices in Emergency and Mass Communication." Regroup Compliance Services.

Children's Institute International. *Armed and Ready for School.* Los Angeles: Pacific Visions Communication, 1996.

Children's Safety Network. *Taking Action to Prevent Adolescent Violence.* Newton, MA: Education Development Center, 1995.

Cloud, John. "Of Arms and the Boy." *Time.* July 6, 1998.

CNN Interactive. "Accused Oregon Shooter Shows No Emotion in Court." May 22, 1998. http://www.cnn.com.

CNN News. "Blood Stains Oregon High School." May 21, 1998. http://www.cnn.com.

———. "18-Year-Old Charged with Police Station Killings." June 7, 2003. http://www.cnn.com/2003/US/South/06/07/alabama.shooting/index.html.

———. "Parents of Shooting Suspect among Those Asking 'Why?.'" March 27, 1998. http://www.cnn.com.

Collins, Nick. "Video Games 'Can Alter Children's Brains.'" *Telegraph.* October 14, 2011. https://www.telegraph.co.uk/news/health/children/8825655/Video-games-can-alter-childrens-brains.html.

Colorado Trust. "Safe2tell Hotline." https://www.coloradotrust.org/strategy/safe2tell.

Colvard, Karen. "Crime Is Down? Don't Confuse Us with the Facts." *Crimes of Violence* 2 (Fall 1997). http://www.hfg.org/hfg_review/2/colvard-2.htm.

Commercial Alert. "Shaping the Mind: Searching for the Why of Buy." http://www.commercialalert.org.

Commonwealth Fund. "2013 Commonwealth Fund Health Policy Survey." November 13, 2013.

Connors, Diane. "Interview: Michael Gazzaniga." *Omni: Special Issue—Science and the Soul* (October 1993).

Cook, Donald E., Clarence Kestenbaum, L. Michael Honiker, and E. Ratcliffe Anderson Jr., *Joint Statement on the Impact of Entertainment Violence on Children Congressional Public Health Summit.* July 26, 2000. https://iianthropology.org/psychology_childrenviolence.html.

Coordinating Council on Juvenile Justice and Delinquency Prevention. *Combating Violence and Delinquency: The National Juvenile Justice Action Plan.* Washington, DC: US Department of Justice, 1996.

Cooper, Anderson. *Anderson Cooper 360 Degrees*, "Bullying: No Escape." Aired October 10, 2010, on CNN.

Cornell, Dewey G. "Psychology of the School Shootings: Testimony presented at the House Judiciary Committee Oversight Hearing to Examine Youth Culture and Violence." US House Judiciary Committee, May 13, 1999.

———. "School Violence Myths." Curry School of Education and Human Development. University of Virginia. Updated July 26, 2015. https://curry.virginia.edu/faculty-research/centers-labs-projects/research-labs/youth-violence-project/violence-schools-and-5.

"Corporate Profits: Breaking Records." *The Economist.* February 10, 2005.

Corrick, James A. *The Human Brain: Mind and Matter.* New York: Arco Publishing, 1983.

Council on Crime in America. *Preventing Crime, Saving Children: Monitoring, Mentoring, and Ministering.* New York: Center for Civic Innovation of the Manhattan Institute, 2001.

———. *Preventing Crime, Saving Children: Monitoring, Mentoring and Ministering.* New York: Center for Criminal Justice Innovation at the Manhattan Institute, 1997.

———. *The State of Violent Crime.* Collingdale, PA: Diane, 1996.

Cowley, Geoffrey, "The Roots of Good and Evil." *Newsweek.* February 26, 1996.

Council on Communications and Media. "Impact of Music, Music Lyrics and Music Videos on Children and Youth." *Pediatrics* 124, no. 5 (November 2007). doi.org/10.1542/peds.2009–2145.

Crawford, Donna K., and Richard J. Bodine. "Conflict Resolution Education: Preparing Youth for the Future." *Juvenile Justice: School Violence; An Overview* 8, no. 1 (2001): 21–29.

Crick, N., and K. A. Dodge. "A Review and Reformulation of Social Information–Processing Mechanisms in Children's Social Adjustment." *Psychological Bulletin* 115 (1994): 74–101.

CSN National Injury and Violence Prevention Resource Center. *Do You Know These Facts about Violence?* Newton, MA: Education Development Center, 1997.

Cullen, Dave. *Columbine.* New York: Twelve, 2010.

Cullen, Francis T., Gray Cavender, William J. Maakestad, and Michael L. Benson. *Corporate Crime under Attack: The Fight to Criminalize Business Violence.* Cincinnati, OH: Anderson, 2006.

Dabbs, James M. Jr., Frank J. Bernieri, Rebecca K. Strong, Rebecca Campo, and Rhonda Milan. "Going on Stage: Testosterone in Greetings and Meetings." *Journal on Research in Personality* 35 (2001): 27–40.

Daily Mail reporter. "Jailed for Life: 'Sadist' Who Murdered 15-Month-Old Toddler Because Her Crying Interrupted Him Playing on His X-Box." *Daily Mail.* April 13, 2010.

Dalai Lama. *The Path to Tranquility: Daily Wisdom.* Edited by Renuka Singh. New York: Penguin, 2002.

Daly, Michael. "Adam Lanza: Newtown Massacre Suspect a Puzzle to Authorities." *Daily Beast.* December 17, 2012.

D'Anastasio, Cecilia. "Experts Have a New Reason to Debate Whether 'Gaming Disorder' is Real." December 27, 2017. https://kataku.com/experts.

Darwin, Charles. *On the Origin of Species by Means of Natural Selection.* New York: Pantheon, 1977.

Davidson, Richard J., David .C. Jackson, and Nancy.H. Kalin. "Emotion, Plasticity, Context and Regulation: Perspectives for Neuroscience." *Psychological Bulletin* 126 (2000): 890–909.

Deats, Richard. "The Culture of Violence." *Fellowship.* Fellowship of Reconciliation. http://www.forusa.org.

Decker, Scott. "Increasing School Safety through Juvenile Accountability Programs." *Juvenile Accountability Incentive Block Grants Program Bulletin.* Washington, DC: US Department of Justice, 2000.

Dees-Thomases, Donna. *Looking for a Few Good Moms.* Emmaus, PA: Rodale Press, 2004.

DeJong, William. "Preventing Interpersonal Violence among Youth: An Introduction to School,

Community, and Mass Media Strategies." *Issues and Practices in Criminal Justice*. Washington, DC: US Department of Justice, 1994.

———. "Building the Peace: The Resolving Conflict Creatively Program (RCCP)." *National Institute of Justice Program Focus*. Washington, DC: US Department of Justice, 1995.

Denby, David. *Snark: A Polemic in Seven Fits*. New York: Simon and Schuster, 2010.

DeParle, Jason. "Hunger in United States at 14-Year High." *New York Times*. November 16, 2009.

DeVaney, Ann. "Reading the Ads: The Bacchanalian Adolescence." *The State of Media Education*. Albuquerque: New Mexico Media Literacy Project, 1995.

DeVoe, Jill, Katharin Peter, Margaret Noonan, Thomas Snyder, and Katrina Baum. *Indicators of School Crime and Safety: 2005*. Washington, DC: Bureau of Justice Statistics and National Center for Education Statistics, 2005. https://nces.ed.gov/pubs2006/2006001.pdf.

Dietrich, David. "Worlds of Whiteness: Race and Character Creation in Online Games." *Social Exclusion, Power, and Video Game Play: New Research in Digital Media and Technology*. Edited by David G. Embrick, J. Talmadge Wright, and Andrus Lukacs, 107–12. Lanham, MD: Lexington Books, 2012.

Dill, Karen E., Brian P. Brown, and Michael A. Collins. "Effects of Exposure to Sex Stereotyped Video Game Characters." *Journal of Experimental Social Psychology* 44, no. 5 (2008): 1402–8.

Dinkes, Rachel, Jana Kemp, Katrina Baum, and Thomas D. Snyder. *Indicators of School Crime and Safety: 2009*. Washington, DC: Bureau of Justice Statistics and National Center for Education Statistics, 2009. https://nces.ed.gov/pubs2010/2010012.pdf.

The Disaster Center. "United States Crime Rates 1960–2018." www.disastercenter.com/crime/uscrime.htm.

Doctors Against Handgun Injury. *Our Position*. New York: DAHI, 2006.

Domhoff, G. William. *The Power Elite and the State: How Policy is Made in America*. Berlin: Aldine deGruyter, 1990.

Dominick, Joseph R. "Videogames, Television Violence and Aggression in Teenagers." *Journal of Communication* 34, no. 2 (1984): 136–47.

Doob, Nick, and Chris Hegedus, dirs. *Al Frankel: God Spoke*. 2006. Balcony Releasing. DVD.

Dooley, Roger. "Focus on NeuroFocus: Interview with A. K. Pradeep." *Neuromarketing*. www.neuromarketing.com.

———. *Brainfluence: 100 Ways to Persuade and Convince Consumers with Neuromarketing*. Hoboken, NJ: Wiley-Blackwell, 2011.

Dowdall, George W. *College Drinking*. Santa Barbara, CA: Praeger, 2008.

Draper, Kevin. "Video Games Aren't Why Shootings Happen: Politicians Still Blame Them." *New York Times*. August 5, 2019.

Dufty, William. *Sugar Blues*. New York: Grand Central, 1986.

Duwe, Grant. *A History: Mass Murder in the United States*. Jefferson, NC: McFarland, 2007.

Eagleman, David. "The Brain on Trial." *The Atlantic*. July/August 2011.

Education Development Center. *Taking Action to Prevent Adolescent Violence: Educational Resources for Schools and Community Organizations*. Washington, DC: United States Department of Health and Human Services, 1996.

———. *Options: Adolescent Violence Prevention Resource Center*. Washington, DC: US Department of Health and Human Services, 1996.

Edwards, Betty. *Drawing on the Right Side of the Brain*. New York: St. Martin's, 1979.

Edwards, Carolyn, Lella Gandini, and George Forman. *The Hundred Languages of Children: The Reggio Emilia Approach*. New York: Ablex, 1998.

Egan, Timothy. "Where Rampages Begin: A Special Report; From Adolescent Angst to Shooting Up Schools." *New York Times*. June 14, 1998.

Ehrenreich, Barbara. *Blood Rites: Origin, History and the Passions of War*. New York: Henry Holt, 1998.

Eller, John. "The School Environment, School Rampage Killings, and Other Forms of School Violence." *School Rampage Shootings and Other Youth Disturbances*. Edited by Kathleen Nader. New York: Routledge, 2012.

Elliott, Delbert S. *Safe Communities—Safe Schools: Some Emerging Lessons and Recommendations*. Boulder: Center for the Study and Prevention of Violence, University of Colorado, 2000.

Elliott, Delbert S., Beatrix A. Hamburg, and Kirk R. Williams. *Violence in American Schools: A New Perspective*. Cambridge, UK: Cambridge University Press, 1998.

Elmer, Vickie. "Games People Play." *New York Times*. November 16, 2014.

Embrick, David G., J. Talmadge Wright, and Andrus Lukacs, eds. *Social Exclusion, Power, and Video Game Play: New Research in Digital Media and Technology*. Lanham, MD: Lexington Books, 2012.

Emery, Fred, and Merrelyn Emery. *A Choice of Futures: To Enlighten or Inform*. Leiden, Netherlands: Martinus Nijhoff Social Sciences Division, 1976.

Erkenberg, Elizabeth. "Discursive Engagements in World of Warcraft: A Semiotic Analysis of Player Relationships." *Social Exclusion, Power, and Video Game Play: New Research in Digital Media and Technology*. Edited by David G. Embrick, J. Talmadge Wright, and Andrus Lukacs. Lanham, MD: Lexington Books, 2012, 13–165.

Ericson, Nels. "Addressing the Problem of Juvenile Bullying." *OJJDP Fact Sheet* 17. Washington, DC: US Department of Justice, 2001.

Erwin, Erica. "Unanswered: Why?" *Workplace Violence News*. April 24, 2008. http://workplaceviolencenews.com.

Esbensen, Finn-Aage, Dana Peterson, Terrance J. Taylor, and Adrienne Feng. *Differences in Offending, Victimization and Gang Membership*. Philadelphia: Temple University Press, 2010.

Esbensen, Finn-Aage, Dana Peterson, Terence J. Taylor, Adrienne Feng, D. Wayne Osgood, and Dena C. Carton. "Evaluation and Evolution of the Gang Resistance Education and Training (G.R.E.A.T.) Program. *Journal of School Violence*, 10, no. 1 (2011): 53–70.

EU Kids Online. "A Poll Conducted in February 2013." London School of Economics and Political Science. http://www.lse.ac.uk/media-and-communications/research/research-projects/

eu-kids-online.

Ewing, Stuart. *All Consuming Images: The Politics of Style in Contemporary Culture.* New York: Basic, 1999.

Farrington, D. P. "Implications of Biological Findings for Criminological Research." *The Causes of Crime: New Biological Approaches.* Edited by S. A. Mednick, T. E. Moffitt, and S. A. Stack, 42–64. New York: Cambridge University Press, 1987.

Fast, Jonathon. *Ceremonial Violence: A Psychological Explanation of School Shootings.* Woodstock: Overlook, 2008

Feagin, Joe R., and Clairece Booher Feagin. *Social Problems: A Critical Power-Conflict Perspective.* Upper Saddle River, NJ: Prentice Hall, 1990.

Federal Bureau of Investigation. "Violent Crime Offenses Reported, 1996." *Crime in the United States, 1996.* Uniform Crime Reports. https://ucr.fbi.gov/crime-in-the-u.s/1996.

———. *Crime in the United States, 2016.* Uniform Crime Reports. https://ucr.fbi.gov/crime-in-the-u.s/2016/crime-in-the-u.s.-2016.

Federal Communications Commission, "Before the FCC: 'Revision of Programming Policies for Television Broadcast Stations.'" August 8, 1996.

"Female Gamer Statistics Marketers Must Know." January 9, 2018. Mediakix.com/blog/female-gamers.

Federal Trade Commission. "Marketing Violent Entertainment to Children." September 2000. https://www.ftc.gov/sites/default/files/documents/reports/marketing-violent-entertainment-children/vioreport_0.pdf.

Feingold, Alice. "Gender Differences in Effects of Physical Attractiveness on Romantic Attraction: A Comparison Across Five Research Paradigms." *Journal of Personality and Social Psychology* 59 (1990): 981–92.

Ferguson, Christopher J., Mark Coulson, and Jane Barnett. "Psychological Profiles of School Shooters: Positive Directions and One Big Wrong Turn." *Journal of Police Crisis Negotiations* 11, no. 2 (2011): 141–58.

Ferguson, Christopher J., and Keith W. Beaver, "Natural Born Killers: The Genetics of Extreme Violence." *Aggression and Violent Behavior* 14, no. 5 (2009): 288.

Ferguson, Christopher J. and Adolfo Garza. "Call of Civic Duty Action Games and Civic Behavior in a Large Sample of Youth." *Computers in Human Behavior* 27, no. 2 (2011): 770–75.

Ferrante, Joan. *Sociology: A Global Perspective.* Belmont, CA: Wadsworth, 1995.

Ferris, Robert. "American Kids See About 2 Alcohol Ads Each Day: Rand Study." CNBC. May 20, 2011. https://www.cnbc.com/2016/05/18/american-kids-see-about-3-ads-for-alcohol-each-day-rand-study.html.

Fetler, Mark. "Television Viewing and School Achievement." *Journal of Communication* 34, no. 2 (1984): 104–18.

Fincher, Jack. *The Brain: Mystery of Matter and Mind.* Washington, DC: US News Books, 1981.

Finkelhor, David. *Childhood Victimization: Violence, Crime and Abuse in the Lives of Young People.* New

York: Oxford University Press, 2008.

Finkelhor, David, and Richard Ormrod. "Homicides of Children and Youth." *Juvenile Justice Bulletin*. Washington, DC: US Department of Justice, 2001.

Finkelhor, David, Heather Turner, Richard Ormrod, Sherry Hamby, and Kristen Kracke. "Children's Exposure to Violence: A Comprehensive National Survey." *Juvenile Justice Bulletin*. Washington, DC: US Department of Justice, 2009.

The First Columbine. Aired April 20, 2009, on WeTV.

Fischer, Peter, and Tobias Greitemeyer. "Music and Aggression: The Impact of Sexual-Aggressive Song Lyrics on Aggression-Related Thoughts, Emotions, and Behavior toward the Same and the Opposite Sex." *Personality and Social Psychology Bulletin* (September 2006). doi.org/10.1177/0146167206288670.

Fischio, Tonya. "Mean Girls Start in Preschool, BYU Study Shows." *Brigham Young University News*, May 5, 2005. https://news.byu.edu/news/mean-girls-start-preschool-byu-study-shows.

Fisher, Roger, William Ury, and Bruce Patton. *Getting to Yes: Negotiating Agreement without Giving In*. New York: Penguin, 1991.

Fite, Katherine V. "Television and the Brain." A paper commissioned by Children's Television Workshop. June 15, 1993.

Fleming, Missy, and Kelley Towey, eds. *Educational Forum on Adolescent Health: Youth Bullying*. Chicago: American Medical Association, 2002.

Flynn, James R. *What is Intelligence*? Cambridge, UK: Cambridge University Press, 2007.

Fogg, B. J. *Expert Guide: The Elements of Human Behavior*. Self-pub., 2017.

Follman, Mark, Gaven Arsonsen, and Deanna Pan. "U.S. Mass Shooters: 1982–2019—Data from *Mother Jones' Investigation*." *Mother Jones*. August 4, 2019, 2. https://www.motherjones.com/politics/2012/12/mass-shootings-mother-jones-full-data/.

Foundation Center. "Child Poverty Rate Up Since 2007." *Philanthropic News Digest*. http://foundationcenter.org.

———. "Hunger in United States at 14-Year High." *Philanthropy News Digest*. November 20, 2009. http://foundationcenter.org/pnd/news/story.jhtml?id=274600020.

———. "Fast Food Chains Market Unhealthy Options to Youth, Study Finds." *Philanthropic News Digest*. November 10, 2010. http://foundationcenter.org/pnd/news/story.jhtml?id=314000004.

———. "Focus on Poverty." www.foundationceter.org. December 10, 2010.

Fox, James Alan. "The Impending Crime Wave Can Be Averted." Unpublished paper, Northeastern University, 1996.

———. *Trends in Juvenile Violence: A Report to the United States Attorney General on Current and Future Rates*. Washington, DC: Bureau of Justice Statistics, US Department of Justice, 1996.

Fox, Matthew. *Creation Spirituality: Liberating Gifts for the Peoples of the Earth*. San Francisco, CA: Harper, 1991.

Frank, Barney. "This Week with George Stephanopoulos." ABC. February 1, 2009.

Frankl, Victor. *Man's Search for Meaning*. Cutchogue: Buccaneer, 1946.

Freire, Paolo. *Education for Critical Consciousness*. New York: Continuum, 1990.

———. *Pedagogy of the Oppressed*. New York: Continuum, 1989.

Fuller, Robert W. *Somebodies and Nobodies: Overcoming the Abuse of Rank*. Gabriola Island, BC: New Society, 2004.

Gabbadini, Alessandro, Brad J. Bushman, Paolo Riva, Luca Andrighetto, and Chiara Volpato. "Grand Theft Auto is a 'Sandbox' Game, but There are Weapons, Criminals, Prostitutes in the Sandbox: Response to Ferguson and Donnellan." *Journal of Youth and Adolescence* 46 (2017).

Gabbiadini, A., P. Riva, L. Andrighetto, C. Volpato, and Brad J. Bushman. "Moral Disengagement Moderates the Effect of Violent Video Games on Self-Control, Cheating, and Aggression." *Social Psychological and Personality Science* (2013). http://spp.sagepub.com/conent/early/2013/10/28/1948550613509286.full.pdddf+html.

Gabbadini, Alessandro, and Paolo Riva. "The Lone Gamer: Social Exclusion Predicts Violent Video Game Preferences and Fuels Aggressive Inclinations in Adolescent Players." *Aggressive Behavior* 44, no. 2 (2018): 113–24.

Garry, Eileen M. "A Compendium of Programs That Work for Youth." *OJJDP Fact Sheet*. Washington, DC: US Department of Justice, 1999.

Gastil, Raymond D. "Homicide and a Regional Culture of Violence." *American Sociological Review* 36, no. 3 (1971): 412–27.

Gauthier, Lily-Ann, David Hicks, Daniel Sanfacon, and Leanne Salel. *100 Promising Crime Prevention Programs from across the World*. Washington, DC: International Centre for the Prevention of Crime and the US Department of Justice, 1999.

Gawin, Frank H. "Cocaine Addiction: Psychology and Neurophysiology." *Science* 251, no. 5001 (1991): 1580–86.

Gazzaniga, Michael S. "Organization of the Human Brain." *Science* 245, no. 4921 (1989): 947–52.

Gentile, Douglas A., and Craig A. Anderson. "Violent Video Games: The Effects on Youth, and Public Policy Implications." *Handbook of Children, Culture and Violence*. Edited by N. Dowd, D. G. Singer, and R. F. Wilson. Thousand Oaks, CA: Sage, 2006.

Gentile, Douglas A., Craig A. Anderson, Shintaro Yukawa, Nobuko Ihori, Muniba Saleem, Lim Kam Ming, Akiko Shibuya, Albert K. Liau, Angeline Khoo, Brad J. Bushman, L. Rowell Huesmann, and Akira Sakamoto. "The Effects of Prosocial Video Games on Prosocial Behavior: International Evidence for Correlational, Longitudinal and Experimental Studies." *Personality and Social Psychology Bulletin* 35, no. 6 (June 2009): 752–63.

Gentile, Douglas A., Paul J. Lynch, Jennifer Ruth Linder, and David A. Walsh. "The Effect of Violent Video Game Habits on Adolescent Hostility, Aggressive Behavior, and School Performance" *Journal of Adolescence* 27, no. 1 (February 2004): 6–22.

Gerbner, George, Larry Gross, Mary Morgan, and Nancy Signorelli. *Television's Mean World: Violence Profile*. Philadelphia, PA: Annenberg School of Communications, University of Pennsylvania, 1986.

Gifford, Rob. "U.S. on List of UNICEF's Worst Countries for Kids." National Public Radio. February 14, 2007. http://www.npr.org.

Gilchrist, Michael A., Lisa M. Sevigny, and Mark G. Gilchrist. "Television—What Children See and Learn." *Pediatrics, Developmental and Behavioral Pediatrics*, 2007. http://childdocs.com.

Gillespie, Mark. "School Violence Still a Worry for American Parents." Gallup News Service. September 7, 1999. https://news.gallup.com/poll/3613/school-violence-still-worry-american-parents.aspx.

Gimbutas, Marija. *The Language of the Goddess*. New York: HarperCollins, 1989.

Gitlin, Todd. *Inside Prime Time*. New York: Pantheon, 1983.

Goddard, Richard A. (Associate professor of history and archaeology). In discussion with the author. November 21, 2008 and March 3, 2009.

Gonzales, David. "Gunmakers and a Culture on Trial." *New York Times*. February 3, 1999.

Goodall, Jane. *The Chimpanzees of Gombe: Patterns of Behavior*. Cambridge, MA: Harvard University Press, 1986.

Goodman, Peter S. "Millions of Unemployed Face Year without Jobs." *New York Times*. February 23, 2010.

Gould, Elise, and Jessica Schieder. "Poverty Persists 50 Years after the Poor People's Campaign." Economic Policy Institute. May 17, 2018.

Grabe, Shelly, L. Monique Ward, and Janet Shibley Hyde. "The Role of the Media in Body Image Concerns of Young Women: A Meta-Analysis." *Psychological Bulletin* 134, no. 3 (2008): 460–76. https://doi.org/10.1037/0033-2909.134.3.460.

Grace, Julie, Sylvester Monroe, and Timothy Roche. "Campus Shooters." *Time*. July 6, 1998.

Granic, Isabella, Adam Lobel, and C. M. E. Engels Rutger. "The Benefits of Playing Video Games." *American Psychologist* 69, no. 1 (2014): 1–66.

Graves, Annie. "Diabetes without the Sugar Coating." *Remedies: The Best Nutrition for Health and Renewal* 1, no. 1 (2005).

Grawert, Ames, Matthew Friedman, and James Cullen. "Crime Trends: 1990–2016." *Brennan Center Report*. Brennan Center for Justice. April 18, 2017.

Greenbaum, Stuart. "Kids and Guns: From Playgrounds to Battlegrounds." *Journal of the Office of Juvenile Justice and Delinquency Prevention* 3, no. 2 (1997).

Greene, Judith. "Bailing Out Private Jails." First published in *American Prospect*, September 2001. Cited here in Herivel and Wright, *Prison Nation*, 139.

Greenwald, Robert, Larry V. Hedges, and Richard D. Laine. "The Effects of School Resources on Student Achievement." *Review of Educational Research* 61, no. 3 (1996): 361–96.

Grohol, J. "Expert: 40 Percent of World of Warcraft Players Addicted." *Psych Central*. August 10, 2006. https://psychcentralcom/blog/archives/2006/08/10/expert-40-percent-of-world-of-warcraft-players-addicted/.

Gross, Martin L. *The Psychological Society*. New York: Touchstone, 1978.

Grossman, Dave, and Gloria DeGaetano. *Stop Teaching Our Kids to Kill: A Call to Action Against TV,*

Movie and Video Game Violence. New York: Crown, 1999.

Grossman, Dave. *On Killing: The Psychological Cost of Learning to Kill in War and Society*. Boston: Little, Brown, 1996.

Grossman, Dave. "Teaching Kids to Kill." *Phi Cappa Phi National Forum*, Fall 2000.

Group for the Advancement of Psychiatry. *The Child and Television Drama: The Psychosocial Impact of Cumulative Viewing*. New York: Mental Health Materials Center, 1982.

Grubb, Jeff. "Gaming Lobby Video Game Voters Network Surpasses 500k Members." *Venture Beat*. March 18, 2013. https://venturebeat.com/2013/03/18/vgvn-500k-members/.

Gutmann, Babette. *Trends in the Well-Being of America's Children and Youth*. Washington, DC: US Department of Health and Human Services, Office of the Assistant Secretary for Planning and Evaluation, 2001.

Hajdu, David. "Songs of Aggression." *The Nation*. December 8, 2017. https://www.thenation.com.

Hall, Karen. "For Real Life?: War Toys in the Peace-Loving Household." Syracuse Peace Council. http://www.peacecouncil.net.

Han, Doug Hyun, Yang Soo Kim, Yong Sik Lee, Kyung Joon Min and Perry F. Renshaw. "Changes in Cue-Induced, Prefrontal Cortex Activity With Video-Game Play." *Cyberpsychological Behavior Social Network* 13, no. 6 (2010): 656–61.

Haninger, Kimberly, and Kevin Thompson. "Violence in E-Rated Video Games." *JAMA* 286 (204): 561.

Hanson, Katherine, and Anne McAuliffe. "Gender and Violence: Implications for Peaceful Schools." *The Fourth R* 52 (1994).

Hasan, Youssef, Laurent Bègue, and Brad J. Bushman. "Viewing the World Though Blood-Red Glasses: The Hostile Expectation Bias Mediates the Link between Violent Video Game Exposure and Aggression." *Journal of Experimental Psychology* 49, no. 4 (July 2012): 953–56.

Hasan, Youssef, Laurent Bègue, Michael Scharkow, and Brad J. Bushman. "The More You Play, the More Aggressive You Become: A Long-Term Experimental Study of Cumulative Violent Video Game Effects on Hostile Expectations and Aggressive Behavior." *Journal of Experimental Social Psychology* 49 (March 2017): 224–27.

"Harper's Index." *Harper's Bazaar*. December 1991.

Harris, S., G. Petrie, and W. Willoughby. "Bullying among 9th Graders: An Exploratory Study." *NASSP Bulletin* 86 (2002): 630.

Harrison, Bennett. *Education, Training and the Urban Ghetto*. Baltimore: Johns Hopkins University Press, 1972.

Hart, Sarah V. "Violence Theory Workshop." National Institute of Justice, 2002.

Harty, Cheyenne Morales. "The Causes and Effects of Get-Tough: A Look at How Tough-on-Crime Policies Rose to the Agenda and an Evaluation of Their Effects on Prison Populations and Crime." Master's thesis, University of Southern Florida, 2012. USF Libraries Scholar Commons (https://scholarcommons.usf.edu/etd/4066).

Hatch, Orrin, and US Senate Committee on the Judiciary. "Children, Violence, and the Media: A Report for Parents and Policy Makers." September 14, 1999. http://judiciary.senate.gov/oldsite/mediavio.htm.

Haugen, David. M., ed. *At Issue: Video Games*. Detroit: Greenhaven Press, 2008.

Hawkins, David J., David P. Farrington, and Richard F. Catalano. "Reducing Violence Through the Schools." *Violence in American Schools: A New Perspective*. Edited by Elliott, Delbert S., Beatrix A. Hamburg, and Kirk R. Williams. Cambridge, UK: Cambridge University Press, 1998.

Hawkins, J. David., Todd. I. Herrenkohl, David P. Farrington, Devon Brewer, Richard F. Catalano, Tracy W. Harachi, and Lynn Cothern. "Predictors of Youth Violence." *Juvenile Justice Bulletin*. Washington, DC: US Department of Justice, 2000.

Healy, James R. "Jazzy New Little Suzuki SX4 SportBack Packs a Nice Punch." *USA Today*. May 21, 2010.

Healy, Jane M. *Endangered Minds: Why Our Children Don't Think*. New York: Simon and Schuster, 1990.

Helliwell, John F., Richard Layard, and Jeffrey D. Sachs, eds. *World Happiness Report 2019*. New York: United Nations Sustainable Development Solutions Network, 2019.

Herival, Tara, and Paul Wright. *Prison Nation: The Warehousing of America's Poor*. New York: Routledge, 2003.

Herman, Edward S., and Noam Chomsky. *Manufacturing Consent: The Political Economy of the Mass Media*. New York: Pantheon, 1988.

Herz, J. C. *Joystick Nation: How Videogames Ate Our Quarters, Won Our Hearts, and Rewired Our Minds*. New York: Little, Brown, 1997.

Hilkirk, John. "It's Time to Put a Hold on the Pentagon's Blank Check." *USA Today*. May 21, 2010.

Hill, Catherine. "Crossing the Line: Sexual Harassment at School." American Association of University Women, 2011.

Hills, Stuart L., ed. *Corporate Violence: Injury and Death for Profit*. New York: Rowman and Littlefield, 1987.

Hindman, Jarrod. *Child and Adolescent Violence in Colorado: A 2005 Status Report*. Denver: Colorado Department of Public Health and Environment, 2005.

Hirschfield, Paul. "School Surveillance in America: Disparate and Unequal." *Schools under Surveillance: Cultures of Control in Public Education*. Edited by T. Monahan and R. D. Torres. New Brunswick, NJ: Rutgers University Press, 2010.

Hobbs, Tawnell D., and Leslie Brody. "Some Teachers Are Already Armed." *The Wall Street Journal*. February 23, 2018.

Hodder, Ian. "A Journey to 9,000 Years Ago." *Turkish Daily News*. January 17, 2008.

Holstrum, Amanda. "The Effects of the Media on Body Image: A Meta-Analysis." *Journal of Broadcasting and Electronic Media* 48, no. 2 (June 2004): 196–217.

Hopf, Werner H., Günter L. Huber, and Rudolf H. Weiss. "Media Violence and Youth Violence: A 2-Year Longitudinal Study." *Journal of Media Psychology: Theories, Methods and Applications* 20, no. 3 (2008): 79–96.

Hopp, Toby, Scott Parrott, and Yuan Wang. "Use of Military-Themed First-Person Shooter Games and

Militarism: An Investigation of Two Potential Facilitating Mechanisms." *Computers in Human Behavior* 78 (2018): 192–99.

Horn, Patricia. "Caging America: The U.S. Imprisonment Binge." *Dollars and Sense*. September 1991.

Horney, Karen. *Neurosis and Human Growth*. New York: Norton, 1991.

Horton, Robert, and Egin Wohl. "Para-Social Interaction." *Journal of the American Medical Association* 201, no. 14 (1958).

Howell, John C., ed. *Guide for Implementing the Comprehensive Strategy for Serious, Violent, and Chronic Juvenile Offenders*. Washington, DC: Office of Juvenile Justice and Delinquency Prevention, 1995.

Hsu, Jeremy. "Video Games Lack Female and Minority Characters." *Live Science*. August 3, 2009.

Huesmann, Lawrence. "Psychological Processes Promoting the Relation Between Exposure to Media Violence and Aggressive Behavior by the Viewer. *Journal of Social Issues* 42 (1986): 125–40.

Huesmann, L. Rowell. "Nailing the Coffin Shut on Debates That Violent Video Games Stimulate Aggression: Comment on Anderson et al." *Psychological Bulletin* 136, no. 2 (February 2010): 179–81.

Huesmann, L. Rowell, Jessica Moise, Cheryl Lynn Podolski, and Leonard E. Eron. "Longitudinal Relations Between Children's Exposure to TV Violence and Their Aggressive and Violent Behavior in Young Adulthood: 1977–1992." *Developmental Psychology* 39, no. 2 (2003): 201–21.

Hummer, Tom, Yang Wang, Wilbur G. Kronenberger, Kristine M. Masier, Andrew J. Kalnin, David W. Dunn, and Vincent P. Matthews. "Short-Term Violent Video Game Play by Adolescent Alters Prefrontal Activity during Cognitive Inhibition." Media Psychololgy 13, no. 2 (May 2010): 136–54.

Hummer, Tom, William Kronenberger, Kristine Mosler, and Vincent P. Matthews. "Violent Video Games Alter Brain Function in Young Men." *Radiological Society of North America*. November 28, 2011. http://www.rsna.org.

Humphrey, Peter J. *Mass Media and Media Policy in Western Europe*. New York: St. Martin's, 1996.

Huxley, Aldous. *Brave New World*. New York: Harper Perennial Modern Classics, 1998.

"Interview with George Lucas." *Daily Show with Jon Stewart*. Aired January 5, 2010, on Comedy Central.

Illich, Ivan. *Deschooling Society*. London: Harrow Books, 1971.

Ingersoll, Sarah. "The National Juvenile Justice Action Plan: A Comprehensive Response to a Critical Challenge." *Juvenile Justice* 3, no. 2 (September 1997).

International Safe Schools. "International Safe Schools: A Project in Collaboration with the World Health Organization Collaborating Centre on Community Safety Practices," 2002.

Irwin, Mary Jane. "Classic Rock Rising—Thanks to Video Games." NBC News. March 11, 2008. http://www.nbcnews.com/.

Israel, Barbara, dir. *Beauty Mark: Body Imaging and the Race for Perfection*. 2009. Media Education Foundation. DVD.

Isanski, Jackub, and Mateusz Leskowicz. "'Keeping Up With the Jonseses': A Sociological Content Analysis of Advertising Catalogues with the Eye-Tracking Method." *Qualitative Sociology Review* 7, no. 2 (August 2011).

Jackson, Kevin. "Senators, Pro-Family Activists Rally against 'Disturbing' TV Trends." *Christian Post.* June 27, 2007.

Jansz, Jereen. "The Emotional Appeal of Violent Video Games for Adolescent Males." *Communications Theory* 15, no. 3 (2006): 218–41.

Jhally, Sut. *The Date Rape Backlash: Media and the Denial of Rape.* 2006. Media Education Foundation. DVD.

———. *Dreamworlds: Desire, Sex and Power in Music Videos.* Media Education Foundation, 1997; 2007. DVD.

Jimerson, Shane R., Susan M. Swearer, and Dorothy L. Espelage, eds. *Handbook of Bullying in Schools: An International Perspective.* New York: Routledge, 2010.

Johnson, Chalmers. "We Have the Money If Only We Didn't Waste It on the Defense Budget." Tom Dispatch. September 29, 2008. http://www.TomDispatch.com.

Jonson, Cheryl Lero. "Preventing School Shootings: The Effectiveness of Security Measures." *Victims and Offenders* 12, no. 6 (2017): 956–73.

Jolly, David. "Credit Agency Warns U.S. and Others of Risk to Top Rating." *New York Times.* March 15, 2010.

Jones, Seth G., and Martin C. Libicki. *How Terrorist Groups End: Lessons for Countering al Qa'ida.* Arlington, VA: RAND, 2008.

Jones, Tim, Peggy A. Cunningham, and Kathrine Gallagher. "Violence in Advertising: A Multilayered Content Analysis." *Journal of Advertising* 39, no. 4 (November 2010): 11–36.

Kachur, Steven P., G. M. Stennies, K. E. Powell, W. Modzeleski, R. Stephens, R. Murphy, M. Kresnow, D. Sleet, R. Lowry. "School-Associated Violent Deaths in the United States, 1992–1994. *Journal of the American Medical Association* 275, no. 22 (June 1996): 1729–33.

Kaestle, Christin C., Carolyn T. Halpern, and Jane D. Brown. "Music Videos, Pro Wrestling, and Acceptance of Date Rape among Middle School Male and Female Students." *Adolescent Health* 40 (2007): 81–83.

Kahn, Chris. "Documents Tell of Shootings." *Denver Post.* August 7, 2006.

Kaku, Michio. *Visions of the Future: The Computer Revolution.* Episode "Tele-Immersion." Aired January 4, 2009, on Science Channel.

Kalish, Rachel, and Michael Kimmel. "Suicide by Mass Murder: Masculinity, Aggrieved Entitlement, and Rampage School Shootings." *Health Sociology Review* 19, no. 4 (December 2010): 451–64.

Kann, Laura, Tim McManus, William A. Harris, et al. "Youth Risk Surveillance—United States, 2017." *Morbidity and Mortality Weekly Report Surveillance Summaries* 67, no. 8 (2018).

Kaufman, Phillip, Xianglei Chen, Susan P. Choy, Kathryn A. Chandler, Christopher D. Chapman, Michael R. Rand, and Cheryl Ringel. *Indicators of School Crime and Safety, 1998.* Washington, DC: National Center for Education Statistics and Bureau of Justice Statistics, 1998.

Kaufman, Phillip, Xianglei Chen, Susan P. Chou, Sally A. Ruddy, Amanda K. Miller, Jill K. Fleury, Kathryn A. Chandler, Michael R. Rand, Patsy Klaus, and Michael G. Planty. *Indicators of School Crime and*

Safety, 2000. Washington, DC: US Department of Education and US Department of Justice, 2000. https://nces.ed.gov/pubs2001/2001017a.pdf.

Kegan, Paul. "Quake." *Mother Jones*. November/December 1999.

Kelley, Barbara Tatem, David Huizinga, Terence P. Thornberry, and Rolf Loeber. "Epidemiology of Serious Violence." *Juvenile Justice Bulletin*. Washington, DC: US Department of Justice, 1997.

Kenney, Dennis. "Crime in the Schools: A Problem-Solving Approach." *National Institute of Justice Research Preview*. Washington DC: National Institute of Justice, US Department of Justice, 1998.

Kent, Steven. *The Ultimate History of Video Games*. Roseville, CA: Prima, 2001.

Kernis, M. H., ed. *Efficacy, Agency and Self-Esteem*. New York: Plenum, 1995.

Kiefer, Heather M. "Public: Society Powerless to Stop School Shootings: Three-Fourths Say School Shootings Likely to Happen in Their Communities." *Gallup News*. April 5, 2005.

Kilbourne, Jean. "Still Killing Us Softly: Advertising and the Obsession with Thinness." *Feminist Perspectives on Eating Disorders*. Edited by P. Fallon, M. A. Katzman, S. C. Wooley, 395–418. New York: Guilford, 1994.

King, Brent. (Psychology Department, Adams State College). In discussion with the author, Alamosa, CO. November 4, 2008.

King, John. "Violent Crime Rising at US Schools." CNN. April 12, 1998. http://www.cnn.com.

King, Marianna. "A Neuropsychological Assessment of Television Viewing." Master's thesis, University of California, 1983.

Klare, Michael T. "The Two-War Strategy." *The Nation*. October 4, 1993.

Klein, Naomi. *No Logo: Taking Aim at the Brand Bullies*. New York: Knopf Canada. 1999.

Kline, Stephen. "Media Consumption as a Health and Safety Risk Factor." Simon Fraser University, Media Analysis Lab, 2003.

Knoll, James L. "Pseudo-Commandos Mass Murder: Part I. The Psychology of Revenge and Obliteration." *Journal of the American Academy of Psychiatry and the Law*. 38, no. 1 (March 2010): 87–94.

Konijn, Elly, Marie Nije Bijvank, and Brad J. Bushman. "I Wish I Were a Warrior: The Role of Wishful Identification in the Effects of Violent Video Games on Aggression in Adolescent Boys." *Developmental Psychology* 43 (2007): 1038–44.

Kohn, Alfie. "Unconditional Teaching." *Educational Leadership* 63, no. 1 (2005): 20–24.

Krantzler, Dave. "The Fed is Running Out of Bullets." *The Daily Coin,* June 19, 2019.

Kronenberger, William G., Vincent P. Matthews, David W. Dunn, Yang Wang, Elisabeth A. Wood, Ann L. Giauque, Joelle J. Larsen, Mary E. Rembusch, Mark J. Lowe, and Tie-Quiang Li. "Media Violence Exposure and Executive Functioning in Aggressive and Control Adolescents." *Journal of Clinical Psychology* 61, no. 6 (2005): 725–37.

Krugman, Harold D. "Brainwave Measures of Media Involvement." *Journal of Advertising Research* 11 (1971): 3–9.

———. "The Impact of Television Advertising: Learning without Involvement." *Public Opinion*

Quarterly 29 (1965): 349–56.

Kumpfer, Karol L. *Strengthening America's Families: Promising Parenting Strategies for Delinquency Prevention; User's Guide*. Washington, DC: Office of Juvenile Justice and Delinquency Prevention, US Department of Justice, 1993.

Kumpfer, Karol L., and Rose Alvarado. "Effective Family Strengthening Interventions." *Juvenile Justice Bulletin*. Washington DC: US Department of Justice, 1998.

Kumpfer, Karol L., and Connie M. Tait. "Family Skills Training for Parents." *Juvenile Justice Bulletin*. Washignton, DC: US Department of Justice, 2002.

LaBahn, Jeri. "Education and Parental Involvement in Secondary Schools: Problems, Solutions and Effects." *Educational Psychology Interactive*. Valdosta, GA: Valdosta State University, 1995. http://www.edpsycinteractive.org/files/parinvol.html.

Lacayo, Richard, and Barbara Maddux. "Still Under the Gun." *Time Magazine*, July 6, 1998.

Lafsky, Melissa. "Economic Crises (Like This One) Lead to Higher Murder and Suicide Rates." *Discover Magazine*, November 16, 2009.

Lam, Katherine. "Florida School Shooting Suspect Nikolas Cruz' Cryptic Love Letters from Jail to UK Woman Revealed." Fox News. April 9, 2018. https://www.foxnews.com/.

Langan, Patrick A., and David P. Farrington. "Crime and Justice in the United States and in England and Wales, 1981–1996." *Bureau of Justice Statistics Executive Summary*. Washington DC: US Department of Justice, 1997.

Langman, Peter. *Why Kids Kill: Inside the Minds of School Shooters*. New York: St. Martin's, 2009.

Langstaff, John, and Tish Sleeper. "The National Center on Child Fatality Review." *OJJDP Fact Sheet*. Washington, DC: US Department of Justice, 2001.

Lankford, Adam. "Are America's Public Mass Shooters Unique? A Comparative Analysis of Offenders in the United States and Other Countries." *International Journal of Comparative and Applied Criminal Justice* 40, no. 2 (October 2015).

———. "Mass Shootings in the U.S.: 1966–2010." *Justice Quarterly* 32, no. 2 (2015): 360–79.

———. "Mass Shooters and Firearms: A Comprehensive National Study of 171 Countries." *Violence and Victims* 31, no. 2 (2016): 187–99.

———. "Public Mass Shooters and Firearms: A Cross-National Study of 171 Countries." *Violence and Victims* 31, no. 2 (2015). doi:10.1891/0886-6708.VV-D-15-00093.

Larsen, Roy E., prod. *March of Time* newsreel. "The Youth Problem." Released 1942.

Leacock, Eleanor. *Myths of Male Dominance*. New York: Monthly Review, 1981.

Leakey, Richard E., and Roger Lewin. *People of the Lake*. New York: Anchor Press, 1978.

Leary, Mark R., Robin M. Kowalski, Laura Smith, and Stephen Phillips. "Teasing, Rejection, and Violence: Case Studies of the School Shootings." *Aggressive Behavior* 29, no. 3 (2003): 202–14.

Leitman, Robert, and Katherine Binns. *The Metropolitan Life Survey of the American Teacher: Violence in America's Public Schools*. New York: Metropolitan Life Insurance, 1993.

Lenhart, Amanda, Joseph Kahne, Ellen Middaugh, Alexandra Rankin MacGill, Chris Evans, and

Jessica Vitak. "Teens, Video Games, and Civics: Teens' Gaming Experiences are Diverse and Include Significant Social Interaction and Civic Engagement." Pew Internet and American Life Project, September 16, 2008. https://www.pewresearch.org/internet/2008/09/16/teens-video-games-and-civics/.

Leo, John. "Madison Avenue Corrupting Society." Associated Press. May 6, 1996.

———. "Modern Ads Thrive on Porn, Aggression." Associated Press. April 2, 1996.

Lerner, Gerda. *The Creation of Patriarchy*. New York: Oxford, 1986.

Levenson, Robert W., Karl Heider, Paul Ekman, and Wallace V. Friesen. "Emotion and Autonomic Nervous System Activity in the Minankabau of West Sumatra." *Journal of Personality and Social Psychology* 62, no. 6, (1992): 972–88.

Levin, Diane, and Carol Copple. *Remote Control Childhood? Combating the Hazards of Media Culture*. Washington, DC: National Association for the Education of Young Children, 1998.

Lewin, Kurt. *Principles of Topological Psychology*. New York: McGraw-Hill, 1936.

Li, Qing. "Cyberbullying in Schools: A Research of Gender Differences." *School Psychology International* 27, no. 2 (May 2006): 157–70.

Lichenstein, Alexander C., and Michael A. Kroll. "The Fortress Economy: The Economic Role of the U.S. Prison System." *Criminal Injustice: Confronting the Prison Crisis*. Edited by Elihu Rosenblatt. New York: South End, 1996.

"Life in the Digital Age." Aired February 2, 2010, on Science Channel.

Limber, Susan P. "Addressing Youth Bullying Behaviors." *Educational Forum on Adolescent Health: Youth Bullying*. Edited by Missy Fleming and Kelley Towey. Chicago: American Medical Association, 2002.

Limber, Susan P., and Maury M. Nation. "Bullying among Children and Youth." *Juvenile Justice Bulletin*. Washington, DC: US Department of Justice, 1998.

Lineberry, Timothy W., and Stephen S. O'Connor. "Suicide in the U.S. and the U.S. Army." *Mayo Clinic Proceedings* 87, no. 9 (September 2012).

Long, Seth. "Raise the Vote for Peace!" *Peace Action Blog*. December 25, 2007.

Lorenz, Konrad. *On Aggression*. New York: Harcourt, Brace and World, 1966.

Lowe, Carl. "The Blood Sugar Blues." *Energy Times*. July/August 2003.

Luckenbill, David F., and Daniel Doyle. "Structural Position and Violence: Developing a Cultural Explanation." *Criminology* 27 (1989): 419–36.

Lungren, Daniel E. *Violence Prevention: A Vision of Hope*. Crime and Violence Prevention Center, 1995.

Lynch, Teresa, Jessica E. Tompkins, Irene I. Van Driel, and Niki Fritz. "Sexy, Strong and Secondary: A Content Analysis of Female Characters in Video Games across 31 Years." *Journal of Communication* 66, no. 4 (June 2016): 564–84.

Macleod, Marlee. "Charles Whitman: The Texas Tower Sniper." *Crime Library*. TruTV. http://www.trutv.com.

Madfis, Eric. "Triple Entitlement and Homicidal Anger: An Exploration of Intersectional Identifies of

American Mass Murderers." *Men and Masculinities* (March 24, 2014): 67–86.

Maguire, Kathleen, and Ann L. Pastore. *Sourcebook of Criminal Justice, 1995*. Washington, DC: US Department of Justice, 1996.

———. *Sourcebook of Criminal Justice Statistics, 2000*. Washington, DC: US Department of Justice, Bureau of Justice Statistics, 2001.

Marshall, S. L. A. *Men Against Fire: The Problem of Battle Command*. New York: William Morrow, 1947.

Martin, Paul Kawika. "InSane." *Peace Action Peace Blog*. February 18, 2010. http://peaceblog.wordpress.com.

Martinez, Edecio. "Game Over for Teen Who Killed Mother Over Video Game." CBS News, June 17, 2009. https://www.cbsnews.com/news/game-over-for-teen-who-killed-mother-over-video-game/.

Maslow, Abraham. "A Theory of Human Motivation." *Psychological Review* 50 (1943): 370–96.

Masons, Pinsent. "Europe to Ban Sales of Violent Video Games to Kids." *Out-Law News*, January 18, 2007.

Masters, Roger D. "Acetylcholines, Toxins and Human Behavior," *Journal of Clinical Toxicology*. doi 10.4172/2161-0495.S6-004.

Marx, Karl. *Selected Writings on Society and Social Philosophy*. Edited by Thomas Bottoms. London: McGraw-Hill, 1964.

Mazur, Anthony A., and Andrew Booth. "Testosterone and Dominance in Men." *Behavioral and Brain Sciences* 21 (1998): 353–63.

McCannon, Robert. "New Mexico Media Literacy Project." University of New Mexico.

McCarthy, Colman. "Teaching Peace." *The Nation*. September 19, 2011.

McChesney, Robert. *Corporate Media and the Threat to Democracy*. New York: Seven Stories, 1998.

McCloud, John. "Of Arms and the Boy." *Time Magazine*. July 6, 1998.

McDonald, Lynn, and Heather E. Frey. *Families and Schools Together: Building Relationships*. Washington, DC: US Department of Justice, 1999.

McDonald, Melissa M., Carlos David Navarrette, and Mark Van Vugt. "Evolution and the Psychology of Intergroup Conflict: The Male Warrior Hypothesis." *Philosophical Transactions of the Royal Society B* 367 (March 5, 2012). doi:10.1098/rstb.2011.0301.

McDonough, Siobhan. "U.S. Prisons Grew By 900 a Week." *Pueblo Chieftain*. April 25, 2005.

McElligott, Paul. "V-Chip Is Not the Answer for TV." *Los Angeles Times*. March 18, 1996.

McGee, John P., and Cecile R. de Bernardo. "Classroom Avenger: A Behavioral Profile of School Based Shootings." *Forensic Examiner*. 8, nos. 5/6 (May/June 1999): 16–18.

McNeil-Lehrer Report. "Youth Violence." Aired December 29, 1994, on PBS.

Meacham, Jon. "Guns, Liquor and the Age of Obama." *Newsweek*. May 30, 2009.

Mead, Margaret. *Coming of Age in Samoa*. New York: Morrow, 1929.

Media Awareness Network. "The Business of Media Violence." 2006. http://www.media-awareness.ca.

———. "Government and Industry Responses to Media Violence." 2010. https://web.archive.org/web/20120514085607/http://www.media-awareness.ca:80/english/issues/violence/

govt_industry_responses.cfm.

———. "How Marketers Target Kids." http://www.media-awareness.ca.

———. "Media Education and Media Violence." http://www.media-awareness.ca.

———. "Research on the Effects of Media Violence." http://www.media-awareness.ca.

———. "Television Violence: A Review of the Effects on Children." http://www.media-wareness.ca.

———. "Violence in Media Entertainment." Accessed May 18, 2011. http://www.media-awareness.ca/english/issues/violence/violence_entertainment.cfm.

Media Education Foundation. "Research on the Effects of Media Violence." https://www.mediaed.org.

Mellaart, James. *Catal Huyuk: A Neolithic Town in Anatolia*. New York: Thames and Hudson, 1967.

Merrell, Kenneth W., Barbara A. Gueldner, Scott N. Ross, and D.M. Isava. "How Effective Are School Bullying Intervention Programs? A Meta-Analysis of Intervention Research." *School Psychology Quarterly* 23 (2008), 26–42.

"Metal/Hip Hop Sales in the U.S." *SoundScan*. March 3, 2014. Blabbermouth.com.

Metropolitan Life Insurance. *The Metropolitan Life Survey of the American Teacher: Violence in America's Public Schools*. New York: Metropolitan Life Insurance, 1993.

Mihalic, Sharon, Katherine Irwin, Delbert Elliott, Abigail Fagan, and Diane Hansen. "Blueprints for Violence Prevention." *Juvenile Justice Bulletin*. Washington, DC: U.S, Department of Justice, 2001.

Mihalic, Sharon, Abigail Fagan, Katherine Irwin, Diane Ballard, and Delbert Elliot. "Blueprints for Violence Prevention." *Office of Juvenile Justice and Delinquency Prevention Report*. Washington, DC: US Department of Justice, Office of Justice Programs, 2004.

Miles, D.R., and G. Carey. "Genetic and Environmental Architecture of Human Aggression." *Journal of Personality and Social Psychology* 72, no. 1 (1997): 207–17.

Mills, C. Wright. *The Power Elite*. New York: Oxford University Press, 1956.

———. *Power Politics and People: The Collected Essays of C. Wright Mills*. New York: Ballantine, 1963.

Milgram, Stanley. "Some Conditions of Obedience and Disobedience to Authority." *Human Relations* 18 (1965): 57–76.

———. *Obedience to Authority*. New York: Harper and Row, 1974.

MIT Press. "Game Studies." www.mitpress.mit.edu/category/discussion/e/game-studies?page=5. Accessed January 17, 2016.

Moenning, David D. "Is the Fed out of Bullets?" *The Daily Decision*.

Molgaard, Virginia K., Richard L. Spoth, and Cleve Redmond. "Competency Training: The Strengthening Families Program for Parents and Youth 10–14." *Juvenile Justice Bulletin*. Washington, DC: US Department of Justice, 2000.

Möller, Ingrid, and Barbara Krahe. "Exposure to Violent Video Games and Aggression in German Adolescents: A Longitudinal Analysis." *Aggressive Behavior* 35, no. 1 (January/February 2009): 75–89.

Moore, Mark H. Carol V. Petrie, Anthony A. Braga, and Brendan L. McLaughlin, eds. *Deadly Lessons: Understanding Lethal School Violence*. Washington, DC: National Academies Press, 2003.

Moore, Michael, dir. *Bowling for Columbine*. 2002. Beverley Hills, CA: MGM Home Entertainment, 2003. DVD.

———. *Sicko*. New York: Weinstein, 2007.

Mortenson, Greg. *Three Cups of Tea*. New York: Penguin, 2007.

Moscowitz, Clara. "How to Tell If You Are Addicted to Technology." *Live Science*. https://www.livescience.com.

Mulholland, Thomas. "Training Visual Attention." *Academic Therapy* 10, no. 1 (1974): 5–17.

Mumola, Christopher J. "Substance Abuse and Treatment, State and Federal Prisoners, 1997." *Special Report*. Washington, DC: US Department of Justice, 1999.

Murray, John P. "TV Violence and Children." *Psychiatric Times* 18, no. 10 (2001).

Murray, John P., Mario M. Liotti, Paul T. Ingmundson, Helen S. Mayberg, Yu Pu, and Frank Zamarripa. "Children's Brain Activation While Viewing Televised Violence Research by fMRI" *Media Psychology* 8 (2006): 25–38.

Muscert, Glenn, Stuart Henry, Nicole Bracy, and Anthony A. Peguero, eds. *Responding to School Violence: Confronting the Columbine Effect*. Boulder, CO: Lynne Rienner, 2013.

Musu-Gillette, Lauren, Anlan Zhang, Ke Wang, Zizhi Zhang, and Barbara A. Oudekerk. *Indicators of School Crime and Safety: 2016*. Washington, DC: Bureau of Justice Statistics and National Center for Education Statistics, 2017. https://nces.ed.gov/pubs2017/2017064.pdf.

———. *Indicators of School Crime and Safety: 2018*. Washington, DC: Bureau of Justice Statistics and National Center for Education Statistics, 2019. https://nces.ed.gov/pubs2019/2019047.pdf.

Myers, David G. *The American Paradox: Spiritual Hunger in an Age of Plenty*. New Haven, CT: Yale University Press, 2000.

———. *Exploring Psychology*. New York: Worth, 2007.

Nagy, James, and Thomas Danitz. "Parental Fears Heightened by Columbine, Poll Shows." 2000. http://www.stateline.org/live/ViewPagek.action?siteNodeId=136&languageID=1&contentID=13994.

Nader, Kathleen, ed. *Rampage School Shootings and Other Youth Disturbances: Early Preventative Interventions*. London: Routledge, 2012.

National Association of Child Care Resource and Referral Agencies. "Media is a Powerful Force." *The Daily Parent* 7 (2006): 1–4.

National Association of School Psychologists. http://www.nasponline.org.

National Census of Domestic Violence Services, "Domestic Violence Count." 2008. https://nnedv.org/wp-content/uploads/2020/04/Library_Census_2008_Full_Report.pdf.

National Center for Injury Prevention and Control. "WISQARS Injury Mortality Reports, 1999–2007." http://webappa.cdc.gov.

National Child Care Information and Technical Assistance Center. "Brain Development." US Department of Health and Human Services. http://nccic.acf.hhs.gov/poptopics/brain.html.

National Commission on Excellence in Education. *A Nation at Risk: The Imperative for Educational Reform*. Washington, DC: National Commission on Excellence in Education, 1983.

National Commission on the Causes and Prevention of Violence. *Violence in America: Final Report of the National Commission on the Causes and Prevention of Violence.* New York: Chelsea House, 1983.

National Criminal Justice Research Service. *Corrections.* 2015.

———. *Serving High Risk Youth: Lessons from Research and Programming.* Washington, DC: US Department of Justice, 2009.

National Institute of Diabetes and Digestive and Kidney Diseases Health Information Center. "Overweight and Obesity Statistics." US Department of Health and Human Services. Updated August 2017. http://win.niddk.nih.gov/statistics.

National Institute of Education. *Violent Schools—Safe Schools: The Safe School Study Report to Congress.* Washington, DC: US Government Printing Office, 1978.

National Institute of Justice. *Violence Theory Workshop.* Washington, DC: US Department of Justice, 2002.

National Institute of Justice. "Preventing School Shootings: A Summary of US Secret Service Safe Schools Initiative Report." *National Institute of Justice Journal* 248 (2002): 11–15.

National Institute on Media and the Family. "Brain Development." Media Family. http://www.mediafamily.org/hot-topics/brain_development.shtml.

———. "Raising Media Wise Kids." Media Family. http://www.mediafamily.org/speakers/raising_mediawise_kids.shtml.

National School Safety Center. "NSSC Review of School Safety Research." Washington, DC: US Department of Education, 2006.

Nation of Islam. "About the Million Man March: A Glimpse of Heaven." https://www.noi.org/about-million-man-march.

Neufeld, Sara. "Seeking to Curb School Violence." *Baltimore Sun.* April 10, 2008.

Neumann, Erich. *The Great Mother.* Princeton, NJ: Princeton University Press, 1991.

New Dream. http://www.newdream.org.

Newman, G. *Understanding Violence.* New York: J.B. Lippincott, 1979.

Newman, Graeme R. *Bomb Threats in Schools: Problem-Oriented Guides for Police.* Problem-Specific Guides Series 32. Washington, DC: US Department of Justice, 2005.

Newman, Katherine S. *Rampage: The Social Roots of School Shootings.* New York: Basic Books. 2004.

———. "Roots of a Rampage." *The Nation.* December 19, 2012

New York Times. "NBC News Special." July 1994.

———. "Boy, 12, Found Guilty of Murder in Fire." August 22, 1997.

Nhat Hanh, Thich. *Creating True Peace: Ending Violence in Yourself, Your Family, Your Community, and the World.* New York: Free Press, 2003.

Nightly Business Report. Aired January 6, 2010, on PBS.

No Bullying. "Cyber Bullying Statistics 2014 Facts." February 24, 2014. https://web.archive.org/web/20150102014254/http://nobullying.com/cyber-bullying-statistics-2014/.

Nocera, Joe. "From Pentagon, a Buy Rating on Contractors." *New York Times*. February 11, 2011.

Nonviolence Magazine. http://www.nonviolencemag.org.

Nord, Mark. "Food Insecurity in Households with Children: Prevalence, Severity and Household Characteristics." *Economic Information Bulletin* (September 2009).

Novotney, Laurence C., Elizabeth Mertinko, James Lange, and Tara Kelly Baker. "Juvenile Mentoring Program: A Progress Review." *Juvenile Justice Bulletin*. Washington, DC: US Department of Justice, 2000.

Office of Juvenile Justice and Delinquency Prevention. *Delinquency Prevention Works: Program Summary*. Washington, DC: US Department of Justice, 1995.

———. *Report to Congress on Juvenile Justice Research*. Washington, DC: US Department of Justice, 1999.

Oliphant, J. Baxter. "Women and Men in Both Parties Say Sexual Harassment Allegations Reflect 'Widespread Problem' in Society." *Factank—News in the Numbers*. Pew Research Center. December 7, 2017.

Olsen, Glenda. "Foods." *Energy Times*. July/August 2003.

Olsen, Kirsten. *Wounded by School: Recapturing the Joy in Learning and Standing Up to Old School Culture*. New York: Teachers College Press, 2009.

Olweus, Dan. *Bullying at School*. Boston: Blackwell, 2006.

Olweus, Dan, Susan Limber, and Steven Mihalic. *The Bullying Prevention Program: Blueprints for Violence Prevention*. Boulder, CO: Center for the Study and Prevention of Violence, 1999.

Opplinger, Patrice. *Girls Gone Skank: The Sexualization of Girls in American Culture*. Jefferson, NC: McFarland, 2008.

Orleans, Myron. "Phenomenology." *Encyclopedia of Sociology*. http://hss.fullerton.edu.

Ostrow, Joanne. "Super Bowl XV Brings Out the Best, Worst Ads." *Denver Post*. February 6, 2011.

Pacific Center for Violence Prevention. "Preventing Youth Violence: Reducing Access to Firearms." San Francisco: California Wellness Foundation, 1994.

Padgett, V.R. "Predicting Organizational Violence: An Application of 11 Powerful Principles of Obedience." Paper presented at the American Psychological Association annual meeting, 1989.

Parsa, Cyrus A. *Artificial Intelligence: Dangers to Humanity*. AI Organization, 2019.

Parsons, Charlie, producer. *Meet the Natives: USA*. Aired November 29–December 20, 2009, on Travel Channel.

Paul, Annie Murphy. "Safety First." *Time*. October 11, 2010.

PC Gamer Magazine (US Edition). https://www.pcgamer.com/magazine/.

Perry Preschool Program. "Curriculum." www.highscope.org.

Persky, Susan, and James Blaskovich. "Consequences of Playing Violent Video Games in Immersive Virtual Environments." *Work and Play in Shared Virtual Environments*. Edited by A. Axelson and Ralph Schroder. New York: Springer, 2005.

Pew Charitable Trusts. "Public Safety, Public Spending: Forecasting America's Prison Population

2007–2011." Washington, DC: Public Safety Performance Project, 2005.

Phillips, Tom. "As Console Ban Lifts, China Reveals 'Hostile' Games Block." *Eurogamers,* January 13, 2014.

Piaget, Jean. *The Child's Conception of the World.* London: Routledge, 1929.

Piepenbrink, Linda. "Violent Video Games Teach Anti-Social Behavior." *At Issue: Video Games.* Edited by David M. Haugent. Detroit: Greenhaven Press, 2008.

Plante, Courtney N., Douglas A. Gentile, Christopher T. Gross, Adam Modlin and Jorge Blanco-Herrera. "Video Games as Coping Mechanism in the Etiology of Video Game Addiction." *Psychology of Popular Media Culture* 8, no. 4 (2019): 385–94.

Pollack, Ira, and Carlos Sundermann. "Creating Safe Schools: A Comprehensive Approach." *Juvenile Justice: School Violence; An Overview* 8, no. 1 (2001): 13–20.

Pollard-Sacks, Deana, Brad J. Bushman, and Craig A. Anderson. "Do Violent Video Games Harm Children? Comparing the Scientific Amicus Curiae 'Experts,' in *Brown v. Entertainment Merchants Association. Northwestern University Law Review* 106 (2011).

Population Reference Bureau. *Kids Count Data Book.* Baltimore, MD: Annie E. Casey Foundation, 2008.

Posner, Marc. "Research Raises Troubling Questions about Violence Prevention Programs." *The Fourth R* 52 (August/September 1994).

Potter, Douglas, Joachim Stader, and Roman Teessler. "PKDGRAV 3: Beyond Billion Particle Cosmological Simulations to the Next Generation of Galaxy Simulations." *Computational Astrophysics and Cosmology* 4, no. 11 (2017).

Pozza, Virginia Dalla, Anna Di Pietro, Sophie Morel, and Emma Psaila. "Cyberbullying among Young People." Report for the European Parliament Policy Department C: Citizens' Rights and Constitutional Affairs, 2016.

Postman, Neil, and Steve Powers. *How to Watch TV News.* New York: Penguin, 1992.

Proctor, Bernadette D., Jessica L. Semega, and Melissa A. Kollar. "Income and Poverty in the United States: 2015." US Census Bureau, report no. P60-256. September 13, 2016.

Professional Data Analysts. "Bullying in U.S. Schools: Declaration of Interests." City Center, MN: Hazelden Betty Ford Foundation, 2015.

Prothrow-Smith, Deborah. "Assimilating Prevention Techniques into the Curriculum." *The Fourth R* 52 (August/September 1994).

Purse, Marcia. "An Overview of Suicidal Ideation." *Very Well Mind,* December 2019. https://www.verywellmind.com/suicidal-ideation-38069.

Puzzanchera, Charles. "Juvenile Arrests, 2017." *Juvenile Justice Statistics National Report Series* (Washington, DC: US Department of Justice, Office of Justice Programs, 2019), 1–3.

Quirk, Matthew. "Video Games Can Shape Players' Beliefs," At Issue: Video Games. Edited by David M. Haugen. Detroit, MI: Greenhaven Press, 2008.

Ramsland, Katherine. *Inside the Minds of Mass Murderers: Why They Kill.* Santa Barbara, CA: Praeger, 2005.

———. "School Killers." *Crime Library*. TruTV. https://web.archive.org/web/20090307073643/http://www.trutv.com:80/library/crime/serial_killers/weird/kids1/index_1.html?print=yes.

Randall, Paula. *Art Works! Prevention Programs for Youth and Communities*. Washington, DC: US Department of Health and Human Services, 1997.

Raunch, Jonathan. "Video Games Will Become More Artistically and Emotionally Satisfying." *At Issue: Video Games*. Edited by David M. Haugen. Detroit: Greenhaven, 2002.

Reiss, A. J., and J. A. Roth. *Understanding and Preventing Violence*. Washington, DC: National Academy Press, 1993.

Restak, Richard M. *The Mind*. New York: Bantam, 1988.

Reynolds, Emily. "Universities are Home to a Rape Epidemic." *The Guardian*. March 2, 2018.

Rideout, Victoria J., Elizabeth Vandewater, and Ellen A. Wartella. *Zero to Six: Electronic Media in the Lives of Infants, Toddlers and Preschoolers*. Washington, DC: Henry J. Kaiser Foundation, 2003.

Robers, Simone, Jinjin Zhang, Jennifer Truman, and Thomas D. Snyder. *Indicators of School Crime and Safety: 2010*. Washington, DC: Bureau of Justice Statistics and National Center for Education Statistics, 2010. https://nces.ed.gov/pubs2011/2011002.pdf.

Robers, Simone, Jana Kemp, Amy Rathbun, Rachel E. Morgan, and Thomas D. Snyder. *Indicators of School Crime and Safety: 2013*. Washington, DC: Bureau of Justice Statistics and National Center for Education Statistics, 2009. https://nces.ed.gov/pubs2014/2014042.pdf.

Roberts, Jeff John. "The Big Economy Squeeze on Workers." *Fortune*. January 2019.

Robinson, Matthew, and Daniel Murphy. *Greed is Good: Maximization and Elite Deviance in America*. Lanham, MD: Rowman and Littlefield, 2008.

Robinson, Nick. *Video Games, Popular Culture and World Politics*. London: Routledge, 2015.

Robinson, Thomas N., and Dina L. G. Borzekowski. "Effects of the SMART Classroom Curriculum to Reduce Child and Family Screen Time." *Journal of Communication* 56, no. 1 (February 2006): 1–26.

Rocque, Michael. "Exploring School Rampage Shootings: Research, Theory and Policy." *Social Science Journal* 47, no. 3 (September 2012): 304–13.

Rogers, Carl R. *On Personal Power: Inner Strength and Its Revolutionary Impact*. New York: Delacorte, 1977.

———. "Client-Centered and Symbolic Perspectives on Social Change." *Innovations in Client-Centered Therapy*. Edited by David A. Wexler and Laura N. Rice. New York: John Wiley, 1974.

Rosen, Louis. "Violence Prevention: School's Newest Challenge." *School Safety News Journal* (Spring 1993).

Rosenblatt, Elihu, ed. *Criminal Injustice: Confronting the Prison Crisis*. New York: South End, 1996.

Roth, James A. "Firearms and Violence: Research in Brief." Washington, DC: US Department of Justice, National Institute of Justice, February 1994.

Roth, Robert. "Why Is the United States the Most Homicidal Nation in the World?." National Institute of Justice Research for the Real World Seminar, December 2, 2013.

Rotter, John B. *Social Learning and Clinical Psychology*. Englewood Cliffs, NJ: Prentice-Hall, 1954.

Rubin, Lyle Jeremy. "A Former Marine Explains All the Weapons of War Being Used by Police in Ferguson." *The Nation*. August 20, 2014. http://www.thenation.com.

Ruskin, Gary. "Commercial Alert Asks Senate Commerce Committee to Investigate Neuromarketing." *Commercial Alert*. July 12, 2004.

Ryan, William. *Blaming the Victim*. New York: Vintage, 1976.

Salam, Maya, and Liam Stack. "Do Video Games Lead to Mass Shootings? Researchers Say No." *New York Times*. February 23, 2018.

Salomon, Gabriel, and Tamar Leigh. "Predisposition about Learning from Print and Television." *Journal of Communication* 34, no 2 (1984): 119–35.

Salwen, Michael W., and Michele DePagne. "The Third-Person Effect Perceptions of the Media's Influence and Immoral Consequences Michael." *Communication Research* 26, no. 5 (January 1999): 523–49.

Samples, Faith, and Larry Aber. "Evaluations of School-Based Violence Prevention Programs." *Violence in American Schools: A New Perspective*. Edited by Delbert S. Elliott, Beatrix Hamburg, Kirk R. Williams. Cambridge, UK: Cambridge University Press, 1998.

Sandler, Lauren. "Popular Video Games Are Often Misogynistic." *At Issue: Video Games*. Edited by David M. Haugen. Detroit: Greenhaven, 2008.

Santa Maria, Cara. "The Mind of a Mass Murderer: Charles Whitman, Bain Damage and Violence." *Huffington Post*. March 28, 2012.

Sarason, Irwin G., and Barbara R. Sarason. *Abnormal Psychology: The Problem of Maladaptive Behavior*. Small River, NJ: Prentice-Hall, 2002.

Savidge, Martin. "Accused Oregon School Shooter Shows No Emotion in Court." CNN Interactive. May 22, 1998. Http://www.cnn.com/US/9805/22/oregon.shooting.pm/.

Schaffhausen, Joanna. "The Biological Basis of Aggression." Brain Connection. http://brainconnection.positscience.com/topics/?main=fa/aggression.

Schell, Terry L., and Terri Tanielian, eds. *A Needs Assessment of New York State Veterans: Final Report to the New York State Health Foundation*. New York: Rand Corporation and the New York State Health Foundation, 2011.

Scherer, Michael. "Why Did They Die?" *Time*. November 24, 2016.

Schiller, Gail. "Nielsen Making Brain Waves." *Commercial Alert*. http://www.commercialalert.org/issues/culture/neuromarketing.

Schiller, Herbert I. *Mass Communication and American Empire*. Boston: Beacon, 1971.

Schlosser, Eric. *Fast Food Nation: The Dark Side of the All-American Meal*. New York: Penguin, 2001.

Schneider, Shari Keller, Lydia O'Donnell, Ann Stueve, and Robert W. S. Coulter. "Cyberbullying, School Bullying and Psychological Distress: A Regional Census of High School Students." *American Journal of Public Health* 102, no. 1 (January 2012): 171–77.

Schoen, Cathy, Melinda K. Abrams, and Karen Davis. "The Commonwealth Fund Survey of the Health of

Adolescent Girls." Commonwealth Fund. November 1, 1997.

School of the Americas Watch. "The U.S. Army School of the Americas: An Introduction by the S.O.A. Watch." Washington, DC: S.O.A. Watch, 1993.

"School Shooters." Aired February 7, 2010, on Discovery Channel.

Schrag, Peter. "Bailing Out of Public Education." *The Nation*. October 4, 1993.

Schutz, Alfred. *On Phenomenology and Social Relations.* Edited and with an introduction by Helmut R. Wagner. University of Chicago Press, 1970.

Seawell, Margaret, ed. *National Television Violence Study*. 3 vols. Thousand Oaks, CA: Sage, 1997.

See, Letha A. (Lee), and Nancy Khashan. "Violence in the Suites: The Corporate Paradigm." *Journal of Human Behavior in the Social Environment* 4, no. 2/3 (2001): 61–83.

Seelinger, Lani. "Survivors Are Standing Up to the NRA." *Bustle*. February 19, 2018.

Semega, Jessica, Melissa Kollar, John Creamer, and Abinash Mohanty. "Income and Poverty in the United States: 2018." US Census Bureau, report no. P60–266. September 10, 2019.

Senate Judiciary Committee. "Media Violence Report." September 14, 1999. http://judiciary.senate.gov/oldsite/mediavio.htm.

Serena, Katie. "Brenda Ann Spencer Shot Up a School. Her Reason? 'I Don't Like Mondays.'" February 7, 2018. www.allthatsinteresting.com/brenda-ann-spencer.

Setoodeh, Ramin. "Young, Gay and Murdered." *Newsweek*. July 28, 2008.

Shanker, Thom. "U.S. Is Top Arms Seller to Developing World." *New York Times*. October 1, 2007.

Shapiro, Jeremy. "The Peacemakers Program: Friends Don't Let Friends Fight." *School Safety Update, 1999*. Center for Research, Quality Improvement and Training, 1999.

Shaw, Margaret. "Bullying Is a Growing Concern Internationally." International Center for the Prevention of Crime. October 1, 2002.

Sheppard, David. "Strategies to Reduce Gun Violence." *OJJDP Fact Sheet*. Washington, DC: US Department of Justice, Office of Juvenile Justice and Delinquency Prevention, 1999.

Sherry, John, L. "The Effects of Violent Video Games on Aggression: A Meta-Analysis." *Human Communication Research* 27 (2001).

Shields, Ann, and Dante Cicchetti. "Emotion Regulation Among School-Age Children: The Development and Validation of a New Criterion Q-Sort Scale." *Developmental Psychology* 33, no. 6 (November 1997): 906–16.

Shipman, Pat. "Scavenger Hunt." *Natural History*. April 1984.

Shea, Molly. "John Oliver Breaks Down the Mental Health Excuse for Mass Shootings." *Yahoo!Life* (blog). October 5, 2015. https://www.yahoo.com/health/john-oliver-breaks-down-the-mental-health-excuse.

Shuen, Michael J. "Confronting a Culture of Violence." *People of God* 13, no. 2, (1995).

Shure, Myrna B. "Preventing Violence the Problem-Solving Way." *Juvenile Justice Bulletin*. Washington, DC: US Department of Justice, Office of Juvenile Justice and Delinquency Prevention, 1999.

Siluva, Suyapa, Jonathon Blutstein, Jason Williams, Chris Ringwalt, Linda Dusenbury, and William

Hansen. *Impacts of a Violence Prevention Program for Middle Schools.* Washington, DC: US Department of Education, National Center for Education Evaluation and Regional Assistance, 2010.

Singer, Katie. *An Electronic Silent Spring: Facing the Dangers and Creating Safe Limits.* Great Barrington, MA: Portal. 2014.

Skinner, B. F. *Science and Human Behavior.* New York: Macmillan, 1953.

Slaby, Ronald. (Harvard Center on Media and Child Health). Telephone conversation with the author, April 3, 2007.

Small, Margaret, and Kellie Dressler Tetick. "School Violence: An Overview." *Juvenile Justice.* Washington, DC: Office of Juvenile Justice and Delinquency Prevention, US Department of Justice, 2000.

Smith, Kate. "U.S. Homicide Rate: Female Victims Rose by 21 Percent." *CBS News.* December 6, 2017.

Smith, Peter K., Debra Pepler, and Ken Rigby, eds. *Bullying in School: How Successful Can Interventions Be?* Cambridge, UK: Cambridge University Press, 2004.

Smith, Peer K., and Katerina Ananiadou. "The Nature of School Bullying and the Effectiveness of School-Based Interventions." *Journal of Applied Psychoanalytic Studies* 5 (2003): 189–209.

Smith, Terence. *NewsHour.* "Powerful Influences." Aired May 10, 1999, on PBS.

Smolowe, Jill, and Moira Bailey. "Confessions of a Bully." *People.* October 18, 2010.

Snell, Tracy L. "Capital Punishment 1997." *Bureau of Justice Statistics Bulletin.* Washington, DC: US Department of Justice, Bureau of Justice Statistics, 1998.

———. "Capital Punishment 2000." *Bureau of Justice Statistics Bulletin.* Washington, DC: US Department of Justice, Bureau of Justice Statistics, 2002.

Snyder, Howard N. "Juvenile Arrests 1995." *Juvenile Justice Bulletin.* Washington, DC: US Department of Justice, Office of Juvenile Justice and Delinquency Prevention, 1997.

———. "Juvenile Arrests 1997." *Juvenile Justice Bulletin.* Washington, DC: US Department of Justice, Office of Juvenile Justice and Delinquency Prevention, 1998.

Snyder, Howard H., and Melissa Sickmund. *Juvenile Offenders and Victims: 2006 National Report.* Washington, DC: US Department of Justice, 2006.

Sparrow, Jeff. "Terror and Rage: What Makes a Mass Murderer Different to a Terrorist?." *The Guardian.* August 4, 2016.

Sperry, Robert W. "Lateral Specialization of Cerebral Function in the Surgically Separated Hemispheres." *The Psychophysiology of Thinking.* Edited by F.J. McGuigan. New York: Academic Press, 1973.

Spurlock, Morgan, dir. *Super Size Me.* The Con, 2004.

Stanfield, James. "Little Bullies: Relational Aggression in the Playground." *Specialists in Special Education* (2017).

Stanford University Medical Center. "School Bullying Affects Majority of Elementary Students." *Science Daily.* April 12, 2007.

State of Colorado. *The Report of Governor Bill Owens' Columbine Review Commission*. May 2001.

Stein, Rob. "38% of Adults Use Alternative Medicine." *Washington Post*. December 11, 2008.

Steinberg, Michele. "Programmed to Kill: Video Games, Drugs and 'The New Violence.'" *21st Century* 13, no. 3 (Fall 2000). https://21sci-tech.com/articles/New_violence.html.

Stolberg, Steven. "Fear Clouds Search for Genetic Roots of Violence." *Los Angeles Times*. December 30, 1993.

Stone, Lisa Cacari, and Deborah Boldt. "Closing the Health Disparity Gap." *Newsletter of Con Alma Health Foundation* (May 2006).

Stone, Merlin. *When God Was a Woman*. New York: Harcourt Brace Jovanovich, 1976.

Stone, Michael. *Most Evil*. Aired 2007, on Investigative Discovery.

Stop Bullying Now!. "Bully Busters Training." http://www.stopbullyingnow.com/.

———. "Stop Bullying Now." http://www.stopbullyingnow.com/.

Strassburger, Victor. "Children, Adolescents and the Media." *Current Problems in Pediatric and Adolescent Health Care* 34, no. 2 (February 2004): 54–103.

Straus, M. A., and R. J. Gelles. "Societal Changes in Family Violence from 1975 to 1985 as Revealed by Two National Surveys." *Journal of Marriage and Family* 48 (1986): 465–79.

Suicide Prevention Action Network, U.S.A. "Suicide is a Major Public Health Problem." http://www.spanusa.org.

Suicide Prevention Advocacy Network. "Statistics Information." http://wwww.spanusa.org.

Sutherland, John. "Why Kinect Is the Future of Game Story." *Gamasutra: John Sutherland's Blog*. November 3, 2010. http://www.gamasutra.com/blogs.

Sykes, Charles J. *Dumbing Down Our Kids*. New York: St. Martin's, 1995.

Szilas, Nicholas. "The Future of Interactive Drama," *Proceedings of the Second Australasian Conference on Interactive Entertainment*. Edited by Yusuf Pisan. Sydney: University of Technology, Sydney: 193–99.

Taubes, Gary. "The New Obesity Campaigns Have It All Wrong." *Newsweek*. May 14, 2012.

Taylor, Shelley E. *The Tending Instinct: Women, Men and the Biology of Relationships*. New York: MacMillan, 2003.

Teen Violence Statistics. "Cyber Bullying Statistics." http://www.teenviolencestatistics.com/content/cyber-bullying-statistics.html.

Terdiman, Daniel. "Will Wright on the Origins of 'Spore.'" February 2, 2009. https://www.cnet.com/news/will-wright-on-the-origins-of-spore/.

Terzian, Mary, Katherine Henth, and Thomson Linney. "What Works for Acting-Out (Externalizing) Behavior: Lessons from Experimental Evaluations of Social Interventions." *Fact Sheet*. Washington, DC: Child Trends, 2011.

Thoman, Elizabeth. "Beyond Blame: Media Literacy as Violence Prevention." *Media and Values* 62 (Spring 1993). http://www.medialit.org/reading-room/beyond-blame-media-literacy-violence-prevention.

Thomas, David. "Players Grapple With Killing, Not Killing and Morality." *Denver Post.* July 4, 2006.

Thompson, Charles. "Student Jailed in a Bomb Plot." *Arizona Republic.* April 1, 2005.

Thornberry, Terence P., Carolyn A. Smith, Craig Rivera, David Huizinga, and Magda Stouthamer-Loeber. "Family Disruption and Delinquency." *Juvenile Justice Bulletin.* Washington, DC: US Department of Justice, 1999.

Thornton, Thomas N., Carole A. Craft, Linda L. Dahlberg, Barbara S. Lynch, and Katie Baer, eds. *Best Practices of Youth Violence Prevention: A Sourcebook for Community Action.* Revised ed. Atlanta: Centers for Disease Control and Prevention, 2002.

Thurman, Elizabeth. "Making Connections: Media's Role in Our Culture of Violence." Center for Media Literacy. http://www.medialit.org/reading_room/article379.html.

Tierney, Joseph P., Jean Baldwin Grossman, and Nancy L. Resch. *Making a Difference: An Impact Study of Big Brothers/Big Sisters.* Philadelphia: Public/Private Ventures, 1995.

"Timeline of Worldwide School and Mass Shootings." https://www.infoplease.com/history/world/timeline-of-worldwide-school-and-mass-shootings.

Tolan, Patrick, and Nancy Guerra. *What Works In Reducing Adolescent Violence: An Empirical Review of the Field.* Boulder: The Center for the Study of Violence and Violence Prevention, 1994.

Tonso, Karen L. "Violent Masculinities as Tropes for School Shooters: The Montreal Massacre, the Columbine Attack, and Rethinking Schools." *American Behavioral Scientist* 52, no. 10 (2009): 1266–85.

Toppo, Greg. "10 Years Later, the Real Story Behind Columbine." *USA Today.* April 14, 2009.

Tresniowski, Alex, Nicole Weisensee, Diane Herbst Egan, Charlotte Triggs, Lesley Messer, Joanne Flower, Daniel S. Levy, and Nadine Shabeeb. "Tormented to Death?." *People.* October 18, 2010.

Turner, Jennifer. "Soldiers of Misfortune: Abusive U.S. Military Recruitment and Failure to Protect Child Soldiers." American Civil Liberties Union. http://www.aclu.org/human-rights/soldiers-misfortune-abusive-us-military-recruitment- and-failure-protect-child-soldiers.

Tynan, Dan. "Screen Wars: How to Win the Screen Time Battle without Alienating Your Teens." *Family Circle.* February 2019.

Ubi Soft. "Ubi Soft Licenses Tom Clancy's Rainbow Six Rogue Speak Game Engine to Train U.S. Soldiers." August 29, 2001. https://web.archive.org/web/20081202104141/http://corp.ubisoft.com/pr_release_010829a.htm.

UCLA Center for Communication Policy. *UCLA Television Violence Monitoring Report.* Los Angeles, CA: UCLA, 1995.

UNICEF. *State of the World's Children, 2016: A Fair Chance for Every Child.* 2016. https://www.unicef.org/publications/files/UNICEF_SOWC_2016.pdf.

United Nations. *Population and Vital Statistics Report.* United Nations Statistics Division, 2007.

University of Utah Health Center. Families Therapy Program. http://www.healthcare.Utah.edu/programs. 2020.

US Army National Guard. "Suicide in Young People." *Hooah 4 Health, Hooah 4 Teens.* 2011. https://web.

archive.org/web/20110727204621/www.hooah4health.com/4life/hooah4teens/teensuicide.htm.

US Department of Education. *Turning around Low-Performing Schools: A Guide for State and Local Leaders*. Washington, DC: US Department of Education, 1998. https://www2.ed.gov/pubs/turning/index.html

US Department of Justice. *Intimate Partner Violence: Attributes of Victimization*. Washington, DC: US Department of Justice, Bureau of Justice Statistics, 1993.

———. *Sourcebook of Criminal Justice Statistics, 2002*. Washington, DC: Bureau of Justice Statistics, 2003.

———. *Trends in Youth Violence*. Washington, DC: US Department of Justice, Office of Juvenile Justice and Delinquency Prevention, 2003.

———. *2000 Annual Report on School Safety*. Washington, DC: US Department of Justice, 2000.

US Department of Justice and US Department of Education. *1998 Annual Report on School Safety*. Washington, DC: US Department of Justice and US Department of Education, 1999.

US House of Representatives. Violent and Repeat Juvenile Offender Accountability and Rehabilitation Act of 1999. H.R. Resolution 1501, 106th Cong., 1999.

US National Commission on the Causes and Prevention of Violence. *Final Report of the National Commission on the Causes and Prevention of Violence*. Washington, DC: US Government Printing Office, 1969.

US National Library of Medicine. "Children and Screen Time." *MediLine Plus*. https://medlineplus.gov/ency/patientinstructions/000355.htm.

Vance, Kaycee, Megan Sutter, Paul B. Perrin, and Martin Heesacker. "The Media's Sexual Objectification of Women, Rape Myth Acceptance, and Interpersonal Violence." *Journal of Aggression, Maltreatment and Trauma* 24, no. 5 (June 10, 2015). https://doi.org/10.1080/10926771.2015.1029179.

Vann, Matthew, and Corky Siemoszco. "Nikolas Cruz, Accused Parkland Shooter, 'Restless' in Solitary, Reports Say." NBC News. March 17, 2018.

Vasquez, Eduardo, William C. Petersen, Brad J. Bushman, Nicolas J. Kelley, Philippine DeMeestre, and Norman Miller. "Lashing Out after Stewing over Public Insults: The Effects of Public Provocation, Public Intensity and Rumination on Triggered Displaced Aggression. *Aggressive Behavior* 39 (2013): 13–29.

Virginia Youth Violence Project. "Middle School Bullying." School of Education, University of Virginia. http://youthviolence.edschool.virginia.edu.

Vossekuil, Bryan, Robert A. Fein, Marissa Ready, Randy Borum, and William Modzelski. *The Final Report and Findings of the Safe School Initiative: Implications for the Prevention of School Attacks in the United States*. Washington, DC: US Secret Service and US Department of Education, 2002.

Vossekuil, Bryan, Marisa Reddy, and Robert Fein. *Safe School Initiative: An Interim Report on the Prevention of Targeted Violence in Schools*. Washington, DC: US Secret Service National Threat Assessment Center, US Department of Education, and the National Institute of Justice, 2000.

Walker, Tim. "Cameras in the Class: Is Big Brother Evaluating You?." *NEA Today*. January 23, 2015.

Waller, Douglas. "Running a School for Dictators." *Newsweek*. August 9, 1993.

Walsh, David Allen. *Physician Guide to Media Violence*. Chicago: American Medical Association, 1996.

Wan, William, Kevin Sullivan, David Weingrad, and Mark Berman. "Florida Shooting Suspect Nikolas Cruz: Guns, Depression and a Life in Trouble." *Washington Post*. February 15, 2018.

War Resisters League. "Where Your Income Tax Money Really Goes." https://www.warresisters.org.

Warrior Science Group. "Media Science Update." 2010. http://www.killolgy.com.

Wasserman, Gail A., Laurie S. Miller, and Lynn Cothern. "Prevention of Serious and Violent Juvenile Offending." *Juvenile Justice Bulletin*. Washington, DC: Office of Juvenile Justice and Delinquency Prevention, 2000.

Watkins, Kevin. *Human Development Report, 2006*. New York: United Nations Development Programme, 2006.

Webster-Stratton, Carolyn, S. Mihalic, A. Fagan, D. Arnold, T. K. Taylor, and C. Tingley. *Blueprints for Violence Prevention: The Incredible Years—Parent, Teacher, and Child Training Series*. Boulder: Center for the Study and Prevention of Violence, 2001.

Webster, David W. "The Unconvincing Case for School-Based Conflict Resolution Programs for Adolescents." *Health Affairs* 12 (1993).

Weimberg, Gary, and Catherine Ryan, dirs. *POV*. "Soldiers of Conscience." Aired October 16, 2008, on PBS.

Weiner, N. A., M. A. Zahn, and R. J. Sagi, eds. *Violence: Patterns, Causes, Public Policy*. San Diego: Harcourt, Brace, Jovanovich, 1990.

Weinstein, David. "Herbert Spencer." *The Stanford Encyclopedia of Philosophy*. Edited by Edward N. Zalta. Stanford University, 2019. https://plato.stanford.edu/archives/fall2019/entries/spencer/.

Weller, Robert. "Columbine: Questions Still Remain." *The Pueblo Chieftain* (Associated Press). April 20, 2007.

West, Beldon. "The Death Penalty: A National Disgrace." *The Nonviolent Activist*. November/December 1993.

Whitaker, Jodi L. and Brad J. Bushman. "'Remain Calm. Be Kind.' Effects of Relaxing Video Games on Aggressive and Prosocial Behavior." *Social Psychological and Personality Science* 3, no. 1 (2012): 88–92.

Widom, Catherine, and M.G. Maxfield. "An Update on the 'Cycle of Violence.'" *Research in Brief*. Washington, DC: US Department of Justice, 2001.

Wihbey, John. "Mass Murder, Shooting Sprees and Rampage Violence: Research Roundup." October 1, 2015. https://journalistsresource.org/studies/government/criminal-justice/mass-murder-shooting-sprees-and-rampage-violence-research-roundup/.

Wilcox, Brian L., Dale Kunkel, Joanne Cantor, Peter Dowrick, Susan Linn, and Edward Palmer. "Report of the APA Task Force on Advertising and Children." American Psychological Association, 2004. https://www.apa.org/pi/families/resources/advertising-children.pdf.

Wilson, James Q. *Thinking About Crime*. New York: Vintage, 1985.

Wilson, John J., James C. Howell. *Comprehensive Strategy for Serious, Violent, and Chronic Juvenile Offenders*. Washington, DC: US Department of Justice, Office of Juvenile Justice and Delinquency Prevention, 1993.

Wilson-Brewer, Renee. "Peer Violence Prevention Programs in Middle and High Schools." *Adolescent Medicine: State of the Art Reviews* 6, no. 2. (1995).

Wired Safety Group. "Stop Cyberbullying." http://www.stopcyberbullying.org.

Wittrock, M. C., Jackson Beatty, Joseph E. Bogen, Michael S. Gazzaniga, Harry J. Jerison, Stephen D. Krashen, Robert D. Nebes, and Timothy J. Teyler. *The Human Brain*. Englewood Cliffs, NJ: Prentice-Hall, 1977.

Woolf, Steven H., Robert E. Johnson, and H. Jack Geiger. "The Rising Prevalence of Severe Poverty in America: A Growing Threat to Public Health." *American Journal of Preventive Medicine* 31, no. 4 (2006): 332–41.

World Health Organization. "Gaming Disorders." *International Classification of Disorders*. 11th ed. Geneva: WHO, 2018.

———. *World Health Organization World Report on Violence and Health*. Geneva: WHO, 2019.

———. *Preventing Violence by Developing Life Skills in Children*. Geneva: WHO, 2009.

Wright, Robert O., Jay Schutz, R. J. Wright, Virginia Bollati, Inger Tarantini, Susan K. Park, Henry Hu, Diane Sparrow, and Paul Vokonas. "Biomarkers of Lead Exposure and DNA Manipulation within Retrotransposins." *Environmental Health Perspectives*. 118, no. 6 (2010): 790–95.

Ybarra, Michele L., L. Rowell Huesmann, Josephine P. Korchmaros, and Sari L. Reisner. "Cross-Sectional Association between Violent Video and Computer Game Playing on Weapon Carrying in a National Cohort of Children." *Aggressive Behavior* 40, no. 4 (July–Aug. 2014): 345–58.

The Youth Problem. Aired in December 2013, on Turner Classic Movies.

Zahn, Margaret A., Henry J. Brownstein, and Shelly L. Jackson, eds. *Violence: From Theory to Research*. Cincinnati, OH: Anderson, 2004.

Zeitlin, Maurice. "Is There a Ruling Class?" *New York Review of Books*. July 17, 1975.

Zero to Three. "Brain Wonders: Nurturing Healthy Brain Development." February 16, 2016. https://www.zerotothree.org/resources/156-brain-wonders-nurturing-healthy-brain-development-from-birth.

Zhang, Anlan, Lauren Musu-Gillette, and Barbara A. Oudekerk. *Indicators of School Crime and Safety: 2015*. Washington, DC: Bureau of Justice Statistics and National Center for Education Statistics, 2016. https://www.bjs.gov/content/pub/pdf/iscs15.pdf.

Zuckerman, Diana. M., Dorothy G. Singer, and Jerome L. Singer. "Television Viewing, Children's Reading, and Related Classroom Behavior." *Journal of Communication* 30, no. 1 (1980): 166–74.

INDEX

A

academic performance, 96, 116, 142, 154, 156, 177, 179–180, 211–213
Accountability Programs, 24
Active Shooter, 185
addiction: drugs, 3, 56; violent video game addiction, 120, 174, 177–179, 210. *See also* fanaticism; gaming disorder
advertisements, 67–68
advertising industry, 67–69, 145, 152
agenda-setting, 131
aggression, 85, 88, 92, 95, 97, 98, 103, 114, 118, 133, 136, 138–139, 142, 144, 151, 156–157, 161–162, 173–176, 177, 199, 205, 209, 217
aggressive personality, 173
alcohol, 70–71. *See also* alcohol-induced rage; Alcohol Industry
alcohol-induced rage, 46
Alcohol Industry, 73, 76, 147
American Academy of Pediatrics, 143–144
American Medical Association, 92, 103, 143
American Psychiatric Association, 144, 178
American Psychological Association, 85, 143, 144
Amusing Ourselves to Death, 135
amygdala, 4, 197–198, 208–209
anger, 5, 8, 11, 14, 15, 173, 183, 192, 205. *See also* rage
anger management, 17
anorexia, 76, 149. *See also* bulimia; eating disorders
anterior cingulated, 198
art education, 34–35
Arts, The, 37
assaults, xi, 56, 61, 73, 133. *See also* sexual assaults
assault weapons, 78. *See also* assault weapons ban
assault weapons ban, 78–79
Australopithecus, 46
autonomic nervous system, 191–192
Auvinen, Pekka Eric, 108

B

banality of evil, 152

Bandura, Albert, 51
bank-teller education, 42, 44–45, 223–224
Barbaro, Anthony, 109
Barbie, 76, 223. *See also* Barbie-type dolls
Barbie-type dolls, 75, 76
Best Practices for Youth Violence Prevention, 24–26
Best Practices for Schools, 33–39
beta brain activity, 205–206
Big Brothers Big Sisters, 27
biological explanations for aggression and violence, 3–7. *See also* neuroscientific explanations
Blueprints for Best Practices, 27–32
Bosse, Sebastian, 189
Bowling for Columbine, 115–116
Boys and Girls Clubs, 30
Bradbury, Ray, 168
brain: cerebral hemispheres, 193–196; child's brain, 201–203; executive functioning, 210–211; women and men, 203–205
brainstem, 197, 199, 200–201
brain structures, 191, 197–201
branding, 136, 151
Bratz dolls, 76
BrightHouse Institute for Thought Sciences, 152
Brookings Institution, 80
Brown v. Entertainment Merchants, 170
bulimia, 76, 148. *See also* anorexia; eating disorders
bullies, 89–90, 96–98, 99, 125, 183. *See also* bullies case studies; bully-victims
bullies case studies, 98–99
Bully Busters, 35
bullycide, 91, 94, 102
bullying: definition, 91–92, 96–98; rates, 94–95; victims, 99–100. *See also* cyberbullying
bully-victims, 102–103

Bush, Catherine, 111
Bushman, Brad J., 173, 176

C

Call of Duty, 164
Cambridge Study in Delinquent Development, 18
Canada, 31, 67, 71, 72
Carneal, Michael, 5, 52, 72, 110, 119, 126, 183; case study, 120–122
cartoons, 70, 113, 136, 137, 150, 161, 217
case studies: bullies, 98–99; bully-victims, 100–102; rampage school shooters, 120–129; violent video gamers, 180
Catal Huyuk, 48
catharsis, 168, 171
causes of violence. *See* biological explanation; neuroscientific explanation; psychological explanations; sociological explanations
cell towers, 88
censorship, 158, 160
Center for Internet Behavior, 179
Center for Media Education, 147–148
Center for Media Literacy, 160
Center for the Study and Prevention of Violence, 10, 27, 33, 100, 103
cerebral cortex, 193, 198–200
cerebral hemispheres, 193, 203–207
Chicago Tribune, 171
child abuse and neglect, 9–10, 14, 27
children, 82–83
Children's Television Act of 1990, 158–59
children's television programming, 135–137, 154, 159, 217. *See also* television: adult programming
China, 179, 189
Cho, Seung-Hui, 112, 126; case study, 127–128
Clinton, Bill, 55, 115, 188
cocaine, 61, 71

cognitive skills, 25–26
cohort analysis, 153–154, 215, 217–218
Columbine, 52, 55, 84, 86, 88. *See also* Columbine effect; Harris, Eric; Klebold, Dylan
Columbine effect, 87
Common Sense Understanding, 2
Community, 22
Community Involvement, 37–38
Community Oriented Policing program (COPS), 216
compassion, 5, 21, 50, 64, 130, 155, 221, 222, 223. *See also* empathy; love
conduct disorders, 63, 202, 211
conflict resolution, 17, 31–32, 96
conflict theory, 11–14
control balance theory, 14
copycat effect, 110–111, 120, 126, 135–136
Cornell, Dewey, 108, 117, 118
Corporate Crime, 73–74
Corporate Media and the Threat to Democracy, 159
Corporate Responsibility, 157–158
Corporate Violence: Injury and Death for Profit, 73
corpus callosum, 193, 203, 207
Cossey, Dillon, 108
counseling, 17, 31, 33, 34, 39
creating peaceful schools, 103–106
crime, xi, 3, 14–15. *See also* crime rates
crime rates, 16, 51, 55, 57–58, 74; juvenile crime, 30, 57, 94, 216; violent crime, 5, 6, 7, 1, 16, 19–20, 27
critical consciousness, 42–43, 196
critical thinking, 21, 33, 36, 42, 142, 156, 213, 223–224
Cruz, Nikolas, 128–129
culture of disrespect, 59, 146, 154, 177
culture of violence: everyday life, 67–70
cumulative risk factors, 18, 113–114
cyberbullying, 93–94, 176

Cyrus, Miley, 136

D

DSM-5 (*Diagnostic Statistical Manual*), 5, 177, 179
Dalai Lama, 223
Darwin, Charles, 12, 41, 45
date rape, 65
death penalty, 57
Death Race, 163
democracy, 36–37, 40, 42, 45, 47, 49–51, 52, 54, 68, 83, 103–104, 155, 221, 224
Democratic Classrooms, 36–37
Denver Youth Survey, 61
depression, 8, 14, 29, 39, 64, 71, 88, 91, 94, 99, 111–114, 117, 125–127, 141, 143, 183, 205
desensitization, 129–130, 209–210, 222
Developing School Capacity, 38
diabetes, 5, 72, 87, 145, 154
Dickens, Charles, 83
disinformation: media violence research, 144–145; video game violence research, 170–171
dissociation, 113
domestic violence, 43, 63, 76, 220
Doom, 121, 125, 164, 166, 217
Double Dragon, 163
Dreamworlds, 4, 138
drugs, 4, 6, 8, 19, 21, 26, 70–71, 76, 90–91, 97, 132, 157, 179, 189

E

early childhood education, 18–21
eating disorders, 64, 76. *See also* anorexia; bulimia
ecstasy, 71, 167
education, 18, 25–26, 42–44; early childhood education, 20–21; gender education, 40; parenting education, 23
Education for a Critical Consciousness, 42
EEG, 205–206, 208

effect of violent electronic entertainment media: violent entertainment media, 138–144; violent video games, 172–179
Ehrenreich, Barbara, 15
Eminem, 132
empathy, 5, 20, 21, 23, 28–29, 36, 47, 50, 59, 64, 86, 104, 112–113, 119, 123, 129, 132, 142–143, 157, 161, 174, 176, 182–186, 209, 221, 223–224
Entertainment Software Ratings Board (ESRB), 187, 189
European Union, 72, 189
evaluation, 18, 20, 23, 25–26, 28, 29–30, 32, 34. *See also* Program Evaluation
EverQuest, 168
Ewing, Stuart, 145
executive functioning, 210–211
expert opinions, 8

F

Fahrenheit 451, 168
Families and Schools Together, 37–38
family, 8–9, 16, 18–19, 26, 27; as protective factor, 20–21
family dysfunction, 15
Family Entertainment Protection Act, 187
family strengthening, 18, 22–23, 25
Family Strengthening Program, 37–38
fanaticism, 178. *See also* gaming disorder; video game addiction
Fanon, Frantz, 42
federal budget, 57, 80–81
Federal Communications Commission, 75, 159
feminist theory, 14–15
Ferguson, Christopher, 144
Ferris, Nathan, 110
First Amendment, 158–159, 170, 189
first-person shooter games, 164, 178, 182, 218
fMRI, 207–208. *See also* MRI

food, 5–7, 13, 65, 71–73, 87, 145–146, 156. *See also* genetically modified food
Food and Drug Administration, 5, 71
food industry, 145–146
Fox, Matthew, 51
Fox News, 170
Freire, Paolo, 42–44, 50, 53, 58, 69, 107, 155, 166, 196, 223, 224
frontal cortex, 194, 202. *See also* prefrontal cortex
frontal lobes, 3, 29, 193, 201–202

G

gaming disorder, 178–179. *See also* fanaticism; video game addiction
Gandhi, Mahatma, 222
gangs, 61–62, 141
gatekeepers, 134. *See also* agenda-setting
General Aggression Model, 7, 173, 209
general strain theory, 14
genetically modified food (GMO), 72. *See also* food
Gerbner, George, 122, 123, 133, 134, 145
Germany, 32, 122, 172, 194
G.I. Joe, 69, 109, 116, 164
Gitlin, Todd, 148
goddess cultures, 43–45
Golden, Andrew, 109, 112–113; case study, 122–123
Grand Theft Auto, 166, 178
Gross, Peter, 8
Grossman, Dave, 183
gun culture, 78, 110, 113, 116
guns, 9–10, 56, 58–59, 66, 69, 78, 90–91, 96, 109, 114–116, 117, 121–122, 124, 125, 188, 195; toy guns, 126, 141, 173–174, 177–178, 185. *See also* weapons
gyrus cingulated, 198, 208

H

Hammurabi Code of Law, 47
Harris, Eric, 166; case study, 125–126
Harvard University Schoolyard Bully Practicum, 103
Healy, Jane, 142
hegemony, 134–135
hierarchy, 4, 10, 12–13, 43, 45–46, 48, 119, 146, 169, 183, 186, 223, 224
hierarchy of needs, 49–50
Hill, Stuart, 73–74
hip-hop, 133
hippocampus, 197–198, 210
homicides, 52. *See also* murder
homicide rate, 55, 58, 60, 62, 65
horizontal violence, 44, 56–57
Horney, Karen, 49, 50
Horton, Miles, 42
hostile bias, 172, 211
hostile expectations, 175
human nature, 41–42, 45–52
humor, 67, 86, 104, 113, 115, 118, 130, 150, 154, 157, 169, 182, 185–186, 211, 220–222, 223
hunter-gatherers, 46–47
Huxley, Aldous, 169
hypothalamus, 193, 197, 199–200

I

Incredible Years, 27–28
injustice, 3, 11, 15, 16, 47, 51, 52, 64, 73–74, 118, 119, 127, 219
Intensive Family Therapy, 28
interactive drama, 168
Interactive Entertainment Merchants Association, 187
internet, 66, 92

J

Jackson, Peter, 169
Jesus, 52
Jhally, Sat, 138
John Hopkins University, 18, 141
Johnson, Mitchell, 119; case study, 122–123
justice, xii, 15, 16, 21, 36, 40, 47, 51, 55, 58, 104, 120, 129, 186, 221–224
Juvenile Justice Act of 1999, 158

K

Kilbourne, Jean, 145, 148, 150
Kinect, 169
Kinkel, Kipland, 113; case study, 124–125
King, Martin Luther, 16, 104, 221
Klebold, Dylan, 125–126
Klein, Naomi, 151

L

language, 12, 43, 67–70, 193, 195–196, 203–204, 206, 208, 213
Las Vegas rampage shooting, 112
Legal Action Project of the Center to Prevent Gun Violence, 79
legislation, 186–188, 189
Levin, Diane E., 125, 137
Lewin, Kurt, 50–51
liberatory education, 42–44, 53, 86, 223
Life Skills Program, 23–24
limbic system, 197–201
lone gamer, 162
Lorenz, Konrad, 3
love, 42, 50–51. *See also* compassion; empathy
low-violence countries, 190
Lucas, George, 158

M

Manson, Marilyn, 124, 132

Marjory Stoneman School shooting, 128, 170, 185
Marshall, S. L. A., 46, 182
Marx, Karl, 12, 69, 80, 149
Maslow, Abraham, 49–50. *See also* hierarchy of needs
massive multiplayer online role-playing games. *See* MMORPGs
mass murder, 55–57, 79, 107, 113, 118, 19, 123–124, 129, 166, 168–169. *See also* rampage school shooters; rampage public shooters
matriarchy, 47
McChesney, Robert, 159
McLuhan, Marshall, 152
Mead, Margaret, 4, 49
mean and threatening world, 133, 137, 141, 150, 154
mean-spiritedness, 81, 154, 157
Mechanical Bride, 152
Medal of Honor, 164
Media Awareness Network, 155
media industry, 134–135, 144–145, 157
media literacy, 155–156
media research: experimental studies, 137; longitudinal, 139–140; meta-analyses, 140–141
mediation, 17, 25. *See also* Peer Mediation
media violence, 135–138; advertising, 145–153; disinformation, 145–146; misinformation, 145–146; research, 137–144
Mentoring, 26–27
Milgram, Stanley, 45
military-industrial complex, 80–81. *See also* military spending, war industry
military spending, 57–80–81. *See also* war industry
Million Man March, 58, 216
Mills, C. Wright, 12

misinformation: media violence research, 144–145; video game violence research, 170–171, 187
misogyny, 132, 133, 139, 166, 167
MMORPGs (massive multiplayer online role-playing games), 158–169
Montessori Schools, 45
Moore, Michael, 115–116, 136
moral disengagement, 148, 177
Mortal Kombat, 163–164, 165, 172, 217
Mother Mary, 62
MRI, 153, 207. *See also* fMRI
MS-13 gang, 52
MTV, 132
murder, 55–58, 60, 69, 70, 112, 115, 117, 119, 135–136, 137. *See also* homicides; mass murder
murder rate, 140
Murray, John, 167
music, 113, 122–123, 127, 132, 181, 187, 193, 206, 207. *See also* music videos
music videos, 131, 132
mutated revenge, 47, 52, 118, 186
myth of male dominance, 47–48

N

narcissism, 112, 177, 178, 183, 186
narcotics. *See* drugs
National Academies of Science, xii
National Association of Broadcasters, 157, 217
National Center for Education Statistics, 95
national debt, 80–81
National Parent Teachers Association (PTA), 223
National Research Council, 10, 86, 108, 109, 115, 117, 120
National Rifle Association (NRA), 170
National School Board Association, 2
Nation at Risk, A, 96
Natural Born Killers, 121, 126

Neolithic Period, 47
nervous system: 6, 142, 191, 192, 199, 210, 213; autonomic, 192, 200, 211; parasycmpathetic, 192; sympathetic, 192
Neuromarketing, 139–140
neuroscientific explanations for violence, 205–208
Neurosociology, 196–197
neurotoxins, 5, 6, 13
neurotransmitters, 6
"new female offender," 2, 64
New Poverty, 65–66
news industry, 135
New York Times, 144, 170
1967 President's Commission on the Causes and Prevention of Violence, 16
Nintendo, 146–147, 162. *See also* Nintendo era; Nintendo kids
Nintendo era, 163
Nintendo kids, 119
No Logo, 151
nonhuman nature, 186
Nurturing Parenting Programs, 22–23

O

objectification, 43, 148, 149, 150, 165
occipital lobes, 193–194
Office of Juvenile Justice and Delinquency Prevention (OJJDP), 20, 24
Olweus, Dan, 92, 94
Olweus Bullying Prevention, 33–35
On Aggression, 3
operational stage of brain development, 202–203. *See also* pre-operational stage
Operation Desert Storm, 115, 217
oppression, 16, 42–43, 52, 87, 224
Orwell, George, 69, 157

P

Paleolithic Period, 47
parasympathetic nervous system, 192
parenting, 18–23, 25
parents, 8, 9, 18, 20, 24–26, 28, 33, 34, 37, 39, 61, 84, 103, 201, 221, 223
parietal lobes, 193, 194
patriarchy, 47–48
Paul VI (pope), 54, 222
PBS NewsHour, 144
PC Gamer, 167
peaceful schools, 52–53
Pedagogy of the Oppressed, 42
Peer Mediation, 32. *See also* mediation
perfect, 67, 69, 137–138, 154
Perry Preschool Program, 20
phenomenology, 13, 133
Physicians for Safe Technology, 87
Piaget, Jean, 141, 202–203
police brutality, 52
Politics of Style, The, 145
Pong, 162
pornography, 73, 124, 166, 188
posterior cingulated, 199, 208
Postman, Neil, 135
post-traumatic stress disorder (PTSD), 47, 141, 208
Poverty, 64–65, 77, 81, 85. *See also* New Poverty
power, 1, 7, 9, 12–15, 26, 31, 33–34, 43–48, 51, 57, 61, 66–68, 75, 85–86, 89, 91–93, 96, 97, 102, 121, 125, 127, 129, 133, 137–138, 150–151, 168, 169, 177, 181–183, 186, 225
prefrontal cortex, 3, 182, 210–211
pre-operational stage of brain development, 202
primary causal factor, xiii, 113, 120, 129, 130, 219
primary risk factor, 181, 184
prison industry, 76–77, 147
problem-solving education, 42–43

profit, 189. *See also* profit at any cost; profit motive
profit at any cost, 73
profit motive, 189
Program Evaluation, 39. *See also* evaluation
Promoting Alternative Thinking Strategies (PATHS), 29–30
prosocial video games, 19–20
protective factors, 115, 154, 181
pro-war, 161–162
psychological explanations for violence, 7–8, 10
Psychological Society, The, 7

R

radiation, 80
rage, 6, 56, 66, 69. *See also* alcohol-induced rage; anger; road rage; steroid rage
rampage public shooters, 57–58
rampage school shooters, xii, 107–112, 119–120, 182, 183–184, 218; case studies, 120–129; history of, 83–84, 109–112; National Research Council case studies, 117
rankism, 61
rape, 63, 65. *See also* rape culture; rape myth
rape culture, 132
rape myth, 148, 176
reflexive shooting, 182, 218
Reggio Emilia, 44, 50
reinforcement, 28, 52, 182
rejection, 13, 49, 52, 113–114, 117–118, 128, 129, 181. *See also* rejection sensitivity
rejection sensitivity, 118
resonance, 135, 167, 178
revenge, 10, 15, 47, 52, 56, 64, 103, 111, 118–119, 121, 125–126, 146, 186. *See also* mutated revenge
risk factors, 5, 7, 9, 18–19, 21, 22, 37, 88, 113, 113, 117, 129, 154, 174, 181, 183–184. *See also* cumulative risk factors; primary risk factor
road rage, 66
Rogers, Carl, 39, 49, 222
root cause, xii, 16, 219
routine activities theory, 15
ruling elites, 13

S

Safe School Study Report to Congress, 77
scavengers/foragers, 46–47
Schiller, Herbert, 123
School, 21, 22
school-associated violent deaths, 83–84, 110, 111, 216–217
School Environment, 85–88
School shooters. *See* rampage school shooters
school staff, 33–34, 35, 88–89, 101, 129
school violence, xi, xiii, 8–12, 37–38, 216–217; bullying, 91–95; history of, 84–85; school environment, 85–86; school staff, 88–89; suicide, 91
school violence prevention, xii, 17–18, 30, 33–39, 40, 52–53, 104, 115
Second Step Program, 36
security measures, 90, 30–31, 66, 84, 86–87, 90
serial killers, 62
sexism, 15. *See also* violent-sexist video games
sex offenders, 4
sexual assaults, 70, 132
Shuhen, Michael, 223
Slaby, Ron, 8
snark, 67
social disorganization theory, 14–15
social learning theory, 13–14
sociological explanations for violence, 12–15
Socrates, 132, 111
Soldier of Fortune, 165
Solomon, Anthony, 86; case study, 126–127

South Sea Islanders, 4
Spencer, Brenda, 109
Spencer, George Herbert, 11
Spore, 167, 168
Spurlock, Morgan, 5
Stanford University's Student Media Awareness to Reduce Television (SMART), 156
Steinhazuser, Robert, 108
steroid rage, 4
steroids, 4
Still Killing Us Softly, 148
Stop Bullying Now!, 35–36
Strengthening Families Program, 22–23, 25
structural-functional theory, 11–12
student-centered education, 36, 223
Subliminal Seduction, 153
submerged consciousness, 196
substance abuse, 5, 7, 59, 71, 154. *See also* drugs
substance abuse prevention, 22–23, 27
sugar, 5, 6–7, 45, 71–72, 87, 88, 113, 146, 192
Sugar Blues, 5
suicide, 54–55
Supersize Me, 5–6
Supreme Court, 171, 189. *See also* misinformation
Surgeon General, 139, 143, 172
symbolic interaction theory, 12
sympathetic nervous system, 192

T

technological development, 153, 157, 164, 185, 189
Telecommunications Act of 1996, 158–159, 187–188
television: adult programming, 137–138. *See also* children's television programming
temporal lobes, 193
"terrible twos," 29, 201–202
testosterone, 4, 203
thalamus, 193, 197, 199–201

Thich Nhat Hanh, 223
third-person effect, 131
"thrill killings," 5, 56, 143
toddlers, 27, 50, 63, 97, 141, 162
Tosh.0, 138
toy industry, 75–76. *See also* Barbie; guns: toy guns; war toy industry
"triple entitlement," 116

U

UCLA Television Monitoring Project, 125
United Nations Convention of the Rights of the Child, 189
United States Department of Education, 17
United States Department of Justice, 17–18, 20. *See also* Office of Juvenile Justice and Delinquency Prevention (OJJDP)
United States Secret Service National Threat Assessment Center, 109, 112, 116
United States Supreme Court, 170, 189. *See also* Supreme Court

V

V-chip, 158–159
video game addiction, 178–179. *See also* fanaticism; gaming disorder
video game research: experimental, 172–173; longitudinal, 174–175; meta-analyses, 175–176
video game violence, 161–162; case studies, 179–180; disinformation, 170–171; history, 162–167; legislation, 186–189; misinformation, 170–171; primary risk factor, 180–181; relationship to school violence, 183–184; research, 171–170
violence, xi–xiii; biological explanations, 3–7; against children, 58, 62–64; against girls, 91; against teachers, 88–89; against women,

59, 63–64; alcohol and other drugs, 70–72; causes, 7–40; domestic violence, 43, 44, 64, 76, 189, 219; future of, 219. *See also* youth violence

Violence against Girls, 91

violence industries, 73; alcohol industry, 76; corporate crime, 73–74; prison industry, 76–77, toy industry, 75–76; violent entertainment industry, 135–136, 144–146, 157–160; violent video game industry, 162–167, 170–171, 185–189; war industry, 79–81; war toy industry, 75; weapons industry, 78–79

violence prevention programs, 17–32

violent-sexist video games, 165–166, 176

virtual reality, 167–169. *See also* virtual worlds

virtual worlds, 69, 125, 133–134, 160. *See also* virtual reality

Visiting Nurses, 27

W

war, 12, 48, 57. *See also* pro-war; war industry; war toys

war industry, 67, 73–74, 78–79, 81. *See also* military spending

warrior-hero, 124, 176, 181, 185, 218

warrior ideal, 15, 75, 93, 115, 119, 136, 182, 195

war toys, 75, 98, 161–162, 217. *See also* war toy industry

war toy industry, 75. *See also* toy industry

weapons, 3, 8, 11, 30, 46, 56, 60, 75, 185, 90, 165; assault weapons, 62, 111–112, 215; fascination with, 113; invention of, 45; on campus, 85, 87, 90, 178; rampage school shooters, 120–121, 125, 127–128, 183. *See also* assault weapons ban; guns; weapons effect; weapons industry

weapons effect, 178–179

weapons industry, 78–79

white heterosexual masculinity, 116. *See also* "triple entitlement"

Whitman, Charles, 3–4

Wi-Fi, 88

Wikipedia, 171

Williams, Andy, 111

wishful identification, 176, 218

Wolfenstein, 164, 218

Women and Girls, 63–64

Woodham, Luke, 111

World Health Organization, 178–179

World of Warcraft, 168; addiction to, 178

World War II, 46, 55, 75, 79, 80, 115, 182, 212, 214

Wounded by School, 86

Wright, Will, 168

Wurst, Andrew Jerome, 113; case study, 123–124

X

Xtreme Beach Volleyball, 166

Y

youth suicide, 70, 76

youth violence, 24, 25, 53, 55–63, 110, 113–114, 215, 216; future of, 219; history of, 57–58; risk factors and protective factors, 18–20; youth violence prevention, 27–39, 115. *See also* school violence